The McGraw-Hill Handbook

Second Edition

Elaine P. Maimon
Governors State University

Janice H. Peritz
Queens College,
City University of New York

Kathleen Blake Yancey
Florida State University

With notes for multilingual students
and *Guide for Multilingual Writers* by
Maria Zlateva, Boston University

Connect
Learn
Succeed™

Published by McGraw-Hill, an imprint of The McGraw-Hill Companies, Inc.,
1221 Avenue of the Americas, New York, NY 10020. Copyright © 2010. All rights
reserved.

This book is printed on acid-free paper.

1 2 3 4 5 6 7 8 9 0 DOW / DOW 0 9

Hardcover
ISBN-13: 978-0-07-739577-3
MHID: 0-07-739577-8

Softcover
ISBN-13: 978-0-07-739578-0
MHID: 0-07-739578-6

Vice President and Editor in Chief: *Michael Ryan*
Publisher: *David S. Patterson*
Senior Sponsoring Editor: *Christopher Bennem*
Director of Development: *Dawn Groundwater*
Development Editor: *Anne Kemper*
Executive Marketing Manager: *Allison Jones*
Market Development Manager: *Molly Meneely*
Lead Production Editor: *Brett Coker, Rachel J. Castillo*
Manuscript Editor: *Barbara Armentrout*
Lead Designer: *Cassandra Chu*
Interior and Cover Designer: *Maureen McCutcheon*
Art and Photo Editor: *Sonia Brown*
Production Supervisors: *Randy Hurst, Richard DeVitto, Louis Swaim*
Lead Media Project Manager: *Thomas Brierly*
Composition: *9/11 New Century Schoolbook by Thompson Type*
Printing: *45# Pub Matte Thin Bulk by R.R. Donnelley & Sons*

Cover images: *(from top to bottom)* © *Visual Landscape;* © *Philadelphia Museum
of Art/CORBIS;* © *NASA/Roger Ressmeyer/CORBIS; Nevros/Folio, Inc;* © *Jon
Hicks/CORBIS*

Credits: The credits section for this book begins on page C-1 and is considered an
extension of the copyright page.

Library of Congress Cataloging-in-Publication Data
Maimon, Elaine P.
    [New McGraw-Hill handbook]
    The McGraw-Hill handbook / Elaine Maimon, Janice Peritz, Kathleen Yancey.
—2nd ed.
        p. cm.
    Originally published as: 1st ed.The new McGraw-Hill handbook, c2007
    Includes bibliographical references and index.
    ISBN-13: 978-0-07-338381-1 (alk. paper)   ISBN-13: 978-0-07-739577-3
    ISBN-10: 0-07-338381-3 (alk. paper)   ISBN-10: 0-07-739577-8
1. English language—Rhetoric—Handbooks, manuals, etc. 2. Academic writing—
Handbooks, manuals, etc. 3. Report writing—Handbooks, manuals, etc. I. Peritz,
Janice. II. Yancey, Kathleen Blake, 1950- III. Title.

PE1408.M3364 2009
808'.042—dc22   2008047891

Contents

PART 2 ▪ Common Assignments across the Curriculum

PART 4 ▪ Documenting across the Curriculum

PART 5 ■ Writing beyond College

PART 6 ■ Grammar Basics

PART 7 ▪ Editing for Grammar Conventions

PART 8 ▪ Editing for Clarity

PART 9 ▪ Editing for Word Choice

PART 10 ▪ Sentence Punctuation

PART 11 ▪ Mechanics and Spelling

PART 12 ▪ Guide for Multilingual Writers

PART 13 ▪ Further Resources for Learning

Preface

As we wrote the first edition of *The McGraw-Hill Handbook,* our students were always on our minds. We knew that today's students' perspectives on college life were different from those of previous generations of students, and so were their expectations. Most college students today have never known a world without the Internet. Advances in technologies ensure that they are constantly connected to a wealth of information on almost any topic, as well as to one another. Raised on the Web, television, and advertising, they are highly attuned to visual images. At the same time, students with careers and families are entering, and reentering, academia with their own rich set of experiences and expectations. More than ever before, today's students represent an abundance of linguistic and cultural backgrounds, needing a variety of approaches to writing and editing at the college level. Multitasking at unprecedented levels, they need a handbook they can rely on in all their courses: whether that means learning about revision in their English composition class, preparing PowerPoints for a speech course, or looking for help with integrating sources into a history assignment.

Students are different,

the tools are different,

but the goals are the same:

writing well and succeeding in college and beyond.

As students change, so, too, do the tools that students use for writing and research. Research occurs online via databases and the Web, and the greatest challenges students face are not in finding sources, but in choosing and evaluating the most appropriate sources and using them effectively in their projects. Word processing, presentation software, and writing for the Web have increased the importance of visuals and design in writing. Many composition courses make use of digital technologies such as electronic portfolios or blogs and use Blackboard or other course-management systems to foster student collaboration and on-line peer review.

Even though the occasions, tools, and audiences for writing seem more varied than ever, the fundamental goals of composition courses persist. Instructors strive to produce students who can think criti-cally, recognize rhetorical situations, communicate clearly and effec-tively, write in a variety of genres, and edit their own work. Students must be discerning and ethical researchers, acknowledging the contri-butions of others and documenting sources appropriately. And compo-sition courses still aim to build writing skills that students will carry with them into their other courses, their work in the community, and their professional lives. In response to these goals—suggested by the WPA Outcomes Statement for First-Year Composition (reproduced on pp. xxxii–xxxiii) and those of many colleges and universities— *The McGraw-Hill Handbook* pays new attention to commonly identified outcomes for composition to help stu-dents track their progress and under-stand how they may be assessed.

Today's students need a handbook with state-of-the-art, accessible resources on writing, researching, editing, and design—a handbook they can rely on for all their aca-demic writing.

In revising this text, we have dedicated ourselves to making *The McGraw-Hill Handbook* an even stronger, more current, and more versatile resource for achieving excellence in the ever-changing environments that students encoun-ter in college.

Features of *The McGraw-Hill Handbook*

Specific, student- and instructor-tested features of *The McGraw-Hill Handbook* equip today's students with tools for learning, writing, re-searching, and editing. The book also provides students and teachers with access to powerful online resources.

A Ready Resource

The second edition of *The McGraw-Hill Handbook* meets the needs of busy students with new, quickly accessible features that make it an even more convenient reference tool.

New Resources for Writers: Identifying and Editing Common Problems foldout

This handy reference presents easy access to fixes for the most common errors students make when editing for clarity, word choice, grammatical conventions, and correctness (punctuation, mechanics, and spelling). On the back of this foldout, students will find **Quick Reference for Multilingual Writers,** a chart offering help with the most common problems that affect Generation 1.5 students and English language learners alike.

New Resources for Writers foldouts for documenting in MLA and APA style

These foldouts reflect the most recent changes to these two styles of citation. On the front of each foldout, **Identifying and Documenting Sources,** flowcharts help guide students to the correct model citations in the text. On the reverse side, each panel includes visual guidelines for citing sources, showing where students can find the bibliographic information for a book, periodical article, Web site, selection from an online database (MLA), or online article with Digital Object Identifier (APA).

New Resources for Writers: Discipline-Specific Resources and World Map foldout

Since research forms a vital part of college writing, this pull-out section includes up-to-date information on reference works and resources from a variety of disciplines. More reliable than a Google search, this listing of academically vetted sources provides students with a quick-reference guide to the places online and in the library where research might reasonably start. A revised, full-color map of the world is found on the back of the foldout.

New attention to key writing outcomes

Writing Outcomes boxes at the beginning of each section indicate where students can find key material that will help them master aspects of writing such as rhetorical knowledge, the writing process, and critical thinking. Based on the Writing Program Administrators Outcomes Statement for First-Year Composition (reproduced on pp. xxxii–xxxiii), this feature helps students find the support they need to address the key issues in their writing on which they are likely to be assessed.

New checklists for self-assessment

These checklists on topics such as editing for style and avoiding plagiarism help students evaluate their own work and reflect on processes for improving their writing.

New online interactive tutorials

The handbook offers important guidance for students throughout college and beyond, and these online guides help students get the most out of this valuable resource. Brief visual overviews to using the text accompany interactive quizzes that help students become more familiar with it.

A Resource for Writing

The McGraw-Hill Handbook recognizes the importance of critical thinking and academic writing in first-year composition.

Guidelines for the most common college writing assignments
Part 2: Common Assignments across the Curriculum gives students step-by-step advice on writing the three most commonly assigned types of papers (informative, interpretive, and argumentative essays), as well as guidance on other common assignments including personal essays, case studies, lab reports, in-class essay exams, oral presentations with PowerPoint, and multimedia assignments. Eight full student papers appear in this section as models.

A focus on critical thinking and effective writing across the curriculum
Although instructors in various disciplines may approach subject matter differently, thinking critically and writing logically are underlying expectations across the curriculum. For this reason, Part 2 begins with a chapter on the connections among critical reading, thinking, and writing.

More sample papers and samples of writing than any other handbook
The McGraw-Hill Handbook provides plentiful samples of student and professional writing for a variety of purposes—to inform, interpret, and argue—from a wide range of disciplines. The writing process chapters follow the development of a student essay from conception to final draft; the document design chapter contains a student's reflective essay from an electronic portfolio; the common assignments chapters include eight student papers; and the MLA and APA documentation chapters each feature a complete student research report.

This edition includes four *new* sample student papers:

- Reflective essay from an electronic portfolio
- Informative report in the social sciences
- Interpretive analysis in the sciences
- Argument paper in the social sciences

New Expanded coverage of argument and visual argument
The second edition further equips students for success in this important genre, with fuller treatment of the classical appeals, fallacies, counterarguments, and the classical, Toulmin, and Rogerian structures of argument. New material on visual argument in Chapter 10: Arguments invites students to recognize the persuasive visual messages that surround them and help them to use those techniques in their own arguments.

👁 *New* **visual rhetoric icon complements integrated coverage of visual rhetoric**
This image appears throughout the text and in the table of contents on pages v–xxi. It guides students and instructors to sections dealing with the use of visuals—a complete listing also appears in the Quick Guide to Key Resources at the back of the book. *The McGraw-Hill Handbook* includes a section on learning in a multimedia world in Chapter 1: Learning across the Curriculum and a chapter on finding and creating effective visuals in Part 3: Researching. Coverage is also integrated throughout the text, particularly in Part 1: Writing and Designing Texts. In addition, the book itself includes visuals drawn from various disciplines, time periods, and cultures.

New updated coverage of today's technologies
Today's students have more opportunities to write than ever before, including *Facebook* and *MySpace* pages, e-mail and texting, chat rooms and blogs. The text gives updated advice on using online tools for learning; practical suggestions for using electronic resources to collaborate and revise; a chapter on designing papers and preparing print and electronic portfolios; advice for writing scannable résumés; and TextConnex boxes with advice on technology and useful links throughout the text.

Preparation for writing at work and in the community
Part 5: Writing beyond College demonstrates how writing in college prepares students for success in the professional world. Special topics include applying for internships, producing résumés, service learning, and creating brochures and newsletters. In addition, Writing beyond College boxes throughout the book illustrate the variety of writing situations students are likely to encounter outside college.

A Resource for Researching

The McGraw-Hill Handbook helps students navigate the complexities of research today.

New updated and expanded coverage of MLA, APA, and CSE documentation
Part 4: Documenting across the Curriculum now conforms to the seventh edition of the *MLA Handbook for Writers of Research Papers* (2009), the sixth edition of the *Publication Manual of the American Psychological Association* (2010), and the seventh edition of the *CSE Manual for Authors, Editors, and Publishers* (2006). (The text also includes up-to-date coverage of *Chicago Manual of Style* documentation.) This expanded section contains 120 MLA citation models and 69 APA citation models.

New Source Smart boxes
Appearing throughout Part 3: Researching, these boxes offer students tips on researching wisely. Topics include creating a research

strategy, conducting interviews, avoiding plagiarism, and integrating sources via summary, paraphrase, and quotation.

New **expanded sections on integrating sources and avoiding plagiarism**
In Chapter 21: Working with Sources and Avoiding Plagiarism, more examples and guidelines give students additional advice on using sources effectively in their papers. Thorough explanation of acceptable and unacceptable paraphrases, summaries, and quotations enables students to avoid accidental plagiarism. An expanded overview of copyright, plagiarism, and fair use appears in Chapter 20: Plagiarism, Copyright, and Intellectual Property.

New **expanded sections on how to evaluate and use online sources appropriately**
Chapter 18: Evaluating Sources now includes an examination of the reliability of three Web sites. These guidelines help students conduct Web research wisely. Chapter 21 helps students draw on a full range of media in their writing, with examples that include blog entries and audio podcasts.

New **discussion of annotated bibliography**
Chapter 21 includes a sample annotated bibliography. The text shows students how to complete this common research assignment, enabling them to assess and track their sources.

A unique chapter on finding and creating effective visuals
Chapter 17: Finding and Creating Effective Visuals includes discussions of why and when students should—or should not—use images to reinforce a point and gives them practical advice on displaying information visually.

A Resource for Editing

The McGraw-Hill Handbook helps today's students see how grammar fits into the writing process, so they can learn to become effective editors of their own work.

Grammar in the context of editing
Most of the chapters in Parts 7–11, which cover the conventions of English grammar, usage, punctuation, and mechanics, are structured first to teach students to identify a particular problem and then to edit to eliminate the problem in a way that strengthens their writing.

Identify and Edit boxes
These boxes appear in key style, grammar, and punctuation chapters. They give students (especially visual learners) strategies for identifying their most serious sentence problems and are especially useful for quick reference.

✓ *New* **Common Issues icon**
This new icon appears throughout the text and in the table of contents, highlighting sections that discuss students' most common difficulties with grammar, style, word choice, punctuation, and mechanics. These sections are listed in the Quick Guide to Key Resources at the back of the book and referenced, for quick consultation, on the Resources for Writers: Identifying and Editing Common Problems foldout.

New **interactive online Test Yourself diagnostic quizzes**
Now online, these interactive diagnostics provide immediate feedback to students to let them know where they need improvement, and where to find help in those areas. They help students gauge their own strengths and weaknesses on the conventions of grammar, style, punctuation, and mechanics. Two new quizzes cover the MLA and APA documentation styles.

Practice exercises
Practice exercises throughout the book include content from subjects across the curriculum that students are likely to encounter in their first-year courses. For students who need additional practice, *Catalyst 2.0* offers more than 4,500 exercises with immediate explanatory feedback in response to incorrect answers.

A Resource for Learning

The McGraw-Hill Handbook is unique in the amount of support it provides students to help them meet the challenges of learning in college.

A guide for success in college through writing
Chapter 1: Learning across the Curriculum introduces students to the new territory of college and to college writing. In this unique section, we define concepts such as *discipline* and explain how to use writing as a tool for learning. New tips in Chapter 1 help students set priorities, take notes, and succeed in all their courses.

Abundant resources for multilingual writers
The McGraw-Hill Handbook offers non-native speakers of English extensive support for learning and writing in college. Chapter 1 advises multilingual students on how to use writing to deal with their unique challenges. Numerous For Multilingual Students boxes throughout the book and Part 12, a three-chapter Guide for Multilingual Writers (prepared by Maria Zlateva, Director of ESL at Boston University), provide targeted advice on every stage of the writing process. A separate index for multilingual writers follows the main index. A complete list of all the For Multilingual Students boxes also appears in the Quick Guide to Key Resources at the back of the book. The Quick Reference for Multilingual Writers foldout offers handy grammar tips in a convenient format.

New **attention to Generation 1.5 of English language learners**
Chapter 1c: Learning in a Multilingual World now addresses both traditional ESL students and members of Generation 1.5, who have marginal proficiency in English as well as one or more other languages.

Further Resources for Learning
The innovative final section of the book, Part 13: Further Resources for Learning, provides students with a variety of aids—a timeline of world history, a glossary of selected terms from across the curriculum, a map of the world, and a directory of print and online discipline-specific resources—that will come in handy for students in a wide variety of courses.

Charting the Territory boxes
These boxes provide students with examples of how requirements and conventions vary across the curriculum. They present relevant information on such topics as informative assignments in different disciplines and the function of the passive voice in scientific writing.

A Resource for Technology

Online Learning Center (www.mhhe.com/mhhb2)

Throughout *The McGraw-Hill Handbook*, Web references in the margin let students know where they can find additional resources on the text's comprehensive Web site. Access to the site—which is powered by *Catalyst 2.0*, an online resource for writing, research, and editing—is free with every copy of *The McGraw-Hill Handbook*. The site includes the following resources for students:

- Interactive tutorials on document design and visual rhetoric
- Guides for avoiding plagiarism and evaluating sources
- Electronic writing tutors for composing informative, interpretive, and argumentative papers
- Over 4,500 exercises with feedback in grammar, usage, and punctuation

Additional Options Online

Connect Composition for *The McGraw-Hill Handbook*
This online premium companion to the text provides students and instructors with:

- **Interactive exercises and assignments keyed to the chapters of the text** which allow students to practice the material in the text and submit assignments online.

- **Online diagnostics and study plans** which allow students to test themselves and find where they might need help; Connect Composition will then suggest a course of study including video instruction, practice exercises, and a post-test.

- **Online tools for administering peer review** in a flexible, easy-to-use electronic format that help students throughout the process of inventing, drafting, and revising their work.

- **Live, online tutors** via Net Tutor that offer students help with their writing when instructors or writing centers might not be available.

- **Numerous additional interactive resources for writing and research,** including interactive writing tutors, as well as tutorials for visual rhetoric and avoiding plagiarism.

Connect Composition Plus: *The McGraw-Hill Handbook Online*
This interactive, economical alternative to the print text includes all of the features contained in Connect Composition *plus:*

- **All the content of the full handbook online,** optimized for online reading—with material broken out in easy-to-read chunks of information, and with interactive elements integrated contextually throughout.

- **A state-of-the-art search portal** which allows students to explore the whole text using numerous digital navigational tools including text and advanced text search options, hyperlinked indexes and table of contents, interactive Resources for Writers pages for help with the most common problems, and multimedia quick links that offer instant access to all of the text's multimedia instruction in one place.

- **Over 100 Ask the Author video segments** integrated throughout the digital text, providing students with instant-access multimedia guidance on the most commonly asked questions about writing, researching, editing, and designing their work.

- **An economical price** providing students access to the interactive text for approximately half the price of the print text.

Visit ShopMcGraw-Hill.com to purchase registration codes for this exciting new product. Or contact English@mcgraw-hill.com.

CourseSmart is a new way for faculty to find and review eTextbooks. It's also a great option for students who are interested in accessing their course materials digitally and saving money. CourseSmart offers thousands of the most commonly adopted textbooks across hundreds of courses from a wide variety of higher education publishers. It is the only place for faculty to review and compare the full text of a textbook online, providing immediate access without the environmental impact of requesting a print exam copy. At CourseSmart, students can save up to 50% off the cost of a print book, reduce their impact on the environment, and gain access to powerful Web tools for learning including full text search, notes and highlighting, and e-mail tools for sharing notes among classmates.

Tegrity Campus is a service that makes class time available all the time by automatically capturing every lecture in a searchable format for students to review when they study and complete assignments. With a simple one-click start and stop process, you capture all computer screens and corresponding audio. Students replay any part of any class with easy-to-use browser-based viewing on a PC or Mac.

Educators know that the more students can see, hear, and experience class resources, the better they learn. With Tegrity Campus, students quickly recall key moments by using Tegrity Campus's unique search feature. This search helps students efficiently find what they need, when they need it across an entire semester of class recordings. Help turn all your students' study time into learning moments immediately supported by your lecture.

To learn more about Tegrity, watch a two-minute Flash demo at http://tegritycampus.mhhe.com.

WPA Outcomes Statement for First-Year Composition

Adopted by the Council of Writing Program Administrators (WPA), April 2000. For further information about the development of the Outcomes Statement, please see http:// comppile.tamucc.edu/ WPAoutcomes/continue.html

For further information about the Council of Writing Program Administrators, please see http://www.wpacouncil.org

A version of this statement was published in WPA: Writing Program Administration 23.1/2 (fall/winter 1999): 59-66

Introduction

This statement describes the common knowledge, skills, and attitudes sought by first-year composition programs in American postsecondary education. To some extent, we seek to regularize what can be expected to be taught in first-year composition; to this end the document is not merely a compilation or summary of what currently takes place. Rather, the following statement articulates what composition teachers nationwide have learned from practice, research, and theory. This document intentionally defines only "outcomes," or types of results, and not "standards," or precise levels of achievement. The setting of standards should be left to specific institutions or specific groups of institutions.

Learning to write is a complex process, both individual and social, that takes place over time with continued practice and informed guidance. Therefore, it is important that teachers, administrators, and a concerned public do not imagine that these outcomes can be taught in reduced or simple ways. Helping students demonstrate these outcomes requires expert understanding of how students actually learn to write. For this reason we expect the primary audience for this document to be well-prepared college writing teachers and college writing program administrators. In some places, we have chosen to write in their professional language. Among such readers, terms such as "rhetorical" and "genre" convey a rich meaning that is not easily simplified. While we have also aimed at writing a document that the general public can understand, in limited cases we have aimed first at communicating effectively with expert writing teachers and writing program administrators.

These statements describe only what we expect to find at the end of first-year composition, at most schools a required general education course or sequence of courses. As writers move beyond first-year composition, their writing abilities do not merely improve. Rather, students' abilities not only diversify along disciplinary and professional lines but also move into whole new levels where expected outcomes expand, multiply, and diverge. For this reason, each statement of outcomes for first-year composition is followed by suggestions for further work that builds on these outcomes.

Rhetorical Knowledge

By the end of first year composition, students should
- Focus on a purpose
- Respond to the needs of different audiences
- Respond appropriately to different kinds of rhetorical situations
- Use conventions of format and structure appropriate to the rhetorical situation
- Adopt appropriate voice, tone, and level of formality

- Understand how genres shape reading and writing
- Write in several genres

Faculty in all programs and departments can build on this preparation by helping students learn
- The main features of writing in their fields
- The main uses of writing in their fields
- The expectations of readers in their fields

Critical Thinking, Reading, and Writing

By the end of first year composition, students should
- Use writing and reading for inquiry, learning, thinking, and communicating
- Understand a writing assignment as a series of tasks, including finding, evaluating, analyzing, and synthesizing appropriate primary and secondary sources
- Integrate their own ideas with those of others
- Understand the relationships among language, knowledge, and power

Faculty in all programs and departments can build on this preparation by helping students learn
- The uses of writing as a critical thinking method
- The interactions among critical thinking, critical reading, and writing
- The relationships among language, knowledge, and power in their fields

Processes

By the end of first year composition, students should
- Be aware that it usually takes multiple drafts to create and complete a successful text
- Develop flexible strategies for generating, revising, editing, and proof-reading
- Understand writing as an open process that permits writers to use later invention and re-thinking to revise their work
- Understand the collaborative and social aspects of writing processes
- Learn to critique their own and others' works
- Learn to balance the advantages of relying on others with the responsibility of doing their part
- Use a variety of technologies to address a range of audiences

Faculty in all programs and departments can build on this preparation by helping students learn
- To build final results in stages
- To review work-in-progress in collaborative peer groups for purposes other than editing
- To save extensive editing for later parts of the writing process
- To apply the technologies commonly used to research and communicate within their fields

Knowledge of Conventions

By the end of first year composition, students should
- Learn common formats for different kinds of texts
- Develop knowledge of genre conventions ranging from structure and paragraphing to tone and mechanics
- Practice appropriate means of documenting their work
- Control such surface features as syntax, grammar, punctuation, and spelling

Faculty in all programs and departments can build on this preparation by helping students learn
- The conventions of usage, specialized vocabulary, format, and documentation in their fields
- Strategies through which better control of conventions can be achieved
  [http://www.wpacouncil.org/positions/outcomes.html, accessed 10/17/2008]

Supplements to *The McGraw-Hill Handbook*

Instructor's Manual (available online in printable format)
(www.mhhe.com/mhhb2)
Deborah Coxwell Teague, Florida State University; Dan
Melzer, California State University, Sacramento; Lynette Reini-
Grandell, Normandale Community College

MLA Quick Reference Guide (ISBN 0-07-730080-7)
Carol Schuck, Ivy Tech Community College
This handy card features the basic guidelines for MLA citation
in a convenient, portable format.

APA Quick Reference Guide (ISBN 0-07-730076-9)
Carol Schuck, Ivy Tech Community College
This handy card features the basic guidelines for APA citation in
a convenient, portable format.

*Partners in Teaching: Instructor Resource Portal for
Composition*
(www.mhhe.com/englishcommunity)
McGraw-Hill is proud to partner with many of the top names
in the field to build a *community of teachers helping teachers.*
Partners in Teaching features up-to-date scholarly discourse,
practical teaching advice, and community support for new and
experienced instructors.

The McGraw-Hill Exercise Book (ISBN 0-07-326032-0)
Santi Buscemi, Middlesex College and Susan Popham,
University of Memphis
This workbook features numerous sentence-level and paragraph-
level editing exercises, as well as exercises in research, docu-
mentation, and the writing process.

The McGraw-Hill Exercise Book for Multilingual Writers
(ISBN 0-07-326030-4)
Maggie Sokolik, University of California, Berkeley
This workbook features numerous sentence-level and paragraph-
level editing exercises tailored specifically for multilingual
students.

The McGraw-Hill Writer's Journal (ISBN 0-07-326031-2)
Lynée Gaillet, Georgia State University
This elegant journal for students includes quotes on writing
from famous authors, as well as advice and tips on writing and
the writing process.

Dictionary and Vocabulary Resources

Merriam-Webster's Collegiate® Dictionary, Eleventh Edition (ISBN 978-0-877-79808-8)
The new edition of America's best-selling dictionary merges print, CD-ROM, and online formats to deliver unprecedented accessibility and flexibility. Fully revised content features more than 225,000 clear and precise definitions and more than 10,000 new words and meanings. Includes an easy-to-install Windows/Macintosh CD-ROM and a free one-year subscription to the Collegiate Web site.

The Merriam-Webster Dictionary (Paperback) (ISBN 978-0-877-79930-6)
This completely revised edition of the best-selling dictionary of all time covers the core vocabulary of everyday life.

The Merriam-Webster Thesaurus (Paperback). (ISBN 978-0-877-79637-4)
The new edition of this classic thesaurus features over 150,000 synonyms, antonyms, and related and contrasted words.

Merriam-Webster's Notebook Dictionary. (ISBN 978-0-8777-9650-3)
This handy, quick-reference word resource is conveniently designed for three-ring binders. Includes definitions for 40,000 words.

Merriam-Webster's Notebook Thesaurus (ISBN 978-0-8777-9671-8)
Conveniently designed for three-ring binders, this quick-reference compendium provides synonyms, related words, and antonyms for over 100,000 words.

Merriam-Webster's Dictionary and Thesaurus (ISBN 978-0-8777-9851-4)
This incredible new addition to the Merriam-Webster family features two essential references in one handy volume. 60,000 alphabetical dictionary entries integrated with more than 13,000 thesaurus entries.

Merriam-Webster's Vocabulary Builder (ISBN 978-0-877-79910-8)
Introducing 3,000 words and including quizzes to test progress, this excellent resource will help students improve their vocabulary skills.

Merriam-Webster's Dictionary of Basic English (ISBN 978-0-8777-9605-3)
Over 33,000 entries offer concise, easy-to-understand definitions. More than 10,000 word-use examples, over 400 black-and-white

illustrations, word histories, abbreviations, and proper names make this a great resource for multilingual students.

Acknowledgments

When we wrote *The McGraw-Hill Handbook,* we started with the premise that it takes a campus to teach a writer. It is also the case that it takes a community to write a handbook. This text has been a major collaborative effort for all three of us. And over the years, that ever-widening circle of collaboration has included reviewers, editors, librarians, faculty colleagues, and family members.

Let us start close to home. Mort Maimon brought to this project his years of insight and experience as a writer and as a secondary and post-secondary English teacher. Gillian Maimon, a first-grade teacher, a PhD candidate, and a writing workshop leader, and Alan Maimon, a journalist who is expert in using every resource available to writers, inspired and encouraged their mother in this project. Elaine also drew inspiration from her young granddaughters, Dasia and Madison Stewart and Annabelle Elaine Maimon, who already show promise of becoming writers. Rudy Peritz and Lynne Haney reviewed drafts of a number of chapters, bringing to our cross-curricular mix the pedagogical and writerly perspectives of, respectively, a law professor and a sociologist. Jess Peritz, a recent college graduate, was consulted on numerous occasions for her expert advice on making examples both up-to-date and understandable. David, Genevieve, and Matthew Yancey—whose combined writing experience includes the fields of biology, psychology, medicine, computer engineering, mathematics, industrial engineering, and information technology—helped with examples as well as with their understandings of writing both inside and outside of the academy.

At Governors State University, Diane Dates Casey, dean of Library Science and Academic Computing, provided research support, while Executive Assistant Penny Purdue gave overall encouragement. At Arizona State University West, Beverly Buddee, executive assistant to the provost, worried with us over this project for many years. Our deepest gratitude goes to Lisa Kammerlocher and Dennis Isbell for the guidelines on critically evaluating Web resources in Chapter 18, as well as to Sharon Wilson. Thanks, too, go to C. J. Jeney and Cheryl Warren for providing assistance. ASU West professors Thomas McGovern and Martin Meznar shared assignments and student papers with us. In the chancellor's office at the University of Alaska Anchorage, Denise Burger, and Christine Tullius showed admirable support and patience.

Several colleagues at Queens College and elsewhere not only shared their insights on teaching and writing, but also gave us valuable classroom materials to use as we saw fit. Our thanks go to Fred

Buell, Stuart Cochran, Nancy Comley, Ann Davison, Joan Dupre, Hugh English, Sue Goldhaber, Marci Goodman, Steve Kruger, Eric Lehman, Norman Lewis, Charles Molesworth, Beth Stickney, Amy Tucker, and Stan Walker. We are also grateful to Jane Collins, Jane Hathaway, Jan Tecklin, Christine Timm, Scott Zaluda, Diane Zannoni, and Richard Zeikowitz. The Queens College librarians also gave us help with the researching and documentation chapters, and we thank them, especially Sharon Bonk, Alexandra DeLuise, Izabella Taler, and Manny Sanudo.

We give special thanks to the students whose papers we include in full: Rajeev Bector, Diane Chen, Sam Chodoff, McKenna Doherty, Josh Feldman, Audrey Galeano, Josephine Hearn, Esther Hoffman, Carlos Jasperson, Ignacio Sanderson, Mark Shemwell, Jon Paul Terrell, and Ken Tinnes. We also acknowledge the following students who allowed us to use substantial excerpts from their work: Ilona Bouzoukashvili, Lara Deforest, Baz Dreisinger, Sheila Foster, Jacob Grossman, Jennifer Koehler, Holly Musetti, and Umawattie Roopnarian.

Our thanks also go to Judy Williamson and Trent Batson for contributing their expertise on writing and computers as well as for sharing what they learned from the Epiphany Project. We are grateful to Harvey Wiener and the late Richard Marius for their permission to draw on their explanations of grammatical points in *The McGraw-Hill Handbook.* We also appreciate the work of Andras Tapolcai, who collected many of the examples used in the documentation chapters, and the contributions of Maria Zlateva of Boston University; Karen Batchelor of City College of San Francisco; and Daria Ruzicka for their work on Part 12: A Guide for Multilingual Writers and on the For Multilingual Students boxes that appear throughout the text. Thanks to Charlotte Smith of Adirondack Community College for her help on several sections of the book. Thanks also go to librarians Debora Person, University of Wyoming, and Ronelle K. H. Thompson, Augustana College, who provided us with helpful comments on Part 3: Researching. Our colleague Don McQuade has inspired us, advised us, and encouraged us throughout the years of this project.

Within the McGraw-Hill organization, many wonderful people have been our true teammates. Tim Julet believed in this project initially and signed us on to what has become a major life commitment. From 1999, Lisa Moore, first as executive editor for the composition list, then as publisher for English, and now as publisher for special projects in Art, Humanities, and Literature, has creatively, expertly, and tirelessly led the group of development editors and in-house experts who have helped us find the appropriate form to bring our insights as composition teachers to the widest possible group of students. We have learned a great deal from Lisa. Thanks also to

Christopher Bennem, who had the unenviable job of filling Lisa's shoes as sponsoring editor. Crucial support also came from Beth Mejia, editorial director; David Patterson, publisher for English; Dawn Groundwater, director of development for English; and Molly Meneely, market development manager. This book has benefited enormously from three extraordinary development editors: Anne Kemper, development editor; Carla Samodulski, senior development editor; and David Chodoff, senior development editor. All were true collaborators; as the chapters on editing show, the book has benefited enormously from their care and intelligence. Other editorial kudos go out to Meredith Grant, Drew Henry, Karen Herter, Bruce Thaler, Joanna Imm, Judy Voss, Sarah Caldwell, Laura Olson, Elsa Peterson, Aaron Zook, Karen Mauk, Steven Kemper, Anne Stameshkin, and Margaret Farley for their tireless work on this project. Thanks as well to Paul Banks, Andrea Pasquarelli, Todd Vaccaro, Alex Rohrs, and Manoj Mehta, without whom there would be no *Catalyst 2.0*. Chanda Feldman and Brett Coker, lead project managers, monitored every detail of production; Cassandra Chu, lead designer, supervised every aspect of the striking text design and cover; and Robin Mouat and Sonia Brown, art editors, were responsible for the stunning visuals that appear throughout the book. Allison Jones, executive marketing manager; and Ray Kelley, Paula Radosevich, Byron Hopkins, Barbara Siry, and Brian Gore, field publishers, have worked tirelessly and enthusiastically to market *The McGraw-Hill Handbook*. Jeff Brick provided valuable promotional support. We also appreciate the hands-on attention of McGraw-Hill senior executives Mike Ryan, editor-in-chief of the Humanities, Social Sciences, and World Languages group; and Steve Debow, president of the Humanities, Social Sciences, and World Languages group.

Finally, many, many thanks go to the reviewers who read this text, generously shared their perceptions, and had confidence in us as we shaped this book to address the needs of their students. We wish to thank the following instructors:

Content Consultants and Reviewers

Angela Albright, North West Arkansas Community College

Regina Alston, North Carolina Central University

Don Bennett, Jacksonville State University

Doug Branch, Southwest Tennessee Community College, Macon

Ashlee Brand, Cuyahoga Community College

Carolyn Briggs, Marshalltown Community College

Christy Burns, Jacksonville State University

Licia Calloway, The Citadel

Yvonne Cassidy, Alfred State College

Constance Chapman, Clark Atlanta University

April Childress, Greenville Technical College

P.J. Colbert, Marshalltown Community College

Aniko Constantine, Alfred State College

Julia Cote, Houston Community College

Darin Cozzens, Surry Community College

Nancy Davies, Miami Dade College

Editorial Board of Advisors

Ellen Laird, Hudson Valley Community College

Shellie Michael, Volunteer State Community College

Kathleen Moore, University of California, Riverside

Michael Ronan, Houston Community College

Linda Strahan, University of California, Riverside

Freshman Composition Symposia

Every year McGraw-Hill conducts Freshman Composition Symposia, which are attended by instructors from across the country. These events are an opportunity for editors from McGraw-Hill to gather information about the needs and challenges of instructors teaching the Freshman Composition course. They also offer a forum for the attendees to exchange ideas and experiences with colleagues they might not have otherwise met. The feedback we have received has been invaluable and has contributed—directly or indirectly—to the development of *The McGraw-Hill Handbook* and its supplements.

Ellen Arnold, Coastal Carolina University

Tony Atkins, University of North Carolina, Wilmington

Edith Baker, Bradley University

Evan Balkan, Community College of Baltimore

Carolyn Barr, Broward Community College

Laura Basso, Joliet Junior College

Linda Bergmann, Purdue University

Karen Bilda, Cardinal Stritch University

Carol Bledsoe, Florida Gulf Coast University

Kimberly Bovee, Tidewater Community College

Charley Boyd, Genesee Community College

Charlotte Brammer, Samford University

Amy Braziller, Red Rocks Community College

Bob Broad, Illinois State University

Cheryl Brown, Towson University

Liz Bryant, Purdue University, Calumet-Hammod

JoAnn Buck, Guilford Technical Community College

Monica Busby, University of Louisiana, Lafayette

Jonathan Bush, Western Michigan University

Steve Calatrello, Calhoun Community College

Susan Callendar, Sinclair Community College

Diane Canow, Johnson County Community College

Richard Carpenter, Valdosta State University

Sandy Clark, Anderson University

Keith Comer, University of Canterbury

Jennifer Cooper, University of Texas, Arlington

Deborah Coxwell-Teague, Florida State University

Mary Ann Crawford, Central Michigan University

Susan Jaye Dauer, Valencia Community College

Michael Day, Northern Illinois University

Rosemary Day, Central New Mexico Community College

Michel de Benedictis, Miami-Dade College

Anne Dearing, Hudson Valley Community College

Nancy DeJoy, Michigan State University

Christy Desmet, University of Georgia

Brock Dethier, Utah State University

Carlton Downey, Houston Community College

Robert Eddy, Washington State University

Anthony Edgington, University of Toledo

Dan Ferguson, Amarillo College

Bonnie Finkelstein, Montgomery County Community College

Steve Fox, Indiana University–Purdue University, Indianapolis

Sherrin Frances, San Jacinto College, Pasadena

Elaine Fredericksen, University of Texas, El Paso

Karen Gardiner, University of Alabama, Tuscaloosa

Judith Gardner, University of Texas, San Antonio

Elizabeth Gassel, Darton College

Joanna Gibson, Texas A&M University

Lois Gilmore, Bucks County Community College

Chuck Gonzalez, Central Florida Community College, Ocala

John Gooch, University of Texas, Dallas

Cathy Gorvine, Delgado Community College

Frank Gunshanan, Daytona State College

Emily Gwinn, Glendale Community College

Audley Hall, North West Arkansas Community College

Carolyn Handa, University of Alabama, Tuscaloosa

Rebecca Heintz, Polk Community College

Dedria Humphries, Lansing Community College

Kim Jameson, Oklahoma City Community College

Nanette Jaynes, Wesleyan College

Theodore Johnston, El Paso Community College

Peggy Jolly, University of Alabama, Birmingham

Joseph Jones, University of Memphis

Rebecca Kajs, Anne Arundel Community College

Pam Kannady, Tulsa Community College

Shelley Kelly, College of Southern Nevada

Elizabeth Kessler, University of Houston

Kirk Kidwell, Michigan State University

Roxanne Kirkwood, Marshall University

Sandra Lakey, Pennsylvania College of Technology

William Lennertz, Santiago Canyon College

Tom Lovin, Southwestern Illinois College

Heidi Marshall, Florida Community College

Denise Martone, New York University

Barry Mauer, University of Central Florida

Michael McCready, University of Mississippi

Sharon McGee, Southern Illinois University, Edwardsville

Janice McIntire-Strasburg, St. Louis University

Patrick McLaughlin, Lakeland Community College

Shellie Michael, Volunteer State Community College

John Miles, University of New Mexico

Susan Miller, Santa Fe Community College

Susan Miller-Cochran, North Carolina State University, Raleigh

Jennifer Nelson, College of Southern Nevada

Donna Nelson-Beene, Bowling Green State University

Lindee Owens, University of Central Florida

Matthew Parfitt, Boston University

Irvin Peckham, Louisiana State University

Chere Peguesse, Valdosta State University

Bruce Peppard, El Camino College

Rich Peraud, St. Louis Community College, Meramec

David Peterson, University of Nebraska, Omaha

Helen Frances Poehlman, Blinn College

Susan Popham, University of Memphis

Mara Rainwater, Keiser University

Christa Raney, University of North Alabama

Beverly Reed, College of Dupage

Patricia Reid, University of Toledo

David Reinheimer, Southeast Missouri State University

Mandi Riley, Florida A&M University

Dixil Rodriguez, Tarrant County College

Denise Rogers, University of Louisiana

Lou Ethel Rolliston, Bergen Community College

Shirley Rose, Purdue University

Kathleen Ryan, University of Montana

Mary Sauer, Indiana University–Purdue University, Indianapolis

Mark Saunders, Front Range Community College

Matthew Schmeer, Johnson County Community College

Jane Schreck, Bismark State College

Carol Schuck, Ivy Tech Community College

Marc Scott, New Mexico State University

Susan Sebok, South Suburban College

Wendy Sharer, East Carolina University

E. Stone Shiflet, Capella University

Patrick Slattery, University of Arkansas

Beverly Slaughter, Brevard Community College, Melbourne

James Sodon, St. Louis Community College, Florissant Valley

Ann Spurlock, Mississippi State

Wayne Stein, University of Central Oklahoma

Kip Strasma, Illinois Central College

Beverly Stroud, Greenville Technical College

Paul Tanner, Utah Valley University

Todd Taylor, University of North Carolina

William Thelin, University of Akron

Gordon Thomas, University of Idaho

Donna Thomsen, Johnson & Wales University

Martha Tolleson, Collin College

Pauline Uchmanowicz, State University of New York, New Paltz

Frank Vaughn, Campbell University

Stephanie Venza, Brookhaven College

Philip Virgen, Wilbur Wright College

Judy Welch, Miami-Dade College

Christina Wells, Northern Virginia Community College

Jeff Wiemelt, Southeastern Louisiana University

John Ziebell, College of Southern Nevada

Supplements Team

Preston Allen, Miami Dade College

Santi Buscemi, Middlesex College

Deborah Coxwell Teague, Florida State University

Thomas Dinsmore, University of Cincinnati, Clermont College

Lynée Gaillet, Georgia State University

Dan Melzer, California State University, Sacramento

Susan Popham, University of Memphis

Lynette Reini-Grandell, Normandale Community College

Carol Schuck, Ivy Tech Community College

Maggie Sokolik, University of California, Berkeley

Technology Consultants

Cheryl Ball, Illinois State University

Dene Grigar, Washington State University

Elizabeth Nist, Anoka-Ramsey Community College

Donna Reiss, Tidewater Community College

Rich Rice, Texas Tech University

Heather Robinson, City University of New York, York College

James Sodon, St. Louis Community College, Florissant Valley

ESL Consultants

Karen Batchelor, City College of San Francisco

Cherry Campbell, University of California, Los Angeles

Christine T. Francisco, City College of San Francisco

Candace A. Henry, Westmoreland Community College

Maria Zlateva, Boston University

Design and Cover Reviewers

Yvonne Cassidy, Alfred State College

Constance Chapman, Clark Atlanta University

April Childress, Greenville Technical College

Aniko Constantine, Alfred State College

Julia Cote, Houston Community College

Michael Day, Northern Illinois University

Anne Dearing, Hudson Valley Community College

Nancy Rosenberg England, University of Texas, Arlington

Mary Evans, Hudson Valley Community College

Holly French, Bossier Parish Community College

Jeannine Horn, Houston Community College

Gloria Horton, Jacksonville State University

Sandy Jordan, University of Houston

Lori Kanitz, Oral Roberts University

Mary Lang, Wharton County Junior College

Chester Mills, Southern University, New Orleans

Jennifer Mooney, Wharton County Junior College

Thomas Moretti, University of Maryland

Sandra Offiah-Hawkins, Daytona State College

Terrie Leigh Relf, San Diego City College

John Schaffer, Blinn College

Linda Tetzlaff, Normandale Community College

Christopher Twiggs, Florida Community College, Jacksonville

Focus Group and Seminar Participants

Joyce Adams, Brigham Young University

Jeannette Adkins, Tarrant County Community College

Jim Allen, College of Dupage

Sonja Andrus, Collin College

Marcy Bauman, Lansing Community College

Sue Beebe, Texas State University, San Marcos

Candace Bergstrom, Houston Community College

Bruce Bogdon, Houston Community College

Barbara Bonallo, Miami-Dade College

Sarah Bruton, Fayetteville Tech Community College

Joe Bryan, El Paso Community College

Alma Bryant, University of South Florida

Lauryn Angel Cann, Collin College

Diane Carr, Midlands Technical College

Lucia Cherciu, Dutchess Community College

Regina Clemens Fox, Arizona State University

Terry Cole, Laguardia Community College

Keith Comer, University of Canterbury

Genevieve Coogan, Houston Community College

Dagmar Corrigan, University of Houston

Marla DeSoto, Glendale Community College

Debra Dew, University of Colorado, Colorado Springs

Erika Dieters, Moraine Valley Community College

Michael Donnelly, Ball State University

Marilyn Douglas-Jones, Houston Community College

Carlton Downey, Houston Community College

Lisa Dresdner, Norwalk Community College

Heather Eaton, Daytona State College

George Edwards, Tarrant County Community College

Richard Enos, Texas Christian University

Nancy Enright, Seton Hall University

Paula Eschliman, Richland College

Karin Evans, College of Dupage

Jennie Fauls, Columbia College–Chicago

Africa Fine, Florida Atlantic University

Stacha Floyd, Wayne County Community College

John Freeman, El Paso Community College

Casey Furlong, Glendale Community College

Karen Gardiner, University of Alabama, Tuscaloosa

Mary Lee Geary, Front Range Community College

Ruth Gerik, University of Texas, Arlington

Phyllis Gooden, Atlantic International University, Chicago

Lisa Gordon, Columbus State Community College

Jay Gordon, Youngstown State University

Steffen Guenzel, University of Alabama, Tuscaloosa

John Hagerty, Auburn University

Jonathan Hall, Rutgers University, Newark

Dustin Hanvey, Pasadena Area Community College

Bryant Hayes, Bernard M. Baruch College

Shawn Hellman, Pima Community College

Maren Henry, University of West Georgia

Kevin Hicks, Alabama State University

Brandy James, University of West Georgia

Peggy Jolly, University of Alabama, Birmingham

Nicole Khoury, Arizona State University

Jessica Kidd, University of
Alabama, Tuscaloosa

Lindsay Lewan, Arapahoe
Community College

Victoria Lisle, Auburn
University

Colleen Lloyd, Cuyahoga
Community College

Margaret Lowry,
University of Texas,
Arlington

Andrew Manno, Raritan
Valley Community
College

Shirley McBride, Collin
College

Dan Melzer, California
State University,
Sacramento

Erica Messenger, Bowling
Green State University

Joyce Miller, Collin
College

Dorothy Minor, Tulsa
Community College

Webster Newbold, Ball
State University

Gordon O'Neal, Collin
College

Maryann Perlman, Wayne
County Community
College

Joann Pinkston-McDuffie,
Daytona State College

Deborah Prickett,
Jacksonville State
University

Roberta Proctor, Palm
Beach Community
College, Lake Worth

Helen Raica-Klotz,
Saginaw Valley State
University

Sharon Roberts, Auburn
University

Cassanda Robison, Central
Florida Community
College

Michael Ronan, Houston
Community College

Jane Rosencrans, J.S.
Reynolds Community
College

Mark Saunders, Front
Range Community
College

Mary Beth Schillacci,
Houston Community
College

Shelita Shaw, Moraine
Valley Community
College

Jenny Sheppard, New
Mexico State University

Michelle Sidler, Auburn
University

Jean Sorensen, Grayson
County College

Cathy Stablein, College of
Dupage

Wayne Stein, University of
Central Oklahoma

Martha Tolleson, Collin
College

Saundra Towns, Bernard
M. Baruch College

George Trail, University of
Houston

Bryon Turman, North
Carolina A&T University

Christopher Twiggs,
Florida Community
College

Kathryn Valentine, New
Mexico State University

Kevin Waltman,
University of Alabama

Maryann Whitaker,
University of Alabama,
Tuscaloosa

Joseph White, Fayetteville
Tech Community College

Virginia Wicher, Tarrant
County Community
College

Reginald Williams,
Daytona State College

Elizabeth Woodworth,
Auburn University,
Montgomery

Elaine P. Maimon
Janice H. Peritz
Kathleen Blake Yancey

About the Authors

Elaine P. Maimon is president of Governors State University in the south suburbs of Chicago, where she is also professor of English. Previously she was chancellor of the University of Alaska Anchorage, provost (chief campus officer) at Arizona State University West, and vice president of Arizona State University as a whole. In the 1970s, she initiated and then directed the Beaver College writing-across-the-curriculum program, one of the first WAC programs in the nation. A founding executive board member of the National Council of Writing
Program Administrators (WPA), she has directed national institutes to improve the teaching of writing and to disseminate the principles of writing across the curriculum. With a PhD in English from the University of Pennsylvania, where she later helped to create the Writing Across the University (WATU) program, she has also taught and served as an academic administrator at Haverford College, Brown University, and Queens College.

Janice Haney Peritz is an associate professor of English who has taught college writing for more than thirty years, first at Stanford University, where she received her PhD in 1978, and then at the University of Texas at Austin; Beaver College; and Queens College, City University of New York. From 1989 to 2002, she directed the Composition Program at Queens College, where in 1996, she also initiated the college's writing-across-the-curriculum program and the English department's involvement with the Epiphany Project and cyber-composition. She also worked with a group
of CUNY colleagues to develop The Write Site, an online learning center, and more recently directed the CUNY Honors College at Queens College for three years. Currently, she is back in the English department doing what she loves most: full-time classroom teaching of writing, literature, and culture.

Kathleen Blake Yancey is the Kellogg W. Hunt Professor of English and director of the Graduate Program in Rhetoric and Composition at Florida State University. She is past president of the Council of Writing Program Administrators (WPA), past chair of the Conference on College Composition and Communication (CCCC), and past president of the National Council of Teachers of English (NCTE). In addition, she co-directs the Inter/National Coalition on Electronic Portfolio Research. She has directed several institutes focused on electronic portfolios and on service
learning and reflection, and with her colleagues in English education, she is working on developing a program in new literacies. Previously, she has taught at UNC Charlotte and at Clemson University, where she directed the Pearce Center for Professional Communication and created the Class of 1941 Studio for Student Communication, both of which are dedicated to supporting communication across the curriculum.

The way the butterfly in this image emerges on a computer screen, as if from a cocoon of written text, suggests the way writers transform words and visuals into finished works through careful planning, drafting, revision, and design.

PART

1

I like to do first drafts at night, when I'm tired, and then do the surgical work in the morning when I'm sharp.

—ALEX HALEY

Writing and Designing Texts

1 Learning across the Curriculum

1a Use writing to learn as you learn to write.

College is a place for exploration. You will travel through many courses, participating in numerous conversations—oral and written—about nature, society, and culture. As you navigate your college experience, use this book as your map and guide.

- As a map, this text will help you understand different approaches to knowledge and see how your studies relate to the larger world of learning.

- As a guide, this text will help you write everything from notes to exams to research papers.

www.mhhe.com/
mhhb2

For discipline-related resources, go to

Links across the
Curriculum

1. Studying the world through a range of academic disciplines

Each department in your college represents a specialized territory of academic study, or area of inquiry, called a **discipline.** A discipline has its own history, terminology, issues, and subgroups. The discipline of sociology, for example, is concerned with the conditions,

WRITING OUTCOMES

Part 1: Writing and Designing Texts
This section will help you answer questions such as:

Rhetorical Knowledge
- How do I respond appropriately to different writing situations? **(2b–h)**
- What type of visuals will help my writing achieve its purpose? **(3d)**

Critical Thinking, Reading, and Writing
- What is a thesis statement, and how do I think of one? **(3b)**
- How do I provide constructive feedback on my classmates' work? **(5a)**

Processes
- What are the components of the writing process? **(2a)**
- How can technology help me in the writing process? **(4a, 5b, 5c, 6b)**

Knowledge of Conventions
- How can I write effective, organized paragraphs? **(4c)**
- What aspects of document design can help my writing communicate more effectively? **(6c)**

CHARTING the TERRITORY

Getting the Most from a Course

When you take a course, your purpose is not just to amass information. Your purpose is also to understand the kinds of questions people who work in the discipline ask.

- In an art history class, for example, you might ask how a work relates to an artist's life and times.
- In a math class, you might ask about the practical applications of a particular concept.

patterns, and problems of people in groups and societies. Sociologists collect, analyze, and interpret data about groups and societies; they also debate the data's reliability and various interpretations in journals, books, conferences, and classrooms.

Your college curriculum is likely to include distribution requirements that will expose you to a range of disciplines. You may be asked to take one or two courses in the humanities (the disciplines of literature, music, and philosophy, for example), the social sciences (sociology, economics, and psychology, for example), and the natural sciences (physics, biology, and chemistry, for example). When you write in each discipline—taking notes, writing papers, answering essay-exam questions—you will join the academic conversation, deepen your understanding of how knowledge is constructed, and learn to see and think about the world from different vantage points.

2. Using writing as a tool for learning

One goal of this handbook is to help you create well-researched and interesting texts. As you go from course to course, however, remember that writing itself is a great aid to learning. Think of the way a simple shopping list helps your memory once you get to the store, or recall the last time you were asked to keep the minutes of a meeting. Because of your heightened attention, you undoubtedly knew more about what happened at that meeting than did anyone else who attended it. Writing helps you remember, understand, and create.

www.mhhe.com/
mhhb2
For more on learning
in college, go to
Learning

- **Writing aids memory.** From taking class notes (*see Figure 1.1 on p. 4*) to jotting down ideas for later development, writing ensures that you will be able to retrieve important information. Many students use an informal outline for lecture notes (*see Figure 1.1*) and then go back to fill in the details after class. Write down ideas inspired by your course work—in any form or order. These ideas can be the seeds for a research project or other critical inquiry.

www.mhhe.com/
mhhb2
For activities to help
strengthen your use
of writing as a tool
for learning, go to
Learning > Writing
to Learn Exercises

👁 *Sections dealing with visual rhetoric*

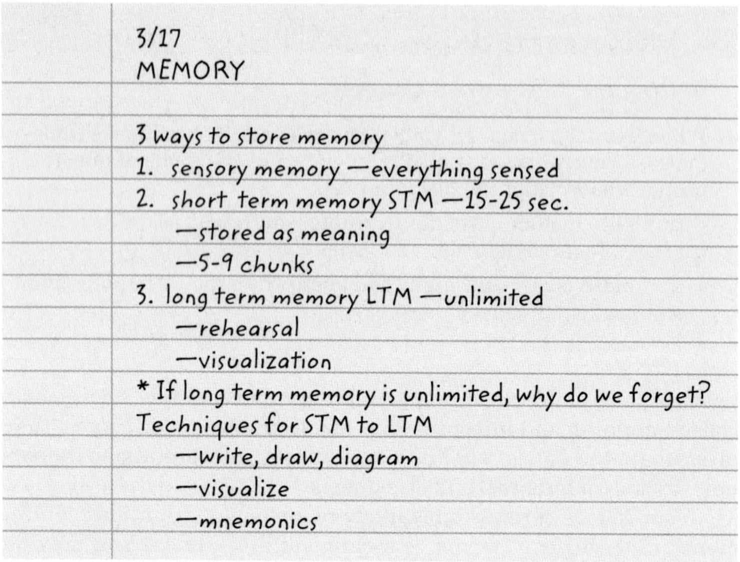

3/17
MEMORY

3 ways to store memory
1. sensory memory —everything sensed
2. short term memory STM —15-25 sec.
   —stored as meaning
   —5-9 chunks
3. long term memory LTM —unlimited
   —rehearsal
   —visualization
* If long term memory is unlimited, why do we forget?
Techniques for STM to LTM
   —write, draw, diagram
   —visualize
   —mnemonics

FIGURE 1.1 Lecture notes. Jotting down the main ideas of a lecture and the questions they raise helps you become a more active listener.

- **Writing sharpens observations.** When you record what you see, hear, taste, smell, and feel, you increase the powers of your senses. Note the smells during a chemistry experiment, and you will more readily detect changes caused by reactions.

- **Writing clarifies thought.** Carefully reading your own early drafts helps you pinpoint what you really want to say. The last paragraph of a first draft often becomes the first paragraph of the next draft.

- **Writing uncovers connections.** Maybe a character in a short story reminds you of your neighbor, or an image in a poem makes you feel sad. Writing down the reasons you make connections like these can help you learn more about the work and, possibly, more about yourself.

- **Writing improves reading.** When you read, taking notes on the main ideas and drafting a brief summary of the writer's points sharpen your reading skills and help you retain what you have read. Writing a personal reaction to the reading enhances your understanding. (*For a detailed discussion of critical reading and writing, see Chapter 7.*)

- **Writing strengthens argument.** In the academic disciplines, an argument is not a fiery disagreement but rather a path of reasoning to a position. When you write an argument, you work out the connections between your ideas—uncovering both flaws that force you to rethink your position and new connections that make your position stronger. Writing also requires you to consider your audience and the objections they might raise. (*For a detailed discussion of argument, see Chapter 10.*)

3. Taking responsibility for reading, writing, and research

www.mhhe.com/
mhhb2
For more on study
skills, go to
Learning > Study
Skills Tutor

The academic community assumes that you are an independent learner, capable of managing your workload without supervision. For most courses, the course syllabus will be the primary guide to what is expected of you, serving as a contract between you and your instructor. It will tell you what reading you need to do in advance of each class, when tests are scheduled, and when papers or stages of papers (for example, topic and research plan, draft, and final paper) are due. Use the syllabus to map out your weekly schedule for reading, research, and writing. (*For tips on how to schedule a research paper, see Chapter 15.*)

If you are collaborating with a group on a project, plan a series of meetings well in advance to avoid schedule conflicts. Also make time for your solo projects, away from the distractions of phones, e-mail, and visitors. You will be much more efficient if you work in shorter blocks of concentrated time than if you let your reading and writing drag on for hours filled with interruptions.

4. Recognizing that writing improves with practice

Composition courses are extremely valuable in helping you learn to write at the college level, but your development as a writer does not end there. Writing in all your courses, throughout your academic career, will enable you to mature as a writer while preparing you for more writing after college.

Exercise 1.1 Examining a syllabus

Refer to the syllabus for your writing class and answer the following questions:

1. How can you get in touch with your instructor? When should you contact him or her?
2. How much is class participation worth in your overall course grade?
3. What happens if you turn in a paper late?
4. How are final course grades determined? Is there a final exam or culminating project?

Tips LEARNING in COLLEGE

Study Skills

Whether academic pursuits are a struggle or come easily to you, whether you are fresh out of high school or are returning to school after many years, college is a challenge. Here are a few hints and strategies for taking on some of the challenges you will encounter.

- **Make the most of your time by setting clear priorities.** Deal with surprises by saying "no," getting away from it all, taking control of phone and e-mail interruptions, and leaving slack in your schedule to accommodate the unexpected.

- **Recognize how you prefer to learn.** *Tactile learners* prefer hands-on learning that comes about through touching, manipulating objects, and doing things. *Visual learners* like to see information in their mind, favoring reading and watching over touching and listening. *Auditory learners* favor listening as the best approach. Work on improving your less-preferred learning styles.

- **Evaluate the information you gather.** Consider how authoritative the source is, whether the author has any potential biases, how recent the information is, and whether anything important is missing from the research. In college, critical thinking is essential.

- **Take good notes.** The central feature of good note taking is listening and distilling important information—not writing down everything that is said.

- **Build reading and listening skills.** When you read, identify the main ideas, prioritize them, think critically about the arguments, and explain the writer's ideas to someone else. Listen actively: focus on what is being said, pay attention to nonverbal messages, listen for what is not being said, and take notes.

- **Improve your memory.** Rehearsal is the key strategy in remembering information. Repeat the information, summarize it, associate it with other memories, and above all, think about it when you first come across it.

Source: Based on Robert S. Feldman, *P.O.W.E.R. Learning: Strategies for Success in College and Life,* 2nd ed., New York: McGraw-Hill, 2003.

👁 **1b** Explore ways of learning in a multimedia world.

More people than ever are using electronic media to write in school, social situations, and the workplace. Composition today includes such diverse activities as sending a text message to a friend, posting a

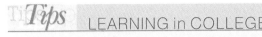

Tips LEARNING in COLLEGE

Dealing with Stress

Whether you are fresh out of high school or graduated years ago, college is a challenge. It helps to develop responses to the stress that often results.

- **Make flexible schedules.** Schedules help you control your time and avoid procrastination by breaking big projects into manageable bits. Be sure to leave room for the unexpected so that the schedule itself does not become a source of stress.
- **Take care of yourself.** Eating healthful food, exercising regularly, and getting plenty of sleep are well-known stress relievers. Some people find meditation to be very effective.
- **Reach out for support.** If you find it difficult to cope with stress, seek professional help. Colleges have trained counselors on staff as well as twenty-four-hour crisis lines.

photo on a social-networking site like *Facebook*, and adding an original video to a content-sharing site like *YouTube*. These sites are part of Web 2.0, a "second generation" of Internet sites and tools that foster user creativity and community. Their growth has led many more people to write for different purposes and audiences: to stay in touch with friends or to develop a research project with an international colleague. Today's college writers read and compose verbal, audio, and visual texts.

Although you probably have used digital communication tools in social situations, bear in mind that academic and professional writing requires greater formality. For example, an e-mail to your instructor or employer should contain standard capitalization, punctuation, and spelling (use *you* and *through*, not *u* and *thru*). *(For more on this topic, see Chapter 29 and the box on p. 12.)*

1. Becoming aware of the persuasive power of images

As a student, you will be analyzing images as well as creating them. We live in a world in which images—in advertising, in politics, in books and classrooms—join with words as tools of persuasion as well as instruction. Images, like words, require careful, critical analysis. A misleading graph (*see Figure 1.2, p. 8*) or an altered photograph can easily distort your perception of a subject. The ability not only to understand visual information but also to evaluate its credibility is an essential tool for learning and writing. *(For details on evaluating visuals, see Chapter 7: Reading, Thinking, Writing, pp. 121–37.)*

7

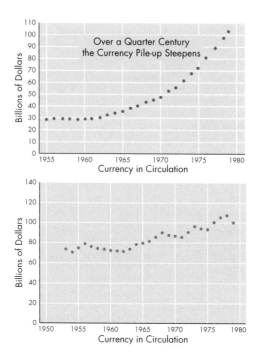

FIGURE 1.2 A misleading graph. The graph on top, which appeared in a 1979 article in the *Wall Street Journal*, shows a dramatic and accelerating increase in currency in circulation in the United States between 1953 and 1979. As a measure of the purchasing power of the individual Americans who held the currency, however, the graph is misleading because it fails to take inflation into account. The second graph, corrected for inflation (based on the dollar's purchasing power in 1979), reveals a generally steady but far less dramatic rate of increase.

Exercise 1.2   Recognizing misleading images

Conduct a Web search using the keywords "misleading images" and "misleading charts," and collect examples of three different types of misleading visuals. Be prepared to share your examples with the class.

---

2. Making effective use of multimedia elements

Technology allows you to include images and other nonverbal elements in your writing to convey certain ideas more efficiently or powerfully. You can create these elements yourself or import them from other sources and place them where you want them. Always cite the source of any elements from another source. (*See Chapters 20–21 for*

FIGURE 1.3 **New Orleans immediately after Hurricane Katrina (top) and one year later (bottom).**

information on how to do so.) The source credits for this book begin at the back on page C-1.

A photo or diagram or chart can contain information that adds details or makes relationships clearer. In a project for a geography course, for example, photographs like the ones above (*Figure 1.3*) can illustrate at a glance the effects of a hurricane and the scale of recovery.

A graph (*see Figure 1.4, p. 10*) can effectively illustrate important trends for a history assignment. A timeline, like the one in the Further Resources for Learning section at the end of this book, can help your readers grasp the relationships among important events.

If you can post your text online or deliver it as an electronic file to be read on the computer, you can include an even greater variety of media. You could supplement a musical passage, for example, with a link to an audio file. You could supplement a paper about political speeches for an American Government course with a link to a video clip of a politician giving a speech.

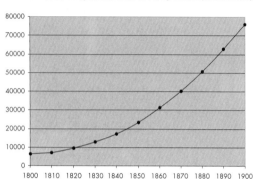

Total U.S. Resident Population 1800–1900, by decade (in thousands)

FIGURE 1.4 A line graph showing trends over time. To learn how to create a graph like this one, see Figure 17.2.

www.mhhe.com/
mhhb2
For an interactive
tutorial on using
visuals, go to

Writing > Visual
Rhetoric Tutorial >
Visualizing Data

Presentation software such as PowerPoint allows you to integrate audio and visual features into oral or stand-alone presentations. Effects such as animation can enliven your presentation, but avoid using multimedia elements in a merely decorative manner.

(*For details on creating effective visuals, see Chapter 3: Planning and Shaping the Whole Essay; Chapter 4: Drafting Paragraphs and Visuals; and Chapter 5: Revising and Editing. For information on creating oral and multimedia presentations, see Chapter 13: Oral Presentation, and Chapter 14: Multimedia Writing. For help with finding appropriate visuals, see Chapter 17: Finding and Creating Effective Visuals.*)

Exercise 1.3   Deciding when to use visuals

1. Decide whether each of the following would be best presented as a visual, as written text, or as both. For those that call for a visual, which type of visual would you use?

    a. Instructions for constructing a birdhouse

    b. An inventory of the different species of birds that appear in your yard during a one-month period

    c. A description of a songbird's call

    d. A discussion of how a bird's wings enable it to fly

    e. A proposal on ways to protect endangered songbirds from predation by cats

2. Go to the Further Resources for Learning section at the end of this book; read the entry for the term *Aristotelian* in the glossary of Selected Terms from across the Curriculum (*p. FR-18*); and note the entry for Aristotle on the Timeline of World

History (*p. FR-3*). How does the timeline help you place the term in historical context? What can you learn from the timeline about significant developments in geometry, theater, physics, and religion that occurred within a few hundred years of Aristotle's lifetime?

3. Taking advantage of online and other electronic tools for learning

www.mhhe.com/
mhhb2

For more about
online learning
resources, go to

Additional Links
on Learning

Technology now makes it possible to transcend the constraints of the clock, the calendar, and the car and to engage in educational activities 24/7, or twenty-four hours a day, seven days a week. Different electronic tools work best for different purposes (*see the TextConnex box below*).

- **E-mail.** E-mail is one of the most frequently used forms of written communication in the world today. In some classes, you can use e-mail to communicate with your professor, other students, or a consultant in your school's writing center.

- **Instant messaging.** Instant messaging (IM) can be used to further your learning in much the same way as e-mail. Some instructors may encourage you to contact them in this way, but otherwise, use IM sparingly in an academic setting. Like other technologies, it can distract you from work.

 TEXTCONNEX

Digital Communication Tools: Best Uses

	PEER REVIEW	GROUP PROJECT	FORMAL CONVER- SATION	INFORMAL CONVER- SATION	QUICK QUESTION	EXTENDED DISCUSSION
E-mail	X	X	X	X	X	X
Instant message/ Chat	X	X		X	X	
Text message				X	X	
Listserv		X	X	X	X	X
Blog	X	X		X		X
Wiki	X	X				X

This table shows the most appropriate academic uses of six electronic communication tools.

11

TextConnex

Netiquette

The term *netiquette* combines the words *Internet* and *etiquette* to form a new word that stands for good manners online. Here are some netiquette guidelines:

- **Remember that most forms of electronic communication can be reproduced.** Avoid saying anything you would not want attributed to you or forwarded to others. Do not forward another person's words without consent.
- **Remember that you are interacting with real humans,** not machines, and practice kindness, patience, and good humor.
- **Use words economically,** and edit carefully. Readers become impatient and their eyes tire when they encounter all lowercase letters or text that lacks appropriate punctuation.
- **Bear in mind that without cues such as facial expressions, body language, and vocal intonation, your message can easily be misunderstood.** Be extra careful about humor that could be misread as sarcasm. Misunderstandings can escalate quickly into *flaming*, the sending of angry, inflammatory posts that use heated language.
- **Avoid ALL CAPS.** Typing in all caps is considered shouting.
- **Always seek permission to use other people's ideas,** and acknowledge them properly.
- **Never copy other people's words and present them as your own.** This practice, known as *plagiarism*, is always wrong. (*See Part 4: Documenting across the Curriculum, for help with citing Internet sources.*)
- **Limit e-mails to a single topic and use accurate subject headers. Include a sufficient portion of the previous text** when responding to an e-mail, or use a dash to keep the conversation flowing and to provide context. **Include your name and contact information at the end of every e-mail you send.**
- **When sending text messages, use abbreviations in moderation.** Keep messages brief, but do not use so many abbreviations and emoticons that your meaning is obscured.

- **Course Web sites.** Your instructor may have a Web site for your course. If so, check it for late-breaking announcements, the course syllabus, assignments (and their due dates), and course-related links as well as other Web resources. For course Web sites that are part of Web-based software offered by companies like Blackboard, see "Using Web-based course software" on page 14.

- **Networked classrooms and virtual classrooms.** Some colleges and instructors use **networked classrooms** in which each student works at one of a network of linked computers. Instructors can post daily assignments and discussion topics, and students might be assigned to work collaboratively on a writing project. Computers and the Internet also make it possible for students to engage in distance learning—from almost anywhere in the world—in classes conducted entirely online in **virtual classrooms.** Because you are interacting in writing rather than in spoken discussion, you can more easily save ideas and comments and use them in the first draft of a paper.

- **Blogs.** A **blog** is a continually updated site that features dated entries with commentary on a variety of topics, links to Web sites the authors find interesting, and (sometimes) a way for readers to add comments. These readers, as well as the blog's author, may or may not be experts on the topics. (*For information on assessing a blog's credibility, see Chapter 18, pp. 289–98.*) Students sometimes use blogs to summarize and reflect on readings. A class blog may allow students to comment on one another's drafts. Faculty also may use blogs as sites for sharing assignments, where students can access them at any time and ask for clarification via comments. (*See Chapter 14, pp. 244–47.*)

- **Podcasts.** Instructors may record their lectures as downloadable audio or video **podcasts,** making them available to the class for repeated listening or viewing on a computer or an MP3 player. Popular radio shows, television shows, and newspapers frequently include podcasts; the *New York Times*, for example, has a print book review section and a podcast of reviews. Reputable podcasts, such as these, are important sources for research projects.

- **Text messages.** Texting is especially useful for very short messages, and its abbreviations can be used in class notes to make note-taking faster. Abbreviations and emoticons (combinations of characters that look like images, such as :-)) should not be used in more formal writing situations.

- **Videos.** Outside school and in some college classes, many students and instructors create short videos, which they may post on video sharing sites such as *YouTube*. Although compositions usually have a specific intended audience, many Web sites allow these texts to be viewed by anyone with Internet access. When students create their own videos, they become better prepared to analyze the informative and persuasive videos that surround us today.

13

TEXTCONNEX

Web 2.0

The Machine Is Us/ing Us— This video by Michael Wesch of Kansas State University shows some defining features of Web 2.0 <http://mediatedcultures.net/mediatedculture.htm>

■ **Social networking sites.** Sometimes students use **social networking sites** (like *MySpace* and *Facebook*) to discuss writing projects, conduct surveys, and locate experts. Postings may be private, from person to person; or public, from one person to many. Be careful what you post on these sites, as this information is potentially public and visible to prospective employers.

■ **Wikis.** A **wiki** comprises interlinking Web pages created collaboratively, which form databases of information. Because multiple people create and edit pages on the site, college students and instructors often use wikis to create collaborative projects. The popular online encyclopedia *Wikipedia* is not always accurate because almost anyone can create or edit its content. The content of some other, more reliable wikis is created and monitored by experts. Always learn enough about a wiki to assess its reliability (*see Chapter 18: Evaluating Sources, pp. 289–98*).

■ **Virtual environments.** Some college students and instructors use virtual spaces for group projects. These include graphic **virtual worlds** such as Second Life, as well as older text-based technologies such as MUDs (multiuser dimensions) and MOOs (object-oriented multiuser dimensions). (*See Chapter 16: Finding and Managing Print and Online Sources, p. 280.*)

4. Using Web-based course software

Many colleges offer some kind of course management software (CMS) like Blackboard. Although these programs vary, they typically include common features that students can access at any time via a password-protected course Web page. "Distribution" features allow instructors to present the course syllabus, assignments, and readings. "Contribution" features promote class participation and communication. These features may include e-mail systems; bulletin boards and chat rooms for class discussions; and folders where students can post their work to be read and commented upon by classmates and the instructor. **Chat rooms** are online spaces that permit real-time communication. All participants in a chat see the text of the others as they type. Often the CMS will save a transcript of the chat for future reference.

Some CMS platforms include tools for **peer review,** in which students comment on one another's writing at specific stages in the writing process. Specialized software, like the writing environment in the *Catalyst* Web site that accompanies this book, makes peer review an efficient and accessible learning tool.

If your course has a home page, take time at the beginning of the semester to become familiar with its features—as well as any related course requirements. (*For more on chat rooms, see Chapter 3: Planning and Shaping the Whole Essay, p. 33 and p. 41.*)

www.mhhe.com/
mhhb2

To explore
Catalyst, go to
Home

| **Exercise 1.4** | Using *Catalyst* |

Go to *Catalyst*, the Web site that supports this text. Once you have entered the student home page, explore the site's five resource areas: Learning, Writing, Research, Editing, and More Resources. If you have a personal digital assistant (PDA), you can download a reference version of the grammar and documentation portions of this handbook from the site. Indicate where you would look for help with the following:

1. Choosing a topic to research
2. Deciding if a sentence you have written has a comma splice
3. Evaluating the source of some demographic data about your town
4. Searching for online sources for a psychology paper
5. Writing an interpretive paper about a short story
6. Developing a thesis for a paper
7. Avoiding plagiarism when you make use of sources in a research paper

1c Use strategies for learning in a multilingual world.

To some extent, all college students navigate multiple cultures and languages. The language of anthropology, for example, probably sounds strange and new to most students. In college, students who know two or more languages have an advantage over those who know only English. Multilingual students are able to contribute insights about other cultures and often have interesting career opportunities in our rapidly globalizing world.

This book uses the term *multilingual* to address students from varied cultural, national, and linguistic backgrounds. You may be an international student learning to speak and write English. You may have grown up speaking standard American English at school and another language or dialect at home. Perhaps your family has close ties to another part of the world. You may have moved between the United States and another country more than once. If you came to the United States at a young age, you may read and write English better than you do your parents' native language. You may speak a blended language such as "Spanglish," a mixture of English and Spanish.

Because the way we talk influences the way we write, blended and other nonstandard forms of English often appear in college students' writing. There is no single "correct" English, but there is a type typically used in academic contexts. Academic language is formal, with an expanded vocabulary as well as complex grammar patterns and culturally specific usage patterns. Learning to read and write academic English may pose special challenges to multilingual students, but the learning strategies discussed in this section can help you meet those challenges.

1. Becoming aware of cultural differences in communication

If you are familiar with at least two languages and cultures, you already know that there is more than one way to interact politely and effectively with other people. Your classmates may pride themselves on being direct, but you may think that they sound almost impolite in their enthusiasm to make a point. They may consider themselves to be explicit and precise; you may wonder why they are explaining things attentive people should be able to figure out on their own.

Colleges in the United States emphasize openly exchanging views, clearly stating opinions, and explicitly supporting judgments with examples, observations, and reasons. You may be concerned about an accent or about the fine points of grammar or pronunciation. Don't worry. Gather up your confidence and join the conversation. In some cultures, asking a question indicates that the student has not done the homework or has not been paying attention. In contrast, instructors in the United States generally encourage students to ask questions and participate in class discussion. Students who need advice can approach the instructor or fellow students outside class.

During the first few sessions of a class, observe how students show their interest through body language. Usually, American students are expected to sit up straight, look at the instructor, and take notes. Note your classmates' posture, their facial expressions, and the gestures they make. Do they raise their hands to ask a question?

Do they wait until the end of class and speak with the instructor privately?

Just as students are not all the same, neither are instructors. Does the instructor tell students to ask their questions after class? Another good way to learn an instructor's preferences is to visit his or her office hours and ask questions.

Instructors in the United States often ask students to form small groups to discuss an issue or solve a problem. All the members of such a group are expected to contribute to the conversation and offer ideas. Students usually speak and interact much more informally in these groups than they do with the instructor in class. (For example, you would not raise your hand before speaking in a small group.)

In every class, students must read and think critically. You will be asked to question the statements in the textbook or the author's reasons for writing. You will also be expected to write about what you have read and share your opinions.

2. Using reading, writing, and speaking to learn more about English

To develop your fluency in English, get into the habit of reading, writing, and speaking in English every day.

- **Keep a reading and writing notebook.** Write down thoughts, comments, and questions about the reading assignments in your courses. Try to put ideas from the readings into your own words (and note the source). Make a list of new words and phrases that you find in your reading or that you overhear. Many of them may be **idioms,** words and phrases that have a special meaning not always included in a simple dictionary definition. Go over these lists with a tutor, a friend, or your writing group.

- **Write a personal journal or blog.** Using English to explore your thoughts, feelings, and questions about your studies and your life in college will help make you feel more at home in the language.

- **Join a study group.** Most college students can benefit from belonging to a study group. When you get together and discuss an assignment, you often understand it better. Study groups also provide opportunities to practice some of those new words on your list.

- **Write letters in English.** Letters are a good way to practice the informal style used in conversation. Write to out-of-town acquaintances who do not speak your first language. Write a letter to the college newspaper. You can also write brief notes either on paper or through e-mail to instructors, tutors, librarians, secretaries, and other native speakers of English.

17

www.mhhe.com/
mhhb2
For access to online
dictionaries and
thesauri, go to

Dictionaries
and Thesauri

3. Using learning tools that are available for multilingual students

The following reference books can also help you as you write papers for your college courses. You can purchase them in your college's bookstore or find copies in the reference room of your college's library.

ESL dictionary A good dictionary designed especially for second-language students can be a useful source of information about word meanings. Ordinary dictionaries frequently define difficult words with other difficult words. In the *American Heritage Dictionary,* for example, the word *haze* is defined as "atmospheric moisture, dust, smoke, and vapor suspended to form a partially opaque condition." An ESL dictionary defines it more simply as "a light mist or smoke."

Do not confuse ESL dictionaries with bilingual, or "translation," dictionaries. Translation dictionaries frequently oversimplify word meanings. So too do abridged dictionaries that do not indicate shades of meaning.

Like all standard English dictionaries, an ESL dictionary includes instructions for its use. These instructions explain the abbreviations used in the entries. They also list the special notations used for words classified as slang, vulgar, informal, nonstandard, or other categories worthy of special attention. In the ESL/Learner's Edition of the *Random House Webster's Dictionary of American English* (1997), you will find "pig out" as the sixth entry under the word *pig*:

> **Pig out** (no obj) Slang. to eat too much food: *We pigged out on pizza last night.*

The entry tells you that "pig out" does not take a direct object ("no obj") and that its use is very informal ("Slang"), appropriate in talking with classmates but not in writing formal texts. You will hear a great deal of slang on your college campus, on the radio, and on TV. Make a list of slang phrases, and look them up later. If you don't find them listed in your standard or ESL dictionary, check for them in a dictionary of American slang.

The dictionary will help you with spelling, syllabication, pronunciation, definitions, word origins, and usage. The several meanings of a word are arranged first according to part of speech and then from most common to least common meaning. Examine the entry for the word *academic* in the ESL/Learner's Edition:

> **ac·a·dem·ic** /ˌækəˈdɛmɪk/ *adj.* **1.** (before a noun) of or relating to a school, esp. one for higher education: *an academic institution.* **2.** Of or relating to school subjects that teach general intellectual skills rather than specific job skills: *academic subjects like English and mathematics.* **3.** Not practical or

18

directly useful: *Whether she wanted to come or not is an academic question because she's here now.*—*n.* (count) **4.** A student or teacher at a college or university—**ac'a·dem'i·cal·ly,** *adv.*

Note that nouns are identified as count or noncount, indicating whether you can place a number in front of the noun and make it plural. You can say "Four academics joined the group," so when *academic* is used as a noun, it is a count noun. *Honesty* is a noncount noun.

When you look up words or phrases in the dictionary, add them to your personal list. Talk about the list with classmates. They will be happy to explain particular, up-to-date uses of the words and phrases you are learning.

Thesaurus Look up a word in a thesaurus to find other words with related meanings. The thesaurus can help you expand your vocabulary. However, always look up synonyms in a dictionary before using them because all synonyms differ slightly in meaning.

Dictionary of American idioms As explained earlier, an idiom is an expression that is peculiar to a particular language and cannot be understood by looking at the individual words. "To catch a bus" is an idiom.

Desk encyclopedias You will find one-volume encyclopedias on every subject from U.S. history to classical or biblical allusions in the reference room of your college's library. You may find it useful to look up people, places, and events that are new to you, especially if the person, place, or event is referred to often in U.S. culture.

Exercise 1.5   Using learning tools

Choose one of the following statements and use one of the learning tools discussed in this section to determine what any unfamiliar terms or concepts in the statement mean.

1. "Like those typical New Deal liberals, Smith wants to remake the way we do things in this hospital!"
2. "I need to get the straight dope on that situation before I can proceed."
3. "I plan to sign up for another tour of duty in the Navy."
4. "Let's not pour any more money down that rat hole."
5. "We need to protect our rights under the Fourteenth Amendment."

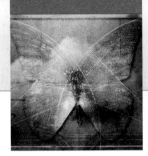

2 Understanding Writing Assignments

No matter what your course of study, writing assignments help you learn about a topic and demonstrate what you have learned. They will be an important part of your college experience. Understanding what is being asked of you as a writer is a critical ingredient in your success.

www.mhhe.com/
mhhb2

For help with the writing process, go to

Writing > Writing Tutors

2a Recognize that writing is a process.

Words do not flow effortlessly from the pens—or keyboards—of even the most experienced writers. As you begin working on a project, remember that writing is a process, a series of manageable activities that result in a finished product. Although **writing processes** vary in scope and sequence from writer to writer and assignment to assignment, these activities should be part of every lengthy writing project:

- **Understand the assignment** (Chapter 2). Begin by analyzing the assignment so you are clear about your **writing situation:** your topic and purpose as well as the audience you will address, the tone you will take, and the genre—or type of writing—you will produce. Note other important details about deadline, length, and format.

- **Generate ideas and plan your approach** (Chapter 3). Give yourself time to explore your topic, using a variety of brainstorming techniques. Decide on a working thesis that will help you focus your first draft, and sketch an informal or a formal plan for the sequence of your ideas.

- **Draft paragraphs and visuals** (Chapter 4). Use paragraph development as a way of moving your writing forward. Use various strategies such as description and comparison to develop and shape your ideas. Consider when visuals such as tables and graphs will be an efficient way to present data and support your ideas. After you draft the body of your composition, develop an effective introduction and conclusion.

- **Revise, edit, and proofread** (Chapter 5). Develop your first draft and tailor it for your readers in one or more subsequent drafts. Analyze the overall development from paragraph to paragraph; then look at individual paragraphs, sentences, and words. Use revising and editing checklists in this process.

- **Design your document** (Chapter 6). A clear, uncluttered format will make your text more appealing to readers. Lists and headings may help them see the structure of longer documents.

WRITING beyond COLLEGE

Writing Skills in College and Beyond

The writing that you do in college is excellent preparation for your professional life, even if you do not choose a career in academia. Business leaders say that strong writing skills are an essential component of job performance, and the amount of writing increases with job advancement. The skills you develop by responding to college writing assignments—analyzing the writing situation, gathering information, generating ideas, drafting unified and coherent paragraphs, and revising and editing with your audience in mind—will serve you well after graduation.

Exercise 2.1   Exploring your writing process

Learn about yourself as a writer by telling the story of your writing experiences. The following questions will help you write a brief narrative.

1. How were you taught to write in school? Were you encouraged to explore ideas and use your imagination, or was the focus primarily on writing correct sentences? Did you struggle with writing assignments, or did they come easily to you? Have you ever written for pleasure, not just in response to a school assignment?

2. Describe the writing process you use for academic papers. Does your process vary according to the assignment? If so, how? Do you engage in all the activities described on page 20? If not, which ones do you skip? Which activities are the most difficult for you? Why? Which are the easiest? Why?

Tips LEARNING in COLLEGE

Understanding Assignments

It is often helpful to talk with the instructor after receiving and looking over a new assignment. It is far better to ask for clarification before you begin an assignment than to have to start over, or to turn in something that does not fulfill the requirements.

2b   Understand the writing situation.

Writers respond to **writing situations.** When you write a lab report for a science class, create a flyer for a candidate for student government, or send an e-mail inviting a friend for coffee, you shape the communication (**message**) to suit the purpose, audience, and context. The results

21

for each situation will differ. All communication arises because something is at stake (the **exigence**). The **audience** receives the message. Audience members may be friendly or hostile to the writer's message, and their cultures and backgrounds will influence their reactions. Your **purpose** may be to inform them or to move them to action. **Context** includes the means of communication, current events, and the environment in which the communication takes place. See an illustration of how these elements are related in Figure 2.1:

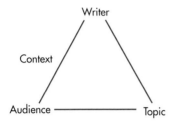

FIGURE 2.1 Elements of a writing situation.

CHECKLIST

Understanding the Writing Situation

Ask yourself these questions as you approach a writing assignment.

Topic (*see 2c*)

☐ What are you being asked to write about?

☐ Have you narrowed your topic to a question that interests you?

☐ What kind of visuals, if any, would be appropriate for this topic?

☐ What types of sources will help you explore this topic? Where will you look for them?

☐ What genre or format would suit this assignment? (*see 2e*)

Purpose (*see 2d*)

☐ What do you want your writing to accomplish? Are you trying to inform, analyze, or argue? (What key words in your assignment indicate the purpose?)

☐ Do you want to intensify, clarify, complicate, or change your audience's assumptions or opinions?

Audience and Tone *(see 2f and 2g)*

☐ What are your audience's demographics (education level, social status, gender, cultural background, and language)? How diverse is your audience?

☐ What does your audience know about the topic at hand?

☐ What common assumptions and different opinions do these audience members bring to the issue? Are they likely to agree with you, or will you have to persuade them?

☐ What is your relationship to them?

☐ What sort of voice would appeal to this audience: informal, entertaining, reasonable, or forceful? Why?

Context *(see 2h)*

☐ Does your topic deal with issues of interest to the public or to members of an academic discipline?

☐ What have other writers said recently about this topic?

☐ How much time do you have to complete the assignment?

☐ What is the specified number of pages?

☐ What medium are you using (print essay, video podcast, Web site, presentation software)?

2c Find an appropriate topic.

Many college writing assignments allow students to find a topic of interest to them within the framework of the course. Here is an example:

ASSIGNMENT   Visit a local photography exhibit or check out the photography archives in the library. Choose one or more photographs to analyze, and discuss the role of the photographer. Consider the formal elements of the photograph(s) as well as the social context.

23

FIGURE 2.2 The Web site for a photography exhibit. Diane Chen found this Web site about Sebastião Salgado's exhibit *Migrations:*

After locating some photography exhibits in her area, reading a few reviews of them, and exploring information about them on the Web, Diane Chen selected an exhibit called *Migrations: Humanity in Transition (Figure 2.2)* because of its relevance to her family's immigrant history. (We will follow Diane Chen's work on this assignment from start to finish in the following chapters. *For guidelines on analyzing photographs, see Chapter 14, pp. 228–31.*) A topic does not need to have personal relevance to be intellectually interesting, of course. A student with an interest in science who is assigned to write about one factor in the decline of the Roman Empire might focus on the epidemics that ravaged the Roman population. Someone interested in military history might focus instead on the instability caused by a succession of military emperors who seized power by force.

1. Finding a manageable topic

Thinking of questions on a topic will help you generate interesting ideas. Play the "I wonder/They say/I think" game:

- **I wonder:** Starting with the subject matter of the course or the assignment, list concepts and issues that you wonder about.

- **They say:** Reviewing your class notes, course reading, online discussion-group postings, and scholarly bibliographies, see what topics and issues others in the field say are important. Jot down relevant information, ideas, and issues.
- **I think:** Choosing an item or two that you have listed, figure out what you think about it, giving your curiosity free rein. Connect your interests to what you are learning in the course.

2. Narrowing your topic

When choosing a topic, consider whether it is narrow enough to fit your assignment. A topic such as Thomas Jefferson's presidency would be appropriate for a book-length treatment but could not be covered in adequate detail in an essay. Consider the following examples:

BROAD TOPICS	NARROW TOPICS
Sports injuries	The most common types of field injuries in soccer and how to administer emergency care
Reading problems	Approaches to treating dyslexia in middle-school students

The following strategy can help you narrow your subject area:

1. Browse your course texts and class notes to find topics and then ask specific questions about the topics. Use the "five *w*'s and an *h*" strategy by asking about the *who, what, why, when, where,* and *how* of a topic (*see Chapter 3, p. 36*). See the box on the bottom of page 26 for examples of questions.
2. Make sure that you are posing a challenging question that will interest your readers. An appropriate question cannot be answered with a simple yes or no, a dictionary-like definition, or a handful of well-known facts.
3. Speculate about the answer to your question, which will give you a hypothesis to work with during the research process. A **hypothesis** is a speculation, or guess, that you must test and revise as you explore your topic.

Exercise 2.2   Narrowing a topic

Narrow the topics below to make them appropriate for a composition of approximately ten double-spaced pages.

1. For a course in criminal justice: crime-prevention programs
2. For a psychology course: studies on memory
3. For a nutrition course: obesity in the United States

25

4. For a film course: filmmaking in the 1990s
5. For a history course: Civil War battles

2d Be clear about the purpose of your assignment.

If your instructor has provided a written description of the assignment, look for key terms that might give you a clue about the composition's **purpose.** Are you expected to inform, interpret, or argue? Each of these purposes is linked to a common writing assignment found in many different disciplines.

■ In an **informative report,** the writer's purpose is to pass on what he or she has learned about a topic or issue. The following terms are often associated with the task of informing:

Classify   Illustrate   Report   Survey

EXAMPLE   A psychology student might *survey* recent research about the effects on adolescents of violence in video games.

EXAMPLE   A business major might *illustrate* the theory of supply-side economics with an example from recent history.

■ An **interpretive analysis** explores the meaning of written documents, cultural artifacts, social situations, or natural

CHARTING the TERRITORY

Posing Discipline-Specific Questions

The particular course you are taking defines a range of questions that are appropriate within a given discipline. Here are examples of the way your course would help define the questions you might ask if, for example, you were writing about Thomas Jefferson:

U.S. history: How did Jefferson's ownership of slaves affect his public stance on slavery?

Political science: To what extent did Jefferson's conflict with the courts redefine the balance of power among the three branches of government?

Art history: What architectural influences do you see at work in Jefferson's design for his home at Monticello?

CHARTING the TERRITORY

Writing to Express: Personal Essays

Another purpose for writing is to express thoughts and feelings about personal experiences. Your first writing assignment for college—the essay required by the Admissions Department as part of your college application form—probably had this purpose. The personal essay is one of the most literary kinds of writing and therefore is often assigned in English composition courses. (*For more on personal essays and writing with an expressive purpose, see Chapter 11, pp. 212–16.*)

events. The following terms often appear when the purpose is interpreting:

Analyze   Compare   Explain   Reflect

EXAMPLE   A philosophy student might *explain* the allegory of the cave in Plato's *Republic*.

EXAMPLE   A science student might *analyze* satellite images in order to make weather predictions.

▪ An **argument** proves a point or supports an opinion through logic and concrete evidence. The following terms usually indicate that the purpose of a paper is to argue a position:

Agree   Assess   Defend   Refute

EXAMPLE   A political science student might *defend* the electoral college system.

EXAMPLE   A nutrition student might *refute* the claims of low-carb weight-loss diets.

Exercise 2.3   Identifying the purpose

For each of the following assignments, state whether the primary task is to inform, interpret, or argue a position.

1. Defend or refute the claim that the colonies would inevitably have declared independence no matter how Britain had responded to their demands.

2. Explain the Declaration of Independence as a product of the European Enlightenment.

3. Survey and classify the variety of ways in which Americans responded to the Declaration of Independence and the outbreak of the Revolutionary War.

2e Use the appropriate genre.

When you know your composition's purpose, you can select a genre that supports that purpose. **Genre** simply means kind of writing. Poems, stories, and plays are genres of literature, and audiences have different expectations for each. Most of the writing you will be asked to produce in college will be nonfiction, that is, writing about real events, people, and things for the purpose of argument, information, or interpretation. Within nonfiction, however, there are many additional genres of writing such as letters, brochures, case studies, lab reports, and literary analyses. Some types of writing, like the case study, are common in a particular field such as sociology. Understanding the genre that an assignment calls for is an important step in successfully fulfilling it. If you are supposed to be writing a description of a snake for a field guide, you will not be successful if you write a poem—even a very good poem—about a snake.

Some Common Genres of Writing

Letters	Profiles	Brochures
Memoirs	Proposals	Case studies
Essays	Instructions	
Reviews	Reports	

Sometimes an assignment will specify a genre. For example, you may be asked to write a report (an informative genre), a comparative analysis (an interpretive genre), or a critique (an argumentative genre). In other instances you might be asked to select the genre yourself. Make sure the one you choose—whether it be a multimedia presentation or a researched essay—is appropriate to the purpose of your assignment.

Some genres have very specific conventions for formatting and design. Whether you need to follow the formatting conventions and documentation style recommended by the Modern Language Association (MLA), the American Psychological Association (APA), the editors of *The Chicago Manual of Style,* the Council of Science Editors (CSE), or some other authority will depend largely on the disciplinary context of your writing. Your instructor will typically let you know which style you should use. You can find coverage of the MLA, APA, Chicago, and CSE styles in Part 4: Documenting across the Curriculum. (*For more on when to use a specific documentation style for a discipline, see Chapter 22: Writing the Paper, pp. 337–40.*)

If you are unfamiliar with the conventions of a particular genre, seek out examples from your instructor or college writing center. Many genres of academic writing are covered in Part 2: Common Assignments across the Curriculum; additional genres are covered in Part 5: Writing beyond College.

2f Ask questions about your audience.

Whether we realize it or not, most of us are experts at adjusting what we say to suit the audience we are addressing. In everyday conversation, for example, your description of a car accident would be different if you were talking to a young child instead of an adult. For most college assignments, your instructor is your primary audience, but he or she also represents a larger group of readers who have an interest or stake in your topic. Consider *why* your topic might interest your audience as you answer the following questions (*see also the checklist on p. 22*):

1. **Are your readers specialists, or are they members of a general audience?** How much prior knowledge and specialized vocabulary can you assume your audience has? An education professor, for example, might ask you to write for a general audience of your students' parents. You can assume that they have a general knowledge of your subject but that you will need to explain concepts such as "authentic assessment" or "content standards." If you were presenting to a specialist audience of school principals, you would not need to define these common terms from within the discipline.

   Consider, for example, how audience accounts for the differences in these two passages about snakes:

   > Many people become discouraged by the challenge of caring for a snake which just grows and grows and grows. Giant pythons can get bigger than their owners, eat bunnies, and need large cages, plus it's hard to find pet sitters for them when you go out of town.
   >
   > —DANA PAYNE, Woodland Park Zoo Web site

   > The skull of *Python m. bivittatus* is very highly ossified, with dense bone and complex sutures. Like other snakes, it has lost the upper temporal bar, jugal, squamosal, and epipterygoid. A bony interorbital septum is present.
   >
   > —SUSAN EVAN, NSF Digital Library at UT Austin

   The first passage, written for a general audience, gives practical advice in simple, nontechnical language and with a humorous tone. The second passage focuses on physical details of primary interest to other scientists who study snakes and uses technical language and a serious tone.

2. **Are the demographics** (age, gender, sexual orientation, ethnicity, cultural background, religion, group membership) **of your audience relevant to your presentation?** What experiences, assumptions, interests, opinions, and attitudes might your audience members have in common? What are

29

Purposes and Genres

The common purposes of academic writing are also the common purposes for most genres of communication that you will encounter outside college. (*See Part 5: Writing beyond College.*)

- A blog presents an individual's interpretation of world events.
- A brochure can inform its reader about a particular subject.
- A grant proposal argues for an allocation of funds or other resources.

their needs? Will any of your ideas be controversial? Background information can help you build rapport with your audience and anticipate any objections they may have, especially when you are writing an argument. In some high-stakes situations, writers may use interviews or questionnaires to gather information about their audience. More typically, writers use peer review to gauge audience reactions and make adjustments (*see Learning in College: An Audience of Your Peers on p. 31*).

2g Determine the appropriate tone.

The identity, knowledge level, and needs of your audience will determine the tone of your composition. In speech, the sentence "I am surprised at you" can express anger, excitement, or disappointment depending on your tone of voice. In writing, your content, style, and word choice communicate **tone.**

Consider the differences in tone in the following passages on the subject of a cafeteria makeover:

SARCASTIC
: "I am special," the poster headline under the smirking face announces. Well, good for you. And I'm specially glad that cafeteria prices are up because so much money was spent on motivational signs and new paint colors.

SERIOUS
: Although the new colors in the cafeteria are electric and clashing, color in general does brighten the space and distinguish it from the classrooms. But the motivational posters are not inspiring and should be removed.

Tips LEARNING in COLLEGE

An Audience of Your Peers

In some courses, you may have the opportunity to get feedback on your drafts from a peer audience—classmates with similar levels of expertise in the course content. Comments from readers can help you see where passages are unclear, paragraphs need more detail, and sentences delight or offend. Audiences are not monolithic: opinions vary; individuals react to and notice different things. Look for recurring comments and themes among the responses. You may want to address those issues before submitting your paper to its final audience.

The tone in the first passage is sarcastic and obviously intended for other students. An audience of school administrators probably would not appreciate the slang or the humor. The second passage is more serious and respectful in tone while still offering a critique.

For most college writing, your tone should reflect seriousness about the subject matter and purpose, as well as respect for your readers. You can indicate your seriousness by stating information accurately, presenting reasonable arguments and interpretations, dealing fairly with opposing views, and citing sources for your ideas. Unless you are writing a personal essay, the topic, not yourself or your feelings, should be the center of attention.

Writing with sincerity and authority does not mean being condescending or pompous to readers, as in the following examples:

CONDESCENDING   Along with many opportunities, obstacles exist that have restricted the amount of foreign direct investment, as I already explained to you.

POMPOUS   It behooves investors to cogitate over the momentousness of their determinations.

These sentences use a more appropriate tone for college writing:

APPROPRIATE   Along with many opportunities, obstacles exist that have restricted the amount of foreign direct investment, as noted earlier.

APPROPRIATE   Investors should consider the consequences of their decisions.

(For more on appropriate language, see Chapter 48.)

31

Exercise 2.4   Analyzing audience and tone

Find an article from one of the following sources and rewrite a paragraph in the article for the specified audience.

1. An article on a diet or exercise that appears in a magazine for teenagers (30- to 40-year-old adults)

2. An article on a celebrity's court trial that appears in a supermarket tabloid (the audience of a highly respected newspaper such as the *New York Times* or the *Wall Street Journal*)

3. A discussion of clinical depression from a psychology journal (your classmates)

2h   Consider the context.

The context, or surrounding circumstances, influences how an audience receives your communication. Your assignment goes a long way toward establishing the context in which you write. Your instructor probably has specified a length, due date, and genre. Medium also affects writing: an assignment asking you to create a Web site requires different decisions on your part from one asking you to write a print essay. If you create a Web site, you have the option of including audio and video, for example.

Context also involves broader conversations about your topic. Your course gives you background on what others in the discipline have said and what issues have been debated. Current events, on campus and in society as a whole, provide a context for public writing. You may wish, for example, to e-mail the student newspaper in response to a new school policy or on an issue of general concern.

2i   Meet early to discuss coauthored projects.

In many fields, **collaborative writing** is essential. Here are some suggestions to help you make the most of this activity:

- Working with your partners, decide on ground rules, including meeting times, deadlines, and ways of reconciling differences, whether by majority rule or some other method. Is there an interested and respected third party you can consult if the group's dynamics break down?

- Divide the work fairly so that everyone has a part to contribute to the project. Each group member should do some researching, drafting, revising, and editing.

- In your personal journal, record, analyze, and evaluate the intellectual and interpersonal workings of the group as you see and experience them.

32

For Coauthoring Online

Computer networks make it easy for two or more writers to coauthor texts. Wikis allow writers to contribute to a common structure and edit one another's work. Most courseware (such as Blackboard) includes chat rooms and public space for posting and commenting on drafts. Word-processing software also allows writers to make tracked changes in files. (*See Chapter 5, pp. 76–79 for more on peer review.*)

If your group meets online, make sure that you save a transcript of the discussion. If you exchange ideas via e-mail, you will automatically have a record of how the piece developed and how well the group worked together. Archive these transcripts and e-mails into designated folders. In all online communications, be especially careful with your tone. Without the benefit of facial expression and tone of voice, readers can easily misinterpret critical comments.

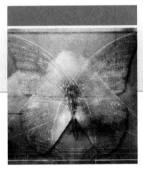

3 Planning and Shaping the Whole Essay

This chapter will help you get started on writing the first draft of your composition. It offers strategies for exploring your topic, developing a thesis, and planning a preliminary structure. These strategies are useful at the beginning of the writing process, but you may also need to return to them at a later stage of your project, especially if you find yourself staring at a blank screen. Writing is a messy business, and planning, drafting, revising, and designing rarely proceed in a straight line; writers often need to circle back to an earlier stage.

3a Explore your ideas.

The following strategies, sometimes called **invention techniques** or **prewriting activities,** are designed to get you thinking and writing about your topic. Remember that what you write at this stage is for your eyes only—no one will be judging your work. You can do much

www.mhhe.com/
mhhb2
For help generating
ideas, go to
Writing >
Paragraph/Essay
Development >
Prewriting

CHECKLIST

Activities for Exploring Your Ideas

☐ Freewrite. (*3a1*)

☐ List. (*3a2*)

☐ Cluster. (*3a3*)

☐ Question. (*3a4*)

☐ Review your notes and annotations. (*3a5*)

☐ Keep a journal. (*3a6*)

☐ Browse in the library. (*3a7*)

☐ Search the Internet. (*3a8*)

☐ Exchange ideas. (*3a9*)

TEXTCONNEX

Invisible Writing

If you find your mind wandering when you freewrite, or if you find it hard to resist the urge to stop and reread what you have written, try turning down the brightness and contrast on your monitor or using white as your font color. (Highlight the document and select black when you are done.)

of your exploratory writing in a **journal** (print or electronic), which is simply a place to record your thoughts on a regular basis. (*For more on journals, see p. 39.*) Your class notes constitute a type of academic journal, as do the notes you take on your reading and research.

As you explore, turn off your internal critic and generate as much material as possible. Later you can select the best ideas from what you produce. We will witness this process by following the development of student Diane Chen's composition.

1. Freewriting

To figure out what you are thinking, try **freewriting.** Just write whatever occurs to you about a topic. If nothing comes to mind, then write "nothing comes to mind" until you think of something else. The

For MULTILINGUAL STUDENTS

Using Another Language to Explore Ideas

Consider exploring your topic using your native language. You won't have to worry about grammar, spelling, or vocabulary, so these issues won't interfere with your creative thought. Once you have some ideas, it is best to work with them in English.

trick is to keep pushing forward without stopping. Do not worry about spelling, punctuation, or grammar rules as you freewrite. Your objective is to explore ideas freely and to "loosen up" in the same way that a jogger does before a long run.

Once you have some ideas down on paper, you might try doing some **focused freewriting.** Begin with a point or a specific question. You might explore more deeply one of the ideas or questions that you discovered while freewriting. The following is a portion of Diane Chen's freewriting about her photography paper:

> I want to talk about what it's like to look at all these pictures of people suffering, but to also admire how beautifully the photographs have been composed. Those two things feel like they shouldn't go together. But it's also what makes the photographs so great—because you're feeling two different emotions at the same time. It makes it harder to stop looking at what it is he's trying to show us.

You can see ideas beginning to take shape that Diane might be able to use in her paper. She needed several sessions of general freewriting, however, before she was able to reach this point.

2. Listing

Another strategy is to **brainstorm** by starting with a topic and listing the words, phrases, images, and ideas that come to mind. Later, you can review this list and highlight the items you would like to explore. When you brainstorm in this way, don't worry about whether the individual thoughts or ideas are "right." Just get them down on paper or into an electronic file.

Once you have composed a fairly lengthy list, go through it looking for patterns and connections. If you have written your list on paper, highlight or connect related ideas. If you have typed them into a document, group related material together. Move apparently extraneous material or ideas to the end of the list or to a separate page.

Now zero in on the areas of most interest, and add any new ideas that occur to you. Arrange the items into main points and subpoints if necessary. Later, this material may form the basis of an outline for your paper.

35

Here is part of a list that Diane Chen produced for her paper about a photography exhibit:

Migrations—still photographs, dynamic subject
why migrate/emigrate?
my family—hope of a better life
fear & doubt in new places; uprooting
beautiful photos but horrible reality
Sebastião Salgado as photojournalist
black & white pictures
strong vertical & horizontal lines
lighting choices are meaningful

TEXTCONNEX

Digital Tools for Exploring Ideas

Some students use a separate file on a word processor to record ideas, which can then be copied and pasted into a draft. Others use Web sites, such as bubbl.us (http://www.bubbl.us), that allow individuals and groups to generate ideas and link them in a visual cluster. This cluster can be e-mailed to one or more recipients.

3. Clustering

Having something down in writing enables you to look for categories and connections. **Clustering,** sometimes called **mapping,** is a brainstorming technique that generates categories and connections from the beginning. To make an idea cluster, do the following:

- Write your topic in the center of a piece of paper, and draw a circle around it.

- Surround the topic with subtopics that interest you. Circle each, and draw a line from it to the center circle.

- Brainstorm more ideas. As you do so, connect each one to a subtopic already on the sheet, or make it a new subtopic of its own.

Web sites such as bubbl.us allow you to use this technique on the computer, alone or in groups (*see the box above*). As she explored her ideas about the Sebastião Salgado exhibit, Diane Chen prepared the cluster that appears in Figure 3.1 on the next page.

4. Questioning

Asking questions is a good way to explore a topic further. The journalist's five *w*'s and an *h* (*who? what? where? when? why?* and *how?*) can help you find specific ideas and details. For example, here are some questions that would apply to the photography exhibit:

- Who is the photographer, who are his subjects, and who is his audience?
- What is the photographer's attitude toward his subjects?
- Where were these pictures shot and first published?
- When did these events take place?
- Why are the people in these pictures migrating?
- How did I react to these images?

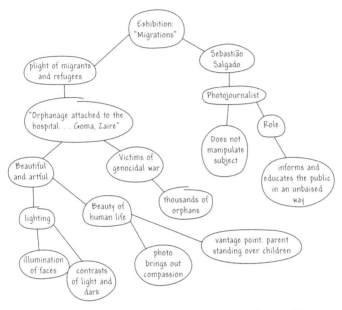

FIGURE 3.1 Diane Chen's cluster about the Salgado exhibit.

CHARTING the TERRITORY

Different Questions Lead to Different Answers

Always consider what questions make the most sense in the context of the course you are taking.

- **Sociology:** A sociologist might ask questions about the ways recent immigrants interact with more established immigrants from the same country.
- **History:** A historian might ask how and why immigration to the United States has changed over the past century.
- **Economics:** An economist might wonder what effect refugees have on the economy of their host country.

TEXTCONNEX

Blogging as a Writing Process Tool

As a site for invention, a blog provides space for your notes. It also can function as a research notebook in which you link to online sources and record your own ideas, and it allows you to ask readers questions about issues you encounter in an assignment. (*For more on blogs, see Chapter 14: Multimedia Writing, pp. 244–47.*)

Another questioning technique is looking at a topic dramatically, as an action (*what*) with actors (*who*), a scene (*where*), a time period (*when*), means (*how*), and a purpose (*why*). Also take note of the problems or questions your professor poses to get class discussion going.

5. Reviewing your notes and annotations

If your assignment involves reading one or more texts or researching multiple sources, review your notes and annotations. (*For details on annotating, see Chapter 7. For details on researching and keeping a research journal, see Chapter 21.*) If you are writing about something you have observed, review any notes or sketches you have made. These immediate comments and reactions are some of your best sources for ideas. Look for patterns.

CHARTING the TERRITORY

Varieties of Notes

Here are some examples of the different kinds of notes you might take when preparing paper assignments for courses in two different disciplines:

- **For a paper on conflict resolution** among four-year-olds for a course in human development, you observe and record the play activities of one child during several play periods in a preschool class. Your careful written observations will help you understand principles in the course text and may later contribute to a case study (*see Chapter 11*).

- **For an article on journalistic styles** for a news reporting class, you read an account of the same event in the *New York Times*, the *Arizona Republic*, and *Time* magazine, annotating each with notes on its style and point of view. Analyzing the treatment of the same story in different publications will help you identify stylistic differences.

6. Keeping a journal or notebook

You may find it helpful to go beyond note taking and start recording ideas and questions inspired by your classes or your exploratory writing in a journal. For example, you might write about connections between what has happened in your personal life and your academic subjects, connections among your subjects, or ideas touched on in class that you would like to know more about. Jotting down one or two thoughts at the end of class and taking a few minutes later in the day to explore those ideas at greater length will help you build a store of writing ideas.

> Prof. says some Civil War photographers posed the corpses on the battleground. Does that change the meaning or value of their work? Did their audiences know they did this, and if so, what did they think of the practice?

For MULTILINGUAL STUDENTS

Private Writing in English

Multilingual students can also use a journal to develop fluency in thinking and writing in English. Keep in mind that no one will be correcting your work, so you can focus on writing as much as possible. You can also use your journal to collect and comment on idioms and to express your thoughts on your experience as a multilingual student.

Exercise 3.1   Keeping an academic journal

Start a print or electronic journal and write in it daily for at least two weeks. Using your course work as a springboard, record anything that comes to mind, including personal reactions and memories. At the end of the two weeks, reread your journal and write about the journal-keeping experience. Does your journal contain any ideas or information that might be useful for the papers you are writing? Has the journal helped you gain any insight into your courses or your life as a student?

---

7. Browsing in the library

Your college library is filled with ideas—and it can provide inspiration when you need to come up with your own. Sometimes it helps to take a break: leave your study carrel, stretch your legs, and browse the bookshelves. You can also explore online resources via your library's Web site. Keep careful track of the sources of compelling ideas so that you will be able to provide proper credit if you use them in your writing. Using others' ideas without acknowledging them is plagiarism.

FIGURE 3.2 Initial results of an Internet search. This screen shows the first three results of Diane Chen's search on *Google*.

(*See Chapter 21: Working with Sources and Avoiding Plagiarism, pp. 314–32.*) (*For help with library research, see Chapter 16: Finding and Managing Print and Online Sources, pp. 259–80.*)

8. Searching the Internet

Type keywords related to your topic into a search engine such as *Google,* and visit several sites on the list that results. (*See Chapter 16: Finding and Managing Print and Online Sources, pp. 259–80.*) When Diane Chen searched *Google* using the keywords "Salgado" and "migrations," for example, she got the results in Figure 3.2.

Evaluate information from the Web with a critical eye, as Web sites are not screened for reliability. Keyword searches of library resources are more likely to yield accurate information. (*See Chapter 18: Evaluating Sources, pp. 289–98.*)

9. Exchanging ideas in person or online

Seek out opportunities to talk about your writing with your classmates, friends, and family.

- Visit your college writing center to discuss your work in progress.

- Brainstorm within your peer response group, if your instructor has set up such groups. Come prepared with ideas and information about your topic to get the discussion started.

- Contact graduate students and professionals with expertise in your discipline and discuss with them their approaches to writing assignments.

Online tools that are available to writers offer additional ways for you to collaborate with others on your papers. Discuss your assignments by exchanging e-mail. Especially if your course has a class Web site, you might exchange ideas in chat rooms. Other options include instant messaging (IM), text messaging, and virtual environments. You also might use a blog to exchange ideas and drafts with your classmates (*See the TextConnex box on p. 38*).

Writing e-mail When you work on papers with classmates, use e-mail in the following ways:

- To check out your understanding of the assignment
- To ask each other useful questions about ideas and topics
- To share your freewriting, listing, and other exploratory writing
- To respond to each other's ideas

Chatting about ideas You can also use online chats as well as other virtual spaces to share ideas. Your instructor may include **chat room** activities, where you go into virtual rooms to work on assignments in small groups or visit and interact with classes at other colleges.

You can also exchange ideas in virtual worlds such as *Second Life* (secondlife.com). Instant messaging (IM) also permits real-time online communication. Exchanging ideas with other writers via IM can help you clarify your thinking on a topic. In the exchange in Figure 3.3, for example, two students share ideas about work.

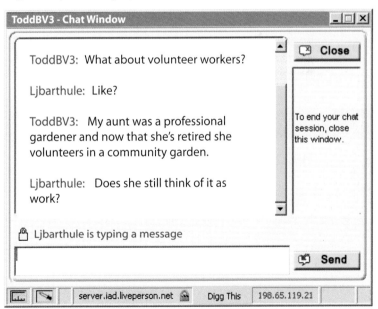

FIGURE 3.3 **Exchanging ideas in an online discussion.**

41

TEXTCONNEX

Exchanging Text Messages

Text messaging—the exchange of brief messages between cell phones—can be a helpful tool. You can text your ideas for an assignment to a classmate (or, with permission, your instructor) for response. Although you can employ abbreviations commonly used in texting for speedier note taking, *never* use such shorthand in assignments.

Exercise 3.2   Generating ideas

For a paper that you are currently writing or a topic you are interested in, brainstorm by listing, clustering, freewriting, questioning, and searching the Internet or browsing in the library. Be sure to put your responses in writing, even if your instructor will not be reading your work. If possible, exchange ideas with classmates, either in person or online. Write a summary of what techniques worked best for you and why.

---

www.mhhe.com/
mhhb2

For help with
developing a thesis,
go to

Writing >
Paragraph/Essay
Development >
Thesis/Central Idea

3b   Decide on a thesis.

The **thesis** is the central idea of your paper. It should communicate a specific point about your topic and suit the purpose of the assignment. As you explore your topic, ideas for your thesis will begin to emerge. You can focus these ideas by drafting a preliminary, or working, **thesis statement,** which can be one or more sentences long. As you

CHECKLIST

A Strong Thesis

A strong thesis does the following:

☐ It fits the purpose of the assignment.

☐ It makes a specific point about the topic and gives readers a sense of the direction of your paper.

☐ It asserts something that could make a difference in what

draft and revise your paper, you may revise or even change your thesis several times.

1. Making sure your thesis fits the purpose of the assignment

All theses are arguments in the sense that they make an assertion about a topic. But there are different kinds of assertions or theses: a thesis for an informative or interpretive paper usually previews the paper's content or expresses the writer's insight, while a thesis for an argument takes a position on a debatable issue or recommends an action. (*For information on assignment purposes, see 2d, p. 26.*)

THESIS TO INFORM	The exhibit *Migrations* offers images of the world's poor people.
THESIS TO INTERPRET	Sebastião Salgado's photographs ask us to understand the pain and suffering that refugees experience.
THESIS TO ARGUE	Military intervention by the United States and other nations can prevent further increases in the number of refugees.

 For MULTILINGUAL STUDENTS

State Your Thesis Directly

In U.S. academic and business settings, readers expect writers to state the main idea right away. Some other cultures may use an indirect style, telling stories and giving facts but not stating the central idea in an obvious way. When assessing a writing situation, consider your readers' expectations and values.

2. Making sure that your thesis is specific

Avoid thesis statements that simply announce your topic, state an obvious fact about it, or offer a general observation:

ANNOUNCEMENT

I will discuss the photography exhibit *Migrations* by Sebastião Salgado. [*What is the writer's point about the photography exhibit?*]

STATEMENT OF FACT

The exhibit of photographs by Sebastião Salgado is about people in migration. [*This information does not make a specific point about the exhibit.*]

GENERAL OBSERVATION

Sebastião Salgado's photographs of people in migration are beautiful and informative. [*This point could apply to many photographs. What makes these photographs special?*]

By contrast, a specific thesis signals a focused, well-developed paper.

SPECIFIC

Like a photojournalist, Salgado brings us images of newsworthy events, but he goes beyond objective reporting, imparting his compassion for refugees and migrants.

In this example, the thesis expresses the writer's particular point— Salgado's intention to move the viewer.

> *Note:* A thesis statement can be longer than one sentence (if necessary) to provide a framework for your main idea. All of the sentences taken together, though, should build to one specific, significant point that fits the purpose of your assignment. (Some instructors may prefer that you limit your thesis statements to one sentence.)

3. Making sure your thesis is significant

A significant thesis makes an assertion that could change what readers know, understand, or believe. A topic that makes a difference to you is much more likely to make a difference to your readers. When you are looking for possible theses, be sure to challenge yourself to develop one that you care about.

Exercise 3.3   Evaluating thesis statements

Evaluate the thesis statements that accompany each of the following assignments. If the thesis statement is inappropriate or weak, explain why and suggest how it could be stronger.

1. *Assignment:* For a social ethics course, find an essay by a philosopher on a contemporary social issue, and argue either for or against the writer's position.
   Thesis: In "Active and Passive Euthanasia," James Rachels argues against the standard view that voluntary euthanasia is always wrong.

2. *Assignment:* For an economics course, find an essay on the gap between rich and poor in the United States, and argue either for or against the writer's position.
   Thesis: George Will's argument that economic inequality is healthy for the United States depends on two false analogies.

LEARNING in COLLEGE

Finding a Thesis through Questioning

Think of the thesis as an answer to a question. In the following examples, the topic of the thesis is in italics and the assertion about that topic is underlined.

QUESTION
What did Alfred Stieglitz contribute to the art of photography?

THESIS
Alfred Stieglitz's struggle to promote photography as an art involved starting a journal, opening a gallery, and making common cause with avant-garde modernist artists.

QUESTION
What makes a photograph significant?

THESIS
The significance of a photograph depends on both its formal and its documentary features.

QUESTION
Is Susan Sontag right that photography obstructs critical thinking?

THESIS
Susan Sontag's critique of photography is unconvincing, partly because it assumes that most people are visually unsophisticated and thoughtlessly voyeuristic.

3. *Assignment:* For a nutrition course, report on recent research on an herbal supplement.
Thesis: Although several researchers believe that echinacea supplements may help reduce the duration of a cold, all agree that the quality and the content of these supplements vary widely.

4. *Assignment:* For a literature course, analyze the significance of setting in a short story.
Thesis: William Faulkner's "A Rose for Emily" is set in the fictional town of Jefferson, Mississippi, a once-elegant town that is in decline.

5. *Assignment:* For a history course, describe the factors that led to the fall of the Achaemenid Empire.
Thesis: Goverments that attempt to build far-flung empires will suffer the same fate as the Achaemenids.

Exercise 3.4 Thinking about your own thesis statements

Identify the thesis statements in two of your recent papers, and evaluate how well they meet the criteria for thesis statements given in the checklist on page 42. Freewrite about the process of arriving at a thesis

45

in those papers: Did you start drafting your paper with a preliminary thesis? If not, would a working thesis have made it easier or harder to produce a first draft? At what point did you arrive at the final thesis? Did your thesis change over the course of several drafts?

3c Plan a structure that suits your assignment.

Many writers feel that they are more efficient when they know in advance how to develop their thesis and where to fit the information they have gathered. For some, that means organizing their notes into a sequence that makes sense. Others prefer to sketch out a list of ideas in a rough outline; still others prefer to prepare a formal outline.

Every paper needs the following components:

- A beginning, or **introduction,** that hooks the reader and usually states the thesis
- A middle, or **body,** that develops the main idea of the paper in a series of paragraphs—each making a point that is supported by specific details
- An ending, or **conclusion,** that gives the reader a sense of completion, often by offering a final comment on the thesis

1. Deciding on an organizational scheme

Give some thought to how you will lay out the body of the paper, using one or a combination of the following organizational schemes:

- **Chronological organization:** A chronological organization takes the reader through a series of events while explaining their significance to the thesis. A text that walks the reader scene by scene through a movie or play employs a chronological scheme, as does a biography or a case study. A survey of the literature for an informative report might also proceed chronologically, from the earliest to the most recent articles on a topic.
- **Problem-solution organization:** The problem-solution scheme is an efficient way to present a rationale for change. For example, an argument paper for a U.S. government course could explain the problems with electronic voting devices and then describe solutions for overcoming each difficulty.
- **Thematic organization:** A thematic structure takes the reader through a series of examples that build from simple to complex, from general to specific, or from specific to general. For example, in her paper about the *Migrations* exhibit, Diane Chen begins with a general discussion of Salgado's work and then focuses on one specific photograph.

TEXTCONNEX

Using Presentation Software as a Writing Process Tool

Presentation-software slides provide a useful tool for exploring and organizing your ideas before you start drafting. The slides also give you another way to get feedback from peer reviewers and others. Here are the steps to follow:

- Well before a paper is due, create a very brief, three- to five-slide presentation—with visuals if appropriate—that previews the key points you intend to make in the paper.
- Present the preview to an audience—friends, other students in the class, perhaps even the course instructor—and ask for suggestions for improvement.

2. Deciding on a type of outline

It is not essential to have an outline before you begin drafting, but a scratch outline can help you get started and keep you moving forward. After you have a first draft, outlining what you've written can help you spot organizational problems or places where the support for your thesis is weak.

A **scratch outline** is a simple list of points, without the levels of subordination that are found in more complex outlines. Scratch outlines are useful for briefer papers. Here is a scratch outline for Diane Chen's paper on the *Migrations* exhibit:

1. Photojournalism should be factual and informative, but it can be beautiful and artful too, as Salgado's *Migrations* exhibit illustrates.
2. The exhibit overall—powerful pictures of people uprooted, taken in 39 countries over 7 years. Salgado documents a global crisis: over 100 million displaced due to war, resource depletion, overpopulation, natural disasters, extreme poverty.
3. Specific picture—"Orphanage"—describe subjects, framing, lighting, emotions it evokes.
4. Salgado on the purpose of his photographs. Quote.

A **formal outline** classifies and divides the information you have gathered, showing main points, supporting ideas, and specific details by organizing them into levels of subordination. You may be required to include a formal outline for some assignments.

Formal outlines come in two types. A formal **topic outline** uses single words or phrases; a formal **sentence outline** states every idea in sentence form. Because the process of division always results in at least two parts, in a formal outline every I must have a II; every A, a B; and so on. Also, items placed at the same level must be of the same kind; for example, if I is London, then II can be New York City but not the Bronx or Wall Street. Items at the same level should

www.mhhe.com/
mhhb2
For more on outlines, go to
Writing >
Paragraph/Essay Development >
Outlines

www.mhhe.com/
mhhb2
For help with outlining, go to
Writing >
Outlining Tutor

also be grammatically parallel; for example, if A is "Choosing Screen Icons," then B can be "Creating Away Messages" but not "Away Messages."

Here are two outlines for Diane Chen's paper on the *Migrations* exhibit, a formal topic outline first, followed by a formal sentence outline:

FORMAL TOPIC OUTLINE

Thesis: Like a photojournalist, Salgado brings us images of newsworthy events, but he goes beyond objective reporting, imparting his compassion for refugees and migrants.

   I. Sophistication of Salgado's photographs
  II. Power of "Orphanage attached to the hospital" photo
      A. Three infant victims of Rwanda War
          1. Label: abstract statistics
          2. Photo: making abstractions real
      B. Documentary vividness and dramatic contrasts of black and white
          1. Black-and-white stripes of blankets
          2. White eyes and dark blankets
          3. Faces
             a. Heart-wrenching look of baby on left
             b. Startled look of baby in center
             c. Glazed and sickly look of baby on right
      C. Intimate vantage point
          1. A parent's perspective
          2. Stress on innocence and vulnerability
  III. Salgado's ability to illustrate big issues with intimate images

FORMAL SENTENCE OUTLINE

Thesis: Like a photojournalist, Salgado brings us images of newsworthy events, but he goes beyond objective reporting, imparting his compassion for refugees and migrants.

   I. The images in *Migrations,* an exhibit of his work, suggest that Salgado does more than simply point and shoot.
  II. Salgado's photograph "Orphanage attached to the hospital at Kibumba, Number One Camp, Goma, Zaire" illustrates the power of his work.
      A. The photograph depicts three infants who are victims of the war in Rwanda.
          1. The label indicates that there are 4,000 orphans in the camp and 100,000 orphans overall.
          2. The numbers are abstractions that the photo makes real.
      B. Salgado's use of black and white gives the photo a documentary feel, but he also uses contrasts of light and dark to create a dramatic image of the babies.

1. The vertical black-and-white stripes of the blanket direct viewers' eyes to the infants' faces and hands.
2. The whites of the infants' eyes stand out against the darkness of the blankets.
3. The camera's lens focuses sharply on the babies' faces, highlighting their expressions.
   a. The baby on the left has a heart-wrenching look.
   b. The baby in the center has a startled look.
   c. The baby on the right has a glazed and sunken look and appears to be near death.
C. The vantage point of this photograph is one of a parent standing directly over his or her child.
   1. The infants seem to belong to the viewer.
   2. The photo is framed so that the babies take up the entire space, consuming the viewer with their innocence and vulnerability.
III. Salgado uses his artistic skill to get viewers to look closely at painful subjects, illustrating a big, complex topic with a collection of intimate, intensely moving images.

Tips LEARNING in COLLEGE

Formatting Rules for Formal Outlines

- Place the thesis statement at the beginning of the outline. It should not be numbered.
- Start the outline with the first body paragraph. Do not include the introduction or conclusion.
- For a topic outline, capitalize the first word of each new point and all proper nouns. Do not use periods to end each point.
- For a sentence outline, capitalize and punctuate each item as you would any sentence.
- Different styles of numbers and letters indicate levels of generality and importance, as in the examples on pages 48–49. Use capital Roman numerals (I, II, III) for each main point, capital letters (A, B, C) for each supporting idea, arabic numbers (1, 2, 3) for each specific detail, and lowercase letters (a, b, c) for parts of details. Place a period and a space after each number or letter.
- Indent consistently. Roman numerals should line up under the first letter in the thesis statement. Capital letters should line up under the first letter of the first word of the main point, and so on. See the example on page 48 for a model of outline format.

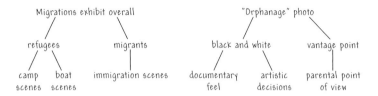

A **tree diagram** is a nonlinear method of planning your paper's organization. In a tree diagram (*see Figures 3.4 and 3.5*), you can see the relationship between topics and subtopics, but the sequence of topics is not specified. Tree diagrams are useful when you want to group ideas but prefer to make decisions about their sequence as you draft.

TEXTCONNEX

Formatting an Outline

Most word-processing software has a feature that will indent and number your outline automatically. Spend a little time investigating this feature before you attempt to set up a numbered outline so that the program can help rather than hinder your efforts.

Exercise 3.5   Shaping notes into an outline

Arrange the following items into a properly formatted formal topic outline, with several levels of subordination.

> thesis: used with supervision, instant messaging can offer adolescents many advantages
> build social ties
> strengthen existing friendships
> maintain long-distance relationships
> chat with several friends simultaneously
> extend social network
> meet friends' friends
> talk to new classmates
> explore identity
> create an online persona
> pick screen icon
> create screen name
> experiment with multiple personas
> adopt public screen name
> assume private or secret screen name

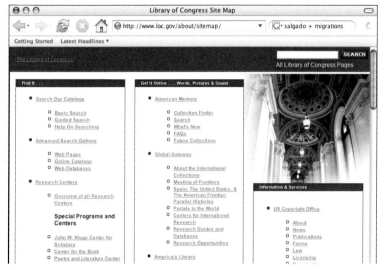

FIGURE 3.5 A site map. Site maps such as this one for the Library of

---

Exercise 3.6   Reflecting on your own work: Outlining

Generate an outline for one of your current assignments—before or after you write your first draft—and freewrite about your experiences. Were you able to generate an outline before you started drafting paragraphs? If so, did you stick with your outline, or did you deviate from it? What kind of outline are you most comfortable with? If you were not able to create an outline before you started drafting, why not?

3d   Consider using visuals.

Visuals such as tables, charts, and graphs can clarify complex data or ideas. Effective visuals are used for a specific purpose, not for decoration, and each type of visual illustrates some kinds of material better than others. For example, compare the table and the line graph on page 52. Both present similar types of data, but does one strike you as clearer or more powerful than the other?

When you use photographs or illustrations, always credit your source, and be aware that most photographs and illustrations are protected by copyright. If you plan to use a photograph as part of a Web page, for example, you will usually need to obtain permission from the copyright holder. (*The credit information for most illustrations in this book appears in the Credits list at the back of the book.*)

51

Types of Visuals and Their Uses

TABLES

Tables organize precise data for readers. Because the measurements in the example include decimals, it would be difficult to plot them on a graph.

Emissions from Waste (Tg CO_2 Eq.)

Gas/Source	1990	1995	2000	2001	2002	2003	2004	2005
CH$_4$	185.8	182.2	158.3	153.5	156.2	160.5	157.8	157.4
Landfills	161.0	157.1	131.9	127.6	130.4	134.9	132.1	132.0
Wastewater treatment	24.8	25.1	26.4	25.9	25.8	25.6	25.7	25.4
N$_2$O	6.4	6.9	7.6	7.6	7.7	7.8	7.9	8.0
Domestic wastewater treatment	6.4	6.9	7.6	7.6	7.7	7.8	7.9	8.0
Total	192.2	189.1	165.9	161.1	163.9	168.4	165.7	165.4

Note: Totals may not sum due to independent rounding.
SOURCE: U.S. Environmental Protection Agency. *Inventory of U.S. Greenhouse Gas Emissions and Sinks: 1996-2005.* U.S. Environmental Protection Agency, 15 Apr. 2008. Web. 9 June 2008. p. 8-1.

BAR GRAPHS

Bar graphs highlight comparisons between two or more variables, such as the cost of tuition and fees at different public universities. They allow readers to see relative sizes quickly.

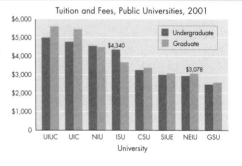

Tuition and Fees, Public Universities, 2001

PIE CHARTS

Pie charts show the size of parts in relation to the whole. The segments must add up to 100% of something; differences in segment size must be significant; and there should not be too many segments.

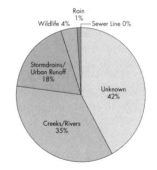

Sources of Contamination Resulting in Warnings Posted Statewide in Year 2000 (Based on Beach Mile Days)

LINE GRAPHS

Line graphs show changes in one or more variables over time. The example shows three sources of nitrous oxide emissions over a sixteen-year period.

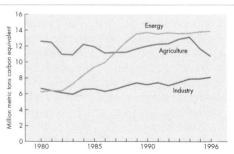

DIAGRAMS
Diagrams show processes
or structures visually.
Common in technical writ-
ing, they include time lines,
organization charts, and
decision trees. The example
shows the factors involved
in the decision to commit a
burglary.

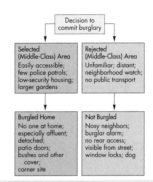

PHOTOS
Photos can reinforce your
point by showing readers
what your subject actually
looks like or how it has
been affected. This image
could support a portrayal of
Kurt Cobain as a talented
but conflicted artist.

MAPS
Maps highlight locations
and spatial relationships,
and they show relationships
between ideas. This one
shows the size of Hurricane
Frances when it struck the
United States in 2004.

ILLUSTRATIONS
Like photographs, illustrations make a point dramatically. (*See p. 192 for more
about this image.*)

*A complete directory of visual rhetoric resources in this text appears in
the back of the book following the Index for Multilingual Writers.*

53

Note that different illustrations of the same subject or charts depicting the same data can serve different purposes. The satellite image of Hurricane Frances on page 53 depicts the storm's size and the region affected; the photos of the area affected by Hurricane Katrina (*p. 9 in Chapter 1*) convey the destructive power of the storm and the progress of recovery. The map serves an informative purpose, whereas the photos might offer support to an argument about funding rebuilding efforts after devastating storms.

TEXTCONNEX

Preparing Pie Charts

Several types of computer programs allow you to create pie charts. When you insert a pie chart in PowerPoint 2007, for example, you will see a premade slide. Change the title and size of each section by deleting the text in the spreadsheet that is displayed along with the pie chart and typing in your own numbers and category labels.

Caution: Because the use of visual elements is more accepted in some fields than in others, you may want to ask your instructor for advice before planning to include visuals in your composition.

Exercise 3.7   Using visuals

For each of the following kinds of information, decide which type of visual would be most effective. (You do not need to prepare the visual itself.)

1. For an education paper, show the percentage of teaching time per week devoted to math, language arts, science, social studies, world languages, art, music, and physical education using a _____.

2. For a business paper, show the gross domestic product (GDP) for ten leading industrial countries over a five-year period using a _____.

3. For a criminal justice paper, compare the incidence of three different types of crime in one precinct during a three-month period using a _____.

4. For a health paper, chart the number of new cases of AIDS in North America and Africa over a ten-year period in order to show which continent has had the greater increase using a _____.

4 Drafting Paragraphs and Visuals

Except during an exam, you will usually refine your essay by working through several drafts. (*See Chapter 5: Revising and Editing, for an example of a paper in successive drafts.*) Think of your first draft as an attempt to discover a beginning, a middle, and an end for what you have to say. Avoid putting pressure on yourself to make it perfect the first time through.

This chapter offers strategies for developing paragraphs, the building blocks of a composition. It will also help you decide when to use visuals to present information and what kinds of visuals suit different purposes. In Chapter 5, we will look at strategies for revising your work. Keep in mind, though, that you may move back and forth between drafting and revising.

4a Use electronic tools for drafting.

www.mhhe.com/
mhhb2

For more on drafting
and revising, go to

Writing >
Paragraph/Essay
Development >
Drafting and
Revising

If you did not set up a folder for your paper as you were researching and generating ideas, be sure to do so now. Use the following tips:

1. **Save your work.** Always protect your drafts from power surges and other acts of technological treachery. Save often, and make backups.

2. **Label revised drafts with different file names.** Use a different file name for each successive version of your paper. For example, Diane Chen saved drafts of her paper as Migrations1, Migrations2, Migrations3, and so on.

3. **Print hard copies early and often.** If you save and print the original, you can feel free to experiment.

TEXTCONNEX

Using Hypertext as a Writing Process Tool

A variety of links in your essays can help you during the writing process. For example, you might include a link to additional research, to a source that refutes an argument, or to interesting information that is not directly relevant to the primary subject. These links can help you refer to supplemental material without undermining the coherence of the text. If a reader of an early draft—an instructor or a colleague—thinks the linked material should be in the essay itself, you can include it in the next draft.

Tips   LEARNING in COLLEGE

Avoiding Writer's Block

Do not put off writing the first draft. If you find it difficult to get started, consider the tips below.

1. **Resist the temptation to be a perfectionist.** The poet William Stafford said, "There's no such thing as writer's block for writers whose standards are low enough." Reserve your high standards for the revising and editing stages of your paper. For your first draft, do not worry about getting the right word, the stylish phrase, or even the correct spelling.

2. **Take it "bird by bird."** Writer Anne Lamott counsels students to break down writing assignments into manageable units and then make a commitment to finishing each unit in one session. She passes along her father's advice to her brother, who had procrastinated on a report about birds and was frozen by the enormity of the project: "Bird by bird, buddy. Just take it bird by bird."

3. **Start anywhere.** If you are stuck on the beginning, pick a section where you have a clearer sense of what you want to say. You can go back later and work out the transitions. Writers often compose the introduction after drafting a complete text.

4. **Generate more ideas.** If you are drawing a blank, you may need to do more reading, research, or brainstorming. Be careful, though, not to use reading and research as a stalling tactic.

5. **Set aside time and work in a quiet place.** Make sure you have somewhere you can work undisturbed for at least half an hour at a stretch.

---

www.mhhe.com/
mhhb2

For more on paragraph
unity, go to

Writing >
Paragraph/Essay
Development >
Unity

4b   Write focused paragraphs.

A **paragraph** is a set of sentences that develop an idea or example in support of the thesis. In academic papers, paragraphs are usually four or more sentences long, allowing for the detailed development of your ideas. Paragraphs break the text into blocks for your readers, allowing them to see how your essay builds step by step. A paragraph indent of one-half inch is typical in academic writing. In business writing and publishing, a line space above the paragraph serves instead. When writing for the Web, use very short paragraphs, and place links at the ends of paragraphs to ensure readers read all of the text.

1. Focusing on one main point or example

In a strong paragraph, the sentences form a unit that explores one main point or elaborates on one main example. When you are drafting, start a new paragraph when you introduce a new reason that supports your thesis, a new step in a process, or a new element in an analysis. New paragraphs also signal shifts in time and place, changing speakers in dialogue, contrasts with earlier material, and changes in level of emphasis. The paragraphs in your first draft may not all be perfectly unified, and you will likely need to revise for paragraph unity later on (*see Chapter 5: Revising and Editing*). However, bear in mind as you draft that a paragraph develops a main point or example.

The paragraph in the following example focuses on a theory that the writer will refer to later in his essay. The main idea is highlighted:

> Current thinking on the topic of loss and mourning rests on foundations constructed by the British psychiatrist John Bowlby. Using examples from animal and human behavior, Bowlby (1977) posited "attachment theory" as a means of understanding the powerful bonds between humans and the disruption that comes when the bonds are jeopardized or destroyed. The bonds are formed because of a need for security and safety, are developed early in life, are long enduring, and are directed toward a few special individuals. In normal maturation, the child becomes ever more independent, moving away from the figure of attachment, and returning periodically for safety and security. If the bonds are threatened, the individual will try to restore them through crying, clinging, or other types of coercion; if they are destroyed, withdrawal, apathy, and despair will follow.

The main idea is introduced in the highlighted sentences.

Details of attachment theory are developed in the rest of the paragraph.

> —JONATHAN FAST, "After Columbine: How People Mourn Sudden Death"

2. Signaling the main idea of your paragraph with a topic sentence

A **topic sentence** can be a helpful starting point as you draft a paragraph. In the paragraph below, the topic sentence (highlighted) provides the writer with a launching point for a series of details:

> The excavation also revealed dramatic evidence for the commemorative rituals that took place after the burial. Four cattle had been decapitated and their skulls symbolically placed in a ditch enclosing the burial pit. In the soil above the skulls archaeologists found the butchered bones of at least 250 slaughtered cattle, evidence for a huge ceremonial feast. Clearly this was an expensive way to commemorate a leader. Indeed, the huge quantity of meat suggests that the entire tribe may have gathered at the grave to take part in a ritual feast. Perhaps this was one way the bonds between scattered communities were strengthened.

The topic sentence announces that the paragraph will focus on a certain kind of evidence.

> —DAMIAN ROBINSON, "Riding into the Afterlife"

57

Sometimes the sentences in a paragraph will lead to a unifying conclusion, a form of topic sentence, as in this example:

> Table 1 presents the 15 mechanisms for gaining prestige that were reported for girls and for boys. There were few differences in the avenues to prestige between those in public and private high schools, particularly for girls. Avenues to prestige for girls that focus on their physical attributes, such as attractiveness, popularity with boys, clothes, sexual activity, and participation in sports, were more prominent in public schools than in private schools. In private schools the avenues more indicative of personality attributes, such as general sociability, having a good reputation/virginity, and participating in school clubs/government and cheerleading, were more prominent. Contrary to what parents may expect, avenues considered to be more negative, such as partying and being class clown, appeared more prevalent in private schools than in public schools. However, only clothes remained a significantly more important route to prestige for girls in public schools compared to girls in private schools once controls were introduced for region, size of community, year of graduation, and gender of respondent. Thus, taken together, type of high school had little effect on the ways in which girls accrued prestige in high school.
>
> —J. Jill Suitor, Rebecca Powers, and Rachel Brown, "Avenues to Prestige among Adolescents"

If a topic sentence would simply state the obvious, it can be omitted. In the following example, it is not necessary to state that the paragraph is about Igor Stravinsky's early life:

> Stravinsky was born in Russia, near St. Petersburg, grew up in a musical atmosphere, and studied with Nikolai Rimsky-Korsakov. He had his first important opportunity in 1909, when the great impresario Sergei Diaghilev heard his music.
>
> —Roger Kamien, *Music: An Appreciation*

Exercise 4.1　　Paragraph unity

Underline the topic sentences in the following paragraphs. If there is no topic sentence, state the main idea.

1.　　Based on the results of this study, it appears that a substantial amount of bullying by both students and teachers may be occurring in college. Over 60% of the students reported having observed a student being bullied by another student, and over 44% had seen a teacher bully a student. More than 6% of the students reported having been bullied by another student occasionally or very frequently, and almost 5% reported being bullied by a teacher occasionally or very frequently, while over 5% of the students stated that they bullied students occasionally or very frequently.

—MARK CHAPELL ET AL., "Bullying in College by Students and Teachers"

2.   ARS [the Agricultural Research Service] launched the first areawide IPM [Integrated Pest Management] attacks against the codling moth, a pest in apple and pear orchards, on 7,700 acres in the Pacific Northwest. Other programs include a major assault against the corn rootworm on over 40,000 acres in the Corn Belt, fruit flies in the Hawaiian Islands, and leafy spurge in the Northern Plains area. In 2001, an areawide IPM project began for fire ants in Florida, Mississippi, Oklahoma, South Carolina, and Texas on pastures using natural enemies, microbial pesticides, and attracticides.

—ROBERT FAUST, "Integrated Pest Management Programs Strive to Solve Agricultural Problems"

4c Write paragraphs that have a clear organization.

The sentences in your final draft need to be clearly related to one another. As you are drafting, make connections among your ideas and information as a way of moving your writing forward. One way to make your ideas work together is to organize them using one of the common organizational schemes for paragraphs. (*For advice on using repetition, pronouns, and transitions to relate sentences to one another, see Chapter 5.*)

1. Developing a chronological or spatial organization

The sentences in a paragraph with a **chronological organization** describe a series of events, steps, or observations as they occur in time: this happened, then that, and so on. The sentences in a paragraph with a **spatial organization** present details as they appear to a viewer: from top to bottom, outside to inside, east to west, and so on. In the following example, the authors use a chronological organization to describe how they found research subjects for their study:

Recruitment of students with ADHD and their teachers occurred through two mechanisms. The first mechanism

First step

involved making initial contact with school systems and/or principals to determine potential interest for participation. Contacts were made with administrators (principals, special education directors, or superintendents) from school systems in the Boston suburban area. Approximately half of the contacted school systems expressed initial interest in participating. The principal investigator described the study at faculty meetings at the schools within each system to solicit the participation of teachers. To protect against potential confounds (i.e., differences between teachers who agreed and did not agree to participate), all teachers in each school had to agree to participate for the school to be included in the study. Approximately 85% of schools agreed to participate after hearing the project described.

Result of first step

Second step

Result of second step

> —Ross Greene et al., "Are Students with ADHD More Stressful to Teach?"

You can see an example of spatial organization in paragraphs 5–7 of Diane Chen's student paper about Sebastião Salgado, on pages 102–03.

2. Developing a general-to-specific organization

As we have seen, paragraphs often start with a general topic sentence that states the main idea and then proceed with specifics that elaborate on that idea. The general topic sentence can include a question that the paragraph then answers or a problem that the paragraph goes on to solve. A variation of the general-to-specific organization includes a **limiting sentence** that seems to oppose the main idea. This structure allows you to bring in a different perspective on the main idea but then go on to defend it with specific examples, as in this paragraph:

General topic sentence

Limiting sentence

Specifics

> Parents do not have the moral right to make decisions for their children simply because of their status as parents. This idea may seem to go against our basic understanding of how families should operate. However, there are a number of actual cases that illustrate the weaknesses in the argument for absolute parental rights. [*The following paragraphs present a series of examples.*]

> — Sheila Foster, "Limiting Parental Rights," student paper

3. Developing a specific-to-general organization

Putting the general topic sentence at the end of the paragraph, preceded by the specific details leading up to that general conclusion, is especially effective when you are preparing your reader for a revelation. The following example is a variation on this organization;

the paragraph begins and ends with general statements that offer an interpretive framework:

> Even the subtlest details of Goya's portrait convey tension between revealing and concealing, between public and private personae. Dona Josefa's right eye avoids our gaze while her left eye engages it. Half of her ear is revealed while half is obscured by her hair. Above the sitter's arms, her torso faces us directly; her legs, however, turn away from us toward the left. The closed fan that Dona Josefa holds atop her stomach, pointed toward her enclosed womb, seems a mere trapping of formality in an otherwise informal setting. The fan reminds viewers that though we intrude on a private domain, Dona Josefa remains aware that she is indeed receiving company. Thus while our glimpse of her is, in many ways, an intimate one, Goya never allows us to forget that through the act of portraiture, this private self is being brought into the social sphere—and that our voyeurism has not gone unnoticed.

Introductory general statement

Specific details

Concluding general statement

> —BAZ DREISINGER, "The Private Made Public: Goya's *Josefa Castilla Portugal de Garcini y Wanasbrok*," student paper

4. Developing other organizational schemes

Many other methods of organizing paragraphs are available. These include the problem-solution scheme, in which the topic sentence defines an issue and the rest of the paragraph presents a solution (*discussed in Chapter 3, p. 46, as it applies to entire essays*). Other schemes include simple to complex, most familiar to least familiar, and least important to most important.

| **Exercise 4.2** | Paragraph organization |

Go back to the paragraphs in Exercise 4.1 (*pp. 58–59*) and identify the organizational strategy used in each one.

👁 **4d** Develop ideas and use visuals strategically.

When you develop ideas, you give your writing texture and depth as well as provide support for your thesis. Depending on the purpose of your text, you may use a few of these strategies or a mix of all of them. Photographs and other kinds of visuals can also support your ideas. Keep in mind, though, that visuals should always serve the overall purpose of your work. (*See 3d, pp. 51–54, for more on types of visuals and their purposes.*)

www.mhhe.com/
mhhb2

For more information on developing paragraphs, go to

Writing > Paragraph Patterns

61

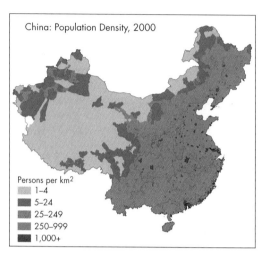

China: Population Density, 2000

Persons per km²
1–4
5–24
25–249
250–999
1,000+

FIGURE 4.1 Visuals that illustrate. This map illustrates the population densities in various regions of China in the year 2000.

1. Illustration

To appeal to readers, you often have to show as well as tell. Detailed examples (and well-chosen visuals—see Figure 4.1) can make abstractions more concrete and generalizations more specific, as the following paragraph shows:

> As Rubin explains, "for much of the Accord era, the ideal-typical family . . . was composed of a 'stay-at-home-mom,' a working father, and dependent children. He earned wages; she cooked, cleaned, cared for the home, managed the family's social life, and nurtured the family members" (97). Just such an arrangement characterized my grandmother's married life. My grandmother, who had four children, stayed at home with them, while her husband went off to work as a safety engineer. Sadly, when he died, she was left with nothing. She needed to support herself, yet had no work experience, no credit, and little education. But even though society frowned on her for seeking employment, my grandmother eventually found a clerical position—a low-level job with few perks.
>
> —JENNIFER KOEHLER, "Women's Work in the United States: The 1950s and 1990s"

www.mhhe.com/
mhhb2
For help with the use of illustration, go to

Writing >
Writing Tutors >
Exemplification

> *Caution:* Although any image you choose to include in your paper will be illustrative, images should not function merely as decoration. Ask yourself whether each image you are considering truly adds information to your text.

FIGURE 4.2 **Visuals that narrate.** Using images that narrate can be a powerful way to reinforce a message or portray events you discuss in your paper. Images like this one help tell one of many stories about the war in Iraq.

2. Narration

When you narrate, you tell a story. (*See Figure 4.2 for an example of a narrative visual.*) The following paragraph comes from a personal essay on the goods that result from "a lifetime of production":

> My dad changed too. He had come to that job feeling—as I do now—that everything was still possible. He'd served his time in the air force during the Korean War. Then, while my mother worked as a secretary to support them, he earned a college degree courtesy of the GI Bill. After graduation, my father painted houses for a season until he was offered a position scheduling the production of corrugated board. He took it, though he has told me that he never planned to stay. It was not something he envisioned as his life's work. I try to imagine what it is like suddenly to look up from a stack of orders and discover that the job you started one December day has watched you age.
>
> —MICHELLE M. DUCHARME, "A Lifetime of Production"

Notice that Ducharme begins with two sentences that state the topic and point of her narration. Then, using the past tense, she recounts in chronological sequence some key events that led to her father's taking a job in the box manufacturing business.

www.mhhe.com/
mhhb2

For help with use of narration, go to

Writing >
Writing Tutors >
Narration

63

FIGURE 4.3 Visuals that describe. Pay attention to the effect your selection will have on your paper. This photograph by Sebastião Salgado appeals to the viewer's emotions, evoking sympathy for the refugee children's plight.

www.mhhe.com/
mhhb2
For help with the use of
description, go to

Writing >
Writing Tutors >
Description

3. Description

To make an object, a person, or an activity vivid for your readers, describe it in concrete, specific words that appeal to the senses of sight, sound, taste, smell, and touch. In the following example, Diane Chen describes her impression of the photograph in Figure 4.3:

> The vertical black-and-white stripes of the blanket direct our eyes to the infants' faces and hands, which are framed by a horizontal white stripe. The whites of their eyes in particular stand out against the darkness created by the shell of the blankets. The camera's lens also seems to be in sharper focus on the faces than on the blankets, again drawing our attention to the babies' expressions.
>
> —DIANE CHEN, "The Caring Eye of Sebastião Salgado," student paper

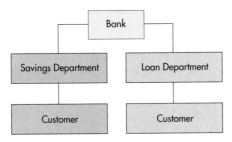

FIGURE 4.4 Visuals that classify or divide. An image can help you make the categories in or parts of complex systems or organizations easier to understand. The image shown here, for example, helps readers comprehend the structure of a business.

4. Classification

Classification is a useful way of grouping individual entities into identifiable categories (*see Figure 4.4*). Classifying occurs in all academic disciplines and often appears with its complement—**division,** which breaks a whole entity into its parts. **Analysis** interprets the meaning and importance of these parts.

www.mhhe.com/
mhhb2

For help with the use
of classification, go to

Writing >
Writing Tutors >
Classification

> [M]ost of America's traditional, routinized manufacturing jobs will disappear. So will routinized service jobs that can be done from remote locations, like keypunching of data transmitted by satellite. Instead, you will be engaged in one of two broad categories of work: either complex services, some of which will be sold to the rest of the world to pay for whatever Americans want to buy from the rest of the world, or person-to-person services, which foreigners can't provide for us because (apart from new immigrants and illegal aliens) they aren't here to provide them.
>
> Complex services involve the manipulation of data and abstract symbols. Included in this category are insurance, engineering, law, finance, computer programming, and advertising. Such activities now account for almost 25 percent of our GNP, up from 13 percent in 1950. They have already surpassed manufacturing (down to about 20 percent of GNP). Even *within* the manufacturing sector, executive, managerial, and engineering positions are increasing at a rate almost three times that of total manufacturing employment. Most of these jobs, too, involve manipulating symbols.
>
> —ROBERT REICH, "The Future of Work"

To make his ideas clear, Reich first classifies future work into two broad categories: complex services and person-to-person services. Then in the next paragraph, he develops the idea of complex services in more detail, in part by dividing that category into more specific— and familiar—categories like engineering and advertising.

65

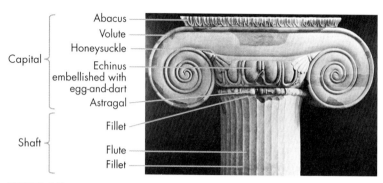

Capital
- Abacus
- Volute
- Honeysuckle
- Echinus embellished with egg-and-dart
- Astragal

Shaft
- Fillet
- Flute
- Fillet

FIGURE 4.5 Visuals that define. Visuals can be extremely effective when used to support a written definition or to identify parts of a whole. This image uses labels and leader lines to identify the characteristics of an Ionic column, an example of one of the five orders of classical architecture.

www.mhhe.com/
mhhb2

For help with the use of
definition, go to

Writing >
Writing Tutors >
Definition

5. Definition

You should define any concepts that the reader must understand to follow your ideas. (*See Figure 4.5 for an example of the use of a visual to define.*) Interpretations and arguments often depend on one or two key ideas that cannot be quickly and easily defined. In the following example, John Berger defines "image," a key idea in his televised lectures on the way we see things:

> An image is a sight which has been recreated or reproduced. It is an appearance, or a set of appearances, which has been detached from the place and time in which it first made its appearance and preserved—for a few moments or centuries. Every image embodies a way of seeing. Even a photograph. For photographs are not, as is often assumed, a mechanical record. Every time we look at a photograph, we are aware, however slightly, of the photographer selecting that sight from an infinity of other possible sights. This is true even in the most casual family snapshot. The photographer's way of seeing is reflected in his choice of subject.
>
> —JOHN BERGER, *Ways of Seeing*

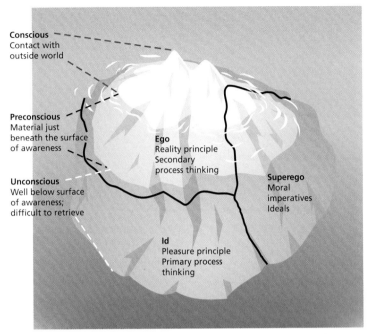

Conscious
Contact with
outside world

Preconscious
Material just
beneath the surface
of awareness

Unconscious
Well below surface
of awareness;
difficult to retrieve

Ego
Reality principle
Secondary
process thinking

Superego
Moral
imperatives
Ideals

Id
Pleasure principle
Primary process
thinking

FIGURE 4.6 Visuals as analogies. Visual analogies operate in the same way as written analogies. This figure uses the image of an iceberg to illustrate Freud's theory of the unconscious. The portion of the iceberg below the surface of the water represents the preconscious and unconscious mind.

6. Analogy

An **analogy** compares topics that at first glance seem quite different (*see Figure 4.6*). A well-chosen analogy can make unfamiliar or technical information seem more commonplace and understandable.

The human eye provides a good starting point for learning how a camera works. The lens of the eye is like the *lens* of the camera. In both instruments the lens focuses an image of the surroundings on a *light-sensitive surface*—the *retina* of the eye and the *film* in the camera. In both, the light-sensitive material is protected within a light-tight container—the *eyeball* of the eye and the *body* of the camera. Both eye and camera have a mechanism for shutting off light passing through the lens to the interior of the container—the *lid* of the eye and the *shutter* of the camera. In both, the size of the lens opening, or *aperture*, is regulated by an *iris diaphragm*.

—MARVIN ROSEN, *Introduction to Photography*

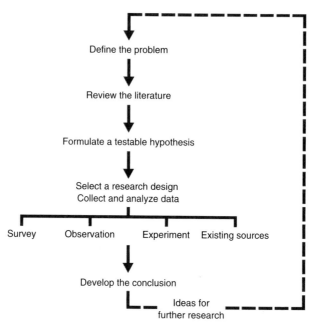

FIGURE 4.7 Visuals that show a process. Flow charts and diagrams are especially useful when illustrating a process. This one shows the scientific method used in disciplines throughout the sciences and social sciences.

www.mhhe.com/
mhhb2
For help with describing
a process, go to
Writing > Writing
Tutors > Process
Analysis

7. Process

To explain how to do something or show readers how something is done, you use process analysis (*see Figure 4.7*), explaining each step of the process in chronological order, as in the following example:

> To end our Hawan ritual of thanks, *aarti* is performed. First, my mother lights a piece of camphor in a metal plate called a *taree*. Holding the taree with her right hand, she moves the fire in a circular, clockwise movement in front of the altar. Next, she stands in front of my father and again moves the fiery *taree* in a circular, clockwise direction. After touching his feet and receiving his blessing, she attends to each of us children in turn, moving the fire in a clockwise direction before kissing us, one by one. When she is done, my father performs his *aarti* in a similar way, and then my sister and I do ours. When everyone is done, we say some prayers and sit down.
>
> —U. ROOPNARIAN, "Family Rituals," student paper

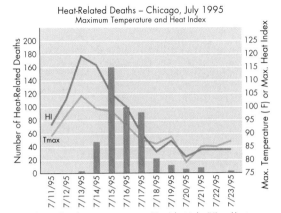

Heat-Related Deaths – Chicago, July 1995
Maximum Temperature and Heat Index

This graph tracks maximum temperature (Tmax), heat index (HI), and heat-related deaths in Chicago each day from July 11 to 23, 1995. The orange line shows maximum daily temperature, the green line shows the heat index, and the bars indicate number of deaths for the day.

FIGURE 4.8 Visuals that show cause and effect. Visuals can provide powerful evidence when you are writing about causes and effects. Although graphs like this one may seem self-explanatory, you still need to analyze and interpret them for your readers.

8. Cause and effect

Use a cause-and-effect strategy when you need to trace the causes of some event or situation, to describe its effects, or both (*see Figure 4.8*). In the following example, Rajeev Bector explains the reasons for a character's feelings and actions in a short story:

> Given the differences between Mrs. Chestny's and her son's values, as well as the oppressiveness of Mrs. Chestny's racist views, we can understand why Julian struggles to "teach" his mother "a lesson" (185) throughout the entire bus ride. Goffman would point out that "each individual is engaged in providing evidence to establish a definition of himself at the expense of what can remain for the other" (29). But in the end, neither character wins the contest. Julian's mother loses her sense of self when she is pushed down to the ground by a "colored woman" wearing a hat identical to hers (187). Faced with his mother's breakdown, Julian feels his own identity being overwhelmed by "the world of guilt and sorrow."
>
> —RAJEEV BECTOR, "The Character Contest in Flannery O'Connor's 'Everything That Rises Must Converge,'" student paper

www.mhhe.com/
mhhb2

For more information on how to work with visuals, go to

Writing > Visual Rhetoric Tutorial > Understanding Images

www.mhhe.com/
mhhb2

For help analyzing cause and effect, go to

Writing > Writing Tutors > Causal Analysis

Caution: When you use graphs or other visuals to summarize numeric data or show possible causal relationships, be sure to discuss the visuals in the body of your text.

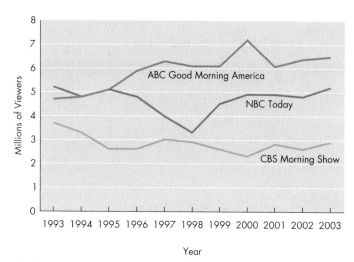

FIGURE 4.9 Visuals that compare and contrast. Graphs and charts are effective ways of comparing parallel sets of data. This line graph tracks the population of viewers for the three most popular morning shows over ten years.

www.mhhe.com/
mhhb2
For help with the use
of comparison and
contrast, go to
Writing >
Writing Tutors >
Comparison/
Contrast

9. Comparison and contrast

When you *compare*, you explore the similarities and differences among various items. When used with the term *contrast*, however, *compare* has a narrower meaning: "to spell out key similarities." *Contrast* always means "to itemize important differences." (*See Figure 4.9.*)

In the following example, the student writer uses a **subject-by-subject** pattern to contrast the ideas of two social commentators, Jeremy Rifkin and George Will:

> Rifkin and Will have different opinions about unemployment due to downsizing and the widening income gap between rich and poor. Rifkin sees both the decrease in employment and the increase in income disparity as evils that must be immediately dealt with lest society fall apart: "If no measures are taken to provide financial opportunities for millions of Americans in an era of diminishing jobs, then . . . violent crime is going to increase" (3). Will, on the other hand, seems to believe that both unemployment and income differences are necessary to the health of American society. Will writes, "A society that chafes against stratification derived from disparities of talents will be a society that discourages individual talents" (92). Apparently, the society that Rifkin wants is just the kind of society that Will rejects.
>
> —JACOB GROSSMAN, "Dark Comes before Dawn,"
> student paper

70

Notice that Grossman comments on Rifkin first and then turns to his second subject, George Will. To ensure paragraph unity, he begins with a topic sentence that mentions both subjects.

In the following paragraph, the student writer organizes her comparison of two photographs **point by point** rather than subject by subject. Instead of saying everything about Smith's picture before commenting on the Associated Press (AP) photo, the writer moves back and forth between the two images as she makes and supports two points: first, that the images differ in figure and scene and second, that they are similar in theme.

> Divided by an ocean, two photographers took pictures that at first glance seem absolutely different. W. Eugene Smith's well-known *Tomoko in the Bath* and the less well-known AP photo *A Paratrooper Works to Save the Life of a Buddy* portray distinctively different settings and people. Smith brings us into a darkened room where a Japanese woman is lovingly bathing her malformed child, while the AP staff photographer captures two soldiers on the battlefield, one intently performing CPR on his wounded friend. But even though the two images seem as different as women and men, peace and war, or life and death, both pictures show something similar: a time of suffering. It is the early 1970s— a time when the hopes and dreams that modernity promoted are being exposed as deadly to human beings. Perhaps that is why the bodies in both pictures seem humbled. Grief pulls you down onto your knees. Terror impels you to crawl along the ground.
>
> —ILONA BOUZOUKASHVILI, "On Reading Photographs," student paper

---

Exercise 4.3 Developing ideas

Experiment with the development strategies just discussed— illustration, narration, description, classification, definition, analogy, process, cause and effect, and comparison and contrast—in a paper you are currently drafting. Are some strategies inappropriate to your assignment? Have you combined any of the strategies in a single paragraph?

4e Integrate visuals effectively.

If you decide to use a table, chart, diagram, or photograph, keep this general advice in mind:

1. **Number and label tables and other figures** consecutively throughout your paper: Table 1, Table 2, and so on. Do not abbreviate *Table*. *Figure* may be abbreviated as *Fig*.

www.mhhe.com/
mhhb2

For an interactive tutorial on using visuals, go to

Writing > Visual Rhetoric Tutorial > Document Design

71

2. **Refer to the visual element in your text** before it appears, placing the visual as close as possible to the text in which you state why you are including it. If your project contains many visuals or complex tables, you may want to group them in an appendix. Always refer to a visual by its label: for example, "See Fig. 1."

3. **Give each visual a title or caption** that clearly explains what the visual shows. A visual with its caption should be clear without the discussion in the text, and the discussion of the visual in the text should be clear without the visual itself.

4. **Include explanatory notes below the visuals.** If you want to explain a specific element within the visual, use a superscript *letter* (not a number) both after the specific element and before the note. The explanation should appear directly beneath the graphic, not at the foot of the page or at the end of your paper. Do not use your word processor's Insert/Footnote commands to create the footnote because the program will put the note in the wrong place.

5. **Credit sources for visuals.** If you use a visual element from a source, be sure to credit the source. Unless you have specific guidelines to follow, you can use the word *Source*, followed by a colon and complete documentation of the source, including the author, title, publication information, and page number if applicable.

Note: The Modern Language Association (MLA) and the American Psychological Association (APA) provide guidelines for figure captions and crediting sources of visuals that differ from the previous guidelines (*see Chapter 23: MLA Documentation Style, pp. 341–90, and Chapter 24: APA Documentation Style, pp. 391–410*).

www.mhhe.com/mhhb2

For more information on crafting introductions, go to

Writing > Paragraph/Essay Development > Introductions

4f Craft an introduction that establishes your purpose.

As you begin your first draft, you may want to skip the introduction and start by writing the body of your paper. After your paper has taken shape, you can then go back and sketch out the main ideas for your introduction.

For most types of compositions, your opening paragraph or paragraphs will include your thesis statement. If your thesis has changed in the course of writing your first draft, adjust it as necessary.

An introduction that begins with broad assertions and then narrows the focus to conclude with the thesis is called a **funnel opener.** If your purpose is analytic, however, you may prefer to build up to your thesis, placing it near the end of the paper. Some types of writing, such as narratives, may not require an explicitly stated thesis if the main idea is obvious without it.

Focus on presenting the main ideas of your introduction in a way that will hook readers. Because the introduction establishes your credibility, avoid either understating or overstating your authority ("I'm not completely sure about this, but . . ."; "As an expert on the topic, I think . . ."). Instead, encourage readers to share your view of the topic's importance. An introduction that begins by referring to the paper title or that baldly states "The purpose of my essay is . . ." could benefit from a more creative approach. Here are some opening strategies:

- Tell a brief story related to the question your thesis answers.
- Begin with a relevant and attention-getting quotation.
- Begin with a paraphrase of a commonly held view that you immediately question.
- State a working hypothesis.
- Define a key term, but avoid the tired opener that begins "According to the dictionary. . . ."
- Pose an important question.

The following paragraphs from an informative essay begin with an attention-getting fact, followed by a definition of key terms, a key question, and a working hypothesis:

> Every year huge rotating storms packing winds greater than 74 miles per hour sweep across tropical seas and onto shorelines—often devastating large swaths of territory. When these roiling tempests—called hurricanes in the Atlantic and the eastern Pacific oceans, typhoons in the western Pacific and cyclones in the Indian Ocean—strike heavily populated areas, they can kill thousands and cause billions of dollars of property damage. And nothing, absolutely nothing, stands in their way.
>
> But must these fearful forces of nature be forever beyond our control? My research colleagues and I think not. Our team is investigating how we might learn to nudge hurricanes onto more benign paths or otherwise defuse them. Although this bold goal probably lies decades in the future, we think our results show that it is not too early to study the possibilities.
>
> —Ross N. Hoffman, "Controlling Hurricanes"

The following paragraphs from an analytical essay begin with a vivid quotation that illustrates a commonly held view. The writer then calls that view into question:

> "Loathsome hordes, dark swarms of worms that emerge from the narrow crevices of their holes when the sun is high,

TEXTCONNEX

Web Sites: Beginnings, Middles, and Ends

If you are creating a Web site, remember that readers may enter it in the "middle" and never find the "end." Web sites simply do not have the kind of linear structure that papers do, and readers tend to want information in short chunks rather than in lengthy paragraphs. However, readers visiting a Web site still expect to be able to go to an introductory page, or **home page,** that makes the overall purpose and contents of the site clear. Make sure that your home page loads quickly—in under ten seconds or less. Provide clear navigational links on every page of the site, and always include one link that returns the user to the home page.

preferring to cover their villainous faces with hair rather than their private parts and surrounding areas with clothes." So wrote the sixth-century British churchman Gildas, lamenting the depredations of Pictish and other Scotland-based barbarian "butchers" a century earlier following Rome's abandonment of its British provinces in A.D. 410. This characterization of the Picts as illiterate, uncivilized, scantily clothed, and promiscuous heathens has clung to them to the present day. Although over the past half century scholars have regarded the cleric Gildas as a somewhat biased commentator, most haven't tended to see the Picts as outstandingly civilized either.

Now, however, one of the most detailed surveys of their art has revealed that these archetypal barbarians actually developed a deep knowledge of the Bible and of some aspects of Roman classical literature. . . .

—DAVID KEYS, "Rethinking the Picts"

www.mhhe.com/
mhhb2

For more information on conclusions, go to

Writing >
Paragraph/Essay
Development >
Conclusions

4g   Conclude by answering "So what?"

Your closing makes a final impression and motivates the reader to think further. You should not merely repeat the main idea, nor should you introduce a completely new topic. Instead, remind readers of the paper's significance (without overstating it) and satisfy those who might be asking, "So what?" Here are some common strategies for concluding a paper effectively:

- Refer to the story or quotation you used in your introduction.

- Answer the question you posed in your introduction.

- Summarize your main point.

- Call for some action on your reader's part.

- Present a powerful image or forceful example.
- Suggest some implications for the future.

The following conclusion refers to a quotation used in the introduction on pages 73–74 as it summarizes the main point:

> Burghead, the current excavations at Tarbat, and new art-history research demonstrate the extraordinary diversity and sophistication of Dark Age Pictish culture. Even if the Picts had once been scantily clothed "butchers," as Gildas and others no doubt perceived them, they evolved into something quite different.
>
> —DAVID KEYS, "Rethinking the Picts"

If your paper is brief—five hundred words or fewer—a few concluding sentences may be enough to satisfy the reader. You might also end a brief paper with a powerful supporting point and vivid image. A short composition presenting two sides of the argument over whether cell phones make us more secure concludes with a quotation supporting the pro–cell phone side:

> "If you are left to your own, what would you think about?" said Kenneth J. Gergen, a professor of psychology at Swarthmore College, and author of *The Saturated Self*. "You have to have other voices, reports and news. The best decisions are made in a whole set of dialogues."
>
> —KEN BELSON, "Saved, and Enslaved, by the Cell"

Exercise 4.4   Analyzing introductions and conclusions

Find an essay that has an introduction or a conclusion that engaged you and one with an introduction or conclusion that failed to draw you in. What strategies did the successful essay employ? What strategies could the writer of the unsuccessful essay have used? Next look at the introduction and conclusion of an essay you are currently writing. Do these paragraphs use any of the strategies discussed in this section? If not, try one of these strategies when you revise.

 For MULTILINGUAL STUDENTS

Special Features of Introductions and Conclusions

U.S. readers expect introductory paragraphs to tackle the topic directly. Therefore, avoid offering long background explanations or making broad generalizations. Readers expect the concluding paragraph to revisit the thesis and, for complex papers, to summarize the main points. Bringing the text to an orchestrated close gives the reader a final opportunity to grasp your message.

5 Revising and Editing

Once you have a draft, you can approach it with a critical eye. In the **revising** stage, you review the whole composition and its parts, adding, deleting, and moving text as necessary. After you are satisfied with the substance of your paper, **editing** begins. When you edit, you polish sentences so that you say what you want to say as effectively as possible.

This chapter focuses on revising and includes a complete student essay in several drafts. It also introduces the concepts and principles of editing, which are covered in much greater detail in Parts 6 through 12.

5a Get comments from readers.

Asking actual readers to comment on your draft is the best way to get fresh perspectives on your writing. (Be sure that your professor allows this kind of collaboration.)

1. Trying peer review

Whether it is required or optional, online or face-to-face, **peer review** is a form of **collaborative learning** that involves reading and critiquing your classmates' work while they review yours. Consider including some of your peers' responses with your final draft so that your teacher knows you have taken the initiative to work with other writers.

Help your readers help you by asking them specific questions. The best compliment readers can pay you is to take your work seriously enough to make constructive suggestions. When you share a draft with readers, provide responses to the following questions:

- **What is the assignment?** Readers need to understand your purpose and audience.

- **How close is the project to being finished?** Help readers understand where you are in the writing process and how to assist you in taking the next step.

- **What steps do you plan to take to complete the project?** If readers know your plans, they can either question the direction you are taking or give you more specific advice, for example, additional sources that you might consult.

- **What kind of feedback do you need?** Do you want readers to summarize your main points so you can determine whether you have communicated them clearly? Do you want to know what readers were thinking and feeling as they read or heard your draft? Do you want a response to the logic of your argument or the development of your thesis?

Tips LEARNING in COLLEGE

Re-Visioning Your Paper

Revising is a process of "re-visioning"—of looking at your work through the eyes of your audience. Here are some tips for getting a fresh perspective on your paper:

1. **Get feedback from other readers.** Candid, respectful feedback can help you discover the strong and weak areas of your paper. See "Responding to readers" below and the box on page 78 for advice on making use of readers' reactions to your drafts.

2. **Let your draft cool.** Whenever possible, try to schedule a break between drafting and revising. A good night's sleep, a movie break, or some physical exercise will help you view your paper more objectively.

3. **Read your paper aloud.** Some people find that reading aloud helps them hear their paper the way their audience will.

4. **Use revising and editing checklists.** The checklists on pages 82, 93, 94–95, and 99 will assist you in evaluating your paper systematically.

Reading other writers' drafts will help you view your own work more objectively, and comments from readers will help you see your own writing as others see it. As you gain more objectivity, you will become more adept at revising your work. The approaches that you see your classmates taking to the assignment will broaden your perspective and give you ideas for new directions in your own writing.

The writing environment in the *Catalyst* Web site that accompanies this book can make it easier for you to obtain and review comments from your readers. Many Web-based tools such as *Google Docs* enable groups to share, edit, and revise their work online.

2. Responding to readers

Consider and evaluate your readers' suggestions, but remember that you are under no obligation to do what they say. One reader may like a particular sentence; a second reader may suggest that you eliminate the very same sentence. Is there common ground? Yes. Both readers stopped at that sentence. Ask yourself why—and whether you want readers to pause there. You are the one who is ultimately responsible for your paper, so make decisions accordingly.

5b Use resources available on your campus, on the Internet, and in your community.

www.mhhe.com/
mhhb2

For links to online resources on writing, go to

Writing > Writing Web Links

You can call on a number of different resources outside the writing classroom for feedback on your paper.

CHECKLIST

Giving Feedback

☐ **Focus on strengths as well as weaknesses.** Let writers know what parts of their paper are strongest so that they can retain those sections and use them as models to improve weaker sections. Do not withhold constructive criticism, or you will deprive the writer of an opportunity to improve the paper.

☐ **Be specific.** Give examples to back up your general reactions.

☐ **Be constructive.** Phrase negative reactions to help the writer see a solution. Instead of saying that an example is a bad choice, explain that you did not understand how the example was connected to the main point and suggest a way to clarify the connection.

☐ **Ask questions.** Jot down any questions that occur to you as you read. Ask for clarification, or note an objection that other readers might make.

See also: Checklist—Revising Your Draft for Content and Organization, on page 82.

Receiving Feedback

☐ **Resist being defensive.** Keep in mind that readers are discussing your paper, not you, and their feedback offers a way for you to see your paper differently. Be respectful of their time and efforts. Remember that you, not your reviewers, are in charge of decisions about your paper.

☐ **Ask for more feedback if you need it.** Some students may be hesitant to share all their reactions, and you may need to do some coaxing.

1. Using the campus writing center
Tutors in the campus writing center can read and comment on drafts of your work. They can also help you find and correct problems with grammar, punctuation, and mechanics.

2. Using online writing labs, or OWLs
Most OWLs present information about writing that you can access anytime, including lists of online resources. OWLs with tutors on staff can be useful in the following ways:

For MULTILINGUAL STUDENTS

Peer Review

Respectful peer review will challenge you to view your writing critically and present ideas to a diverse audience. It also will show you that many of your errors are quite common; it will improve your ability to detect mistakes and decide what to correct first. Your unique perspective can help native speakers improve their writing, as they can help you with the subtleties of English idioms.

- You can submit a draft by e-mail for feedback. OWL tutors will return your work, often within forty-eight hours.

- OWLs may post your paper in a public access space where you will receive feedback from more than just one or two readers.

- You can read papers online and learn how others are handling writing issues.

You can learn more about what OWLs have to offer by checking out the following Web sites:

- *Purdue University's Online Writing Lab (Figure 5.1 on p. 80)* http://owl.english.purdue.edu

- *Writing Labs and Writing Centers on the Web* (you can visit almost fifty OWLs) http://owl.english.purdue.edu/internet/owls/writing-labs.html

3. Working with experts and instructors

In addition to sharing your work with peers in class, through e-mail, or in online environments, you can use e-mail to consult your instructor or other experts. Your instructor's comments on an early draft are especially valuable, but remember, it is your responsibility to address the issues your instructor raises and to revise your work.

5c Use electronic tools for revising.

Even though word-processing programs can make a first draft look finished, it is still a first draft. Check below the surface for problems in content, structure, and style. Move paragraphs around, add details, and delete irrelevant sentences. Print out a copy of your draft to see the big picture—your paper as a whole.

Become familiar with the revising and editing tools in your word-processing program.

www.mhhe.com/
mhhb2
For help with revising, go to

Writing >
Paragraph/Essay
Development >
Drafting and
Revising

79

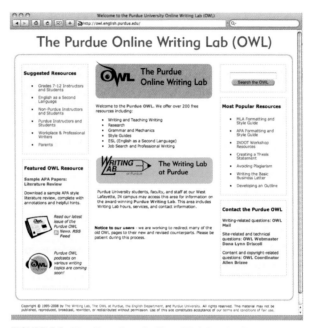

FIGURE 5.1 The Purdue Online Writing Lab.
http://owl.english.purdue.edu/

- **Comments:** Many word-processing programs have a Comments feature (*see Figure 5.2*) that allows you to add notes to sections of text. This feature is very useful for giving feedback on someone else's draft. Some writers use it to make notes to themselves.

- **Track Changes:** The Track Changes feature (*see Figure 5.3*) allows you to edit a piece of writing while maintaining the original text. You can judge whether a suggested edit has improved the paper. If you change your mind, you can restore the deleted text. When collaborating with another writer, take care to delete comments and to accept or reject all changes before turning in a paper to your instructor. You can preserve a record of the edits by saving the Track Changes version as a seperate file.

5d   Focus on the purpose of your writing.

As you revise your paper, consider your purpose. Is your primary purpose to inform, to interpret, or to argue? (*For more on assignment purposes, see Chapter 2, pp. 26–27.*)

FIGURE 5.2 **Using Microsoft Word 2007's Comments feature.**

Clarity about your purpose is especially important when an assignment calls for interpretation. A description is not the same as an interpretation. With this principle in mind, Diane Chen read over the first draft of her paper on the *Migrations* photography exhibit. Here is part of her description of the photograph she chose to discuss in detail:

FIRST DRAFT

The photograph is black and white, as are the others in the show. The faces of the babies are in sharp focus while the blanket is a bit defocused. Light, which is essential to photography, is disseminated from a single source coming from the upper left-hand corner of the picture. The light source is not too bright as to bathe the babies in light, but just bright enough to illuminate their faces, which have expressions of interest and puzzlement. Perhaps they are wondering who Salgado is or what is that strange contraption he is holding.

Keeping her purpose in mind, Chen realized that she needed to discuss the significance of her observations—to interpret the details and offer an analysis. She wanted to show her readers how the formal elements of the photograph functioned. Her revision clarifies this interpretation.

REVISION

The orphanage photograph is shot in black and white, as are the other images in the show, giving it a documentary feel that emphasizes the truth of the situation. But Salgado's choice of black-and-white photography is also an artistic decision. He uses the contrasts of light and dark to create a dramatic image of the three babies.

FIGURE 5.3 **Showing revisions with Track Changes.**

The vertical black-and-white stripes of the blanket direct our eyes to the infants' faces and hands, which are framed by a horizontal white stripe . . .

www.mhhe.com/
mhhb2

For help developing a
strong thesis, go to
Writing >
Paragraph/Essay
Development >
Thesis/Central
Idea

5e Make sure you have a strong thesis.

Remember that a thesis makes an assertion about a topic. It links the *what* and the *why*. Is your thesis evident on the first page of your draft? Before readers get very far along, they expect an answer to the question, "What is the point of all this?" If you do not find the point on the first page, its absence is a signal to revise, unless you are deliberately waiting until the end to reveal your thesis. (*For more on strong theses, see Chapter 3, pp. 42–46.*)

CHECKLIST

Revising Your Draft for Content and Organization

☐ **Purpose:** What is the purpose of the text, and how clearly does the writing communicate it? What aspects of the text convey the purpose? What would make it more apparent?

☐ **Thesis:** What is the thesis? Is it clear and specific, and does it appear early in the draft? If not, is there a reason for withholding it? What revisions would make the thesis clearer?

☐ **Audience:** How does the approach—including evidence and tone—appeal to the intended audience? How might the composition appeal to this audience more effectively?

☐ **Structure:** How does the order of the key points support the thesis, and would another order do so more effectively? Do any sections not support the thesis, and if so, which ones? How might overly long or short sections be revised?

☐ **Paragraphs:** How might the development, unity, and coherence of each paragraph be improved?

☐ **Visuals:** Do visuals communicate the intended meaning clearly and without unnecessary clutter? How might they be improved?

☐ **Introduction and conclusion:** How does the introduction draw the reader in? What main idea does it convey? What changes might clarify the main idea? How does the conclusion answer the "So what?" question?

When Diane Chen looked over the first draft of her paper, she decided that she needed to strengthen her thesis statement. She had included two sentences that could serve as a thesis, and it wasn't clear which one was to be the central idea of her paper:

POSSIBLE THESIS
[A] photograph taken with an aesthetic awareness does not debase the severity of war and worldwide suffering.

POSSIBLE THESIS
Whether capturing the millions of refugee tents in Africa that seem to stretch on for miles or the disheartened faces of small immigrant children, Salgado brings an artistic element to his pictures that suggests he does so much more with his camera than just point and shoot.

Chen decided to change her introduction to sharpen the focus on one main idea:

FINAL THESIS Like a photojournalist, Salgado brings us images of newsworthy events, but he goes beyond objective reporting, imparting his compassion for refugees and migrants to the viewer.

(To compare Diane's first and second drafts, see p. 100 and pp. 101–102.)

Tips LEARNING in COLLEGE

Selecting a Title

Your essay title should engage your readers' interest and prepare them for the thesis of your paper. The title should not simply state a broad topic ("Lake Superior Zooplankton") but rather should indicate your angle on that topic ("Changes in the Lake Superior Crustacean Zooplankton Community"). Here are some suggestions for strengthening your title:

1. Include a phrase that communicates the purpose of your paper.
   - Alcohol Myopia Theory: A Review of the Literature
   - From Palm to iPhone: A Brief History of PDAs

2. Use a question to indicate that your paper weighs different sides of an argument.
   - Does the Patriot Act Strengthen America?
   - Performance-Based Funding for the Arts: Wise Fiscal Policy or Unwise Gamble?

3. Use a quotation and/or a play on words or a vivid image.
   - Much Ado about "Noting": Perception in Shakespeare's Comedy
   - Many Happy Returns: An Inventory Management Success Story
   - A Fly Trapped in Amber: On Investigating Soft-Bodied Fossils

Readers need to see a statement of the main idea on the first page, but they also expect the writer to return to the thesis near the end. Here is Diane Chen's restatement of her thesis from the end of her revised draft:

> Salgado uses his skills as an artist to get us not only to look at these difficult subjects, but also to feel compassion for them. He is able to bring a story as big and complex as the epic displacement of the world's people to us through a collection of intimate and intensely moving images. As he says in his introduction to the exhibit catalog, "We hold the key to humanity's future, but for that we must understand the present. We cannot afford to look away" (15).

Exercise 5.1   Revising thesis statements

Examine some of your recent papers to see whether the thesis is clearly stated. Is the thesis significant? Can you follow the development of this idea throughout the paper? Does the version of your thesis in the conclusion answer the "So what?" question?

5f   Review the structure of your project as a whole.

Does your draft have a beginning, a middle, and an end, with bridges between those parts? When you revise, you can refine and even change this structure so that it supports what you want to say more effectively.

One way to review the structure is by outlining your first draft. (*For help with outlining, see Chapter 3, pp. 47–51.*) Try listing the key points in sentence form; whenever possible, use sentences that actually appear in the draft. Ask yourself if the key points are arranged effectively or if another arrangement would work better. The following structures are typical ways of organizing papers:

- **Informative:** Sets out the key parts of a topic.
- **Exploratory:** Begins with a question or problem and works step by step to discover or explain an answer or a solution.
- **Argumentative:** Presents a set of linked reasons plus supporting evidence.

5g   Revise your composition for paragraph development, paragraph unity, and coherence.

As you revise, examine each paragraph, asking yourself what role it plays—or should play—in the paper as a whole. Keeping this role in mind, check the paragraph for development and unity. You should also check each paragraph for coherence—and consider whether all the paragraphs taken together contribute to the paper as a whole.

1. Paragraph development

Paragraphs in academic papers are usually about a hundred words long. Consider dividing any that exceed two hundred words or that are especially dense. When paragraphs are short for no apparent stylistic reason, you may need to develop them or combine them with other paragraphs. Would more information make the point clearer? Perhaps a term should be defined. Do generalizations need to be supported with examples?

Note how this writer developed one of her draft paragraphs, adding details and examples to clarify her points and make a more effective argument.

FIRST DRAFT

A 1913 advertisement for Shredded Wheat illustrates Kellner's claim that advertisements sell self-images. The ad suggests that serving Shredded Wheat will give women the same sense of accomplishment as gaining the right to vote.

REVISION

According to Kellner, "advertising is as concerned with selling lifestyles and socially desirable identities . . . as with selling the products themselves" (193). A 1913 ad for Shredded Wheat shows how the selling of self-images works. At first glance, this ad seems to be promoting the women's suffrage movement. In big, bold letters, "Votes for Women" is emblazoned across the top of the ad. But a closer look reveals that the ad is for Shredded Wheat cereal. Holding a piece of the cereal in her hand, a woman stands behind a large bowlful of Shredded Wheat biscuits that is made to look like a voting box. The text claims that "every biscuit is a vote for health, happiness and domestic freedom." Like the rest of the advertisement, this claim suggests that serving Shredded Wheat will give women the same sense of accomplishment as gaining the right to vote.

—HOLLY MUSETTI, "Targeting Women," student paper

2. Paragraph unity

To check for **unity,** identify the paragraph's topic sentence (*see p. 57*). Everything in the paragraph should be clearly and closely connected to the topic sentence. In particular, check very long paragraphs (over two hundred words) for unity. Items unrelated to the topic sentence should be deleted or developed into separate paragraphs. Another option is to revise the topic sentence.

Compare the first draft of the following paragraph with its revision, and note how the addition of a topic sentence (in bold in the revision) makes the paragraph more clearly focused and therefore easier

www.mhhe.com/ mhhb2
For help developing paragraph unity, go to

Writing > Paragraph/Essay Development > Unity

85

for the writer to revise further. Note also that the writer deleted ideas that did not directly relate to the paragraph's main point (underlined in the first draft):

FIRST DRAFT

Germany is ranked first on worldwide production levels. Automobiles, aircraft, and electronic equipment are among Germany's most important products for export. As the standard of living of the citizens of what was formerly East Germany increases due to reunification, their purchasing power and productivity will increase. A major problem is that east Germany is not as productive or efficient as west Germany, and so it would be better if less money were invested in the east. Germany is involved in most global treaties that protect business interests, and intellectual property is well protected. A plus for potential ventures and production plans is its highly skilled workforce. Another factor that indicates that Germany will remain strong in the arena of productivity and trade is its physical location in the world. "Its terrain and geographical position have combined to make Germany an important crossroads for traffic between the North Sea, the Baltic, and the Mediterranean. International transportation routes pass through all of Germany," thus utilizing a comprehensive and efficient network of transportation, both on land and over water ("Germany," 1995, p. 185). Businesses can operate plants in Germany and have no difficulties transporting goods and services to other parts of the country. Generally, private enterprise, government, banks, and unions cooperate, making the country more amenable to negotiations for business entry or joint ventures.

REVISION

For many reasons, Germany is attractive both as a market for other nations and as a location for production. As the standard of living of the citizens of what was formerly East Germany increases because of reunification, their purchasing power and productivity increase. Intellectual property is well protected, and Germany is involved in most global treaties that protect business interests. Germany's highly skilled workforce is another plus for potential ventures and production plans. Generally, private enterprise, government, banks, and unions cooperate, making the country amenable to negotiations for business entry or joint ventures. Germany also has an excellent physical location that makes it an "important crossroads for traffic between the North Sea, the Baltic, and the Mediterranean" ("Germany," 1995, p. 185). Equally important, a comprehensive and efficient transportation system allows businesses to operate plants in Germany and easily transport their goods and services to other parts of the country and the world.

—JENNIFER KOEHLER, "Germany's Path to
Continuing Prosperity"

3. Coherence

A coherent paragraph flows smoothly, with an organization that is easy to follow and with each sentence clearly related to the next. (*See Chapter 4, pp. 59–61, for tips on how to develop well-organized paragraphs.*) You can improve the **coherence** both within and among the paragraphs in your draft by using repetition, pronouns, parallel structure, and transitions.

www.mhhe.com/
mhhb2
For help writing
coherent paragraphs,
go to
Writing >
Paragraph/Essay
Development >
Coherence

Use repetition to emphasize the main idea   Repeating key words helps your readers stay focused on the topic of your paper and reinforces your thesis. In the example that follows, Rajeev Bector opens his paper with a paragraph that uses repetition (highlighted) to define a key term central to his essay:

> Sociologist Erving Goffman believes that every social interaction establishes our identity and preserves our image, honor, and credibility in the hearts and minds of others. Social interactions, he says, are in essence "character contests" that occur not only in games and sports but also in our everyday dealings with strangers, peers, friends and even family members. Goffman defines character contests as "disputes [that] are sought out and indulged in (often with glee) as a means of establishing where one's boundaries are" (29). Just such a contest occurs in Flannery O'Connor's short story "Everything That Rises Must Converge."

—RAJEEV BECTOR, "The Character Contest in Flannery
O'Connor's 'Everything That Rises Must Converge,'"
student paper

(To see Bector's complete essay, turn to p. 167 in Chapter 9: Interpretive Analyses.)

Use pronouns to avoid unnecessary repetition   Too much repetition can make your sentences sound clumsy and your paragraphs seem monotonous. Use pronouns to stand in for nouns where needed, and to form connections between sentences.

In the next paragraph, Diane Chen uses pronouns (highlighted) to create smooth-sounding sentences that hold the paragraph together:

Salgado uses **his** skills as an artist to get us not only to look at these difficult subjects, but also to feel compassion for **them.** **He** is able to bring a story as big and complex as the epic displacement of the world's people to us through a collection of intimate and intensely moving images. As **he** says in **his** introduction to the exhibit catalog, "We hold the key to humanity's future, but for that we must understand the present. We cannot afford to look away."

Use parallel structure to emphasize connections   Parallel structure helps to form connections within and between the sentences of your paragraph. In the following sentence, for example, the three clauses are grammatically parallel, each consisting of a pronoun (P) and a past-tense verb (V):

>   P - V   P - V   P - V

▶   **We came, we saw, and we conquered.**

Within paragraphs, two or more sentences can have parallel structures, as in the following example:

▶   Because the former West Germany lived through a generation
of prosperity, its people developed high expectations of material
comfort. Because the former East Germany lived through a
generation of deprivation, its people developed a disdain for
material values.

Too much parallelism can seem repetitive, though, so save this device for ideas that you can pair meaningfully. (*For more information on editing for parallelism in your writing, turn to Chapter 42: Faulty Parallelism.*)

Use transitional words and phrases   One-word **transitions** and **transitional expressions** link one idea to another, helping readers understand your logic. (*See the box on p. 89 for a list of common transitional expressions.*) Compare the following two paragraphs, the first version without transitions and the second, revised version with transitions (in bold type):

FIRST DRAFT

Glaser was in a position to affect powerfully Armstrong's career and his life. There is little evidence that the musician submitted to whatever his business manager wanted or demanded. Armstrong seemed to recognize that he gave Glaser whatever power the manager enjoyed over him. Armstrong could and did resist Glaser's control when he wanted to. That may be one reason why he liked and trusted Glaser as much as he did.

TRANSITIONAL EXPRESSIONS

- **To show relationships in space:** above, adjacent to, against, alongside, around, at a distance from, at the . . . , below, beside, beyond, encircling, far off, forward, from the . . . , in front of, in the rear, inside, near the back, near the end, nearby, next to, on, over, surrounding, there, through the . . . , to the left, to the right, up front
- **To show relationships in time:** afterward, at last, before, earlier, first, former, formerly, immediately, in the first place, in the interval, in the meantime, in the next place, in the last place, later on, latter, meanwhile, next, now, often, once, previously, second, simultaneously, sometime later, subsequently, suddenly, then, therefore, third, today, tomorrow, until now, when, years ago, yesterday
- **To show addition or to compare:** again, also, and, and then, besides, further, furthermore, in addition, last, likewise, moreover, next, too
- **To give examples that intensify points:** after all, as an example, certainly, clearly, for example, for instance, indeed, in fact, in truth, it is true that, of course, specifically, that is
- **To show similarities:** alike, in the same way, like, likewise, resembling, similarly
- **To show contrasts:** after all, although, but, conversely, differ(s) from, difference, different, dissimilar, even though, granted, however, in contrast, in spite of, nevertheless, notwithstanding, on the contrary, on the other hand, otherwise, still, though, unlike, while this may be true, yet
- **To indicate cause and effect:** accordingly, as a result, because, consequently, hence, since, then, therefore, thus
- **To conclude or summarize:** finally, in brief, in conclusion, in other words, in short, in summary, that is, to summarize

REVISION

Clearly, Glaser was in a position to affect powerfully Armstrong's career and his life. **However,** there is little evidence that the musician submitted to whatever his business manager wanted or demanded. **In fact,** Armstrong seemed to recognize that he gave Glaser whatever power the manager enjoyed over him. When he wanted to, Armstrong could and did resist Glaser's control, and that may be one reason why he liked and trusted Glaser as much as he did.

—ESTHER HOFFMAN, "Louis Armstrong and Joe Glaser"

(To see Hoffman's complete essay, turn to pp. 379–90 in Chapter 23: MLA Documentation Style.)

89

Use coherence strategies to show how paragraphs are related
You can also use repetition, pronouns, parallelism, and transitions to
show how paragraphs are related to one another. In addition, you can
use **transitional sentences** both to refer to the previous paragraph and
at the same time to move your essay on to the next point. Lengthy essays
may contain short transitional paragraphs to bridge two topics that are
developed in some detail. Notice how the first sentence at the beginning
of the second paragraph below, from Diane Chen's paper about Sebastião
Salgado, both refers to the babies described in the previous paragraph
and serves as a topic sentence for the second paragraph.

> The vertical black-and-white stripes of the blanket direct our eyes to the infants' faces and hands,
> which are framed by a horizontal white stripe. The whites of their eyes in particular stand out against
> the darkness created by the shell of the blankets. The camera's lens also seems to be in sharper focus
> on the faces than on the blankets, again focusing our attention on the babies' expressions.
> Each baby has a different response to the camera. The baby on the left returns our gaze
> with a heart-wrenching look. The baby in the center, whose eyes are open extra-wide, appears
> startled and in need of comforting. But the baby on the right, whose eyes are glazed and sunken,
> doesn't even notice the camera. We glimpse death in that child's face.

Exercise 5.2   Revising paragraphs

Revise the paragraphs below to improve their unity, development,
and coherence.

1.   Vivaldi was famous and influential as a virtuoso violinist
     and composer. Vivaldi died in poverty, having lost popularity in
     the last years before his death. He had been acclaimed during
     his lifetime and forgotten for two hundred years after his death.
     Many composers suffer that fate. The baroque revival of the
     1950s brought his music back to the public's attention.

2.   People who want to adopt an exotic pet need to be aware
     of the consequences. Baby snakes and reptiles can seem fairly
     easy to manage. Lion and tiger cubs are playful and friendly.
     They can seem as harmless as kittens. Domestic cats can revert
     to a wild state quite easily. Adult snakes and reptiles can grow
     large. Many species of reptiles and snakes require carefully
     controlled environments. Big cats can escape. An escaped lion
     or tiger is a danger to itself and to others. Most exotic animals
     need professional care. This kind of care is available in zoos and
     wild-animal parks. The best environment for an exotic animal is
     the wild.

Exercise 5.3   Writing well-developed, coherent paragraphs

Using the strategies for paragraph development and coherence discussed in section 5g, write a paragraph for one of the following topic

sentences. Working with two or more classmates, decide where your paragraph needs more details or improved coherence.

1. Awards shows on television often fail to recognize creativity and innovation.
2. Most people learn only those aspects of a computer program that they need to use every day.
3. First-year students who also work can have an easier time adjusting to the demands of college life than nonworking students.
4. E-mail messages that circulate widely can be broken down into several categories.

👁 **5h** Revise visuals.

Review your visuals during the revision stage to eliminate what scholar Edward Tufte calls **chartjunk,** or distracting visual elements. The "Revising Visuals" Checklist on page 93 presents Tufte's suggestions for editing visuals so that your readers will focus on your data rather than your "data containers."

www.mhhe.com/
mhhb2
For more on using visuals, go to
Writing > Visual Rhetoric Tutorial > Visualizing Data

5i Edit sentences.

Parts 7, 8, and 9 of this handbook address editing for grammar conventions, clarity, and word choice. The section that follows gives you an overview of editing concerns and techniques.

www.mhhe.com/
mhhb2
For additional help with editing, go to
Editing

1. Editing for grammar conventions

Sometimes writers construct a sentence or choose a word form that does not follow the rules of standard written English. In academic writing, these kinds of errors are distracting to readers and can obscure your meaning.

DRAFT
Photographs of illegal immigrants being captured by the United States border patrol, of emotional immigrants on the plane to their new country, and of villagers fleeing rebel gangs. [*This is a sentence fragment because it lacks a verb. It also omits the writer's point about these images.*]

EDITED SENTENCE
Photographs of illegal immigrants being captured by the United States border patrol, of emotional immigrants on the plane to their new country, and of villagers fleeing rebel gangs exemplify the range of migration stories.

Professional editors use abbreviations and symbols to note errors in a manuscript; a list of common ones can be found at the back of this book. Your instructor and other readers may use these abbreviations and symbols, and you may find it helpful to learn them as well.

DRAFT

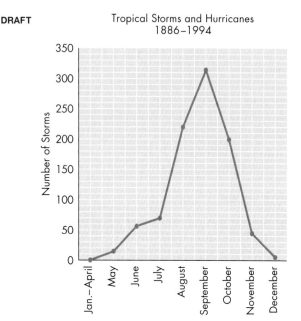

REVISION

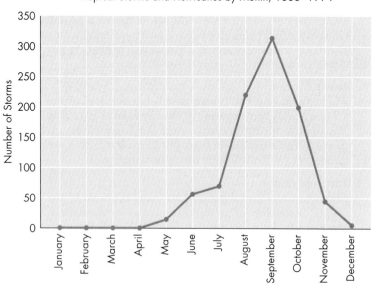

FIGURE 5.4 Eliminating distortion in a line graph.

CHECKLIST

Revising Visuals

☐ **Are grid lines needed in tables?** Eliminate grid lines or, if the lines are needed for clarity, lighten them. Tables should not look like nets, with every number enclosed in a box. Vertical rules are needed only when space is extremely tight between columns.

☐ **Are there unnecessary three-dimensional renderings?** Cubes and shadows can distort the information in a visual. For most charts, including pie charts, a flat image makes it easier for readers to compare parts.

☐ **Is data labeled clearly?** Avoid abbreviations and legends, if possible.

☐ **Does each visual have an informative title?**

☐ **Do bright colors focus attention on the key data?** If you are including a map, use muted colors over large areas, and save strong colors for emphasis.

☐ **Do pictures distract from the visual's purpose?** Clip art and other decorative elements seldom make data more interesting, nor do they make it appear more substantial.

☐ **Are data distorted?** Look out for and correct distortions of the data. In the draft version of the graph in Figure 5.4 (*on the facing page*), eight months of the year are plotted separately, with the months of January, February, March, and April grouped together. This creates a misleading impression of hurricane activity by month. The revision corrects this distortion.

2. Editing for clarity

Concentrate on sentence style. Some of your sentences, though grammatically correct, can probably be improved. A volley of short, choppy sentences, for example, distracts readers from what you have to say, whereas an unbroken stream of long, complicated sentences is likely to dull their senses. Also vary sentence openings and structure. In the example that follows, notice how the revised version connects ideas for readers and, consequently, is easier to read.

DRAFT   My father was a zealous fisherman. He took his fishing rod on every family outing. He often spent the whole outing staring at the water,

93

CHECKLIST

Editing Sentences and Words

The online diagnostic "Test Yourself" quizzes that accompany this handbook, as well as the exercises and Checklists in Parts 7 through 12, can help you determine which conventions give you trouble. To create a personalized editing checklist, fill in the boxes next to your trouble spots in the list that follows. For examples of the most common errors in student writing, see the foldout section at the beginning of Part 6.

1. **Editing for grammar conventions** (*Part 7*): Does the paper contain any of these common errors? Note and correct any sentences that contain errors.

☐ Sentence fragments (*Chapter 32, pp. 514–25*)

☐ Comma splices (*Chapter 33, pp. 526–37*)

☐ Run-on sentences (*Chapter 33, pp. 526–37*)

☐ Subject-verb agreement problems (*Chapter 34, pp. 538–53*)

☐ Incorrect verb forms (*Chapter 35, pp. 553–77*)

☐ Inconsistent verb tenses (*Chapter 35, pp. 553–77*)

☐ Pronoun-antecedent agreement problems (*Chapter 36, pp. 588–93*)

☐ Incorrect pronoun forms (*Chapter 36, pp. 577–99*)

☐ Misused adjectives or adverbs (*Chapter 37, pp. 599–612*)

☐ Other: _____

2. **Editing for clarity** (*Part 8*): Does the paper contain any of the following common causes of unclear sentences? Note sections that could be clearer.

☐ Wordiness (*Chapter 38, pp. 614–22*)

☐ Missing words (*Chapter 39, pp. 622–27*)

☐ Mixed constructions (*Chapter 40, pp. 628–31*)

☐ Confusing shifts (*Chapter 41, pp. 631–39*)

☐ Faulty parallelism (*Chapter 42, pp. 639–47*)

☐ Misplaced or dangling modifiers (*Chapter 43, pp. 647–54*)

☐ Problems with coordination and subordination (*Chapter 44, pp. 655–64*)

☐ Other: _____

3. **Editing for word choice** (*Part 9*):

☐ How can I revise to avoid slang, biased language, clichés, or other inappropriate usages? (*Chapter 48, pp. 691–98*)

☐ Where and how might the choice of words be more precise? (*Chapter 49, pp. 698–709*)

☐ Does the paper misuse any commonly confused words (for example, *advice* vs. *advise*) or use any nonstandard expressions (for example, *could of*)? (*Chapter 50, pp. 709–18*)

If you are in the process of developing fluency in English, consult Part 12: Guide for Multilingual Writers for more advice.

	waiting for a nibble. He went to the kitchen as soon as he got home. He usually cleaned and cooked the fish the same day he caught them.
REVISED	A zealous fisherman, my father took his fishing rod on every family outing. He would often spend the whole afternoon by the shore, waiting for a nibble, and then hurry straight to the kitchen to clean and cook his catch.

You should also condense and focus sentences that are wordy and that lack a clear subject and a vivid verb. Rephrase sentences beginning with *it is, there is,* or *there are* (**expletive constructions**) to begin with the subject and a stronger verb. (Change *There are five cats in the house* to *Five cats reside in the house.*)

DRAFT	Although both vertebral and wrist fractures cause deformity and impair movement, hip fractures, which are one of the most devastating

consequences of osteoporosis, significantly increase the risk of death, since 12%–30% of patients with a hip fracture die within one year after the fracture, while the mortality rate climbs to 40% for the first two years post fracture.

REVISED Hip fractures are one of the most devastating consequences of osteoporosis. Although verte-bral and wrist fractures cause deformity and impair movement, hip fractures significantly increase the risk of death. Within one year after a hip fracture, 12%–20% of the injured die. The mortality rate climbs to 40% after two years.

DRAFT *There are stereotypes* from the days of a divided Germany that must be dealt with.

REVISED *Stereotypes* formed in the days of a divided Germany *persist* and must be dealt with.

TEXTCONNEX

The Pros and Cons of Grammar Checkers and Spell Checkers

Grammar checkers and spell checkers can help you spot some errors, but they miss many others and may even flag correct sentences. Consider the following example:

► **Thee neighbors puts there cats' outsider.**

A spelling and grammar checker did not catch the five real errors in the sentence. (Correct version: *The neighbors put their cats outside.*) The software also flagged the following grammatically correct and eloquent sentence by Alice Walker and suggested the nonsense substitution below.

WALKER'S SENTENCE

► **Consider, if you can bear to imagine it, what might have been the re-sult if singing, too, had been forbidden by law.**

GRAMMAR CHECKER'S SUGGESTION

► **Consider, if you can bear to imagine it, law if singing, too, had forbid what might have been the result.**

If you are aware of your program's limitations, then you can make some use of it as you edit your manuscript. Be sure, however, to review the manuscript carefully yourself.

3. Editing for word choice

Finding precisely the right word and putting that word in the best place is an important part of revision. Different disciplines and occupations have their own terminologies. The word *significant,* for example, has a mathematical meaning for the statistician and a different meaning for the literary critic. When taking courses in a discipline, you should use its terminology accurately. Whenever you are unsure of a word's denotation (its exact meaning), consult a dictionary.

As you review your draft, look for general terms that might need to be made more specific:

DRAFT   Foreign direct investment (FDI) in Germany will probably remain low because of several *factors.* [Factors *is a general word. To get specific, answer the question, what factors?*]

REVISED   Foreign direct investment (FDI) in Germany will probably remain low because of *high labor costs, high taxation, and government regulation.*

Your search for more specific words can lead you to a dictionary and a thesaurus. A dictionary gives the exact definition of a word, its history (etymology), and the parts of speech it belongs to. A thesaurus provides its synonyms, words with the same or nearly the same meaning. (*For more on using a dictionary and a thesaurus, see Chapter 47.*)

One student used both a thesaurus and a dictionary as aids in revising the following sentence:

DRAFT   Malcolm X had a special kind of power.

A thesaurus listed *influence* as a synonym for *power,* and *charisma* as a special kind of influence. In the dictionary, the writer found that *charisma* means a "divinely conferred" power and has an etymological connection with *charismatic,* a term used to describe ecstatic Christian experiences like speaking in tongues. *Charisma* was exactly the word she needed to convey both the spiritual and the popular sides of Malcolm X:

REVISED   Malcolm X had charisma.

As you edit for word choice, make sure that your tone is appropriate for academic writing (*see Chapter 2, p. 30*) and that you have avoided biased language, such as the use of *his* to refer to women as well as men:

BIASED
Every student who wrote *his* name on the class list had to pay a copying fee in advance and pledge to attend every session.

REVISED AS PLURAL

Students who wrote *their* names on the class list had to pay a copying fee in advance and pledge to attend every session.

REVISED TO AVOID PRONOUNS

Every student who signed up for the class had to pay a copying fee in advance and pledge to attend every session.

REVISED WITH *HIS* OR *HER*

Every student who wrote *his or her* name on the class list had to pay a copying fee in advance and pledge to attend every session.

(See Chapter 48: Appropriate Language for advice on editing to eliminate biased language.)

Exercise 5.4   Editing sentences

Type the following sentences into your word processor and activate the grammar and spell-checker feature. Copy the sentence suggested by the software, and then write your own edited version of the sentence.

1. Lighting affects are sense of the shape and texture of the objects depict.

2. A novelist's tells the truth even though he invent stories and characters.

3. There are the question of why bad things happen to good people, which story of Job illustrate.

4. A expensive marketing campaign is of little value if the product stinks.

5. Digestive enzymes melt down the nutrients in food so that the body is able to put in effect a utilization of those nutrients when the body needs energy to do things.

5j Proofread carefully before you turn in your composition.

Once you have revised your paper at the composition, paragraph, and sentence levels, give your work one last check to make sure that it is free of typos and other mechanical errors.

Many writers prefer to **proofread** when their work is in its final format. Even if you are submitting an electronic version of your project, it is still a good idea to proofread a printed version. Placing a ruler under each line can make it easier to focus. You can also start at the end and proofread your way backward to the beginning, sentence by sentence.

CHECKLIST

Proofreading

☐ Have you included your name, the date, your professor's name, and the paper title? (*See Chapters 23–26 for the formats to use for MLA, APA, Chicago, and CSE style.*)

☐ Are all words spelled correctly? Be sure to check the spelling of titles and headings. (*See Chapter 63: Spelling.*)

☐ Have you used the words you intended, or have you substituted words that sound like the ones you want but have a different spelling and meaning, such as *too* for *to, their* for *there,* or *it's* for *its*? (*See Chapter 50: Glossary of Usage.*)

☐ Are all proper names capitalized? Have you capitalized titles of works correctly, and either italicized them or put them in quotation marks, as required? (*See Chapter 57: Capitalization, and Chapter 60: Italics and Underlining.*)

☐ Have you punctuated your sentences correctly? (*See Part 10.*)

☐ Are sources cited correctly? Double-check all source citations and the works-cited or reference list. (*See Chapters 23–26.*)

☐ Have you checked anything you retyped—for example, quotations, data tables—against the original?

5k Learn from one student's revisions.

In this section we will look at several drafts of Diane Chen's paper on the *Migrations* photography exhibit. The photograph that she is discussing appears in the final version of her paper, on page 103.

1. First draft, with revision comments

In Chapter 2, we saw Diane Chen choose the exhibit of photographs by Sebastião Salgado as the topic for a paper (*see 2c, pp. 23–24*). In Chapter 3 , we saw her explore this topic (*see 3a, pp. 33–42*), develop a working thesis (*see 3b, pp. 42–45*), and plan her organization (*see 3c, pp. 46–50*). Here is Diane Chen's first draft, along with notes about general and paragraph-level concerns that she received at her school's writing center.

*Consider using
a title that
is related to
your thesis.*

Sebastião Salgado
Migrations: Humanity in Transition

The role of a photojournalist is to inform and educate the public in an unbiased manner. Photography as a means of documentation requires it to be factual and informative. However, a photograph taken with an aesthetic awareness does not debase the severity of war and worldwide suffering.

*Why is this ar-
tistic element
significant?*

In a recent exhibition of Sebastião Salgado's work entitled, "Migrations: Humanity in Transition," the noted photographer displayed his documentation of the plight of migrants and refugees through beautiful and artful photographs. Whether capturing the (millions) of   *OK?* refugee tents in Africa that seem to stretch on for miles or the disheartened faces of small immigrant children, Salgado (brings an artistic element) to his pictures that suggests he does so much more with his camera than just point and shoot.

*Is this phrase
appropriate ?*

*Does this
apply to all
three faces?*

So many photographs in Salgado's show are certain to impress and touch the viewers with their subject matter and sheer beauty. However, "Orphanage attached to the hospital at Kibumba, Number One Camp, Goma, Zaire," was (my favorite photograph.) It depicts three apparently newborn or several month old babies, who are victims of the genocidal war in Rwanda, arranged neatly in a row, wrapped in a mass of stripe-patterned clothes or blankets. Wide-eyed and bewildered, their three little faces and their tiny hands peek out from under the blankets. The whites of their eyes stand out against the darkness created by the shell of the blankets.

*Excellent
descriptions
but tie them
to analyses.*

The photograph is black and white, as are the others in the show. The faces of the babies are in sharp focus while the blanket is a bit defocused. Light, which is essential to photography, is disseminated from a single source coming from the upper left-hand corner of the picture. The light source is not too bright as to bathe the babies in light, but just bright enough to illuminate their faces, which have expressions of interest and puzzlement. Perhaps they are wondering who Salgado is or what is that strange contraption he is holding. The lighting also creates contrasts of light and dark in the peaks and valleys created by the folds in the blanket.

*Do the
details that
follow support
this idea?*

What I find most impress~~ing~~ive in this picture is Salgado's ability to find the beauty of human life amidst the ugliness of warfare. The vantage point that this photograph was taken from is one of a mother or father directly standing over the child. In this sense the infants become our own. Salgado also makes an interesting point with the framing of this picture. The babies and the blanket occupy the entire photo. The beauty of the infants consumes the viewer. It is unclear if any part of this composition was posed. Logically, a true photojournalist would not manipulate his subject but photograph it as is.

*Point is not
related to
paragraph.*

meaning?

What is it?

Perhaps such aesthetic consciousness is necessary in order for the audience to even be able to look at the photographs. Hardly anyone enjoys looking at gruesome or explicit pictures, an issue newspaper editors have to grapple with in every copy. As art, Salgado's photographs transport us in grand and abstract way. As a photojournalist, Salgado needs to tell it like it is. Finding the right balance between the two means atracting the eye of the viewer while conveying a strong message. Salgado never lets us forget that it is after all, refugee camps and remnants of bloody tribal gang warfare that we are looking at. Beauty needs to accompany truth for it to be bearable.

*Diane,
Your paper is full of great observations about the Salgado picture, but I wasn't sure of your thesis. There seemed to be one at the end of the first paragraph and another at the end of the second. A clear thesis would give you a focus for discussing the significance of your observations. I look forward to reading the next draft.
Seth*

2. Second draft, with edits

For her second draft, Chen revised her introduction and sharpened her thesis statement. She changed the focus of her essay somewhat, from the beauty of the picture to the way that the picture forces the viewer to look closely into the babies' faces and feel compassion for them. She also tightened the focus of her descriptive paragraphs so that the details in each one served her analytic purpose. After revising her paper overall, she edited her second draft.

The Caring Eye of Sebastião Salgado

Photographer Sebastião Salgado spent seven years ~~of his life~~ traveling along migration routes to city slums and refugee camps~~, and migration routes~~ in order to document the lives of people uprooted from their homelands. A selection of his photographs can be seen in the exhibit, ~~"~~*Migrations: Humanity in Transition.*~~"~~ Like a photojournalist, Salgado brings us images of newsworthy events, but he goes beyond objective reporting, imparting his compassion for refugees and migrants to the viewer.

~~So m~~Many of the photographs in Salgado's show are certain to ~~impress and~~ touch ~~the~~ viewers ~~with their subject matter and sheer beauty~~. Whether capturing the thousands~~millions~~ of refugee tents in Africa that seem to stretch on for miles or the disheartened faces of ~~small~~ immigrant children, ~~Salgado brings an artistic element to his pictures that~~the images in *Migrations* suggest~~s~~ that ~~he~~ Salgado does so much more with his camera than ~~just~~ point and shoot.

Salgado's photograph of the most vulnerable of these refugees illustrates the power of his work. "Orphanage attached to the hospital at Kibumba, Number One Camp, Goma Zaire~~,~~" (Fig. 1) depicts three ~~apparently newborn or several month old babies~~infants, who are victims of the genocidal war in neighboring Rwanda. The label for the photograph reveals ~~tells us~~ that there were 4,000 orphans at this camp and an estimated 100,000 Rwandan orphans overall. Those numbers are mind-numbing abstractions, but this picture is not.

The orphanage photograph is shot in black and white, as are the others in the show, ~~and provides the audience with~~giving it a ~~very~~ documentary~~, newspaper type of~~ feel that emphasizes that this is a real~~, newsworthy~~ situation ~~that we need to be aware of~~ deserving our attention. But Salgado's choice of black-and-white photography is also an artistic decision. He uses the contrasts of light and dark to create a dramatic image of the three babies.

The vertical black-and-white stripes of the blanket direct our eyes to the infants' faces and hands, which are framed by a horizontal white stripe. The whites of their eyes in particular stand out against the darkness created by the shell of the blankets. The camera's lens also seems to be in sharper focus on the faces than on the blankets, again focusing our attention on the babies' expressions. Each baby has a different response to the camera. The center baby, with his or her extra-wide eyes, appears startled and in need of comforting. The baby to the right is oblivious to the camera and in fact seems to be starving or ill. The healthy baby on the left returns our gaze.

Diane Chen 4/24/08 9:22 AM
Comment: Reorganize——move from left to right across the picture for a more dramatic conclusion. [...6]

The vantage point ~~of~~~~that~~ this photograph ~~was taken from~~ is one of a ~~mother or father~~par~~ent directly~~ standing directly over his or her~~the~~ child. In this sense the infants become our own. Salgado also ~~makes an interesting point with the framing of~~frames this picture strategically. The babies in their blanket consumes the entire space, so that their innocence and vulnerability consume~~s~~ the viewer.

101

Salgado uses his skills as an artist to get us ~~not only~~ to look at these difficult subjects, ~~but also to feel compassion for them~~. He is able to bring a story as big and complex as the epic displacement of the world's people to us through a collection of intimate and intensely moving images. As he says in his introduction to the exhibit catalog, "We hold the key to humanity's future, but for that we must understand the present. We cannot afford to look away."

3. Final draft

After editing her paper, Chen printed it out, proofread it, corrected some minor errors, and then printed the final version, which is reprinted below. (Chen formatted her paper using the MLA style. The version here, however, does not reflect all the MLA conventions for page breaks, margins, and line spacing. For details on the proper formatting of a paper in MLA style, see Chapter 23 and the sample that begins on p. 379.)

Diane Chen
Professor Bennet
Art 258: History of Photography
5 December 2009

The Caring Eye of Sebastião Salgado

> *Chen identifies the topic and then states her thesis.*

Photographer Sebastião Salgado spent seven years traveling along migration routes to city slums and refugee camps in order to document the lives of people uprooted from their homelands. A selection of his photographs can be seen in the exhibit *Migrations: Humanity in Transition*. Like a photojournalist, Salgado brings us images of newsworthy events, but he goes beyond objective reporting, imparting his compassion for refugees and migrants to the viewer.

> *Chen provides background about the exhibit.*

Many of the photographs in Salgado's show are certain to touch viewers. Whether capturing the thousands of refugee tents in Africa that seem to stretch on for miles or the disheartened faces of immigrant children, the images in *Migrations* suggest that Salgado does so much more than point and shoot.

> *Chen first references the photo that illustrates her main point.*

Salgado's photograph of the most vulnerable among these refugees illustrates the power of his work. "Orphanage attached to the hospital at Kibumba, Number One Camp, Goma, Zaire" (see fig.1) depicts three infants who are victims of the genocidal war in neighboring Rwanda. The label for the photograph reveals that there were 4,000 orphans at this camp and an estimated 100,000 Rwandan orphans overall. Those numbers are mind-numbing abstractions, but this picture is not.

> *The fourth paragraph focuses on the image.*

The orphanage photograph is shot in black and white, as are the others in the show, giving it a documentary feel that emphasizes that this is a real situation deserving our attention. But Salgado's choice of black-and-white photography is also an artistic decision. He uses the contrasts of light and dark to create a dramatic image of the three babies.

> *Chen describes the photograph in the next three paragraphs, using a spatial organization.*

The vertical black-and-white stripes of the blanket direct our eyes to the infants' faces and hands, which are framed by a horizontal white stripe. The whites of their eyes in particular stand out against the darkness created by the shell of the blankets. The camera's lens also seems to be in sharper focus on the faces than on the blankets, again focusing our attention on the babies' expressions.

Fig.1. Sebastião Salgado, *Migrations,* "Orphanage attached to the hospital at Kibumba, Number One Camp, Goma, Zaire."

Each baby has a different response to the camera. The baby on the left returns our gaze with a heart-wrenching look. The baby in the center, whose eyes are open extra-wide, appears startled and in need of comforting. But the baby on the right, whose eyes are glazed and sunken, doesn't even notice the camera. We glimpse death in that child's face.

The vantage point of this photograph is one of a parent standing directly over his or her child. In this sense the infants become our own. Salgado also frames this picture strategically. The babies in their blanket consume the entire space, so that their innocence and vulnerability consume the viewer.

Salgado uses his skills as an artist to get us to look closely at these difficult subjects. He is able to bring a story as big and complex as the epic displacement of the world's people to us through a collection of intimate and intensely moving images. As he says in his introduction to the exhibit catalog, "We hold the key to humanity's future, but for that we must understand the present. We cannot afford to look away" (15).

The concluding paragraph restates the thesis; the paper ends with a compelling quotation.

————————————————[new page]————————————————

Work Cited

Salgado, Sebastião. *Migrations.* New York: Aperture, 2000. Print.

The work-cited entry appears on a new page, listing the source of the quotation used to end the essay.

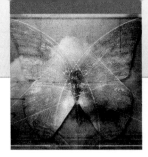

6 Designing Academic Papers and Preparing Portfolios

One of your crucial writing tasks is to format your text so that readers can "see" your ideas clearly. The focus of this chapter is on designing academic papers. (*Advice on designing multimedia presentations and Web sites is in Chapter 14: Multimedia Writing, and advice on designing brochures, newsletters, résumés, and other documents is in Part 5: Writing beyond College.*)

In your writing classes, as well as in other courses and in your professional life, you may be called on to compile a **portfolio,** a collection of your writing and related work. This chapter offers guidelines for designing print and electronic portfolios that showcase your work effectively.

www.mhhe.com/ mhhb2

For links to information on document and Web design, go to

Writing > Writing Web Links > Annotated Links on Design

6a Consider audience and purpose when making design decisions.

Effective design decisions take into account your purpose for writing as well as the needs of your audience. If you are writing an informative paper for a psychology class, your instructor—your primary audience—will probably prefer that you follow the guidelines provided by the American Psychological Association (APA). If you are writing a lab report for a biology or chemistry course, you will very likely need to follow a well-established format and use the documentation style recommended by the Council of Science Editors (CSE) to cite any sources you use. A history paper might call for use of the Chicago style. Interpretive papers for language and literature courses usually use the style recommended by the Modern Language Association (MLA). In any paper, however, your goal is to enhance the content of your text, not decorate it. (*For help with these documentation styles, see Chapters 23–26.*)

6b Use the tools available in your word-processing program.

Most word-processing programs give you a range of options for editing, sharing, and, especially, designing documents. For example, if you are using Microsoft Word 2007, you can access groups of commands by clicking on the various tabs at the top of the screen. Figure 6.1 on the facing page shows the Home tab, which contains basic formatting and editing commands. You can choose different typefaces; add bold, italic, or underlined type; insert numbered or bulleted lists, and so on. Other tabs allow you to add boxes and drawings to your text, make comments, and change the page layout.

Many word-processing programs are organized differently. Some include menus of commands on toolbars instead of on tabs. Take

FIGURE 6.1 **Formatting tools in a word-processing program.**

some time to learn the different formatting options available in your program.

👁 **6c** Think intentionally about design.

For any print or online document that you create, whatever its purpose or audience, apply the same basic **document design** principles:

- Organize information for readers.
- Choose typefaces and use lists and other graphic options to make your text readable and to emphasize key elements.
- Format related design elements consistently.
- Use headings to organize long papers.
- Use restraint.
- Meet the needs of readers with disabilities.

A sample page from a student's report on a local food bank, which includes information that she gathered while serving as a volunteer, illustrates these principles. The content in Figure 6.2 on page 106 is not presented effectively because the author has not adhered to these principles. By contrast, the same material in Figure 6.3 on page 107 is clearer and easier for readers to understand because of its design.

www.mhhe.com/
mhhb2

For more on
designing your paper,
go to

Writing > Visual
Rhetoric Tutorial >
Document Design

1. Organizing information for readers

You can organize information visually and topically by grouping related items using boxes, indents, headings, spacing, and lists. These variations in text appearance help readers scan, locate important information, and dive in when they need to know more about a topic. If a color printer is available to you and your instructor allows you to use color in your paper, then it can serve this purpose as well. Use color with restraint, and remember that colors may look different on screen and in print. Also consider readers with disabilities (*see p. 111*).

You can also use **white space,** areas of a document that do not contain type or graphics, to help organize information for your readers. Generous margins and plenty of white space above headings and around other elements make text easier to read. Use white space to divide your document into chunks of related information. **105**

Emphasis wrong: Title of report is not as prominent as the heading within the report.

Margins are not wide enough, making the page look crowded.

Bar chart is not intro-duced in the text and does not have a caption.

Description of proce-dure is dense, not easy to follow.

Use of bold type and different typeface for no reason.

The Caring Express Food Bank

The Caring Express Food Bank serves a varied population of clients, including chronically homeless people, temporarily homeless people, recent immigrants, elderly people on fixed incomes, and people in need of temporary services.

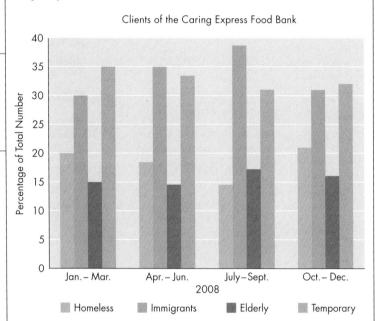

Clients of the Caring Express Food Bank

While the number of homeless, both temporary and permanent, that Caring Express assisted in 2008 decreased during the summer months, the number of immigrant workers increased. The percentage of elderly people and people in need of temporary services remained fairly stable throughout the year.

How Caring Express Helps Clients

When new clients come to Caring Express, a volunteer fills out a **form** with their **address** (if they have one), their **phone number,** their **income,** their **employ-ment situation,** and the help they are receiving, if any, from the local department of human services. Clients who do not live in Maple Valley are referred to a food bank or outreach program in their area. Clients who qualify check off the food they need from a list, and then that food is packed and distributed to them.

FIGURE 6.2 **Example of a poorly designed report.**

The Caring Express Food Bank

The Caring Express Food Bank serves a varied population of clients, including chronically homeless people, temporarily homeless people, recent immigrants, elderly people on fixed incomes, and people in need of temporary services. As Figure 1 shows, while the number of homeless, both temporary and permanent, that Caring Express assisted in 2008 decreased during the summer months, the number of immigrant workers increased. The percentage of elderly people and people in need of temporary services remained fairly stable throughout the year.

Clients of the Caring Express Food Bank

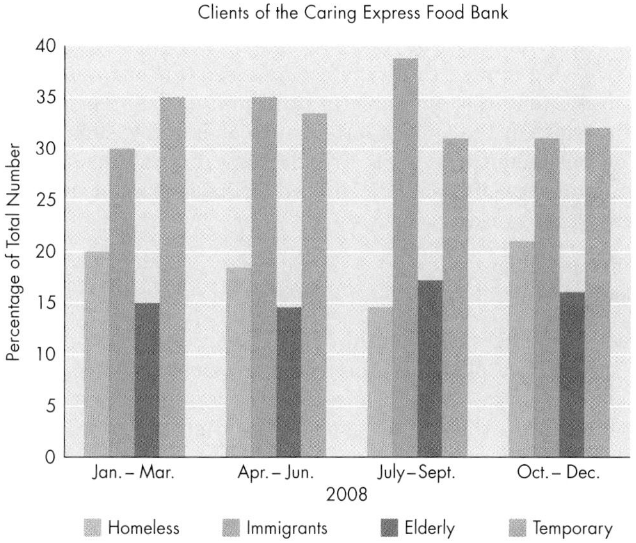

Figure 1. Percentage of clients in each group during 2008

How Caring Express Helps Clients

When new clients come to Caring Express, the volunteers follow this procedure:

1. The volunteer fills out a form with the client's address (if he or she has one), phone number, income, and employment situation.
2. Clients who do not live in Maple Valley are referred to a food bank or outreach program in their area.
3. Clients who qualify check off the food they need from a list.
4. The food is packed and distributed to them.

Title is centered and in larger type than text and heading.

Bar chart is introduced and explained.

White space above and below figure sets it off.

Caption explains figure.

Heading is subordinate to title.

Procedure is explained in a numbered list. Writer uses parallel structure for list entries.

FIGURE 6.3 Example of a well-designed report.

In the résumé on page 466, Laura Amabisca uses white space to group her experience into different categories, such as education, work experience, and internship. This makes her résumé easy to evaluate in the sixty seconds or so that a prospective employer may first look at it.

You should also introduce any visuals within your text and position them so that they appear near—but never before—this text reference. Strive for a pleasing balance between visuals and other text elements; don't try to cram too many visuals onto one page.

2. Using type style and lists to make your text readable and to emphasize key elements

Typefaces are designs that have been established by printers for the letters in the alphabet, numbers, punctuation marks, and special characters. For most academic papers, choose a standard, easy-to-read typeface and a 10- or 12-point size. **Fonts** are all of the variations available in a certain typeface and size (for example, 12-point Times New Roman is available in **bold** and *italics*). Serif typefaces have tiny lines at the ends of letters such as n and y; sans serif typefaces do not have these lines. Standard serif typefaces such as the following have traditionally been used for basic printed text because they are easy to read:

Times New Roman	Courier
Bookman Old Style	Palatino

Sans serif typefaces such as the following are used for headings because they offer a pleasing contrast, or for electronic documents because they are more readable onscreen. (Norms may be changing. For example, Calibri, the default typeface in Microsoft Word 2007, is a sans serif typeface.)

Calibri
Arial
Verdana

Generally, if a document's main portion is in a sans serif typeface, headings should be in serif typeface, and vice versa.

Many typefaces available on your computer are known as *display fonts,* for example:

Curlz	Old English
Lucinda Sans	Monotype Corsiva

These should be used rarely, if ever, in academic papers, on the screen, or in presentations. They can be used effectively in other kinds of documents, however, such as brochures, fliers, and posters.

Elements of type allow you to organize content. You can emphasize a word or phrase in your text by selecting it and making it **bold,** *italicized,* or underlined. Numbered or bulleted lists help you

LEARNING in COLLEGE

Margins, Spacing, Type, and Page Numbers

Here are a few basic guidelines for formatting academic papers.

- **First page:** In a paper that is no longer than five pages, you can usually place a header with your name, your professor's name, your course and section number, and the date on the first page, preceding the text. (*See the final draft of Diane Chen's paper on p. 102.*) If your paper exceeds five pages, page one is usually a title page. (*For an example of a title page for a paper written in APA style, see the first page of Audrey Galeano's paper on p. 412.*)

- **Type:** Select a common typeface, or font, such as Calibri, Times New Roman, or Bookman, and choose a 12-point size.

- **Margins:** Use one-inch margins on all four sides of your text. Adequate margins make your paper easier to read and give your instructor room to write comments and suggestions.

- **Margin justification:** Line up, or justify, the lines of your document along the left margin but not along the right margin. Leaving a "ragged-right"—or uneven—right margin enables you to avoid odd spacing between words.

- **Spacing:** Always double-space your paper unless you are instructed to do otherwise, and indent the first line of each paragraph five spaces. Use the ruler at the top of your screen to set this indent automatically. (Many business documents are single spaced, with an extra line space between paragraphs, which are not indented.) Allow one space after periods, question marks, exclamation points, commas, semicolons, and colons. Add a space before and after an ellipsis mark. Do not allow extra space before or after dashes, hyphens, apostrophes within words, quotation marks, parentheses or brackets, or a mark that is immediately followed by another mark, such as a comma followed by a quotation mark. (*For more on these punctuation marks, see Part 10.*)

- **Page numbers:** Place page numbers in the upper or lower right-hand corner of the page. Some documentation styles require a header next to the page number—see Chapters 23–26 for the requirements of the style you are following.

cluster larger amounts of related information and make the material easier for readers to navigate and understand. You can use a numbered list to display steps in a sequence, present checklists, or suggest recommendations for action. Use parallel structure in your list (give entries the same grammatical form, as in the examples on page 110). Introduce your list with a complete sentence followed by a

109

colon, and put a period at the end of each entry only if the entries are complete sentences. (*For more on parallel structure, see Chapter 42, pp. 637–45.*)

Putting information in a box emphasizes it and also makes it easier for readers to find if they need to refer to it again. Most word-processing programs offer several ways to enclose text within a border or box.

3. Formatting related design elements consistently
In design, simplicity, contrast, and consistency matter. If you emphasize an item by putting it in italic or bold type or in color, or if you use a graphic element such as a box to set it off, consider repeating this effect for similar items to give your document a unified look. Even a simple horizontal line can be a purposeful element in a long document when used consistently to help organize information.

4. Using headings to organize long papers
In short papers, headings are usually not necessary. In longer papers, though, they can help you organize complex information. (*For headings in APA style, see Chapter 25, p. 411.*)

Effective headings are brief and descriptive. Make sure that your headings are consistent in grammatical structure as well as formatting:

Phrases beginning with –*ing* words
Handling Complaints
Fielding Inquiries

Nouns and noun phrases
Complaints
Customer Inquiries

Questions
How Do I Handle Complaints?
How Do I Field Inquiries?

Imperative sentences
Handle Complaints Calmly and Politely
Field Inquiries Efficiently

Headings at different levels can be in different forms. If you have not already done so, preparing a formal topic outline will help you decide what your main points and second-level points are and where headings should go. (*For help with topic outlines, see Chapter 3, pp. 47–51.*) You might center all first-level headings—which correspond to the main points in your outline—and put them in bold type. If you have second-level headings—your supporting points—you might align them at the left margin and underline them.

Standard Headings and Templates

Some types of papers, such as lab reports and case studies, have standard headings, such as Introduction, Abstract, and Methods and Materials (*see Chapter 8, pp. 148–54*). Word-processing programs allow you to create *templates,* or preformatted styles, that establish the structure and settings for the document and apply them automatically. If you frequently write papers that require formatting—lab reports, for example—consider creating a template.

First-Level Heading

Second-Level Heading
Third-Level Heading

If a heading falls at the very bottom of a page, move it to the top of the next page.

5. Using restraint

If you include too many graphics, headings, bullets, boxes, or other elements in a document, you risk making it "noisy." Certain typefaces and fonts have become standard because they are easy on the eye. Variations from these standard fonts are jarring. Bold or italic type, underlining, or any other graphic effect should not continue for more than one or two sentences at a time.

6. Meeting the needs of readers with disabilities

If your potential audience might include the vision- or hearing-impaired, follow these guidelines:

- **Use a large, easily readable font:** The font should be 14 point or larger. Use a sans serif font such as Arial, as readers with poor vision find these fonts easier to read. Make headings larger than the surrounding text (rather than relying on a change in font, bold, italics, or color to set them apart).

- **Use ample spacing between lines:** The American Council of the Blind recommends a line spacing of 1.5.

- **Use appropriate, high-contrast colors:** Black text on a white background is best. If you use color for text or visuals, put light material on a dark background and dark material on a light background. Use colors from different families

111

(such as yellow on purple). Also, avoid red and green because colorblind readers may have trouble distinguishing them.

■ **Include narrative descriptions of all visuals:** Describe each chart, map, photograph, or other visual. Indicate the key information and the point the visual makes, so that users of screen-reader software will be able to follow your meaning.

■ **If you include audio or video files in an electronic document, provide transcripts:** Also include narrative description of what is happening in the video.

For further information, consult the American Council of the Blind (http://acb.org/accessible-formats.html), Lighthouse International (http://www.lighthouse.org/print_leg.htm), and the American Printing House for the Blind (http://www.aph.org/edresearch/lpguide.htm).

👁 **6d** Compile a print or an electronic portfolio that presents your work to your advantage.

Students, job candidates, and professionals are often asked to collect their writing in a portfolio. Although most portfolios consist of a collection of papers in print form, many students create electronic writing portfolios incorporating a variety of media.

Portfolios, regardless of medium, share at least three common features:

■ They are a *collection* of work.

■ They offer a *selection*—or subset—of a larger body of work.

■ Once assembled, they are introduced, narrated, or commented on by a document that offers the writer's *reflection* on his or her work.

As with any type of writing, both print and electronic portfolios serve a purpose and address an audience. For example, you may be asked to prepare a "showcase" or "best-work" portfolio to demonstrate writing proficiency to a prospective employer. Or you might be asked to create a portfolio that documents how your writing has improved during a course, for a grade. You also might use a portfolio to assess your own work and set new writing goals.

1. Assembling a print portfolio

Course requirements vary, so always follow the guidelines your instructor provides. Nevertheless, when creating a print writing portfolio, you will usually need to engage in the five activities in the following Checklist box.

Assembling a Print Portfolio

☐ Gather all your written work.

☐ Make appropriate selections.

☐ Arrange the selections.

☐ Include a reflective essay or letter.

☐ Polish your portfolio.

Gathering your writing To organize your portfolio, create a list, or inventory, of the writing that you might include. For a writing course, you may need to provide your exploratory writing, notes, and comments from peer reviewers, as well as all your drafts for one or more of the papers you include. Make sure that all of your materials have your name on them and that your final draft is error free.

Reviewing your written work and making selections Keep the purpose of the portfolio in mind as well as the criteria that will be used to evaluate it. If you are assembling a presentation portfolio, select your best work. If you are demonstrating your improvement (a process portfolio), select papers that show your development and creativity, such as the exploratory writing, peer comments, and drafts for a particular paper.

If no criteria have been provided, consider the audience for the portfolio when deciding which selections will be most appropriate. Who will read it and what qualities will they be seeking?

Tips LEARNING in COLLEGE

Process Portfolios

If you include multiple drafts in your portfolio, you might use one or more of the following strategies to demonstrate improvement:

- Use a highlighter to note changes you made from one draft to the next.
- Annotate changes to explain why you made them.
- Choose two texts, completed at different times, to demonstrate how your writing has improved over the course of a term or year.

113

Arranging the selections deliberately If you have not been told how to organize your portfolio (for example, chronologically), you can think of it as if it were a single text and decide on an arrangement that will serve your purpose. Does it make sense to organize your work from weakest to strongest? From less important to more important? How will you determine importance?

Whatever arrangement you choose, explain your rationale for it to your audience. You can include this information in a letter to the reader, in a brief introduction, or via annotations in your table of contents.

Writing a reflective essay or letter The reflective statement may take the form of an essay or a letter, depending on your purpose and the assignment. Sometimes, the reflective essay will be the last item in a portfolio so that the reader can review all of the work first and then read the writer's interpretation. Or a reflective letter can open the portfolio. Either way, the reflective text lets you explain something about your writing or about yourself as a writer. Common topics in the reflective text include the following:

- How you developed various papers
- Which papers you believe are particularly strong and why
- What you learned as you worked on these assignments
- Who you are now as a writer

Follow the stages of the writing process in preparing your reflective essay or letter. Once you have completed it, you can assemble all of the components of your portfolio in a folder.

Polishing your portfolio In the process of writing the reflective letter or essay, you might discover a better way to arrange your work, or as you arrange your portfolio, you might want to review all your work again. Do not be surprised if you find yourself repeating some of these tasks. As with any writing, a portfolio will also improve if it is revised based on peer review.

Most students learn about themselves and their writing as they compile their portfolios and write reflections on their work. The process not only makes them better writers, it helps them learn how to demonstrate their strengths as well.

2. Preparing an electronic portfolio

For some courses or professional purposes, you will need to present your work in an electronic format. For example, an education student might be required to provide an electronic portfolio of lesson plans, class handouts, and other instructional materials. Electronic portfolios can be saved on CD or DVD, or published on the Web.

The process of creating an electronic portfolio differs somewhat from that of creating a print portfolio. Digital portfolios allow you to include different kinds of texts, such as audio files and video clips; they can be connected to other texts using hyperlinks; and their success depends on the use of visual elements. See the Checklist box below for the essential steps.

CHECKLIST

Creating an Electronic Portfolio

- ☐ Gather all your written work and audio, video, and visual texts.
- ☐ Make selections and consider connections.
- ☐ Decide on an arrangement, navigation, and presentation.
- ☐ Include a reflective essay or letter.
- ☐ Test your portfolio for usability.

Gathering your written work as well as your audio, video, and visual texts Depending on your assignment and purpose, you will need to make up to four inventories:

- ■ A verbal inventory, consisting of your written work (Be sure to scan in any handwritten work that is not provided as a digital text.)
- ■ An audio inventory (examples: speeches, music, podcasts)
- ■ A video inventory (examples: movie clips, videos you have created)
- ■ A visual inventory (examples: photographs, drawings)

The most important—and typical—components of an electronic portfolio tend to be the verbal and visual texts. Visuals can help you think about the images you will want to use to describe your work. One writer, for instance, might use images of everyday life in two countries to coordinate with texts in two languages in her portfolio.

Selecting appropriate texts and making connections among them Choose works from your inventory based on your portfolio's purpose and the criteria for evaluation. Consider relationships among your selections as well as external materials. These connections should reveal something about you and your writing. Ultimately, they will become the links that help the reader navigate your digital portfolio. Internal links connect one piece of your writing to another. For instance, you might link an earlier draft to a later one or link a PowerPoint presentation to a paper on the same topic. External links connect the reader to related files external to the portfolio but relevant to it. For instance, if you collaborated with a colleague or classmate on a project, you might link to that person's electronic portfolio.

Deciding on arrangement, navigation, and presentation As in a print portfolio, your work can be arranged in a variety of ways including in chronological order or order of importance. Once you have decided on a basic arrangement, help your reader navigate through the portfolio. As you plan, create a flowchart that shows each item in your portfolio and how it is linked to others. (*For sample Web site plans, see Chapter 14, p. 239.*) After you have planned your site's structure, add hyperlinks to your documents. Many word-processing programs have a Hyperlink function. Make the link text descriptive of the destination (a link reading "Résumé" should lead to your résumé).

One very simple, intuitive method for helping readers navigate the portfolio is a table of contents with links to the text for each item. You might then provide links from each final draft to exploratory writing, drafts in progress, and comments from peer reviewers. Alternatively, you might decide to make the table of contents part of an introductory page that also gives information about you and explains the course. You might open with a reflective letter embedded with links that take readers to your written work and other texts. The portfolio in Figure 6.4 on the facing page features a menu of links that appears on each page, as well as links in the reflective text.

Consider how the opening screen will establish your purpose and appeal to your audience, and what kind of guidance you will provide for the reader. Choose colors, images for the front page and successive pages, and typefaces that visually suggest who you are as a writer and establish a tone appropriate for your purpose. (For example, some typefaces and themes suggest a more serious tone, while others are more lighthearted.)

Writing a reflective text As in a print portfolio, the reflective text explains to readers what the writer wants them to know about the selections. A digital environment, however, offers you more possibilities for presenting this reflection. You can make it highly visual; for example, you might have it cascade across a series of screens. Another option would be to link to an audio or video file in which you talk directly to the reader.

FIGURE 6.4 **A reflective essay from a student's electronic portfolio.**

Testing your electronic portfolio before sharing it with the intended audience Make sure your portfolio works—both conceptually and structurally—before releasing it. You should navigate all the way though your portfolio yourself and ask a friend to do so from a different machine. Sometimes links fail to work, or files stored on one machine do not open on another, so this step is very important. In addition, another person may have comments or suggestions about the portfolio's structure or the content of your reflective text. Ultimately, this feedback will help you make the portfolio easy to use.

Auguste Rodin's sculpture The Thinker *evokes the psychological complexity of human thought and suggests the spirit of critical inquiry common to all disciplines across the curriculum.*

PART

2

Anybody who is involved in working across the disciplines is much more likely to have a lively mind and a lively life.
—MARY FIELD BELENKY

Common Assignments across the Curriculum

7 Reading, Thinking, Writing: The Critical Connection

The exchange of ideas in every discipline happens as scholars read and respond to one another's work. This chapter introduces you to the process of critical reading as a way of getting intellectually involved with your studies. In this context, the word *critical* means thoughtful. When you read critically, you recognize the literal meaning of the text, make inferences about implicit or unstated meanings, and then make your own judgments in response.

It is now easier than ever to obtain information in a variety of ways, so you need to be able to "read" critically not just written texts, but visuals, sounds, video, and spoken texts as well.

WRITING OUTCOMES

Part 2: Common Assignments

This section will help you answer questions such as:

Rhetorical Knowledge

- How can I argue persuasively? **(10c)**
- How can I keep my audience interested in my oral presentation? **(13b)**
- What should I *not* put on my blog or social networking page? **(14f)**

Critical Thinking, Reading, and Writing

- How do I analyze printed text and images? **(7b–d)**
- How can annotation and summary help me with reading assignments? **(7d)**
- How can I defend my paper against counterarguments? **(10c)**

Processes

- What is the best way to prepare for essay exams? **(12a)**
- How can I use presentation software (such as PowerPoint) effectively? **(13b, 14d)**
- What steps should I take in planning my Web site? **(14e)**

Knowledge of Conventions

- What is a review of the literature, and where do such reviews appear? **(8d)**
- What special design principles apply to Web sites? **(14e)**

CHECKLIST

Reading Critically

- ☐ **Preview** the piece before you read it.

- ☐ **Read** the selection for its topic and point.

- ☐ **Analyze** the who, what, and why of the piece by **annotating** it as you reread it and **summarizing** what you have read.

- ☐ **Synthesize** through making connections.

- ☐ **Evaluate** what you have read.

7a Recognize that critical reading is a process.

Critical reading is a process. As with writing, you will find yourself moving back and forth among the steps in this process.

Critical readers don't just read; they reread. The writer Ray Bradbury claims that he read Herman Melville's *Moby Dick* eighty to ninety times before he understood it well enough to write the screenplay for John Huston's movie adaptation. Your goals for reading (from simply checking a fact to undertaking a full-scale evaluation of a text) will determine how much time you need to spend.

Writing at every stage of the critical reading process also helps to deepen your involvement with the text. If you are reading a book that you own, write in it as you read, highlighting key ideas and terms and noting your questions or objections. If you are reading a library book, a Web page, or a nonprint text, keep notes in a journal—paper or electronic—to help you remember what you have read and reflect on its significance. Some writers use a double-column notebook, with one column for notes about the text and the other column for their own reactions and ideas. (*See the TextConnex box on p. 130 for other tips on annotating electronic texts.*)

7b Preview the text or visual.

Critical reading begins with **previewing:** looking over the text's author and publication information and quickly scanning its contents to gain a context for understanding and evaluating it.

If the text is a possible source for a paper, you will also need to determine whether it is a **primary source** or a **secondary source**—that is, whether it is a firsthand (primary) account of an event or research or someone else's (secondary) interpretation of that firsthand account. Research reports in the sciences are primary sources; textbooks and encyclopedia articles are secondary sources. Original works of art, literature, theater, film, and music are also primary sources; critical analyses and reviews are secondary sources.

1. Asking questions as you preview a written text
As you preview a text, ask questions to get a sense of the topics and to help you judge the credibility of the evidence and arguments the piece presents.

CHECKLIST

www.mhhe.com/
mhhb2
For more on
evaluating sources,
go to
Research > CARS
Source Evaluation
Tutor

Previewing a Written Text

Author

☐ Who wrote this piece?

☐ What are the author's credentials and occupation?

☐ Who is the author's employer?

☐ What are the author's interests and values?

Purpose

☐ What do the title and first and last paragraphs tell you about the purpose of this piece?

☐ Do the headings and visuals provide clues to the purpose of the piece?

☐ What might have motivated the author to write the piece?

☐ Will the main purpose be to inform, to interpret, to argue, or something else (to entertain or to reflect, for instance)?

Audience

☐ Whom is the author trying to inform or persuade?

☐ Does the vocabulary give you a sense of the kind of knowledge the author expects his or her audience to have?

Content

- [ ] What do the title and headings tell you about the piece?

- [ ] Does the first paragraph include the main point?

- [ ] Do the headings give you the gist of the piece?

- [ ] Does the conclusion tell you what the author is trying to inform you about, interpret for you, or argue?

- [ ] What do you already know and think about the topic?

Context

- [ ] Is the publication date (or most recent update for a Web site) current? Does the date matter?

- [ ] What kind of publication is it? Is it a book, an article in a periodical or library database, a Web site, or something else?

- [ ] Where and by whom was the piece published? If it was published electronically, was it posted by the author or by an organization with a special interest?

2. Asking questions as you preview a visual

You can use most of the previewing questions for written texts to preview visuals. Here are some additional questions you should ask:

- In what context does the visual appear? Was it intended to be viewed on its own or as part of a larger work? Is it part of a series of images (for example, a graphic novel, a music video, or a film)?

- What does the visual depict? What is the first thing you notice in the visual? Is its literal meaning immediately clear, or do you need to spend time looking at it to figure it out?

- Does the visual represent a real event, person, or thing (a news photo, a portrait), or is it fictional (an illustration in a story)?

- Is the visual accompanied by audio or printed text?

A preview of Figure 7.1 (on the next page) might produce these answers:

- **In what context does the visual appear?** This public service advertisement appeared in several publications targeted to college students. As the Peace Corps logo in the lower right-hand corner indicates, the ad was produced by the Peace Corps to recruit volunteers.

www.mhhe.com/
mhhb2

For an interactive tutorial on analyzing visuals, go to
Writing > Visual Rhetoric Tutorial > Understanding Images

FIGURE 7.1 Peace Corps advertisement. The text superimposed on this photograph reads: **What happens in Botswana doesn't stay in Botswana.** When you help make a better life for others abroad, you also develop skills and experience that will serve your community back home. Life is calling. How far will you go?

■ **What does the visual depict? What is the first thing you notice in the visual?**

The scene is a bare school room in Botswana. (*Look at the foldout Resources for Writers: World Map in* Part 13: Further Resources, *to find Botswana in Africa.*) As sun streams from a window, one young man in the foreground looks on as a younger boy erases a blackboard. On the blackboard, a handwritten poster appears with points of advice, for example, "Accept responsibility for your decision."

■ **Is it a representation of a real event, person, or thing, or is it fictional?** The scene represents the reality of African children in need of the Peace Corps' help.

■ **Is the visual accompanied by audio or printed text?**

Bold text appears in the center of the image, followed by smaller print directly addressed to the viewer. The phone number and Web address for the Peace Corps are printed in the lower left, and another appeal to the viewer, followed by the Peace Corps logo, is printed in the lower right.

LEARNING in COLLEGE

Evaluating Context in Different Kinds of Publications

- **For a book:** What is the publisher's reputation? University presses, for example, are very selective and usually publish scholarly works. Vanity presses—which require authors to pay to publish their work—are not selective at all.
- **For an article in a periodical:** Look at the list of editors and their affiliations. What do you know about the journal, magazine, or newspaper in which this writing appears? Are the articles that appear in it reviewed by experts in a particular field before they are published?
- **For a Web site:** Who created the site? A Web site named for a political candidate, for example, may actually have been put on the Web by his or her opponents. (*See the Checklist box, Using the CARS Checklist to Evaluate Web Sites, in Chapter 18: p. 297.*)

The meaning of this image is not immediately clear from a preview. We will need to read it more closely to grasp its message fully.

7c Read and record your initial impressions.

A first reading is similar to a first draft—your primary purpose is to get a sense of the whole. Identify what the text is about and the main point the writer makes about the topic. Note difficult passages to come back to, as well as interesting ideas. Look up any unfamilar terms. Record your initial impressions:

- If the written text or image is an argument, what opinion does it express? Were you persuaded by it?
- Did you have an emotional response to the text or image? Were you surprised, amused, or angered by anything in it?
- What was your initial sense of the writer or speaker?
- What key ideas did you take away from the work?

Exercise 7.1   Preview and first reading of an essay

On the following pages is an essay that appeared in the *Village Voice,* a weekly journal of opinion and commentary published in New York City.

1. Preview the essay, using the questions in the Checklist on pages 122–23.
2. Read through the essay in one sitting, then record your initial impressions, using the questions in 7c (*above*).

Misguided Multiculturalism

NAT HENTOFF

An American-history requirement hallows ethnocentrism just as everyone else is embracing internationalism and preparing students to become citizens of the world.

—Joanne Reitano,
history professor and
chair of the Community
College Caucus, *New
York Post*, May 28 [2000]

Both my parents were immigrants from Russia. In my neighborhood, Yiddish was a first and second language. I grew up in the depths of the Great Depression. There were weeks when my father came home with $5 or less. My mother walked blocks to save a few cents on food.

I went to public school. Some of my friends were sent to the yeshiva—an Orthodox Jewish religious school—but my parents, having experienced the vicious, pervasive anti-Semitism in the Old Country, wanted me to learn what America was all about.

At Boston Latin School and Northeastern University—a working-class college—I took classes that taught a great deal about the fundamental rights and liberties that had to be fought for during this still "unfinished American revolution," as Thurgood Marshall called it. These were required courses, and inspired my lifelong involvement in civil rights and civil liberties.

This is a personal prelude to an intense controversy over a

proposed four-year master plan for the City University of New York by CUNY's Board of Trustees, which will be voted on by the New York State Board of Regents in September. The leading, and impassioned, advocate of the part of the plan that I'm focusing on here is Herman Badillo, chairman of CUNY's Board of Trustees.

A key element in the plan is its call for a core curriculum, including a required course in American history—which is already in place in the state university system. A number—not all—of the faculty members on the various campuses vigorously object. Some say trustees have no business meddling in what should be the prerogative of the faculty. Others call the very idea of a required course in American history absurd. "The assumption," says professor Joanne Reitano, "is that our immigrant students need to be taught what it means to be an American."

Over the years, I have given classes in this city's public schools, from elementary grades through high school. And as a reporter, I have spent considerable time in other classrooms. As is the case throughout the country—from failing schools to the prestigious high schools—the teaching of American history, with few exceptions, is cursory, scattered, and superficial.

It's just as bad in most colleges. A recent survey by the American Council of Trustees and Alumni (David Broder's column, *The*

5

Washington Post, July 2) reveals "historical illiteracy" about this country across the board—even among students at Amherst, Williams, Harvard, Duke, and the University of Michigan. Moreover, "none of the 55 elite colleges and universities (as rated by *U.S. News & World Report*) requires a course in American history before graduation." As for high schools, Broder notes, a report by the National Assessment of Educational Progress disclosed that "fully 57 percent of the high school seniors failed to demonstrate a basic level of understanding of American history and institutions—the lowest category in the test."

The foremothers of women's liberation, Susan B. Anthony and Elizabeth Cady Stanton, as well as civil rights leaders like Frederick Douglass and Malcolm X, used the First Amendment as an essential weapon; but how many Americans, including students, know the embattled history of free speech in this nation?

Also neglected in the vast majority of secondary schools and colleges is the history of the American labor movement—its fight against repression in the 19th century and well into this century.

10 When teaching, I have found interest among a wide array of students in the story of why we have a Fourth Amendment— British officials' random, often savage searches of the colonists' homes and businesses to look for contraband. As Supreme Court Justice William Brennan told me, the resultant fury of those initial Americans was a precipitating cause of the American Revolution.

I told that story and others about resistance to discrimination, and worse, throughout American postrevolutionary history to a large group of predominantly black and Hispanic high school students in Miami a couple of years ago.

Before I started, one of their teachers told me, "Don't be upset if they don't pay attention. What they're mostly interested in is clothes and music."

After more than an hour, there was a standing ovation. Not for me, but because they had discovered America—its triumphs and failures. Talking to some of them later, I was told they'd heard none of those stories in school.

Multiculturalism is a welcome development in American education so long as some of its college courses do not exalt one particular culture and history over others. Then, it is indeed ethnocentric. But to understand where you came from, you also have to understand where you are now. You have to know how the society you live in works, and that requires a full-scale knowledge of its history— from its guiding principles to what still has to be done to make them real. For everybody.

Justice William Brennan said: 15 "We do not yet have justice, equal and practical, for the members of minority groups, for the criminally accused, for the displaced persons of the technological revolution, for alienated youth, for the urban masses, for the unrepresented consumer—for all, in short, who do not take part of the abundance of American life. . . . Ugly inequities continue to mar the face of our nation. We are surely nearer the beginning than the end of the struggle."

To do something about that, CUNY students should know the strategies, successes, and failures of widely diverse Americans who have been part of that struggle. For insisting on core American history courses, Herman Badillo should be cheered, not scorned.

From the *Village Voice*,
July 19–25, 2000

Exercise 7.2   Preview and first reading of an essay

Find an article that interests you in a newspaper or magazine, preview it using the Checklist's questions in 7b, then read through it in one sitting and record your initial impressions using the questions in 7c.

Exercise 7.3   First reading of a visual

Spend some time looking at the image and text for the Peace Corps ad on page 124. Record your responses to the following questions:

1. Did you have an emotional response to the ad?
2. What opinion, if any, did you have of the Peace Corps before you read the ad? Has your opinion changed in any way as a result of the ad?
3. What key ideas does the ad attempt to present?
4. If you recognize the slogan the ad references, what do you think is the impact of its use here? Is it effective? Why or why not?

👁 **7d**   Reread using annotation and summary to analyze and interpret.

Once you understand the literal, or surface, meaning of a text, dig deeper by analyzing and interpreting it. To **analyze** a text is to break it down into significant parts and examine how those parts relate to each other. We analyze a text to **interpret** it and come to a fuller understanding of its meanings.

1. Using annotation and summary

Annotation and **summary** can help with analysis and interpretation.

Annotation   To annotate a text, read through it slowly and carefully while asking yourself the *who, what, how,* and *why* questions. As you read, underline or make separate notes about words, phrases, and sentences that strike you as significant or puzzling, and write down your questions and observations.

EXAMPLE OF AN ANNOTATED PASSAGE

Introductory paragraphs from "Misguided Multiculturalism" by Nat Hentoff

Both my parents were immigrants from Russia. In my neighborhood, Yiddish was a first and second language. I grew up in the depths of the Great Depression. There were weeks when my father came home with $5 or less. My mother walked blocks to save a few cents on food.

I went to public school. Some of my friends were sent to the yeshiva—an Orthodox Jewish religious school—but my parents, having experienced the vicious, pervasive anti-Semitism in the Old Country, wanted me to learn what America was all about.

At Boston Latin School and Northeastern University—a working-class college—I took classes that taught a great deal about the (fundamental) rights and liberties that had to be fought for during this still "unfinished American revolution," as (Thurgood Marshall) called it. These were required courses, and inspired my lifelong involvement in civil rights and civil liberties.

This is a personal (prelude) to an intense controversy over a proposed four-year master plan for the City University of New York by CUNY's Board of Trustees, which will be voted on by the New York State Board of Regents in September. The leading, and impassioned, advocate of the part of the plan that I'm focusing on here is Herman Badillo, chairman of CUNY's Board of Trustees.

Childhood story— establishes his personal experience of multicultural issues.

Essential? Supreme Court. Would they inspire everyone?

=introduction Smooth transition to the real argument.

EXAMPLE OF A NOTEBOOK ENTRY

"Misguided Multiculturalism," by Nat Hentoff: Intro paragraphs

Starts by discussing his own background, telling us about his childhood and his education:
—Son of Russian immigrants, grew up poor
—Spoke Yiddish (bilingual upbringing)
—Parents wanted him to "learn what America was all about"
—Took mandatory courses about U.S. rights and liberties in school

Long build-up before he gets to the real subject of his article: a proposal to make American history course mandatory at a university in New York. Is his story really relevant?

2. Questioning the text
Analysis and interpretation require a thorough understanding of the who, what, how, and why of a text:

- **What is the writer's *stance*, or attitude toward the subject?** Does the writer appear to be objective, or does the writer seem to have personal feelings about the subject?

- **What is the writer's *voice*?** Is it that of a reasonable judge, an enthusiastic preacher, or a reassuring friend? Does the writer seem to be speaking *at, to,* or *with* the audience?

- **What assumptions does the writer seem to be making about the audience?** Does the writer assume a readership of specialists or a general audience? Does the writer assume that the reader agrees with him or her, or does the writer try to build agreement? Does the writer seem to have chosen examples and evidence with a certain audience in mind?

- **What is the author's primary purpose?** Is the purpose to present findings, offer an objective analysis, or argue for a particular action or opinion?

- **How does the author develop ideas?** What kind of support does the author rely on? Does the writer define key terms? Include supporting facts? Provide logical reasons?

- **Does the text appeal to emotions?** Does the writer use words, phrases, clichés, images, or examples that are emotionally charged?

- **Is the text fair?** Does the author consider opposing ideas, arguments, or evidence and do so fairly?

- **Is the evidence strong?** Does the author provide sufficient evidence? What are his or her assumptions? Where is the argument strongest and weakest?

- **Is the text effective?** How do your assumptions and views affect your reading? Has the text challenged or changed your beliefs on this subject?

- **How do the ideas in this text relate to those in other texts?**

Visuals too can be subjected to critical analysis, as the annotations a reader made on the Peace Corps ad indicate (*Figure 7.2 on p. 131.*)

TEXTCONNEX

Annotating Electronic Text

Unless a copyright notice prohibits it, you can download an electronic file for your own use in order to annotate it. Write on a printout of the file, or insert your comments directly in the file using a contrasting typeface or color or the Comments feature of your word-processing program. Record full source information in case you need to find or cite the original. (*See Chapter 21, p. 321.*)

Composition of the photograph like Vermeer's paintings of sunlight illuminating an indoor scene. Subtle appeal to students of art history?

Reference to Las Vegas slogan, "What happens here stays here." Secrets of Las Vegas (superficial fun) stay there because of shame. Working with the Peace Corps in Botswana illuminates your life—and the world (another reference to the sunlight?)

The boy is reaching up to erase or wash something from the blackboard. An older boy watches— also "reaching"? A poster covering part of the board lists principles valuable in Botswana and in the United States.

Smaller print emphasizes the What Happens message above. Elaborates on win/win opportunity of the Peace Corps vs. likelihood of losing games in Las Vegas.

The Peace Corps logo combines the globe with the American flag—a global view of patriotism. How far will you go geographically and personally?

FIGURE 7.2 An annotated image.

Exercise 7.4 Analyzing an essay

Reread "Misguided Multiculturalism" on pages 126–28. Annotate it or take separate notes as you read, and analyze it to determine how its parts work together. Add your own interpretations of Hentoff's statements.

Exercise 7.5 Analyzing an article

Reread the article you selected for Exercise 7.2, analyzing it with annotations or in separate notes.

Exercise 7.6 Analyzing a visual

1. Add to the annotated analysis of the Peace Corps ad in Figure 7.2 on page 131, focusing on the text as well as the photograph.
2. The photograph shown in Figure 7.3 below was taken during the January 30, 2005 elections in Iraq. It shows Kurdish women waiting to vote in the city of Kirkuk. First, preview and record your initial impressions of this photograph using the questions in 7b and 7c. Then analyze and annotate it, either directly on the page or on a separate sheet of paper.

FIGURE 7.3 **Women voting in Kirkuk, Iraq, January 30, 2005.**

Summary A **summary** conveys the basic content of a text. When you summarize, your goal is to communicate the text's main points in your own words, without saying what you think of it. A summary of an essay or article typically runs about one paragraph in length. Even when you are writing a fuller summary of a longer work, you should always use the fewest words possible. Clarity and brevity are important. A summary should never be longer than the original work.

A summary requires simplification, but avoid misrepresenting a writer's points by *oversimplifying* them. Consider this summary of the main point of the Hentoff essay (*from pp. 126–28*).

OVERSIMPLIFIED SUMMARY

A U.S. history course should be required because college students are ignorant.

Although Hentoff does point to a general lack of knowledge about U.S. history among college students, a more accurate summary would indicate *why* Hentoff feels an understanding of U.S. history is important.

Here is a summary of Hentoff's essay that Ignacio Sanderson wrote as he was working on the paper that appears at the end of this chapter:

THOUGHTFUL SUMMARY

In his essay "Misguided Multiculturalism," Nat Hentoff defends a proposal to require all students of the City University of New York to take an American history course. Hentoff begins by noting that he is the son of immigrants from Russia. He goes on to discuss his upbringing and education and how the courses he took in American civics inspired his "lifelong involvement in civil rights and civil liberties" (29). In addition to pointing out how valuable the study of American history was to his own career, Hentoff notes that most college students, even at schools like Duke and Harvard, do not know much about U.S. history. Hentoff acknowledges that multiculturalism is a worthwhile value, but stipulates, "You have to know how the society you live in works, and that requires a full-scale knowledge of its history" (30). While multiculturalism is important, a basic knowledge of U.S. history is essential.

Note: Summaries are especially useful in research as a tool for recording various sources' points of view. A good summary can help you avoid plagiarism as well, because a central characteristic of a summary is that it is expressed in your own words. *(For more on summary, as well as paraphrase and quotation— two other methods of incorporating ideas—see Chapter 21: Working with Sources and Avoiding Plagiarism, pp. 322–28.)*

Exercise 7.7   Summarizing

Evaluate these summaries of passages from the Peace Corps ad (*p. 124*) and "Misguided Multiculturalism" (*pp. 126–28*). Indicate the problem with each faulty summary, and suggest how it should be revised.

1. The Peace Corps ad describes Botswana.

2. In "Misguided Multiculturalism," Nat Hentoff argues that everyone should have an education like his.

3. In paragraph 7 of "Misguided Multiculturalism," Hentoff argues that U.S. college and high school students have little knowledge about U.S. history.

Exercise 7.8   Summarizing

If your word-processing program has a feature like "AutoSummarize," use it to generate a summary of one of your own academic papers. Then identify and describe any problems with the computer-generated summary.

Exercise 7.9   Summarizing

1. Summarize the content and message of the Peace Corps ad (*p. 124*).
2. Summarize the article you selected for Exercise 7.2.
3. Summarize the photograph of Iraqi Kurdish women voting in Figure 7.3 (*p. 132*).

Tips   LEARNING in COLLEGE

Writing a Critical Response Paper

- Summarize the main idea of the text fairly and accurately recognizing its strengths as well as its weaknesses.
- Use your course readings to help formulate an approach to your analysis.
- Narrow your focus to one or two key points rather than responding to every point in the text.
- Use facts as well as personal experience to support your points. Avoid phrases such as "I feel" or "In my opinion."
- Avoid derogatory comments and labels such as "stupid."
- Document the text and any additional sources, using the documentation style required by your instructor. (*See Part 4: Documenting across the Curriculum for guidelines.*)

7e Synthesize your observations in a critical response paper.

To **synthesize** means to bring together, to make something out of different parts. In the last stage of critical reading, you pull your analysis, interpretation, and summary together into a coherent whole. Often this synthesis takes the form of a critical response paper.

A **critical response paper** typically begins with a summary of the text, followed by a thesis. The thesis should encapsulate your response to the text. Here are some possible thesis statements in response to Hentoff's "Misguided Multiculturalism":

POSSIBLE THESIS

Hentoff effectively argues that people need a knowledge of U.S. history to live in the United States and that a required U.S. history course is necessary to give people this knowledge.

POSSIBLE THESIS

Hentoff makes valid points about the necessity and importance of learning about U.S. history, but he underestimates the negative impact a required course would have on immigrants and first- and second-generation Americans.

The rest of the response paper should elaborate on your thesis, supporting it with evidence from the text, your other reading, any related research, and your relevant personal experience.

In the following critical response paper, Ignacio Sanderson synthesizes his reading of Nat Hentoff's "Misguided Multiculturalism" with his own experience.

Ignacio Sanderson

Professor Blackwell

English 99-B

15 March 2009

Critical Response to "Misguided Multiculturalism"

by Nat Hentoff

Multiculturalism is one of the most hotly debated topics in higher education today. As the son of an immigrant to the United States, I take this debate personally. The question of what makes an "American education" strikes a chord in me.

The same is true for Nat Hentoff, as he explains in his article "Misguided Multiculturalism." Hentoff first notes that he is the son of immigrants from Russia. He goes on to discuss his upbringing and education and how the courses he took in American civics inspired his "lifelong involvement in civil rights and civil liberties" (29).

Hentoff then defends a proposal by the City University of New York's Board of Trustees to introduce a mandatory American history course for all the university's students. In addition to pointing out how valuable the study of American history was to

135

Hentoff's
argument
summarized.

his own career, Hentoff notes that most college students, even
at schools like Duke and Harvard, do not know much about U.S.
history. He complains that students are ignorant about the history
of the Bill of Rights and the American labor movement. Hentoff
acknowledges that multiculturalism is a worthwhile value but
stipulates, "You have to know how the society you live in works,
and that requires a full-scale knowledge of its history" (30). While
multiculturalism is important, a basic knowledge of U.S. history
is essential.

Thesis
statement

I have experienced the transition from one culture to another
firsthand. Although I agree with Hentoff that it is crucial to learn about
American history if you want to be an American, requiring an American
history course of everyone sends the wrong message to immigrants
and first- and second-generation Americans. It tells such people that
there is only one important history university students should know:
American history.

Objection
to Hentoff's
argument.

Hentoff is clearly sensitive to the charge of "ethnocentrism,"or
the placing of one culture or ethnicity above all others. In the article,
however, he seems to want to have it both ways: he supports a
multicultural, non-ethnocentric curriculum, but also a required
American history course. These goals are incompatible, however.
Making all students take a course in the history of one society to the
exclusion of those of other societies is inevitably ethnocentric.

Consideration
of Hentoff's
response to
the objection.

Hentoff tries to answer this objection by pointing out that
an American history course might reveal to students the history
of discrimination—and the fight against it—in this country.
He implies that, even if requiring the course is ethnocentric,
the content of the course would not have to be ethnocentric
propaganda. That may be true, but Hentoff does not know what
the course will cover. He discusses the history he would like
students to learn, but offers no evidence that faculty members
will teach it. Unless there is a set syllabus for the course, however,
there is no guarantee that students will be exposed to a balanced
account of U.S. history.

Nat Hentoff's heart is in the right place. It is important for all
Americans to know how the United States became the country it is
today. This knowledge would be better gained by people acting individually, though, rather than within the context of mandated classes.
Students should have the right to manage for themselves the complex
task of becoming American.

Conclusion
reinforces
Sanderson's
point.

--------------------------------[new page]--------------------------------------

Work Cited

Hentoff, Nat. "Misguided Multiculturalism." *Village Voice* 19 July
2000: 29–30. Print.

Works-Cited
list follows
MLA style
and begins
on a new
page.

Exercise 7.10   Writing a critical response to an article

Using the analysis that you prepared in Exercise 7.5 and the summary that you wrote in Exercise 7.9.2, write a critical response to the
article you selected for Exercise 7.2.

Exercise 7.11   Writing a critical response to a visual

1. Using the analysis that you prepared in Exercise 7.6 and the
   summary you wrote in Exercise 7.9.1, write a critical response
   to the Peace Corps ad (*p. 124*).

2. Using the analysis that you prepared in Exercise 7.6.2 and the
   summary you wrote in Exercise 7.9.3, describe your personal
   reaction to the photograph of Iraqi women voting in Figure 7.3
   (*p. 132*).

8 Informative Reports

Imagine what the world would be like without records of what others have learned.
Fortunately, we have many sources of information to draw on, including informative
reports.

8a Understand the assignment.

An **informative report** passes on what someone has learned about a topic or issue; it teaches. An informative report gives you a chance to do the following:

- Learn more about an issue that interests you.
- Make sense of what you have read, heard, and seen.
- Teach others in a clear and unbiased way what you have learned.

(For examples of the types of informative reports assigned in college, see pp. 141 and 150.)

CHARTING the TERRITORY

Informative Reports

Informative reports are commonly written by members of the humanities, social sciences, and natural sciences disciplines, as these examples indicate.

- In a published article, an anthropologist surveys and summarizes information from archeological, historical, and ethnographic sources relating to warfare among the indigenous peoples of the American Southwest.
- For an encyclopedia of British women writers, a professor of literature briefly recounts the life and works of Eliza Fenwick, a recently rediscovered eighteenth-century author.
- In an academic journal for research biologists, two biochemists summarize the findings of more than two hundred recently published articles on defense mechanisms in plants.

www.mhhe.com/
mhhb2
For an interactive
tutorial on writing
informative reports,
go to
Writing >
Writing Tutors >
Informative Reports

8b Approach writing an informative report as a process.

1. Selecting a topic that interests you

The major challenge of writing informative reports is engaging the reader's interest. Selecting a topic that interests you makes it more likely that your report will interest your readers.

Connect what you are learning in one course with a topic you are studying in another course or with your personal experience. For example, one student, John Terrell, majored in political science and aspired to a career in international relations. For his topic, he decided to investigate how one Muslim organization was pursuing human rights for women. (*Terrell's paper begins on p. 141.*)

2. Considering what your readers know about the topic

Assume that your readers have some familiarity with the topic area but that most of them do not have clear, specific knowledge of your particular topic. In his paper on Sisters in Islam, Terrell assumes that his readers probably have seen images of Afghan women in burqas.

3. Developing an objective stance

When writers have an **objective stance,** they do not take sides. They present ideas and facts fairly and emphasize the topic, not the writer. (By contrast, when writers are **subjective,** they let readers know their views.) A commitment to objectivity gives an informative report its authority.

4. Composing a thesis that summarizes your knowledge of the topic

www.mhhe.com/
mhhb2
For more help with developing a thesis, go to
Writing >
Paragraph/Essay Development >
Thesis/Central Idea

An informative thesis typically states an accepted generalization or reports the results of the writer's study. Before you decide on a thesis, review the information you have collected. Compose a thesis statement that summarizes the goal of your paper and forecasts its content. (*For more on thesis statements, see Chapter 3: Planning and Shaping the Whole Essay, pp. 42–46.*)

In his paper about Sisters in Islam (SIS), Terrell develops a general thesis that he supports in the body of his paper with information about how the group does its work:

> Based in Malaysia, SIS has developed three key ways to promote women's rights within the context of the Muslim religion and its holy book, the Qur'an.

Notice how the phrase "three key ways" forecasts the body of Terrell's report. We expect to learn something about each of the three key ways, and the report is structured to give us that information, subtopic by subtopic.

5. Providing context in your introduction

Informative reports usually begin with a relatively simple introduction to the topic and a straightforward statement of the thesis. Provide some relevant context or background, but get to your specific topic as quickly as possible and keep it in the foreground. (*For more on introductions, see Chapter 4: Drafting Paragraphs and Visuals, pp. 72–74.*)

6. Organizing your paper for clarity by classifying and dividing information

Develop ideas in an organized way, by classifying and dividing information into categories, subtopics, or the stages of a process. (*For more on developing your ideas, see Chapter 4: Drafting Paragraphs and Visuals, pp. 61–72.*)

www.mhhe.com/
mhhb2

For more on
using patterns of
development,
go to

Writing >
Paragraph
Patterns

7. Illustrating key ideas with examples

Use specific examples to help readers understand your most important ideas. In his paper on Sisters in Islam, Terrell provides many specific examples, including pertinent quotations from the Qur'an, a discussion of the attempt to establish the Domestic Violence Act, and descriptions of SIS educational programs. Examples make his report interesting as well as educational. (*For more on using examples, see Chapter 4: Drafting Paragraphs and Visuals, p. 62.*)

8. Defining specialized terms and spelling out unfamiliar abbreviations

Explain specialized terms with a synonym or a brief definition. For example, Terrell provides a synonym and a brief description of the term *sharia* in the third paragraph of his informative report on Sisters in Islam. (*For more on definition, see Chapter 4: Drafting Paragraphs and Visuals, p. 66.*) Unfamiliar abbreviations like SIS (Sisters in Islam) and NGO (non-governmental organization) are spelled out the first time they are used, with the abbreviation in parentheses.

www.mhhe.com/
mhhb2

For more information
on conclusions, go to

Writing >
Paragraph/Essay
Development >
Conclusions

9. Concluding by answering "so what?"

Conclude with an image that suggests the information's value or sums it all up. Remind readers of your topic and thesis, and then answer the "So what?" question.

At the end of his report on Sisters in Islam, Terrell answers the "So what?" question by contrasting press stereotypes of the status of women in Islam with the more complex and encouraging view his paper presents.

> But their efforts show that the situation of women in Islamic countries is actually much more complex and encouraging than many recent newspaper images and stories have led us to believe.

(*Also see information on conclusions in Chapter 4: Drafting Paragraphs and Visuals, pp. 74–75.*)

LEARNING in COLLEGE

Informative Reports in the Social Sciences

Informative reports in the social sciences examine a wide range of behavioral and social phenomena, such as consumer spending, courtship rituals, political campaign tactics, and job stress.

Some Types of Informative Reports in the Social Sciences

- *Research reports* describe the process and results of research conducted by the author(s).

- *Reviews of the literature* synthesize the published work on a particular topic (*see 8d*).

Documentation Styles

- APA (*see Chapter 24*) and Chicago (*see Chapter 25*)

8c Write informative reports on social science research.

In the informative report that follows, John Terrell reports what he has learned about a Muslim non-governmental organization dedicated to promoting women's rights. Notice how Terrell provides a context for his topic, cites various sources (using the APA documentation style), divides the information into subtopics, and illustrates his ideas with examples, all hallmarks of a clear, carefully developed paper. The annotations in the margin of this paper point out specific aspects of the informative report. (*For details on the proper formatting of a paper in APA style, see Chapter 24 and the sample paper that begins on p. 412.*)

www.mhhe.com/
mhhb2

For another sample of
informative writing,
go to

Writing >
Writing Samples >
Informative Paper

Sample student informative report

Sisters Redefining the Divine

John Terrell

Political Science 252 Contemporary Issues: Human Rights

Professor Paul

December 20, 2008

------------------------------[new page]-------------------------------

Following APA style, Terrell includes a separate title page. He does not include an abstract, however, because his instructor did not require one for this assignment.

Sisters Redefining the Divine

Topic
introduced.

The rights of women in Islamist and majority-Muslim nations have recently become an issue of concern and contention. Images of women in burqas, along with news stories describing forced marriages, public executions by flogging, and virtual house arrest for women without chaperones have led many Americans to assume that Muslim women have no rights and no way to change that situation. But that is not the whole picture. In many parts of the Islamic world, non-governmental organizations (NGOs) are working hard to make sure that women and their interests have a political voice. Sisters in Islam (SIS) is just such an organization. Based in Malaysia, SIS has developed three key ways to promote women's rights within the context of the Muslim religion and its holy book, the Qur'an.

First use of
unfamiliar
abbreviation
spelled out.

Thesis stated.

First way—
introduces
subtopic.

One way that SIS works to promote women's rights is to show how those rights are rooted in the origins of Islam and the Qur'an. Members note that women fought side by side with the prophet Muhammad in the early struggle to establish Islam's rule and point out that allowing some degree of choice in marriage, permitting divorce, and granting inheritance rights for women were revolutionary concepts when Muslims first introduced them to the world 1,400 years ago (Othman, 1997). Furthermore, they argue that the Qur'an mandates "the principles of equality, justice and freedom" and does not specifically prohibit women from assuming leadership roles or contributing to public service. But they also recognize that the revolutionary possibilities of Islam were curtailed when a small group of men claimed "exclusive control over the interpretation of the Qur'an" (Sisters in Islam, 2007).

Source infor-
mation sum-
marized.

Voices of
Muslim
women are
important to
this topic so
are quoted
directly.

Source
named in sig-
nal phrase.

According to Coleman (2006), the Qur'an contains almost 80 sections on legal issues, but neither it nor the secondary texts and oral traditions of Islam contain instruction on everyday matters. To make matters even more complex, the Qur'an includes many seemingly contradictory passages. Its statements on polygamy are a prime example. One verse in the text says, "Marry those women who are lawful for you, up to two, three, or four, but only if you can treat them equally" (Qur'an 4:3), while a later verse reads, "No matter how you try you will never be able to treat your wives equally" (Qur'an 4:129). In the early years following the death of the prophet Muhammad, legal scholars were called upon to examine issues in need of clarification. They were also encouraged to apply independent thinking and then make non-binding rulings. This practice lasted until the 11th century, at which time Sunni religious scholars consolidated legal judgments into strict schools of thought and placed a ban on independent interpretation. The result was *sharia,* or Muslim law. Over the next nine hundred years, this approach to the law changed little. In application, however, sharia does vary according to regional traditions. In Tunisia, for example, taking more than one wife is banned altogether, while India provides few restrictions upon polygamy (Women Living Under Muslim Laws, 2003). Likewise, rules concerning dress and moral codes vary from state to state, with headscarves for women being obligatory in Iran and optional in Egypt.

National diversity in applying sharia accounts for the second way that SIS promotes women's rights within the framework of Islam: they focus their work for change on one country, Malaysia. Before 1957, Malaysia was a British colony with a court system divided between the federal and the local levels. Local Islamic leaders were allowed to establish courts to preside over cases of family law, while most other legal matters went to the federal courts. After Malaysia gained independence, Article 3 of its constitution named Islam as the state religion, although a clause in the same article guaranteed non-Muslims the right to practice their faiths (Mohamad, 1988). The court system, however, remained the same, meaning that the 60 percent of the population who are Muslim are still subject to local Islamic family courts, while the 40 percent who do not follow Islam are not (U. S. Department of State, 2005).

Example given for clarity and interest.

Unfamiliar term defined.

Second way— introduces subtopic.

Source given for data.

143

Objective
stance: first
person (I)
avoided with
APA style.

Malaysia's legal system complicates the work of SIS, as the 1995 campaign to pass a domestic violence act shows. In matters of violence against women, Muslim family law provides little legal recourse. The usual response by Islamic judges is to send the woman home to reconcile with her husband. So in 1995 the SIS campaigned to pass the Domestic Violence Act, which aimed to provide basic legal protections for women. After a vigorous lobbying campaign, the law was passed. Yet the response from Malaysia's Islamic religious establishment was to say that the law would only apply to non-Muslims (Othman, 1997). Even though this interpretation of the law has not been successfully reversed, SIS continues to work on family law reform, submitting to the government memoranda and reports on such issues as divorce, guardianship, and polygamy. In 2005, for example, SIS and five other NGOs formed a Joint Action Group on Gender Equality (JAG) and prepared a memorandum requesting a review and withdrawal of parts of a bill that was intended to improve the Islamic Family Law Act of 1984. While praising the new requirement that in cases of contracting polygamous marriages, both the existing and future wives must be present in the court, the JAG (2005) objected to other parts of the bill such as a change in wording that would make it easier for men to practice polygamy; instead of having to show that the new marriage was both "just and necessary," the men would only have to show that it was "just or necessary."

Example
given for
clarity and
interest.

Third way—
introduces
subtopic.

Although advocating for changes in the law is certainly important, SIS has developed another key way of promoting women's rights: public research-backed education. Using surveys and interviews, the group began a pilot research project in 2004 on the impact of polygamy on the family institution; that research project has recently gone national. As its Web site documents, SIS also sponsors numerous public lectures and forums on such issues as Islam and the political participation of women, the challenges of modernity, the use of fatwa, and the emergence of genetic engineering. There are also seminars and workshops for specific

Examples
given for
clarity and
interest.

groups such as single parents, study sessions with visiting writers, and a rich array of printed material, including newspaper columns that answer women's questions as well as pamphlets on such concerns as family planning, Qur'an interpretation, and domestic violence. Clearly SIS takes a very public approach to reform, an approach that Zainah Anwar (2004), the executive director, contends is necessary to ensure that Islam does not "remain the exclusive preserve of the *ulama* [traditionally trained religious scholars]" (para. 2).

Instead of waiting patiently for Islamic scholars and judges to work issues out in closed sessions, SIS has developed an activist approach to reform. So it is not surprising that its key ways of effecting change sometimes get as much criticism from conservative Islamists as the proposed changes themselves do (Anwar, 2004). It remains to be seen whether SIS, along with other NGOs working for human rights in Muslim countries, will succeed in moderating what they see as harmful expressions of their faith. But their efforts show that the situation of women in Islamic countries is actually much more complex and encouraging than many recent newspaper images and stories have led us to believe.

Quotation integrated into writer's sentence.

Interpretation provided without bi-ased opinion.

Point and purpose restated in conclusion.

-------------------------------[new page]------------------------------------

References

References list follows APA style and begins on a new page.

Anwar, Z. (2004, September-October). Sisters in Islam: A voice for everyone. *Fellowship Magazine, 70*(5). Retrieved from http://www.forusa.org/fellowship

Coleman, I. (2006, January–February). Women, Islam, and the new Iraq. *Foreign Affairs, 85*(1). Retrieved from http://www.foreignaffairs.org

Joint Action Group on Gender Equality. (2005, December). *Memorandum to Ahli Dewan Negara to review the Islamic Family Law (Federal Territories) (Amendment) Bill*

2005. Retrieved from Sisters in Islam website: http://www
.sistersinislam.org.my/memo/08122005.htm

Mohamad, M. (1988). *Islam, the secular state, and Muslim women in Malaysia*. Retrieved from Women Living Under Muslim Laws website: http://www.wluml.org/english/pubsfulltxt
.shtml?cmd[87]=i-87-2615

Othman, N. (1997). Implementing women's human rights in Malaysia. *Human Rights Dialogue, 1*(9). Retrieved from http://www.cceia.org/resources/publications/dialogue/1_09/articles/567.html

Sisters in Islam. (2007). *Mission*. Retrieved from http://sistersinislam.org.my/mission.htm

U. S. Department of State. Bureau of Democracy, Human Rights, and Labor. (2005). *Malaysia: International Religious Freedom Report 2005*. Retrieved from http://www.state.gov/g/drl/rls/irf/2005/51518.htm

Women Living Under Muslim Laws. (2003). *Knowing our rights: Women, family, laws, and customs in the Muslim world*. Retrieved from http://www.wluml.org/english/pubsfulltxt
.shtml?cmd[87]=i-87-16766

8d Write reviews of the literature to summarize current knowledge in a specific area.

In upper-division courses in the social and natural sciences, instructors sometimes assign a special kind of informative report called a **review of the literature.** Here the term *literature* refers to published research reports, and the term *review* means that you need to survey others' ideas, not evaluate them or argue for your opinion. A review presents an organized account of the current state of knowledge in a specific area, an account that you and other researchers can use to figure out new projects and directions for research. A review of the literature may also be a subsection within a research report.

The following paragraph is an excerpt from the review of the literature section in an article by psychologists investigating the motivations for suicide:

One source of information about suicide motives is suicide notes. International studies of suicide notes suggest that women and men do not differ with regard to love versus achievement motives. For example, in a study of German suicide notes, Linn and Lester (1997) found that women and men did not differ with regard to relationship versus financial or work motives. In a study of Hong Kong suicide notes, Ho, Yip, Chiu, and Halliday (1998) reported no gender or age differences with regard to interpersonal problems or financial/job problems. Similarly, in a UK study, McClelland, Reicher, and Booth (2000) found that men's suicide notes did not differ from women's notes in terms of mentioning career failures. In fact, in the UK study relationship losses were reported more often in men's than in women's suicide notes.

—CANETTO AND LESTER, *Journal of Psychology,*
September 2002

8e Write informative reports in the sciences to share discoveries.

Reading and writing play a role at each stage of scientific inquiry. Scientists observe phenomena and record their findings in notebooks. They ask questions about their observations, read related work by other scientists, and compose hypotheses that explain the observations. To prove or disprove their hypotheses, they conduct experiments, carefully documenting their procedures and findings. Finally, they write research reports to share their work with other scientists.

8f Write lab reports to demonstrate understanding.

As a college student, you may be asked to demonstrate your scientific understanding by showing that you know how to perform and report on an experiment designed to verify some well-established fact or principle. In advanced courses, you may get to design original experiments as well. (*An example of a student lab report can be found on pp. 150–54.*)

> *Note:* When scientists report the results of original experiments designed to provide new insight into issues on the frontiers of scientific knowledge, they go beyond informative reporting to interpretive analysis of the significance of their findings.

Lab reports usually include the following sections: Abstract, Introduction, Methods and Materials, Results, Discussion, Acknowledgments, and References. Begin drafting the report, section by section, while your time in the lab is still fresh in your mind.

147

Throughout your report, use passive voice to describe objects of study, which are more important than the experimenter ("the mixture *was heated* for 10 minutes"). Use the present tense to state established knowledge ("the rye seed *produces*"), but use the past tense to describe your own results and the work of prior researchers ("Kurland *reported*").

Follow the scientific conventions for abbreviations, symbols, and numbers. See if your textbook includes a list of accepted abbreviations and symbols. Use numerals for dates, times, pages, figures, tables, and standard units of measurement. Spell out numbers between one and nine that are not part of a series of larger numbers.

1. Abstract

An abstract is a one-paragraph summary (about 250 words) of your lab report. It answers the following questions: What methods were used in the experiment? What variables were measured? What were the findings? What do the findings imply?

2. Introduction

In the introduction, state your topic, summarize prior research, and present your hypothesis. Sometimes you will include a review of the literature (*see pp. 146–47*).

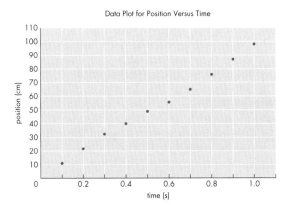

FIGURE 8.1 **The distance traveled by a paper airplane plotted in 0.1 second intervals.**

3. Methods and materials

Select the details that other scientists will need to replicate the experiment. Using the past tense, recount in chronological order what was done with specific materials.

4. Results

In this section, tell your reader about the results that are relevant to your hypothesis, especially those that are statistically significant. Results may be relevant even if they are different from what you expected.

You might summarize results in a table or graph. For example, the graph in Figure 8.1 above, which plots the distance (in centimeters, y-axis) a glider traveled over a period of time (in seconds, x-axis), was used to summarize the results of an engineering assignment.

Every table and figure you include in a lab report must be mentioned in the text. Point out the relevant patterns the figure displays. If you run statistical tests on your findings, be careful not to make the tests themselves the focus of your writing. Also refrain from interpreting why things happened the way they did.

> *Note:* Like the terms *correlated* and *random*, the term *significant* has a specific statistical meaning for scientists and should therefore be used in a lab report only in relation to the appropriate statistical tests.

5. Discussion

In discussing your results, interpret your major findings by explaining how and why each finding does or does not confirm the original hypothesis. Connect your research with prior scientific work and look ahead to new questions for future investigation.

6. Acknowledgments

In professional journals, most research papers include a brief statement acknowledging those who assisted the author or authors.

7. References

Include at the end of your report a listing of the manuals, books, and journal articles you consulted. Use one of the citation formats developed by the Council of Science Editors (CSE style), unless your instructor prefers another citation format.

Sample student lab report

Orientation by Sight in Schooling and Nonschooling Fish

Josephine Hearn

Biology 103

May 5, 2008

Lab partners: Tracy Luckow, Bryan Mignone, Darcy Langford

Experiment summarized.

Abstract

This experiment examined the tendency of schooling and of nonschooling fish to orient by sight toward conspecifics. Schooling species did orient toward conspecifics by sight and nonschooling species did not show any preference, indicating that schooling fish show a positive phototaxis toward conspecifics.

CSE citation-sequence style: superscript numeral indicates source in references list.

Introduction

Vision has been established as the primary method by which many schooling fish maintain a close proximity to one another. Olfaction, sound, and water pressure are secondary factors in schooling[1]. This experiment tested this theory, specifically, to determine whether schooling fish orient by sight toward conspecifics, whether schooling fish orient toward conspecifics more readily in the presence of a nonschooling species than of

another schooling species, and whether schooling fish orient
toward conspecifics more readily than nonschooling fish do. It was
predicted that schooling fish would show a positive phototaxis
to conspecifics, and that nonschooling fish would demonstrate
no definite taxis movement toward conspecifics; furthermore,
schooling fish would orient toward conspecifics more readily in
an environment with nonschooling fish than in one with other
schooling fish; finally, strongly schooling fish would more readily
orient to conspecifics than would less strongly schooling fish.

Background
information
provided:
earlier study,
scope and
hypothesis
of current
experiment.

The hypothesis was tested by placing two species in an
aquarium, one species at each end of the tank, with a test fish
belonging to one of the two species in the center of the tank
allowed to orient by sight toward either species.

Methods and materials

Observations were made of 5 species of fish: *Brachydanio*
sp. (zebra danios), *Barbus tetrazona* (tiger barbs), *Xiphophorus
maculatus* (swordtails), *Hyphessobrycon* sp. (tetras), and *Cichlasoma
nigrofasciatum* (juvenile convict cichlids). The species were ranked
according to the schooling behavior exhibited, determined by
recording the time each species spent schooling. Criteria for ranking
were the proximity of conspecifics to one another and the tendency
to move together. Barbs were ranked as the species with the
strongest schooling tendency, followed closely by tetras, then danios,
swordtails, and cichlids. Cichlids were considered a nonschooling
species. The top 2 ranking species, barbs and tetras, and the last
ranking species, cichlids, were selected for this experiment.

As illustrated in Figure 1, three cylinders were placed inside
a filled 10-gallon aquarium surrounded by a dark curtain to
prevent the entry of light from the sides[2]. Plexiglas cylinders were
used to keep species separated and able to orient to each other
by sight alone. The 2 outermost cylinders contained 4 each of
2 different species. A test fish, belonging to either of those species,
was placed in the central cylinder. The water temperature was
uniformly 22°C and remained so throughout the experiment.

Figure
introduced
(appears
on p. 152).

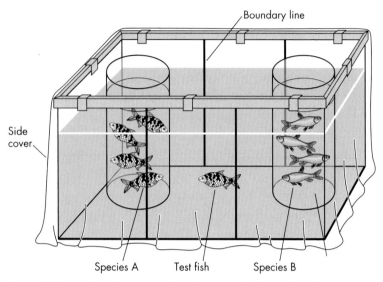

Figure 1 Test tank used to study orientation behavior (from Glase JC; Zimmerman MC, Waldvogel JA[2]).

Specifics about how the experiment was conducted.

When all cylinders were in place, the central cylinder was lifted out of the tank, allowing the test fish to move freely. Over the course of one minute, the time that the test fish spent on the side with conspecifics was recorded. The procedure was repeated with all possible combinations of the 3 species, and 5 replicates of each combination.

Results

Figure 2 shows the results for each of the three species for all of the trials. As predicted, the mean time out of one minute spent on the conspecifics side is higher for the barbs and tetras than for the cichlids. Figure 3 compares the mean times for each of the schooling species when the test fish were with the other schooling species or with the nonschooling species. The mean times for the schooling species are higher when the test fish was with other schooling species than with the nonschooling species.

Outcome of the experiment summarized.

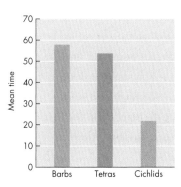

Figure 2 Mean time spent with conspecifics.

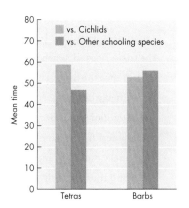

Figure 3 Comparison of mean times.

Discussion

The hypothesis that schooling fish would orient more readily than nonschooling fish to conspecifics was supported. It was shown that barbs and tetras, both schooling fish, spent nearly the entire time on the side with their own species, whereas the cichlids divided their time almost equally between the 2 sides. This result supports the theory that schooling fish orient to each other visually[1]. Furthermore, the barbs, the species with stronger schooling tendencies, showed more orientation than the tetras, the species with weaker schooling tendencies.

Barbs and tetras did not orient more or less readily to conspecifics depending on whether it was the other schooling species or the nonschooling species present in the tank. This indicates that schooling fish are neither attracted to other species of schooling fish nor repelled by nonschooling fish; however, because of the limited data, this subject deserves more investigation. An experiment should be conducted in which schooling fish are placed in a tank with the choice to orient either toward another schooling species or toward a nonschooling species, neither of which are conspecifics to the test fish.

Results of the experiment interpreted and flaws described.

153

Other sources of error may have affected the results of this experiment. First, the species of tetra was changed midway through the trials. Second, when test fish were changed, it was not made certain that the new test fish had not already been used. Third, occasionally test fish were so close to the boundary line dividing the aquarium that it became a subjective decision as to which side the test fish was on. Fourth, during the experiment, fish were continually moved in and out of the water, possibly distressing them and thus affecting their ability to orient.

——————————————[new page]——————————————

References list follows CSE citation-sequence style and begins on a new page.

References

1. Burgess JW, Shaw E. Development and ecology of fish schooling. Oceanus. 1979; 22(2):11–17.

2. Glase JC, Zimmerman MC, Waldvogel JA. Investigations in orientation behavior [Internet]. Association for Biology Laboratory Education (US); c1997 [cited 2008 Apr 28]. Available from: Association for Biology Laboratory Education at http://www.zoo.utoronto.ca/able/volumes/vol-6/1-glase/1-glase.htm

8g Write informative reports on events or findings in the humanities.

In the humanities, informative papers are used primarily to report on an event or finding in one of the humanities disciplines (for example, art, literature, history, philosophy, music, theater, and film). Unlike informative reports in the sciences, informative reports in the humanities may sometimes include subjective responses—your reaction to the event—in addition to specific details that support your points.

In the following example, a journalist explains the recent work of an artist who combines music, video, and readings in live performance.

LEARNING in COLLEGE

Informative Reports in the Humanities

Informative reports in the humanities describe the ideas, stories, and values of people past and present. Topics could include archeological discoveries, accounts of musical performances, and historical findings about art patronage.

Some Types of Informative Reports in the Humanities

- *Concert, theater, or film reports* describe the elements of a single performance or series of performances.
- *Book reports* describe the plot, characters, setting, and themes of a novel or summarize a nonfiction work.

Documentation Styles

- MLA (*see Chapter 23*) and Chicago (*see Chapter 25*)

Sample informative piece

The Sample Life

CARLY BERWICK

Paul D. Miller, a.k.a. DJ Spooky that Subliminal Kid, straddles hip-hop, club culture, and silent film

A young boy danced in the aisle to the DJ's pounding beats until his well-coiffed mother ushered him back to his seat in Lincoln Center's Alice Tully Hall. Behind a series of turntables and computers, Paul D. Miller, a.k.a. DJ Spooky that Subliminal Kid, warmed up his audience for *TransMetropolitan,* a night of music, videos, and readings he likened to a 1960s happening.

Later that week, Miller performed *Rebirth of a Nation,* his live remix of D. W. Griffith's 1915 silent film *Birth of a Nation,* which presents the Ku Klux Klan as the saviors of a South overrun by unruly free blacks. Using the computer to edit and project the movie across three screens, Miller cut and grouped scenes from the nearly three-hour film into repeated gestures, as Robert Johnson's blues echoed beneath rhythmic violin chords Miller created on the computer.

For more than ten years, Miller, a 33-year-old writer, artist, and DJ, has been making the case that sampling and remixing—taking existing sounds or images and

155

DJ Spooky and Ryuichi Sakamoto during the premiere of TransMetropolitan.

reconfiguring them into new ones, like collage—are the way we experience the world today. Originally from Washington, D.C., Miller says sampling provides a "seamless consolidation of cultural patterns." His performance of *TransMetropolitan* at Lincoln Center, for example, brought together writers and musicians from Sri Lanka, Pakistan, England, and Brooklyn. Moreover, he says, our invisible networks of technological communication link us more powerfully than the visible ones. As examples, he lists standard time and wireless Internet networks. "Software," he adds, "has changed all of our cultural patterns."

Films help people respond to certain often-repeated cues. Miller thinks *Birth of a Nation,* one of Hollywood's first blockbusters, "has conditioned people's responses" to race, he says. By reframing the movie, Miller allows contemporary audiences to examine racist gestures established 90 years ago and their persistence in contemporary culture. Miller showed posters and stills from his video, a looped DVD projection, at New York's Paula Cooper Gallery earlier this year, where the prints sold for $1,500 and the edition of five videos was priced at around $10,000.

Miller's music tends to be accessible, with arcane allusions and provocative samples supported by a driving beat. He started working as a DJ to "pay rent," he says, and his desire for people to enjoy the music comes through. "I look at myself as straddling hip-hop, club culture, and the metaphysics of text," says Miller—as he simultaneously scans the paper and answers his cell phone—a relentlessly multitasking interpreter of the wide wired world.

9 Interpretive Analyses and Writing about Literature

Interpretation involves figuring out a way of understanding a written document, literary work, cultural artifact, social situation, or natural event and presenting your understanding so that it is meaningful and convincing to readers.

9a Understand the assignment.

When an assignment asks you to compare, explain, analyze, discuss, or do a reading of something, you are expected to study that subject closely. An interpretive analysis moves beyond simple description and examines or compares particular items for a reason: to enhance your reader's understanding of people's conditions, actions, beliefs, or desires.

9b Approach writing an interpretive analysis as a process.

Writing an interpretive analysis typically begins with critical reading. (*See Chapter 7: Reading, Thinking, Writing: The Critical Connection for a discussion of how to read texts and visuals critically.*)

www.mhhe.com/
mhhb2

For an interactive
tutorial on writing
interpretive analyses,
go to

Writing >
Writing Tutors >
Interpretive
Analysis

1. Discovering an aspect of the subject that is meaningful to you

Think about your own feelings and experiences while you read, listen, or observe. Connecting your own thoughts and experiences to what you are studying can help you develop fresh interpretations.

2. Developing a thoughtful stance

Think of yourself as an explorer. Be thoughtful, inquisitive, and open-minded. You are exploring the possible meaning of something. When you write your paper, invite readers to join you on an intellectual journey, saying, in effect, "Come, think this through with me."

3. Using an intellectual framework

To interpret your subject effectively, use a relevant perspective or an intellectual framework. For example, the basic elements of a work of fiction, such as plot, character, and setting, are often used to analyze stories. Sigmund Freud's theory of conscious and unconscious forces in conflict might be applied to people, poems, and historical periods. In his analysis of Flannery O'Connor's

Interpretive Analyses

You can find interpretive analyses like the following in professional journals like *PMLA* (*Publications of the Modern Language Association*) as well as popular publications like the *New Yorker* and the *Atlantic*:

- A cultural critic contrasts the way AIDS and cancer are talked about, imagined, and therefore treated.

- Two geologists analyze photos of an arctic coastal plain taken from an airplane and infer that the effects of seismic activity vary according to the type of vegetation in the area.

- A musicologist compares the revised endings of two pieces by Beethoven to figure out what makes a work complete and finished.

story "Everything That Rises Must Converge," Rajeev Bector uses sociologist Erving Goffman's ideas about "character contests" to interpret the conflict between a son and his mother. (*Bector's analysis begins on p. 167.*)

No matter what framework you use, analysis often entails taking something apart and then putting it back together by figuring out how the parts make up a cohesive whole. Because the goal of analysis is to create a meaningful interpretation, the writer should treat the whole as more than the sum of its parts and recognize that determining meaning is a complex problem with multiple solutions.

www.mhhe.com/
mhhb2
For more help with
developing a thesis,
go to

Writing >
Paragraph/Essay
Development >
Thesis/Central Idea

4. Listing, comparing, questioning, and classifying to discover your thesis

To figure out a thesis, it is often useful to explore separate aspects of your subject. For example, if you are analyzing literature, you might consider the plot, the characters, the setting, and the tone before deciding to focus your thesis on how a character's personality drives the plot to its conclusion. If you are comparing two subjects, you would look for and list points of likeness and difference. Can you find subtle differences in aspects that at first seem alike? Subtle similarities in aspects that at first seem very different? The answers to these questions might help you figure out your thesis.

As you work on discovering your thesis, try one or more of the following strategies:

- Take notes about what you see or read, and if it helps, write a summary.

- Ask yourself questions about the subject you are analyzing, and write down any interesting answers. Imagine what kinds of questions your instructor or classmates might ask about the artifact, document, performance, or event you are considering. In answering these questions, try to figure out the thesis you will present and support.

- Name the class of things to which the item you are analyzing belongs (for example, memoirs). Then identify important parts or aspects of that class (for example, scene, point of view, turning points).

5. Making your thesis focused and purposeful

To make a point about your subject, focus on one or two questions that are key to understanding it. Resist the temptation to describe everything you see.

FOCUSED THESIS

In O'Connor's short story, plot, setting, and characterization work together to reinforce the impression that racism is a complex and pervasive problem.

Although you want your point to be clear, you also want to make sure that your thesis anticipates the "So what?" question and sets up an interesting context for your interpretation. Unless you relate your specific thesis to some more general issue, idea, or problem, your interpretive analysis may seem pointless to readers. (*For more on developing your thesis, see Chapter 3: Planning and Shaping the Whole Essay, pp. 42–46.*)

6. Introducing the general issue, a clear thesis or question, and relevant context

In interpretive analyses, the introduction often requires more than one paragraph to do the following:

www.mhhe.com/
mhhb2
For more on crafting introductions, go to
Writing > Paragraph/Essay Development > Introductions

- Identify the general issue, concept, or problem at stake. You can also present the intellectual framework that you are applying.

- Provide relevant background information.

- Name the specific item or items you will focus on in your analysis (or the items you will compare).

- State the thesis you will support and develop or the main question(s) your analysis will answer.

You need not do these things in the order listed. Sometimes it is a good idea to introduce the specific focus of your analysis before presenting either the issue or the background information. Even though

159

you may begin with a provocative statement or an example designed to capture your readers' attention, make sure that your introduction does the four things it needs to do. (*For more on introductions, see Chapter 4: Drafting Paragraphs and Visuals, pp. 72–74.*)

For example, the following is the introductory paragraph from a paper on the development of Margaret Sanger's and Gloria Steinem's feminism that was written for a history class:

> In our male-dominated society, almost every woman has experienced some form of oppression. Being oppressed is like having one end of a rope fastened to a pole and the other end fastened to one's belt: it tends to hold a woman back. But a few tenacious and visionary women have fought oppression and have consequently made the lives of others easier. Two of these visionary women are Margaret Sanger and Gloria Steinem. As their autobiographical texts show, Sanger and Steinem felt compassion for women close to them, and that compassion not only shaped their lives but also empowered them to fight for changes in society.

In one paragraph, the student identifies her composition's general issue (the feminist struggle against oppression), introduces the items to be compared (two autobiographical texts), and in the last sentence, states her main point or thesis. Her readers now need additional background information about Sanger and Steinem that will give them a context for the two texts that are being compared.

7. Planning your paper so that each point supports your thesis

After you pose a key question or state your thesis in the introduction, work point by point to answer the question and support your interpretive thesis. From beginning to end, readers must be able to follow your train of thought and see how each point you make is related to your thesis. (*For more on developing your ideas, see Chapter 3: Planning and Shaping the Whole Essay, pp. 46–51.*)

9c Write interpretive papers in the humanities.

Writers in the humanities analyze literature, art, film, theater, music, history, and philosophy. In Part 1, we followed a student's analysis of a photograph through several drafts. In this chapter we look at some examples of literary analysis. The following ideas and practices are useful in writing interpretive papers in the humanities:

■ **Base your analysis on the work itself.** Works of art affect each of us differently, and any interpretation has a subjective element. There are numerous critical theories about the significance of art. However, the possibility

Interpreting in the Visual Arts

Interpreting a painting is similar to interpreting a literary work or any other work of art. For example, your interpretation of this 1965 painting by Andy Warhol, titled *Campbell's Soup Can (Tomato)*, would likely reflect your personal reaction to the work as well as what you know about the artist and his times, but it would have to be grounded in a discussion of details of the work itself. What is the subject of the painting? How has the artist rendered it? How closely does it resemble an actual soup can? What does the painting suggest about the relationship between fine art and popular culture?

of different interpretations does not mean that all interpretations are equally valid. Your reading of the work needs to be grounded in details from the work itself.

■ **Consider how the concepts you are learning in your course apply to the work you are analyzing.** If your course focuses on the formal elements of art, for example, you might look at how those elements function in the painting you have chosen to analyze. If your course focuses on the social context of a work, you might look at how the work shares or subverts the belief system and worldview that was common in its time.

■ **Use the present tense when writing about the work and the past tense when writing about its history.** Use the present tense to talk about the events that happen within a work: *In Aristophanes's plays, characters frequently* **step** *out of the scene and* **address** *the audience directly.* Use the present tense as well to discuss decisions made by the work's creator: *In his version of the Annunciation, Leonardo* **places** *the Virgin outside, in an Italian garden.* Use the past tense, however, to relate historical information about the work or creator: *Kant* **wrote** *about science, history, criminal justice, and politics as well as philosophical ideas.*

161

QUESTIONS for ANALYZING POETRY

Speaker and Tone

How would you describe the speaker's voice? Is it that of a parent or a lover, an adult or a child, a man or a woman? What is the speaker's tone—is it stern or playful, melancholy or elated, nostalgic or hopeful?

Connotations

Although both *trudge* and *saunter* mean "walk slowly," their connotations (associative meanings) are very different. What feelings or ideas do individual words in the poem connote?

Imagery

Does the poem conjure images that appeal to any of your senses—for example, the shocking feeling of a cold cloth on feverish skin or the sharp smell of a gas station? How do the images shape the mood of the poem? What ideas do they suggest?

Figurative Language

Does the poem use **simile** to directly compare two things using *like* or *as* (*his heart is sealed tight like a freezer door*)? Does it use **metaphor** to implicitly link one thing to another (*his ice-hard heart*)? How does the comparison enhance meaning?

Sound, Rhythm, and Meter

What vowel and consonant sounds recur through the poem? Do the lines of the poem resemble the rhythms of ordinary speech, or do they have a more musical quality? Consider how the sounds of the poem create an effect.

Structure

Notice how the poem is organized into parts or stanzas, considering spacing, punctuation, capitalization, and rhyme schemes. How do the parts relate to one another?

Theme

What is the subject of the poem? What does the poet's choice of language and imagery suggest about his or her attitude toward that subject?

www.mhhe.com/
mhhb2
For another sample of interpretive writing, go to

Writing >
Writing Samples >
Interpretive Paper

9d Write a literary interpretation of a poem.

The poet Edwin Arlington Robinson defined poetry as "a language that tells us, through a more or less emotional reaction, something that cannot be said." Although literary analysis can never tell us exactly what a poem is saying, it can help us think about it more deeply.

First read the complete poem without stopping, and then note your initial thoughts and feelings. What is your first sense of the subject of the poem? What ideas and images does the poem suggest?

Reread the poem several times, paying close attention to the rhythms of the lines (reading aloud helps) and the poet's choice of words. Think about how the poem develops. Do the last lines represent a shift from or fulfillment of the poem's opening? Look for connections among the poem's details, and think about their significance. The questions in the box on page 162 may help guide your analysis.

Use the insights you gain from your close reading to develop a working thesis about the poem. In the student essay that begins on page 164, McKenna Doherty develops a thesis about the poem "Testimonial," reprinted below. Doherty's analysis is based on her knowledge of other poems by Rita Dove and her attempt to discover the theme of this particular work. She focuses on how four poetic devices give the theme its emotional impact.

Testimonial

RITA DOVE

Back when the earth was new
and heaven just a whisper,
back when the names of things
hadn't had time to stick;

back when the smallest breezes
melted summer into autumn,
when all the poplars quivered
sweetly in rank and file . . .

the world called, and I answered.
Each glance ignited to a gaze.
I caught my breath and called that life,
swooned between spoonfuls of lemon sorbet.

I was pirouette and flourish,
I was filigree and flame.
How could I count my blessings
when I didn't know their names?

Back when everything was still to come,
luck leaked out everywhere.
I gave my promise to the world,
and the world followed me here.

Sample student analysis of a poem

Rita Dove's "Testimonial": The Music of Childhood

Rita Dove rarely uses obvious, rigid rhyme schemes or strict metrical patterns in her poetry, and her subtle use of language often obscures both the subject and themes of her poetry. However, careful analysis of her work is rewarding, as Dove's poems are dense with ideas and figurative language. Her poem "Testimonial" is a good example of this complexity. Although the poem seems ambiguous on first reading, repeated readings reveal many common and cleverly used poetic techniques that are employed to express a common literary theme: the difference between adult knowledge and childhood innocence.

The first two lines refer to a time when "the earth was new / and heaven just a whisper." At first, these lines appear to refer to the Biblical origins of earth and heaven; however, the title of the poem invites us to take the poem as a personal account of the speaker's experience. The time when "the earth was new" could refer to the speaker's youth. Youth is also the time of life when heaven is "just a whisper," since matters of death and religion are not present in a child's awareness. Thus, Dove's opening lines actually put the reader in the clear, familiar context of childhood.

The lines that follow support the idea that the poem refers to youth. Dove describes the time period of the poem as "when the names of things / hadn't had time to stick" (lines 3–4). Children often forget the names of things and are constantly asking their parents, "What is this? What is that?" The names of objects do not "stick" in their minds. The second stanza, describing a scene of trees and breezes, seems childlike in its sensitivity to nature, particularly to the change of seasons. The trees swaying "sweetly in rank and file" (8) suggest an innocent, simplistic worldview, in which everything, even the random movement of trees in the wind, occurs in an orderly, nonthreatening fashion.

Central sub-
ject of paper
identified.

Examples
provided
to illustrate
theme.

More
examples
given and
interpreted.

Notice that Dove does not state "when I was a child" at the beginning of the poem. Instead, she uses poetic language—alliteration, rhyme, uncommon words, and personification—to evoke the experience of childhood. Figurative language may make the poem more difficult to understand on first reading, but it ultimately makes the poem more personally meaningful.

In line 12, "swooned between spoonfuls of lemon sorbet" not only evokes the experience of childhood, a time when ice cream might literally make one swoon, but the alliteration of "swooned," "spoonfuls," and "sorbet" also makes the poem musical. Dove also uses alliteration in lines 14, 15, and 18. This conventional poetic technique is used relatively briefly and not regularly. The alliteration does not call attention to itself—the music is quiet.

"Testimonial" also uses the best known poetic technique: rhyme. Rhyme is used in many poems—what is unusual about its use in this poem is that, as with alliteration, rhyme appears irregularly. Only a few lines end with rhyming words, and the rhymes are more suggestive than exact: "whisper" and "stick" (2 and 4), "gaze" and "sorbet" (10 and 12), "flame" and "names" (14 and 16), and "everywhere" and "here" (18 and 20). These rhymes, or consonances, stand out because they are isolated and contrast with the other, unrhymed lines.

Dove occasionally uses words that children would probably not know, such as "swooned" (12), "sorbet" (12), "pirouette" (13), "flourish" (13), and "filigree" (14). These words suggest the central theme, which is underscored in the final question of the stanza when the narrator of the poem asks, "How could I count my blessings / when I didn't know their names?" The adult words emphasize the contrast between the speaker's past innocence and present knowledge.

The poem ends with the mysterious lines, "I gave my promise to the world / and the world followed me here" (19-20). The

> Writer presents four poetic techniques, which she explains in the following paragraphs.

Analysis of poem concluded with interpretation of entire poem.

world is personified, given the characteristics of a man or woman capable of accepting a promise and following the speaker. As with the opening lines, these final lines are confusing if they are taken literally, but the lines become clearer when one considers the perspective of the speaker. It is as if the speaker has taken a journey from childhood to adulthood. Just as the speaker has changed during the course of this journey, so too has the world changed. The childhood impressions of the world that make up the poem—the sorbet, the trees swaying in the breeze—do not last into adulthood. The speaker becomes a different person, an adult, and the world also becomes something else. It has "followed" the speaker into adulthood; it has not remained static and unchanging.

Paper concluded briefly, neatly.

In "Testimonial," Dove presents a vision of childhood so beautifully, so musically, that we can experience it with her, if only for the space of a few lines.

————————————————-[new page]————————————————

Works-Cited list follows MLA style and begins on a new page.

Work Cited

Dove, Rita. "Testimonial." *Literature: Approaches to Fiction, Poetry, and Drama*. Ed. Robert DiYanni. New York: McGraw-Hill, 2004. 738. Print.

9e Write a literary interpretation of a work of fiction.

A literary analysis paper is an opportunity to look beyond the plot of a short story or novel and develop a better understanding of it. You may want to read the work, or key sections of it, more than once. The questions in the box on pages 169–70 may help guide your analysis.

The field of literary criticism offers various strategies for analyzing fiction, including formalist theories, reader response theory, and postmodern theories. However, it is also possible to apply the insights offered by other disciplines to your literary analysis paper. In the essay that begins on the next page, Rajeev Bector, a sociology major, applies a theory that he learned in a sociology course to his analysis of a short story.

Sample student analysis of a short story

The Character Contest in Flannery O'Connor's
"Everything That Rises Must Converge"
Sociologist Erving Goffman believes that every social
interaction establishes our identity and preserves our image,
honor, and credibility in the hearts and minds of others. Social
interactions, he says, are in essence "character contests" that occur
not only in games and sports but also in our everyday dealings
with strangers, peers, friends, and even family members. Goffman
defines character contests as "disputes [that] are sought out and
indulged in (often with glee) as a means of establishing where
one's boundaries are" (29). Just such a contest occurs in Flannery
O'Connor's short story "Everything That Rises Must Converge."

> Key idea
> that provides
> intellectual
> framework.

As they travel from home to the Y, Julian and his mother,
Mrs. Chestny, engage in a character contest, a dispute we must
understand in order to figure out the story's theme. Julian is so
frustrated with his mother that he virtually "declare[s] war on
her," "allow[s] no glimmer of sympathy to show on his face," and
"imagine[s] various unlikely ways by which he could teach her a
lesson" (O'Connor 185, 186). But why would Julian want to hurt
his mother, a woman who is already suffering from high blood
pressure?

> Question
> posed.

Julian's conflict with Mrs. Chestny results from pent-up
hostility and tension. As Goffman explains, character contests
are a way of living that often leaves a "residue": "Every day in
many ways we can try to score points and every day we can be
shot down" (29). For many years, Julian has had to live under his
racist mother's authority, and every time he protested her racist
views he was probably shot down because of his "radical ideas"
and "lack of practical experience" (O'Connor 184). As a result,
a residue of defeat and shame has accumulated that fuels a fire
of rebellion against his mother. But even though Julian rebels
against his mother's racist views, it does not mean that he is not

> Interpretation
> organized
> point by point:
> first point.

167

a racist himself. Julian does not realize that in his own way, he is as prejudiced as his mother. He makes it "a point" to sit next to blacks, in contrast to his mother, who purposely sits next to whites (182). They are two extremes, each biased, for if Julian were truly fair to all, he would not care whom he sat next to.

"We" indicates thoughtful stance, not Bector's personal feelings.

When we look at the situation from Mrs. Chestny's viewpoint, we realize that she must maintain her values and beliefs for two important reasons: to uphold her character as Julian's mother and to act out her prescribed role in society. Even if she finds Julian's arguments on race relations and integration valid and plausible, Mrs. Chestny must still refute them. If she did not, she would lose face as Julian's mother—that image of herself as the one with authority. By preserving her self-image, Mrs. Chestny shows that she has what Goffman sees as key to "character": some quality that seems "essential and unchanging" (28).

Second point.

Besides upholding her character as Julian's mother, Mrs. Chestny wants to preserve the honor and dignity of her family tradition. Like an actor performing before an audience, she must play the role prescribed for her—the role of a white supremacist. But her situation is hopeless, for the role she must play fails to acknowledge the racial realities that have transformed her world. According to Goffman, when a "situation" is "hopeless," a character "can gamely give everything . . . and then go down bravely, or proudly, or insolently, or gracefully or with an ironic smile on his lips" (32). For Mrs. Chestny, being game means trying to preserve her honor and dignity as she goes down to physical defeat in the face of hopeless odds.

Third point.

Thesis.

Given the differences between Mrs. Chestny's and her son's values, as well as the oppressiveness of Mrs. Chestny's racist views, we can understand why Julian struggles to "teach" his mother "a lesson" (185) throughout the entire bus ride. Goffman would point out that "each individual is engaged in providing evidence to establish a definition of himself at the expense of what can remain for the other" (29). But in the end, neither character wins the

Conclusion: main point about Julian and his mother related to larger issue of racism.

168

contest. Julian's mother loses her sense of self when she is pushed to the ground by a "colored woman" wearing a hat identical to hers (187). Faced with his mother's breakdown, Julian feels his own identity being overwhelmed by "the world of guilt and sorrow" (191).

————————————[new page]————————————

Works Cited

Goffman, Erving. "Character Contests." *Text Book: An Introduction to Literary Language.* Ed. Robert Scholes, Nancy Comley, and Gregory Ulmer. New York: St. Martin's, 1988. 27–33. Print.

O'Connor, Flannery. "Everything That Rises Must Converge." *Fiction.* Ed. R. S. Gwynn. 2nd ed. New York: Addison, 1998. 179–91. Print.

Works-Cited list follows MLA style and begins on a new page.

QUESTIONS for ANALYZING FICTION

Characters

What are the relationships among the characters? What do the characters' thoughts, actions, and speech reveal about them? What changes take place among or within the characters?

Point of View

Is the story told by a character speaking as "I" (first-person point of view), or by a third-person narrator, who lets the reader know what one (or none) or all of the characters are thinking? How does point of view affect your understanding of what happens in the story?

Plot

What do these particular episodes in the characters' lives reveal? What did you think and feel at different points in the story? What kinds of changes take place over the course of the story?

Setting

What is the significance of the story's setting (its time and place)? What associations does the writer make with each location? How does the social context of the setting affect the characters' choices and attitudes?

QUESTIONS for ANALYZING FICTION *(continued)*

Language

Fiction writers, like poets, use figurative language and imagery to meaningful effect (*see the box "Questions for Analyzing Poetry" on p. 162*). Are there patterns of imagery and metaphor in the story? What significance can you infer from these patterns?

Theme

What sense of the story's significance can you infer from the elements above? Are there any passages in the work that seem to address the theme directly?

9f   Write a literary interpretation of a play.

When we interpret a play, we need to imagine the world of the play—the setting and costumes, the delivery of lines of dialogue, and the movement of characters in relation to one another. Like a poem or story, a play is best read more than once.

Like poetry, drama is meant to be spoken, and the sound and rhythm of its lines are significant. Like fiction, drama unfolds through characters acting in a plot. As in both genres, imagery and figurative language work to convey emotions and meaning. Review the questions for analyzing poetry and fiction (*see pp. 162 and 169–70*), and consider the questions in the box below when analyzing a play.

In the following paper, Sam Chodoff uses dialogue to analyze the theme of honor as it applies to the characters in Shakespeare's *Hamlet*.

QUESTIONS for ANALYZING DRAMA

Dialogue

What does the dialogue reveal about the characters' thoughts and motivations? How do the characters' words incite other characters to action?

Stage Directions

Do the stage directions include references to any objects that may serve as dramatic symbols? How might costume directions suggest mood or symbolize such concepts as freedom, repression, or chivalry, for example? Do the directions call for any music or sounds to add to the atmosphere of the work?

Sample student analysis of a play

Honor in Shakespeare's *Hamlet*

In the world of Shakespeare's *Hamlet*, actions, not motives, are the measure of a character's honor. Good actions bestow honor; evil actions withdraw it. Not all characters in the play, however, are equally equipped to know one from the other. The main characters receive divine enlightenment about what is right and wrong, but the minor characters have to rely on luck, making choices without divine assistance.

Characters fall into one of three categories of honor determined by where their actions fall on the spectrum between good and evil. Hamlet and Fortinbras represent extreme good; Claudius represents extreme evil. These characters have been enlightened by heaven, and their actions are based on this divinely granted knowledge. In the middle of the spectrum are all the other characters, who have chosen a path based on their own, not divine, knowledge, and for whom honor is a matter of luck.

As Hamlet storms into the palace in anger, seeking revenge for the death of his father, Claudius reassures Gertrude, telling her, "Do not fear our person. / There's such divinity doth hedge a king / That treason can but peep to what it would, / Acts little of his will" (4.5.122-25). Claudius knows that by killing his brother and usurping his throne, he has

> Key term—
> "honor"—
> defined.

> Illustration
> of a scene
> discussed in
> the paper.

Fig. 1. Hamlet confronted by his father's ghost as his mother looks on amazed, engraving from John and Josiah Boydell, *Boydell's Shakespeare Prints* (Mineola: Dover, 2004) 73. Print.

171

forfeited any chance to be the rightful king, and behind his façade, he struggles with his own guilt, knowing that heaven will remain closed to him while he still holds the "effects for which [he] did the murder" (3.3.54). Meanwhile, unbeknownst to Claudius, heaven has, through the ghost of Hamlet's father, commanded Hamlet to avenge his father's murder and restore a rightful king to the throne, as shown in fig. 1. This reveals that Claudius is on the lowest end of the honor spectrum, that his honor is false, a mere pretense of honor with nothing but evil underneath. His actions show that an honorable life remains unattainable when the appearance of honor is the only goal, and that, in Hamlet's words, "one may smile, and smile, and be a villain" (1.5.108).

Hamlet and Fortinbras, on the other hand, have been shown by heaven the conflict that they must resolve and are left to do that task without any further divine aid. The engraving in fig. 1 shows Hamlet recoiling at the sight of the ghost. This image emphasizes the way this supernatural contact literally and metaphorically sets Hamlet apart from his mother. With a clear duty whose virtue is unquestionable, the honor of Hamlet and Fortinbras is assured as long as they pursue and complete their objective. The last scene shows that they have achieved this goal, as Fortinbras gives orders to pay tribute to Hamlet: "Let four captains / Bear Hamlet like a soldier to the stage, / . . . and for his passage / The soldier's music and the rite of war / Speak loudly for him" (5.2.400-01, 403-05). While the bodies of the other characters are ignored, Hamlet's is treated with ceremony. This disparity in how the characters are treated confirms that Hamlet and Fortinbras have been placed at the highest end of the honor spectrum, and it shows that the many grave mistakes they both have made (resulting in the death of many innocent people) will be forgiven because the mistakes were made in pursuit of a divine objective. This idea of honor was acceptable in Shakespeare's day, as illustrated in a treatise by Sir William Segar in 1590: "God . . . would give victory to him that justly adventured his life for truth, honor, and justice. . . . the trial by Arms is not only natural, but also necessary and allowable" (qtd. in Corum 153).

Other characters in *Hamlet* are not privy to the true nature of the world and are forced to make decisions without heaven's help. The level of honor these characters attain is determined by luck; with their limited knowledge of good and evil, right and wrong, these characters often act dishonorably. When Rosencrantz and Guildenstern are summoned before the king and asked to spy on Hamlet, they respond positively, saying, "[W]e both obey, / And here give up ourselves in the full bent / To lay our service freely at your feet / To be commanded" (2.2.29-32). In their ignorance, they accept Claudius as the rightful king and thus unintentionally align themselves with the evil he represents, losing any honor they might have gained. Other characters are similarly tricked into obeying Claudius.

Third example given.

Luck can go both ways, however, and several characters end up well, even in the absence of a divine messenger. For example, Horatio chooses from the very beginning to follow Hamlet and not only survives but also attains honor. His honor, though, is by no means assured; there are many instances in which he could have acted differently. He could quite easily have gone to Claudius with the news of the ghost, an act which, while perfectly natural, would have left him devoid of honor.

Another example given of the third category of honor, to strengthen claim.

We would like to think that, by adhering to virtues, we can control how we will be judged. In *Hamlet*, we are shown a world in which lives are spent in the struggle between good and evil, often without clear guidance. But those who have lived honorably are rewarded with a place in heaven, the "undiscover'd country" (3.1.79) that every character both fears and desires. Only those characters either chosen by heaven to be honorable or who by luck become honorable reach paradise, while others burn in hell or wait in purgatory (Greenblatt 51). Very few people in Hamlet's world will be granted a place in heaven.

Essay concluded concisely.

173

—————————————[new page]—————————————

Works Cited

Corum, Richard. *Understanding Hamlet: A Student Casebook to Issues, Sources, and Historical Documents.* Westport, CT: Greenwood, 1998. Print.

Greenblatt, Stephen. *Hamlet in Purgatory.* Princeton: Princeton UP, 2001. Print.

Shakespeare, William. *Hamlet.* Ed. Harold Jenkins. Arden Edition of the Works of William Shakespeare. London: Methuen, 1982. Print.

Works-Cited list follows MLA style and begins a new page.

9g Write case studies and other interpretive analyses in the social sciences.

Social scientists are trained observers and recorders of the behavior of individuals and groups in specific situations and institutions. They use writing not only to see clearly and remember precisely what they observe but also to interpret its meaning, as in this passage from a textbook by anthropologist Conrad Kottak.

Rituals at McDonald's (excerpt)

CONRAD KOTTAK

Each day, on the average, a new McDonald's restaurant opens somewhere in the world. The number of McDonald's outlets today far surpasses the total number of all fast-food restaurants in the United States in 1945. McDonald's has grown from a single hamburger stand in San Bernardino, California, into today's international web of thousands of outlets. Have factors less obvious to American natives than relatively low cost, fast service, and taste contributed to McDonald's success? Could it be that natives—in consuming the products and propaganda of McDonald's—are not just eating but experiencing something comparable in certain respects to participation in religious rituals? To answer this question, we must briefly review the nature of ritual.

[Religious] [r]ituals . . . are formal—stylized, repetitive, and stereotyped. They are performed in special places at set times. Rituals include liturgical orders—set sequences of words and actions laid down by someone other than the current performers. Rituals also convey information about participants and their cultural traditions. Performed year after year, generation after generation, rituals translate messages, values, and sentiments into action. Rituals are social acts. Inevitably, some participants are more strongly committed than others are to the beliefs on which the rituals are founded. However, just by taking part in a joint public act, people signal that they accept an order that transcends their status as mere individuals.

For many years, like millions of other Americans, I have occasionally eaten at McDonald's. Eventually I began to notice certain ritual-like aspects of Americans' behavior at these fast-food restaurants. Tell your fellow Americans that going to McDonald's is similar in some ways to going to church, and their bias as natives will reveal itself in laughter, denials, or questions about your sanity. Just as football is a game and *Star Trek* is "entertainment," McDonald's, for natives, is just a place to eat. However, an analysis of what natives do at McDonald's will reveal a very high degree of formal, uniform behavior by staff members and customers alike. It is particularly interesting that this invariance in word and deed has developed without any theological doctrine. McDonald's ritual aspect is founded on 20th-century technology, particularly automobiles, television, work away from home, and the short lunch break. It is striking, nevertheless, that one commercial organization should be so much more successful than other businesses, the schools, the military, and even many religions in producing behavioral invariance. Factors other than low cost, fast service, and the taste of the food—all of which are approximated by other chains—have contributed to our acceptance of McDonald's and adherence to its rules. . . .

In this passage, Kottak based many of his conclusions on his observations of the way people behave at McDonald's restaurants. When social scientists conduct a systematic study of people's behavior in groups or institutions, they report on and interpret their observations in **case studies**. Anthropologists, for example, often spend extended periods living among and observing the people of one society or group and then report on their findings in a kind of case study called an *ethnography*.

Accurate observations are essential starting points for a case study, and writing helps researchers make clear and precise observations. Here are some things to consider as you undertake a case study assignment.

1. Choosing a topic that raises a question
In doing a case study, your purpose is to connect what you see and hear with issues and concepts in the social sciences. Choose a topic and turn it into a research question. Write down your hypothesis—a tentative answer to your research question—as well as some categories of behavior or other things to look for in your field research.

2. Collecting data

Make a detailed and accurate record of what you observe and when and how you observed it. Whenever you can, count or measure, and take down word for word what is said. Use frequency counts—the number of occurrences of specific, narrowly defined instances of behavior. If you are observing a classroom, for example, you might count the number of teacher-directed questions asked by several children. Your research methodologies course will introduce you to many ways to quantify data. Graphs like Figure 9.1 can help you display and summarize frequency data.

3. Assuming an unbiased stance

In a case study, you are presenting empirical findings, based on careful observation. Your stance is that of an unbiased observer.

4. Discovering meaning in your data

As you review your notes, try to uncover connections, identify inconsistencies, and draw inferences. For example, ask yourself why a subject behaved in a specific way, and consider different explanations

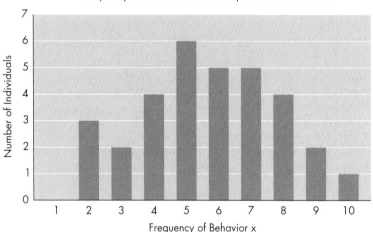

Frequency of Behavior x in a Sample of 32 Individuals

FIGURE 9.1 **Graphing frequency data.** Column graphs like this one can be useful for summarizing behavioral observations. The numbers on the horizontal axis represent the frequency, or number of occurrences, of a particular behavior. (An example might be the number of teacher-directed questions a student asks during a class). The vertical axis represents the number of individuals at each frequency. In this case, three individuals exhibited the behavior twice, two exhibited it three times, and so forth.

for the behavior. You will also need to draw upon the techniques for quantitative analysis that you learn in a statistics course.

5. Presenting your findings in an organized way

There are two basic ways to present your findings in the body of a case study. (1) **As stages of a process:** A student studying gang initiation organized her observations chronologically into appropriate stages. If you organize your study this way, be sure to transform the minute-by-minute history of your observations into a pattern with distinctive stages. (2) **In analytic categories:** A student observing the behavior of a preschool child used the following categories from the course textbook to present his findings: motor coordination, cognition, and socialization.

Note: Develop your stages or categories while you are making your observations. In your paper, be sure to illustrate your stages or categories with material drawn from your observations—with descriptions of people, places, and behavior, as well as with telling quotations.

 CHARTING the TERRITORY

Case Studies

You may be asked to write case studies in a number of social science and science disciplines.

- **In sociology:** You may be asked to analyze a small group to which you have belonged or belong now. In this case, your study will address such issues as the group's norms and values, stratification and roles, and cultural characteristics. Your audience will be your professor, who will want to see how your observations reflect current theories on group norms.

- **In nursing:** You may note details of your care of a patient that corroborate or differ from what you have been taught to expect. Your audience is the supervising nurse, who is interested in your interactions with the patient.

- **In education:** As a student teacher, you may closely observe and write about one student in the context of his or her socioeconomic and family background. Your audience will be your supervising teacher, who seeks more insight into students' behavior.

6. Including a review of the literature, statement of your hypothesis, and description of your methodology in your introduction

The introduction presents the framework, background, and rationale for your study. Begin with the topic, and review related research, working your way to the specific question that your study addresses. Follow that with a statement of your hypothesis, accompanied by a description of your **methodology**—how, when, and where you made your observations and how you recorded them.

7. Discussing your findings in the conclusion

The conclusion of your case study should answer the following three questions: Did you find what you expected? What do your findings show, or what is the bigger picture? Where should researchers working on your topic go now?

9h   Write interpretive analyses in the sciences.

Many research papers in the sciences, like those in the social sciences, are interpretive as well as informative. As mentioned in Chapter 8, for example, interpretation is a crucial aspect of lab reports describing the results of original experiments designed to create new scientific knowledge.

Scientists, however, may also be called upon to analyze trends and make predictions in papers that do not follow the lab or research report model. In the following example, Josh Feldman interprets historical data about hurricanes to see whether they reveal trends in weather patterns.

Sample student interpretive paper in the sciences

Keeping an Eye on the Storms

On August 29, 2005, Hurricane Katrina struck the Gulf

Coast of the United States. It was among the deadliest storms

in American history, responsible for the deaths of close to 2,000

people, and caused tens of billions of dollars in damage[1]. (See

Figure 1.) The images of Katrina's devastation in New Orleans,

across Mississippi, in Florida, and beyond horrified people around

the world. Alarmingly, though, there is reason to fear that the

years ahead could bring even more hurricanes as powerful, or

indeed more powerful, than Katrina. And while we generally

think of hurricanes as natural phenomena over which we have no

Gripping
facts in the
introduction
engage
reader's
attention.

Figure 1 Katrina's winds tear the roof off a building outside New Orleans. (from Thompson, I[2])

control, evidence suggests that humans may in fact be contributing to an increase in the number of deadly hurricanes. The effects of global warming may mean that we will soon see more hurricanes, and ones of greater strength, approaching our shores.

Thesis stated.

To understand why powerful hurricanes may become increasingly common, it is necessary to understand a key fact about hurricane formation: hurricanes depend on warm water. Typically, a hurricane forms only in water that is 80° or warmer[3]. The longer a hurricane remains over warm water, the stronger it becomes. As Katrina moved over the Gulf of Mexico, for example, surface waters there were unusually warm[4]. This is one reason Katrina was such a powerful storm when it made landfall.

The relationship between hurricanes and warm water also connects hurricanes to global warming. The United Nations' Intergovernmental Panel on Climate Change concluded that the evidence of global warming, in the air and in the oceans, was "unequivocal." They also stated the most likely explanation for this warming was human release of greenhouse gases like carbon dioxide into the atmosphere[5].

Authoritative source cited.

Figure 2 shows the global average sea surface temperature from 1860 to 2000. Each line on the graph represents a different

179

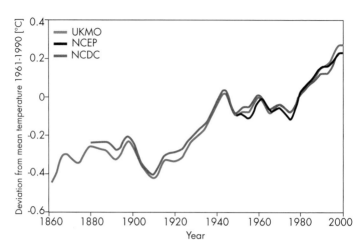

Figure 2 The change in sea surface temperature from 1860 to 2000 (from Intergovernmental Panel on Climate Change[6])

source for this data. The red line shows data from the United States Climatic Data Center; the blue line, data from the United Kingdom Met Office; and the black line, data from the United States National Center for Environmental Prediction[6]. Each line shows that sea surface temperatures are rising, with notable acceleration in the last decades of the 20th century, when human-produced global warming accelerated. Overall, average sea surface temperatures have risen roughly 1° Fahrenheit over the last century[4].

Use of statistics establishes authority.

Prediction made.

Again, hurricanes require warm water for their formation and strength. It stands to reason that as waters across the globe become warmer, there will be more and more opportunities for hurricanes to form and gain power. An article published online by the Pew Center on Global Climate Change states the point clearly: "[Global warming] clearly has created circumstances under which powerful storms are more likely to occur at this point in history (and in the future) than they were in the past[4]." While people often think of global warming in terms of melting ice and unseasonable warmth, it has consequences for every facet of the natural world—including creating oceanic conditions that make hurricanes more likely.

Indeed, humans may already be witnessing the effects of their carbon dioxide production on storm formation. Kerry Emanuel of the Massachusetts Institute of Technology conducted a study that showed that hurricane strength has been on the rise in recent decades. Specifically, Emanuel found a 50% increase in hurricane power and duration since the 1970s[7]. As humans continue to pour carbon dioxide and other greenhouse gases into the atmosphere, there is little reason to believe this trend will be reversed in the near future.

In the aftermath of Katrina, government, the media, and Americans across the country debated what could be done to prevent similar disasters in the future. These discussions largely focused on infrastructure, preparedness, and emergency services. However, it would be wrong to overlook the human role in creating hurricanes in the first place. While there is no scientific link between global warming and Katrina specifically, science does suggest that global warming might make storms like Katrina more common. Working to ensure that there is never another Katrina should also mean working to reduce human effects on the Earth's atmosphere.

----------------------------------[new page]----------------------------------

References

1. Knabb RD, Rhome JR, Brown DP. Tropical cyclone report Hurricane Katrina 23–30 August 2005 [Internet]. Miami (FL): National Hurricane Center (US); c2005 Dec 20 [updated 2006 Aug 10; cited 2008 Apr 29]. Available from: http://www.nhc. noaa.gov/pdf/TCR-AL122005_Katrina.pdf

2. Thompson, I. High winds blow the roof off Backyard Barbeque in Kenner, LA. Dallas Morning News [Internet]. 2005 Aug 29 [cited 2008 Apr 29]. Available from: http://www.dallasnews. com/s/dws/spe/2006/pulitzer

Evidence for prediction.

Issue of global warming placed in context of broader debate about hurricanes.

Conclusion stated succinctly.

Reference list follows CSE ciatation-sequence style and begins on a new page.

181

3. Brain M, Freudenrich C. How hurricanes work [Internet]. Atlanta (GA): HowStuffWorks; c2000 Aug 29 [cited 2008 Apr 29]. Available from: http://science.howstuffworks.com/ hurricane8.htm

4. Pew Center on Global Climate Change. Katrina and global warming [Internet]. Arlington (VA): Pew Center on Global Climate Change; [cited 2008 Apr 29]. Available from: http://www.pewclimate.org/specialreports/katrina.cfm

5. Rosenthal E, Revkin AC. Science panel calls global warming "unequivocal." New York Times [Internet]. 2007 Feb 3 [cited 2008 Apr 29]. Available from: http://www.nytimes.com/ 2007/02/03/science/earth/03climate.html?scp=4&59=global+ warming&st=nyt

6. Intergovernmental Panel on Climate Change. Globally aver-aged sea-surface temperature, according to three data centres: The UK Met Office (UKMO), the US National Center for Environmental Prediction (NCEP), and the US National Climatic Data Center (NCDC) [Internet]. Berlin (Germany): German Advisory Council on Climate Change; c2006 [cited 2008 Apr 29]. Available from: http://www.wbgu.de/wbgu_sn2006_ en/wbgu_sn2006_en_voll_2.html

7. Roach, J. Is global warming making hurricanes worse? National Geographic News [Internet]. Washington (DC): National Geographic Society; 2005 Aug 4 [cited 2008 Apr 29]. Available from: http://news.nationalgeographic.com/ news/2005/08/0804_050804_hurricanewarming.html

10 Arguments

In the college classroom and in ███
debate outside the classroom, a███
ment is a path of reasoning aimed at developing an assertion on an issue under debate. In this chapter, we look at how to construct an argument. Arguments often respond to the thinking of others, so we first look at how to evaluate an argument.

10a Understand the assignment.

In college, reasoned positions matter more than opinions based on personal feelings, and writing arguments is a way to form reasoned positions. When you write an argument paper, your purpose is not to win but to take part in a debate by stating and supporting your position on an issue. In addition to position papers, written arguments appear in various forms, including critiques, reviews, and proposals.

- **Critiques:** Critiques address the question "What is true?" A critique fairly summarizes another's position before either refuting or defending it. *Refutations* either expose the reasoning of the position as inadequate or present evidence that contradicts the position. In his response to Nat Hentoff's article "Misguided Multiculturalism" in Chapter 7, Ignacio Sanderson attempts to refute Hentoff's claims by identifying weaknesses in Hentoff's reasoning (*pp. 135–37*). Matt Shadwell's essay "Person of the Year" (*pp. 201–06*) refutes *Time* magazine's choice of "You" for this annual distinction. *Defenses* clarify the author's key terms and reasoning, present new arguments to support the position, and show that criticisms of the position are unreasonable or unconvincing.

- **Reviews:** Reviews address the question "What is good?" In a review, the writer evaluates an event, artifact, practice, or institution, judging by reasonable principles and criteria. Dale Jamieson's essay on pages 207–08 is an example of a review.

- **Proposals, or policy papers:** Proposals, sometimes called policy papers, address the question "What should be done?" They are designed to cause change in the world. Readers are encouraged to see the situation in a specific way, and to take action. The Council for Biotechnology's argument about genetically modified foods (*see pp. 209–12*) is an example of a proposal.

WRITING beyond COLLEGE

Arguments

Arguments are central to American democracy and its institutions of higher learning because they help create the common ground that is sometimes called public space. Fields inside and outside of the academy value reason and welcome arguments such as the following:

▪ The board of a national dietetic association publishes a position statement identifying obesity as a growing health problem that dieticians should be involved in preventing and treating.

▪ An art critic praises a museum's special exhibition of modern American paintings for its diversity and thematic coherence.

▪ A sociologist proposes four policies that he claims will improve the quality of life and socioeconomic prospects of people living in inner-city neighborhoods.

👁 **10b**   Learn how to evaluate verbal and visual arguments.

Three common ways to analyze verbal and visual arguments are (1) to concentrate on the type of reasoning the writer is using; (2) to question the logical relation of a writer's claims, grounds, and warrants, using the Toulmin method; and (3) to examine the ways an argument appeals to its audience.

1. Recognizing types of reasoning

Writers of arguments may use either inductive or deductive reasoning. When writers use **inductive reasoning,** they do not prove that the statements that make up the argument are true; instead they convince reasonable people that the argument's validity is probable by presenting **evidence** (facts and statistics, anecdotes, and expert opinions). When writers use **deductive reasoning,** they claim that a conclusion follows necessarily from a set of assertions, or **premises**— if the premises are true and the relationship between them is valid, the conclusion must be true.

Consider the following scenarios.

Inductive reasoning A journalism student writing for the school paper makes the following claim:

> As Saturday's game shows, the Buckeyes are on their way to winning the Big Ten title.

Reasoning inductively, the student presents a number of facts—her evidence—that support her claim but do not prove it conclusively:

FACT **1**	With three games remaining, the Buckeyes have a two-game lead over the second-place Badgers.
FACT **2**	The Buckeyes' final three opponents have a combined record of 10 wins and 17 losses.
FACT **3**	The Badgers lost their two star players to season-ending injuries last week.
FACT **4**	The Buckeyes' last three games will be played at home, where they are undefeated this season.

A reader would evaluate this student's argument by judging the quality of her evidence, using the criteria listed in the box on page 186.

Inductive reasoning is a key feature of the **scientific method.** Scientists gather data from experiments, surveys, and careful observations to formulate hypotheses that explain the data. Then they test their hypotheses by collecting additional information.

Deductive reasoning The basic structure of a deductive argument is the **syllogism.** It contains a **major premise,** or general statement; **minor premise,** or specific case; and conclusion, which follows when the general statement is applied to the specific case. Suppose the journalism student were writing about great baseball teams and made the following argument:

MAJOR PREMISE	Any baseball team that wins the World Series more than 25 times in 100 years is one of the greatest teams in history.
MINOR PREMISE	The New York Yankees have won the World Series more than 25 times in the past 100 years.
CONCLUSION	The New York Yankees are one of the greatest baseball teams in history.

This is a deductive argument: if the relationship between its premises is valid and both premises are true, the conclusion must be true. The conclusion must follow from the premises. For example, it is not accurate to say: "The train is late. Jane is late. Therefore, Jane must be on the train." However, if the train is late and Jane is on the train, Jane must be late.

If the logical relationship between the premises is valid, a reader must evaluate their truth. Do you think, for example, that the number of World Series wins is a proper measure of a team's greatness? If not,

185

Tips

Assessing Evidence in an Inductive Argument

- **Is it accurate?** Make sure that any facts presented as evidence are correct and not taken out of context.
- **Is it relevant?** Check to see if the evidence is clearly connected to the point being made.
- **Is it representative?** Make sure that the writer's conclusion is supported by evidence gathered from a sample that accurately reflects the larger population (for example, it has the same proportion of men and women, older and younger people, and so on). If the writer is using an example, make sure that the example is typical and not a unique situation.
- **Is it sufficient?** Evaluate whether there is enough evidence to satisfy questioning readers.

you could claim that the major premise is false and does not support the conclusion.

Deductive reasoning predominates in mathematics and philosophy and some other humanities disciplines. However, you should be alert to both types of reasoning in all your college courses and in your life.

2. Using the Toulmin method to analyze arguments

Philosopher Stephen Toulmin's analysis of arguments is based on claims (assertions about a topic), grounds (reasons and evidence), and warrants (assumptions or principles that link the grounds to the claims).

Consider the following sentence from an argument by a student:

The death penalty should be abolished because if it is not abolished, innocent people could be executed.

This example, like all logical arguments, has three facets:

CLAIM	The death penalty should be abolished.
GROUNDS	Innocent people could be executed (related stories and statistics).
WARRANT	It is not possible to be completely sure of a person's guilt.

1. **The argument makes a claim.** Also known as a *point* or a *thesis*, a **claim** makes an assertion about a topic. A strong claim responds to an issue of real interest to its audience, in terms that are clear and precise. It also allows for some uncertainty by including qualifying words such as *might* or *possibly,* or a

description of circumstances under which the claim is true.
A weak claim is merely a statement of fact or a statement that
few would argue with. Personal feelings are not debatable and
thus are not an appropriate claim for an argument.

WEAK CLAIMS   The death penalty is highly controversial.
The death penalty makes me sick.

2. **The argument presents grounds for the claim.**
Grounds consist of the reasons and evidence (facts and statistics, anecdotes, and expert opinion) that support the claim.
As grounds for the claim in the example, the student would
present stories and statistics related to innocent people being
executed. The box below should help you assess the evidence
supporting a claim.

3. **The argument depends on assumptions that link the
grounds to the claim.** When you analyze an argument,
be aware of the unstated assumptions, or **warrants,** that
underlie both the claim and the grounds that support it.
The warrants underlying the example argument against the
death penalty include the idea that it is wrong to execute
innocent people and that it is not possible to be completely
sure of a person's guilt. Warrants differ from discipline
to discipline and from one school of thought to another. If
you were studying the topic of bullfighting and its place
in Spanish society in a sociology course, for example, you
would probably make different arguments with different
warrants than would the writer of a literary analysis of
Ernest Hemingway's book about bullfighting, *Death in the
Afternoon.* You might argue that bullfighting serves as a safe
outlet for its fans' aggressive feelings. Your warrant would be

TYPES of EVIDENCE for CLAIMS

- **Facts and statistics:** Relevant, current facts and statistics
  can be persuasive support for a claim. People on different
  sides of an issue can interpret the same facts and statistics
  differently, however, or can cite different facts and statistics to
  prove their point.
- **Anecdotes:** An anecdote is a brief narrative used as an illustration to support a claim. Stories appeal to the emotions as
  well as to the intellect and can be very effective. Be especially
  careful to check anecdotes for logical fallacies (*see pp. 188–90*).
- **Expert opinion:** The views of authorities in a given field can
  also be powerful support for a claim. Check that the expert
  cited has proper credentials.

187

hat sports can have socially useful purposes. A more contro-
ersial warrant would be that it is acceptable to kill animals
or entertainment.

As you read the writing of others and as you write
yourself, look for unstated assumptions. What does the
reader have to assume to accept the reason and evidence
in support of the claim? Hidden assumptions sometimes
show **bias,** positive or negative inclinations that can
manipulate unwary readers. Assumptions also differ
across cultures.

3. Analyzing appeals

Arguments support claims by way of three types of appeals to readers, categorized by the Greek words **logos** (logic), **pathos** (emotions),
and **ethos** (character). reasoning

- **Logical appeals** offer facts, including statistics, as well as
  reasoning, such as the inductive and deductive arguments on
  pages 184–86.

- **Emotional appeals** engage an audience's feelings and
  invoke beliefs that the author and audience share.

- **Ethical appeals** present authors as fair and trustworthy,
  and they provide the testimony of experts.

Most arguments draw on all three appeals. A proposal for more nutritious school lunches might cite statistics about childhood obesity
(a logical appeal). The argument might address the audience's sense
of fairness by stating that all children deserve nourishing meals (an
emotional appeal). It might quote a doctor explaining that healthful
food aids concentration (an ethical appeal). When writing an argument, tailor the type and content of appeals to the appropriate audience. Administrators would appreciate logical appeals about the
affordability of nutritious lunches.

4. Avoiding fallacies

In their enthusiasm to make a point, writers sometimes commit
fallacies, or mistakes in reasoning. Fallacies also can be understood
as misuses of the three appeals. Learn to identify fallacies when you
read and to avoid them when you write.

Logical fallacies involve errors in the inductive and deductive reasoning processes discussed above:

- **Non sequitur:** A conclusion that does not logically follow
  from the evidence presented or one that is based on
  irrelevant evidence.

who default on their student loans have no
esponsibility. [*Students who default on loans
faced with high medical bills or prolonged
~nent.*]

`dence is an important tactic of argu-
.ence must be relevant. Non sequiturs
assumptions.

`hoc:` An argument that falsely
e thing happens after another, the
f the second event.

`a` and my headache went away;
`a` makes headaches go away. [*How
headache did not go away for

!escribe causes and effects in
en they oversimplify complex

~~~~~~**-contradiction:** An argument that contradicts itself.

EXAMPLE   No absolute statement can be true. [*The statement
           itself is an absolute.*]

▪ **Circular reasoning:** An argument that restates the point
  rather than supporting it with reasonable evidence.

EXAMPLE   The wealthy should pay more taxes because taxes
           should be higher for people with higher incomes.
           [*Why should wealthy people pay more taxes? The rest
           of the statement does not answer this question; it just
           restates the position.*]

Claims must be backed with evidence, which is missing here.

▪ **Begging the question:** A form of circular reasoning that
  assumes the truth of a questionable opinion.

EXAMPLE   The president's poor relationship with the military
           has weakened the armed forces. [*Does the president
           really have a poor relationship with the military?*]

Some claims contain assumptions that must be proven first.
The author of the above claim must first support the assertion
that the president has a poor relationship with the military.

189

▪ **Hasty generalization:** A conclusion based on inadequate evidence.

EXAMPLE It took me over an hour to find a parking spot downtown. Therefore, the city should build a new parking garage. [*Is this evidence enough to prove this very broad conclusion?*]

▪ **Sweeping generalization:** An overly broad statement made in absolute terms. When about a group of people, a sweeping generalization is a **stereotype.**

EXAMPLE College students are carefree. [*What about students who work to put themselves through school?*]

Legitimate generalizations must be based on evidence that is accurate, relevant, representative, and sufficient (*see the box on p. 186*).

▪ **Either/or fallacy:** The idea that a complicated issue can be resolved by resorting to one of only two options when in reality there are additional choices.

EXAMPLE Either the state legislature will raise taxes or our state's economy will falter. [*Are these really the only two possibilities?*]

Frequently, arguments consider different courses of action. Authors demonstrate their fairness by addressing a range of options.

Ethical fallacies undermine a writer's credibility by showing lack of fairness to opposing views and lack of expertise on the subject of the argument.

▪ **Ad hominem:** A personal attack on someone who disagrees with you rather than on the person's argument.

EXAMPLE The district attorney is a lazy political hack, so naturally she opposes streamlining the court system. [*Even if the district attorney usually supports her party's position, does that make her wrong about this issue?*]

This fallacy stops debate by ignoring the real issue.

▪ **Guilt by association:** Discrediting a person because of problems with that person's associates, friends, or family.

EXAMPLE Smith's friend has been convicted of fraud, so Smith cannot be trusted. [*Is Smith responsible for his friend's actions?*]

This tactic undermines an opponent's credibility and is based on a dubious assumption: if a person's associates are untrustworthy, that person is also untrustworthy.

▪ **False authority:** Presenting the testimony of an unqualified person to support a claim.

EXAMPLE   As the actor who plays Dr. Fine on *The Emergency Room,* I recommend this weight-loss drug because . . . [*Is an actor qualified to judge the benefits and dangers of a diet drug?*]

Although expert testimony can strengthen an argument, the person must be an authority on the subject in question. This fallacy frequently underlies celebrity endorsements of products.

Emotional fallacies stir readers' sympathy at the expense of their reasoning.

▪ **False analogy:** A comparison in which a surface similarity masks a significant difference.

EXAMPLE   Governments and businesses both work within a budget to accomplish their goals. Just as business must focus on the bottom line, so should government. [*Is the goal of government to make a profit? Does government instead have other, more important goals?*]

Analogies can enliven an argument and deepen an audience's understanding of a subject, provided the things being compared actually are similar.

▪ **Bandwagon:** An argument that depends on going along with the crowd, on the false assumption that truth can be determined by a popularity contest.

EXAMPLE   Everybody knows that Toni Morrison is preoccupied with the theme of death in her novels. [*How do we know that "everybody" agrees with this statement?*]

▪ **Red herring:** An argument that diverts attention from the true issue by concentrating on something irrelevant.

EXAMPLE   Hemingway's book *Death in the Afternoon* is unsuccessful because it glorifies the brutal sport of bullfighting. [*Why can't a book about a brutal sport be successful? The statement is irrelevant.*]

5. Reading visual arguments

Like written arguments, visual arguments support claims with reasons and evidence, rely on assumptions, and may contain fallacies. They make logical appeals, such as a graph of experimental data; emotional appeals, such as a photograph of a hungry child; and ethical appeals, such as a corporate logo (*see p. 188*). Like all written works, visual arguments are created by an author for an audience and to achieve a purpose, within a context. (*See Chapter 2, pp. 21–23.*)

Recall that Toulmin's system analyzes arguments based on the claims they make, the grounds (evidence and reasons) for those claims, and the warrants (underlying assumptions) that connect the grounds with the claims. (*See the explanation of Toulmin analysis on pp. 186–88.*) While these elements function similarly in verbal and visual arguments, unstated assumptions play a larger role in visual arguments because claims and grounds often are not stated explicitly.

Consider an example of Toulmin analysis of an image. A photograph of a politician with her family members makes a claim (She is a good public servant) and implicitly offers grounds (because she cares for her family). The warrant is that a person's family life indicates how she will perform in office. This may be a non sequitur (*see p. 188*).

Advertisements combine text and images to promote a product or message to an audience in a social context. They use the resources of visual design: type of image, position, color, light and shadows, fonts, and white space. (*See the questions on previewing a visual in Chapter 7, pp. 123–24 and the discussion of design in Chapter 6, pp. 105–12.*) The public-service ad below was developed by the nonprofit advocacy group Adbusters.

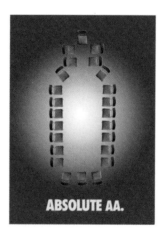

The ad's text and design evoke a popular series of ads for a brand of vodka. Its uncluttered design focuses the viewer's attention on the shape of a bottle, the outline of which consists of chairs. The text at the bottom refers to AA: Alcoholics Anonymous. By association, the text and images in this public-service ad remind readers that liquor can lead to alcoholism (and then to AA). In contrast with those it spoofs, this ad evokes an unexpected threat, creating a powerful emotional appeal.

What claims do you think this ad makes? One might be "alcohol is dangerous." The evidence is supplied by the reader's prior knowledge about alcoholism. The argument's assumptions include familiarity with both the original liquor campaign and the initials "AA" for Alcoholics Anonymous.

Fallacies frequently occur in visual arguments. For example, celebrity endorsements of products rely on our respect for the celebrity's character. However, an athlete's endorsement of a particular type of car is an example of false authority, unless she also happens to be an expert on cars. (*See p. 191.*)

✗✓ CHECKLIST

Reading Visual Arguments Critically

Review the questions for previewing a visual from Chapter 7, pages 123–24, and add the following:

☐ What can you tell about the visual's creator or sponsor?

☐ What seems to be the visual's purpose? Is a product or message promoted?

☐ Who do you think is the intended audience? What aspects of the visual suggest this audience? How?

☐ How do aspects of design such as size, position, color, and shape affect the visual's message?

☐ What is the effect of any text, audio, or video that accompanies the visual?

👁 **10c** Approach writing your own argument as a process.

www.mhhe.com/ mhhb2

For an interactive tutorial on writing arguments, go to

Writing > Writing Tutors > Arguments

Selecting a topic that you care about will give you the energy to think matters through and make cogent arguments. Of course, you will have to go beyond your personal emotions about an issue to make the most convincing case. You will also have to empathize with potential readers who may disagree with you about a subject that is important to you.

1. Figuring out what is at issue

Before you can take a position on a topic like air pollution or population growth, you must figure out what is at issue. Ask questions about your topic. Are there indications that all is not as it should be? Have things always been this way, or have they changed for the worse? From what different perspectives—economic, social, political, cultural, medical, geographic—can problems like world food shortages be understood? Do people interested in the topic disagree about what is true, what is good, or what should be done?

Based on your answers to such questions, identify the issues your topic raises. Then decide which of those issues is most important, interesting, and appropriate to write about in response to your assignment.

2. Developing a reasonable stance that negotiates differences

When writing arguments, you want your readers to respect your intelligence and trust your judgment. By getting readers to trust your character, you build **ethos.** Conducting research on your issue can make you well informed; reading other people's views and thinking critically about them can enhance your thoughtfulness. Pay attention to the places where you disagree with other people's views, but also note what you have in common—topical interests, key questions, or underlying values. (*For more on appeals to your audience, see p. 198.*)

Avoid language that may promote prejudice or fear. Misrepresentations of other people's ideas are out of place, as are personal attacks on their character. Write arguments to open minds; do not slam doors shut. (*See the box on blogs on p. 195.*)

Trying out different perspectives can also help you figure out where you stand on an issue. (*Also see the next section on stating your position.*) Make a list of the arguments for and against a specific position; then compare the lists and decide where you stand. Does one set of arguments seem stronger than the other? Do you want to change or qualify your initial position?

3. Making a strong claim

A successful argument requires a strong, engaging, arguable thesis. As noted in the section on the Toulmin model of argument, personal feelings and accepted facts cannot serve as an argument's thesis because they are not debatable (*see 10b, pp. 186–87*).

PERSONAL FEELING, NOT A DEBATABLE THESIS

I feel that developing nations should not suffer food shortages.

ACCEPTED FACT, NOT A DEBATABLE THESIS

Food shortages are increasing in many developing nations.

Blogs

Blogs frequently function as vehicles for public debate. For example, the online editions of many newspapers include blogs, which invite readers to comment on the news of the day and to present dissenting opinions. While online debate can be freewheeling, it is important to search for common ground with your readers. (*For more on blogs, see Chapter 14, pp. 244–47.*)

Looking at blogs can help you learn about an issue or find common counterarguments to your position. (*See Chapter 16, pp. 278–80.*) However, evaluate blogs carefully before using them as support for an argument (*see Chapter 18, pp. 291–98*). Many blogs rely heavily on personal opinion, and some may not receive careful editing for factual accuracy.

DEBATABLE THESIS

Current food shortages in developing nations are in large part due to climate change and the use of food crops in biofuels.

In proposals and policy papers, the thesis presents a solution in terms of the writer's definition of the problem. The logic behind a thesis for a proposal can be stated like this:

Given these key variables and their underlying cause, one solution to the problem would be . . .

Because this kind of thesis is both complex and qualified, you will often need more than one sentence to state it clearly. You will also need numerous well-supported arguments to make it creditable. Readers will finally want to know that the proposed solution will not cause worse problems than it solves.

4. Supporting and developing your claim

A strong, debatable thesis needs to be supported and developed with sound reasoning and carefully documented evidence. You can think of an argument as a dialogue between writer and readers. A writer states a debatable thesis, and one reader wonders, "Why do you believe that?" Another reader wants to know, "But what about this factor?" Writers need to anticipate readers' questions and answer them by presenting reasons that are substantiated with evidence and by refuting opposing views. They should also be sure to define any abstract terms, such as *freedom*, that figure importantly in their arguments. In his critique of *Time* magazine's choice of "You" for Person of the

Year, Matt Shadwell presents the magazine's definition of Person of the Year and sets out to prove that "You" does not meet these criteria (*pp. 201–06*).

Usually, a well-developed argument paper includes more than one type of reason and one kind of evidence. Besides generalizations based on empirical data or statistics, it often includes authoritative reasons based on the opinions of experts and ethical reasons based on the application of principle. In his paper, Shadwell presents facts about the passivity of *YouTube* users, citing the percentage who contribute information at only 0.07 percent. He also quotes an expert commentator, Frank Rich, who points out that Internet users prefer sites about celebrities to sites that focus on world events (*see p. 204*). In addition, he presents the anecdotal example of an average user, demonstrating that her actions are far from revolutionary. As you conduct research for your argument, note evidence—facts, examples or anecdotes, and expert testimony—that can support each argument for or against your position. Demonstrate your trustworthiness by properly quoting and documenting the information you have gathered from your sources.

Also build your credibility by paying attention to **counterarguments,** substantiated claims that do not support your position. Consider whether a reader could reasonably draw different conclusions from your evidence or disagree with your assumptions. Use the following strategies to take the most important ones into account:

- Qualify your thesis in light of the counterargument by including a word such as *most, some, usually,* or *likely:* "Students with credit cards *usually* have trouble with debt" recognizes that some do not.

- Add to the thesis a statement of the conditions for or exceptions to your position: "Businesses *with over five hundred employees* will save money using the new process."

- Choose one or two counterarguments and refute their truth or their importance.

Introduce a counterargument with a signal phrase like, "Others might contend . . ." (*See Part 3: Researching, p. 330 for a discussion of signal phrases.*) Refute a counterargument's validity by questioning the author's interpretation of the evidence or the author's assumptions. Shadwell refutes the counterargument that passive users of the Internet should be honored as "Person of the Year." He also suggests that the editors of *Time* have assumed that all Internet users create content, and he shows this is not the case.

www.mhhe.com/
mhhb2
For more help with creating an outline, go to

Writing >
Paragraph/Essay
Development >
Outlines

5. Creating an outline that includes a linked set of reasons
Arguments are most effective when they present a chain—a linked set—of reasons. Shadwell presents evidence first and builds to his

thesis at the end of his critique. Although there are multiple ways to order an argument, your outline should include the following parts (arranged below according to **classical structure**):

- An introduction to the topic and the debatable issue, establishing your credibility and seeking common ground with your readers
- A thesis stating your position on the issue
- A point-by-point account of the reasons for your position, including evidence (facts, examples, authorities) to substantiate each major reason
- A fair presentation and refutation of one or two key counterarguments
- A response to the "So what?" question. Why does your argument matter? If appropriate, include a call to action.

If you expect your audience to disagree with you, consider using a **Rogerian structure**:

- An introduction to the topic and the debatable issue
- An attempt to reach common ground by naming values you share and providing a sympathetic portrayal of your readers' (opposing) position
- A statement of your position and presentation of supporting evidence
- A conclusion that restates your view and suggests a compromise or synthesis

(See p. 198 for information on Rogerian argument.)

6. Appealing to your audience

You want your readers to see you as *reasonable, ethical,* and *empathetic*—qualities that promote communication among people who have differences. You display the quality of your logos, ethos, and pathos by the way that you argue for what you believe. (*For more on the classical appeals, see p. 188.*)

Logical appeals include giving reasons and supplying evidence for your position; you also establish your logos when you avoid fallacies. (*For more on fallacies, see pp. 188–91.*) Ethical appeals demonstrate that you are sincere and fair-minded; you build ethos by respecting those who do not share your viewpoint and by avoiding sarcasm and biased language. Emotional appeals show that you care deeply about your thesis and seek to win the hearts of your audience; you may infuse your argument with pathos by relating a compelling anecdote, a memorable quotation, or a concrete description.

When you read your argument, pay attention to the impression you are making. Ask yourself these questions:

- Would a reasonable person be able to follow the logic of the reasons and evidence I offer in support of my thesis?
- Have I presented myself as ethical and fair? What would readers who have never met me think of me after reading what I have to say?
- Have I expressed my feelings about the issue? Have I sought to arouse the reader's feelings?

www.mhhe.com/
mhhb2
For more on crafting
introductions, go to

Writing >
Paragraph/Essay
Development >
Introductions

7. Emphasizing your commitment to dialogue

To promote dialogue with readers, look for common ground—beliefs, concerns, and values you share with those who disagree with you and those who are undecided. Sometimes called **Rogerian argument** after the psychologist Carl Rogers, the common-ground approach is particularly important in your introduction, where it can build bridges with readers who might otherwise become too defensive or annoyed to read further. For example, Dale Jamieson opens his review of a book on Charles Darwin (*p. 207*) by acknowledging the controversy over Darwin's theories. (*See p. 197 for the structure of a Rogerian argument.*)

Keep the dialogue open throughout your essay by maintaining an objective tone and acknowledging opposing views. If possible, point out ways in which your position would be advantageous for both sides (a **win-win solution**). At the end of your argument, leave a favorable impression by referring again to common ground.

8. Concluding by restating your position and emphasizing its importance

Bring your argument to a close by restating your position. The version of your thesis that you present in your conclusion should be more complex and qualified than in your introduction, to encourage readers to appreciate your argument's importance. Readers may not agree with you, but they should know why the issue and your argument matter.

9. Using visuals in your argument

Consider including visuals that support your argument's purpose. Each should relate directly to your argument as a whole or to a point within it. For example, Matt Shadwell takes the cover of *Time* magazine as the subject of his argument, refuting its message. (*See p. 202.*) Visuals also may provide evidence: a photograph can

illustrate an example, and a graph can present statistics t[...]
port an argument.

Visual evidence makes emotional, logical, and ethical [...]
The Absolute AA ad on page 192 makes an emotional appeal by sub-
stituting a warning against alcoholism for the expected commercial message. The graph of Amazon deforestation rates in Audrey
Galeano's paper (*Chapter 24: APA Documentation Style, p. 415*)
makes a logical appeal by presenting evidence that supports her
claim. It also demonstrates the depth of her research (building her
ethos).

Consider how your audience is likely to react to your visuals.
Nonspecialists will need more explanation of charts, graphs, and
other visuals. When possible, have members of your target audience
review your argument and visuals. Help them interpret your visuals
with specific captions that describe each visual and how it supports
your argument. Mention each image in your text. Make sure charts
and graphs are free of distortion or chartjunk (*see Chapter 5: Revising
and Editing, p. 91*). Also acknowledge any data from other sources
and obtain permission when needed. (*See also Chapter 17: Finding
and Creating Visuals, pp. 281–89.*)

10. Reexamining your reasoning

After you have completed the first draft of your paper, take time to
reexamine your reasoning. Step outside yourself and assess your argument objectively. Peer review is also an essential tool for developing critical thinking and writing skills. Use the checklist "Self/Peer
Review of Argument" on page 200 to assess your own arguments and
those of your classmates.

For MULTILINGUAL STUDENTS

*Learning about Cultural Differences through
Peer Review*

U.S. culture encourages writing direct and explicit arguments,
while some other cultures do not. When you share your work
with peers born and raised in the United States, you may learn
that the vocabulary or the style of presentation you have used
makes it difficult for them to understand your point. They may
want you to be more direct. Ask your peers to suggest different
words and approaches. Then decide whether their suggestions
will make your ideas more accessible to others.

CHECKLIST

Self/Peer Review of Argument

☐ **What makes the thesis strong and arguable?**

☐ **Does the essay give a sufficient number of reasons to support its thesis, or does it need one or two more?**

☐ **Are the reasons and evidence suitable for the purpose and audience?**

☐ **Does the argument contain mistakes in logic?** Refer to pages 188–90 to check for logical fallacies.

☐ **How does the essay develop each reason it presents in support of the thesis?** Is the reason clear? Where are its key terms defined? Is the supporting evidence sufficient? Does the argument quote or paraphrase from sources accurately and document them properly? (*For more on quoting, paraphrasing, and documenting sources, see Part 3: Researching, and Part 4: Documenting across the Curriculum.*)

☐ **How does the essay address at least one significant counterargument?** How does it treat opposing views?

☐ **In what way does each visual support the thesis?** How are the visuals tailored to the audience?

☐ **Are logical and emotional appeals consistent?**

www.mhhe.com/ mhhb2

For more samples of argument papers, go to

Writing >
Writing Samples >
Argument Papers

10d Construct arguments to address issues in the social sciences

In the following critique, Matt Shadwell argues that the editors of *Time* magazine made a poor choice in designating "You" as Person of the Year. As you read Shadwell's argument, notice how he defines criteria of accomplishment and then shows that "You" does not fit those standards. In critiquing the *Time* magazine cover, he is also criticizing the passivity of Internet users, refuting the cover's basic claim that "You" are actively engaged in a "flat" world through surfing and blogging.

> *Note:* For details on the proper formatting of a paper in APA style, see Chapter 24 and the sample paper that begins on page 412.

Sample student argument paper

Person of the Year

Matt Shadwell

Communications 110

Professor Bianco

March 11, 2008

Following APA style, Shadwell includes a separate title page. His instructor did not require an abstract for this assignment.

----------------------------[new page]------------------------------------

Time magazine's Persons of the Year have ranged from celebrities, politicians, religious leaders, and humanitarians to more inclusive or abstract selections such as "the American Soldier," "the Peacemakers," and "Endangered Earth." The rationale for selection has varied as widely as the character of its "persons." The Man of the Year in 1938, Adolf Hitler, was chosen for the singular power of his personality and the scale of his terrifying accomplishments; on the other hand, "U.S. Scientists" were named collectively in 1960 for affecting "the life of every human presently inhabiting the planet" through a long list of breakthroughs including the discovery of DNA. In its eighty-year retrospective of this annual cover story, *Time* states that the recognition is "bestowed by the editors on the person or persons who most affected the news and our lives, for good or ill, and embodied what was important about the year." It is therefore baffling to consider *Time's* 2006 honoree, "You" (see Figure 1).

According to the 2006 Person of the Year cover story, the world's boundaries have been broken and its people have united via the Internet. People are flocking to social networking and content-sharing sites like *MySpace* and *YouTube* to broadcast programming and information to millions worldwide. Access to potentially enormous audiences is simpler and more widely available than ever, and *Time's* editors admiringly note that people are finding more uses for this broad public forum every day. Lev Grossman (2006), author of the cover story, wrote:

> Who are these people? Seriously, who actually sits
> down after a long day at work and says, I'm not going to
> watch *Lost* tonight. I'm going to turn on my computer and

Lively beginning inviting readers to consider other Person of the Year choices, including those selected for evil accomplishments.

Topic introduced

201

make a movie starring my pet iguana. I'm going to mash up 50 Cent's vocals with Queen's instrumentals? I'm going to blog about my state of mind or the state of the nation or the steak-frites at the new bistro down the street? Who has that time and energy and passion? The answer is, you do. (para. 3)

Since *Time* is honoring "You" for this achievement, it seems worthwhile to question who precisely the magazine's editors are referring to. In conferring responsibility for this revolution in the control and flow of information, does *Time* mean to honor each and every person in the world who surfed the Internet in 2006, or just the comparatively small number of computer savvy individuals who produced mass quantities of text, film, music, etc. online? At the beginning of "What Is the 1% Rule?" Charles Arthur (2006) wrote that "if you get a group of 100 people online then one will create content, 10 will 'interact' with it (commenting or offering improvements) and the other 89 will just view it" (para. 1). To illustrate the "One Percent Rule," examine the statistics of uploading and downloading content on *YouTube*. According to Antony Mayfield (2006), *YouTube's* hundreds of millions of daily downloads (passive viewings) outnumber its uploads (posting of content) by a margin of 1,538 to 1. That means that the percentage of users on *YouTube* who contribute information is about 0.07 percent—a good deal less than the One Percent Rule would predict. "You" would therefore seem a rather generous way to describe a relatively small number of people.

Alternatively, one might suppose the magazine truly wishes to honor the vast numbers of passive users as well. This, too, seems ill-conceived. Consider a typical Internet user. He or she accesses the Web daily, visiting sites such as *YouTube* on a regular basis. On social networking sites such as *MySpace* and *Facebook*, the user maintains a profile to stay in touch with friends, occasionally adding photos, sending out notices, or posting entries on a blog. Sites like these offer a degree of self-expression through personalized page designs (including music, images, and sometimes

Margin notes:

Presents *Time* magazine's position fairly via an engaging quote.

Poses key question about article's claim.

Presents factual evidence to support point.

Presents and refutes counter-argument.

video); they also typically allow users to control access to their sites, enabling them to designate certain features or their profile at large as either public, private, or selectively public (meaning only visitors designated as "friends" can look at the features).

As novel as such activities may seem to the tens of millions of people who visit such sites daily, it is difficult to see how pasting a *YouTube* video on a *MySpace* profile deserves recognition for "seizing the reins of the global media, for founding and framing the new digital democracy, for working for nothing and beating the pros at their own game" (Grossman, 2006). If *Time* means to include everyone who uses the Internet in their profile, then the editors are simply congratulating people for becoming more eager consumers of an emerging technological market. This is like honoring "Cable TV Viewers" for changing the face of television, or "Hybrid Car Buyers" for revolutionizing the auto industry.

One wonders if the magazine isn't actually expressing wonder over the technology itself, much as it did when it honored "the Computer" in 1982. Since the Internet itself is nothing new, one can only assume *Time*'s editors are terrifically impressed by new applications of existing technology. Web sites such as *YouTube*, which essentially are do-it-yourself video outlets, are visited by millions of viewers every day; but is their content as significant or groundbreaking as the *Time* article seems to claim, or do such sites and their content exist mostly to entertain? Some have argued that the availability of footage from the Iraq war typifies the potential informative power of online video sites. Certainly, in an era in which the Pentagon limits media access to military funerals (Tapper, 2007), and official reports of civilian casualties remain haphazard (and often contradictory), one can argue for the value of access to footage taken by American soldiers and Iraqi civilians in the war zone. Unfortunately, access to information does not necessarily equal interest. *The New York Times* columnist Frank Rich (2006) wrote that a typical Internet search showed that "Britney Spears Nude on Beach" received over a million hits by *YouTube's*

Compelling critique of *Time's* editors for being swayed by novelty of new Internet applications.

Uses expert testimony to support critique.

203

visitors, while "Iraq" clips were viewed by a little over 20,000 users. It would seem, then, that online media exists primarily for entertainment. And it is difficult to see how watching 15-second clips of *I Love Lucy* or montages of Rocky Marciano's knockout punches changes the world for better or worse.

Likewise, *Time*'s assertion that *YouTube* serves as a powerful mirror into the life of the typical American seems overstated. Grossman claimed that "you can learn more about how Americans live just by looking at the backgrounds of *YouTube* videos—those rumpled bedrooms and toy-strewn basement recreation rooms—than you could from 1,000 hours of network television" (2006, para. 5). Is it revelatory to learn that many people keep messy homes? Also, it must be remembered that an individual's control over content can prevent these glimpses into people's everyday lives from being truly spontaneous or accurate. The person behind the camcorder controls what he or she wants us to see.

Finally, it should be noted that while the Internet has certainly made more information instantly available than ever before, in many countries this access falls under government control. In China, for example, search engines such as *Google* have been forced to purge links to any Web sites disapproved of by the government. As a result, it is difficult for the typical Chinese Internet user to find information about Tibet, student protests, or dissident groups such as Falun Gong (Thompson, 2006, para. 5). In the United States, legislation such as the Child Online Protection Act of 1998 has sought to punish online providers of sexually explicit material (American Civil Liberties Union, 2007). Though such laws have been repeatedly struck down by the Supreme Court due to First Amendment concerns, many Web sites, including *MySpace* and *YouTube*, voluntarily police content that its administrators or users identify as explicit or otherwise objectionable. How can one accept the claim that "You" have taken control of the flow of information when governments and service providers still have ultimate power over what is and isn't seen?

Refutes *Time*'s secondary argument that *YouTube* videos reveal 21st century lives.

Refutes claim that "You" are in control of informatin.

It would be difficult to identify single figures who dominated the events of 2006; rather, the continuing conflicts in Iraq and Afghanistan, the deepening diplomatic crises surrounding the nuclear ambitions of North Korea and Iran, and the sudden reversals of political fortunes in Washington all involved numerous individuals, many of them anonymous, slogging through complex issues that are difficult to characterize in a simple way. Perhaps this is the best explanation for *Time* magazine's baffling choice for Person of the Year. It does seem, however, that the rationale for the selection lacks reason, clarity, or meaning. For good or ill, a Person of the Year should actually have accomplished something significant. *Time*'s "You" has not really done so.

----------------------------[new page]-----------------------------------

References

American Civil Liberties Union. (2007, March 22). *ACLU victorious in defense of online free speech* [Press release]. Retrieved from http://www.aclu.org/freespeech/internet/29138prs20070322 .html

Arthur, C. (2006, July 20). What is the 1% rule? *Guardian Unlimited*. Retrieved from http://guardian.co.uk

Grossman, L. (2006, December 13). Time's person of the year: You. *Time*. Retrieved from http://www.time.com

Hochstein, A. (Artist), & Jones, S. (Photographer). (2006, December 25). [Cover of *Time* announcing Person of the Year]. *Time*. Retrieved from http://www.time.com

Mayfield, A. (2006, July 17). 0–60% in under 18 months: *YouTube* dominates online video [Web log message]. Retrieved from http://www.antonymayfield.com/2006/07/17/0-60-in -under-18-months-youtube-dominates-online-video/

Rich, F. (2006, December 24). Yes, you are the person of the year. *The New York Times*. Retrieved from http://nytimes.com

Tapper, J. (2007, November 14). *Pentagon limits media coverage of funerals*. Retrieved from ABC News Online website: http:// abcnews.go.com/WNT/story?id=131450&page=1

Establishes common ground: acknowledges the difficulty of selecting a Person of the Year.

Full statement of thesis refuting the choice.

Underlines the critique's importance: *Time*'s choice misleads readers.

References list begins on a new page and is formatted according to APA style.

Thompson, C. (2006, April 23). Google's China problem (and

China's Google problem). *The New York Times Magazine.*

Retrieved from http://www.nytimes.com

Time's person of the year from 1927 to 2006. (2007,

November 8). *Time.* Retrieved from http://www.time.com

----------------------------[new page]-----------------------------------

Figure 1. Cover of *Time* announcing Person of the Year, December 25, 2006. Retrieved from http://www.time.com

www.mhhe.com/
mhhb2
For online resources
in various disciplines,
go to

Links across the
Curriculum

10e Construct arguments to address issues
in the humanities.

Reviews are arguments in the sense that they involve making principled claims about a specific book or performance. The following review essay by philosopher Dale Jamieson evaluates arguments in a book by another philosopher, James Rachels, and then evaluates the merits of the book overall.

Sample review essay

The Morality of Species

Dale Jamieson

> [A review of] *Created from Animals: The Moral Implications of Darwinism.* By James Rachels. Oxford: Oxford University Press, 1990. 245 pp. $19.95 cloth.

Poor Charles Darwin. For fundamentalists he is the Great Satan, for Social Darwinists the Great Liberator, and for academics, the stuff of dissertations, books, and careers. The sickly gentleman from Downe is roundly loved, hated, reviled, and admired, mostly for bad reasons, by people who never read his books or misread them when they do. Like Matisse, who sometimes claimed forgeries as his own original artworks, Darwin was not always a good judge of what he brought forth: he thought that Spencer was "by far the greatest living philosopher in England: perhaps equal to any that have lived."

In this brilliant but readable book, James Rachels has done much in a few pages to recover the historical Darwin. Although only the first chapter is explicitly about Darwin, his spirit infuses the entire book. Rachels brings out the broadly consequentialist nature of Darwin's moral thinking, and quotes several remarkable passages in which Darwin looks forward to an age in which moral sympathy is "extended to all sentient beings" (p. 165). The Darwin that emerges is not just a biologist cum philosopher. He is also a curious boy, a casual student, an opponent of slavery, and a defender of science. One vignette is especially revealing. Shortly after Darwin's marriage to the devout Emma Wedgewood, who would be his wife for more than forty years, she wrote urging him to reconsider his views about religion. After Darwin's death this letter was found among his papers. Scrawled on the bottom were the words: "When I am dead, know how many times I have kissed and cried over this."

Rachels's first chapter, "Darwin's Discovery," vividly captures the spirit of Darwin's life and work. "How Evolution and Ethics Might Be Related" is a critical but sympathetic discussion of post-Darwinian attempts to connect evolution and ethics. Nodding toward Hume, Rachels rejects deductivist views about what the connection might be but goes on to claim that "Darwinism undermines traditional morality" (p. 97). Chapter three asks, "Must a Darwinian Be Skeptical about Religion?" Yes, is Rachels's answer. Although there is no logical incompatibility between Darwinism and theism, Darwinism "undermines religious belief by removing some of the grounds that previously supported it" (p. 127). "How Different Are Humans from Other Animals?" argues that although some humans are quite different from other animals, the differences are matters of degree rather than kind: "Darwinism leads inevitably to the abandonment of the idea of human dignity and the substitution of a different sort of ethic"

(p. 171). The final chapter, "Morality without the Idea That Humans Are Special," outlines that ethic. It is a view that Rachels calls "moral individualism" and it implies the rejection of speciesism in all its forms.

People who make their living fighting over arguments and texts will find much to quarrel with in Rachels's book. No doubt scholars have found other ways of reading Darwin. Not all moral philosophers will be enamored of Rachels's "moral individualism." I myself would have liked to hear more about the relation of "undermining," and I somehow missed the move from the claim that the value of a life is the value that it has to its subject, to the claim that "the more complex their lives are, the greater the objection to destroying them" (p. 209). Nor is it clear how much weight the distinction between differences of degree and differences of kind can bear: contemplate the difference between the bald and the hirsute. In its treatment of texts, claims, and arguments this book is very good, but Rachels's real accomplishment lies elsewhere.

What Rachels has given us is a framework (a "narrative," as a postmodernist might say) that makes sense of much of the debate in recent moral philosophy, especially in such areas as medical and environmental ethics. What we are witnessing, more than a century after the publication of Darwin's *Origin*, is moral change occasioned by the belated impact of the Darwinian perspective.

Rachels describes moral change in the following way. In the first stage a moral outlook "is supported by a world-view in which everyone . . . has confidence" (p. 221). In the second stage the world-view begins to break up. According to Rachels the "old morality" of human uniqueness and dignity was supported by a world-view with the earth at its center, a specially created home for humans who were made in God's image, with animals given to humans to use as they please. Although this world-view was under attack long before Darwin, it was he who struck the death blow by showing that humans and animals are both products of purposeless natural processes, and indeed are kin. According to Rachels we are now in the third stage of moral change, in which the old morality is no longer taken for granted. It is widely agreed that it requires defense. The fourth stage is one in which a new morality emerges, one that is at home with our best understandings of ourselves and our relation to the world. If Rachels is right, much of this new morality is implicit in Darwin's own thought.

Rachels has given us an important book that provides a new perspective on what we are doing in moral philosophy. It is well written, well argued, and well researched. It deserves a very wide readership.

10f   Construct arguments to address issues in the sciences.

Scientists are called upon to evaluate the research of others and to argue for changes in policy. In the following essay by the Council for Biotechnology Information, the authors argue that biotech crops offer a solution to a looming crisis in food production.

Sample policy paper

Growing More Food*

Council for Biotechnology Information

The world's population more than doubled in the last half century and topped 6 billion in 1999.[1] Each year, it is adding about 73 million people—a population nearly the size of Vietnam's. By 2030, it is projected to reach around 8 billion, and nearly all of that increase is expected to occur in developing countries,[2] which are also expected to see higher incomes and rapid urbanization.

At the same time, the world's hungry and chronically malnourished remain at about 840 million people, despite global pledges and national efforts to improve food security.

These trends mean the world will have to double its food production and also improve food distribution over the next quarter century.[3] These pose staggering challenges for the world's farmers: Much of the world's land suitable for farming is already cultivated and natural resources are under pressure. Soil degradation is widespread, agriculture has already razed 20 to 30 percent of the world's forest areas[4] and water tables in many areas are falling. Agriculture consumes about 70 percent of the fresh water people use every year and, at the current consumption rate, two out of three people will live in water-stressed conditions by 2025.[5]

By 2050, some 4.2 billion people may not have their daily basic needs met.[6]

These projections and complex challenges facing the world's future food supply are prompting international food and agricultural experts and policymakers—including the U.N. Food and Agriculture Organization and the World Health Organization—to call plant biotechnology a critical tool to help feed a growing population in the 21st century.

Governments need to develop policies to ensure greater investment in research and regulatory oversight that's needed to manage the health, environmental and socioeconomic issues associated with biotechnology, according to the Human Development Report 2001, an annual report commissioned by the U.N. Development Programme.[7]

Biotechnology: An eco-efficient option

World crop productivity could increase by as much as 25 percent[8] through the use of biotechnology to grow plants that resist pests and diseases, tolerate harsh growing conditions and delay ripening to reduce spoilage, according to the Consultative Group on International Agricultural Research (CGIAR). All this could be achieved on existing farmland and customized to meet local needs.

---

*The documentation style used in this paper is that which appeared in the original and does not correspond fully to any of the styles discussed elsewhere in the handbook (*see Part 4: Documenting across the Curriculum*).

209

Biotechnology also offers the possibility for scientists to design "farming systems that are responsive to local needs and reflect sustainability requirements," said Calestous Juma, director of the Science, Technology and Innovation Program at the Center for International Development and senior research associate at the Belfer Center for Science and International Affairs, both at Harvard University.[9]

Scientists are developing crops that resist diseases, pests, viruses, bacteria and fungi, all of which reduce global production by more than 35 percent at a cost estimated at more than $200 billion a year.[10] For instance, test fields in Kenya are growing sweet potato varieties that are resistant to a complex set of viruses that can wipe out three-fourths of Kenyan farmers' harvest.

In the United States, crops with built-in insect protection and that tolerate a specific herbicide have helped farmers improve yields and reduce costs. In 2000, direct benefit to growers of insect resistant corn, cotton and potatoes exceeded $300 million, according to the Environmental Protection Agency.[11]

In a study to be released in 2002, the National Center for Food and Agricultural Policy quantified biotechnology's benefits for U.S. farmers through 44 case studies that covered 30 different crops, including papaya, citrus, soybeans and tomatoes. For instance, it found that herbicide tolerant soybeans helped farmers reduce their annual production costs by $15 an acre, which totals $735 million across 49 million acres. Virus-resistant papaya is credited with saving Hawaii's papaya industry, which produces 53 million pounds of the fruit valued at $17 million a year.[12]

Biotechnology: Getting the most from poor growing conditions

Scientists are developing crops that can tolerate extreme conditions, such as drought, flood and harsh soil. For instance, researchers are working on a rice that can survive long periods under water [13] as well as rice and corn that can tolerate aluminum in soil. [14]

A tomato plant has been developed to grow in salty water that is 50 times higher in salt content than conventional plants can tolerate and nearly half as salty as seawater.[15] About a third of the world's irrigated land has become useless to farmers because of high levels of accumulated salt.

Biotech crops "could significantly reduce malnutrition, which still affects more than 800 million people worldwide, and would be especially valuable for poor farmers working marginal lands in sub-Saharan Africa," the Human Development Report stated.

Technology in a seed

While the Green Revolution kept mass starvation at bay and saw global cereal production double as a result of improved crop varieties, fertilizers, pesticides and irrigation, its benefits bypassed such regions as sub-Saharan Africa. The new hybrids needed irrigation and chemical inputs that farmers there couldn't afford.

In contrast, the benefits of biotechnology are passed on through a seed or plant cutting, so that farmers anywhere around the world can easily adopt the technology. That's why biotechnology is particularly attractive to scientists and rural development experts in poor countries where most of the people farm for a living.

Biotech crops are "tailor-made for Africa's farmers, because the new technology is packaged in the seed, which all farmers know how to handle," said Florence Wambugu, a Kenyan plant scientist who helped develop a virus-resistant sweet potato.[16]

Agreeing with Wambugu, the International Society of African Scientists issued a statement in October 2001 calling plant biotechnology a "major opportunity to enhance the production of food crops."[17]

Notes

[1] United Nations Population Fund (UNFPA), "Population Numbers and Trends," <www.unfpa.org/modules/briefkit/05.htm>.

[2] International Food Policy Research Institute, "World Food Prospects: Critical Issues for the Early Twenty-First Century," October 1999, p. 9.

[3] United Nations Population Fund (UNFPA), "State of World Population 2001 Report," November 7, 2001, <www.unfpa.org/swp/swpmain.htm>.

[4] "New Study Reveals That Environmental Damage Threatens Future World Food Production," World Resources Institute, February 14, 2001, <www.wri.org/press/page_agroecosystems.html>.

[5] Global Environment Outlook, 2000—UN Environment Programme, <www.unep.org/geo2000/>.

[6] "State of World Population 2001 Report," United Nations Population Fund (UNFPA), November 7, 2001, <www.unfpa.org/swp/swpmain.htm>.

[7] "The Human Development Report 2001," United Nations Development Programme, July 2001, <www.undp.org/>.

[8] Prakash, C.S., (October 4, 2001). In a media presentation sponsored by the American Medical Association (AMA), cited Consultative Group on International Agricultural Research (CGIAR) as source. See <www.ama-assn.org> media briefings.

[9] Calestous, Juma, director of the Science, Technology and Innovation Program at the Center for International Development and senior research associate at the Belfer Center for Science and International Affairs, "Appropriate Technology for Sustainable Food Security—Modern Biotechnology," both at Harvard University, *2020 Focus 7*, International Food Policy Research Institute (IFPRI). August 2001.

[10] Krattiger, Anatole, "Food Biotechnology: Promising Havoc or Hope for the Poor?" Proteus, 2000.

[11] "Bt Plant-Pesticides Biopesticides Registration Action Document—Executive Summary," United States Environmental Protection Agency, <www.epa.gov/pesticides/biopesticides/otherdocs/bt_brad2/1 overview.pdf>.

[12] Gianessi, Leonard, (October 4, 2001). "The Potential for Biotechnology to Improve Crop Pest Management in the United States," In a media presentation sponsored by the American Medical Association (AMA). See www.ncfap.org and <www.ama-assn.org> media briefings.

[13] "Food in the 21st Century: From Science to Sustainable Agriculture," CGIAR, p. 36, <www.worldbank.org/html/cgiar/publications/shahbook/shahbook.pdf>.

[14] "Food in the 21st Century: From Science to Sustainable Agriculture," CGIAR, p. 36, <www.worldbank.org/html/cgiar/publications/shahbook/shahbook.pdf>

[15] Owens, Susan, "Genetic engineering may help to reclaim agricultural land lost due to salination," *European Molecular Biology Organization (EMBO) Reports 2001,* Vol. 2/No. 10, p. 877–879, <www.embo-reports.oupjournals.org/cgi/content/full/2/10/877>.

[16] "Biotech 'Tailor-Made' for Africa, Researcher Tells Tufts Conference," Council for Biotechnology Information, Washington, D.C., November 19, 2001 <index.asp?id=1156&redirect=con1309mid17%2E.html>.

[17] "Position Statement on Agricultural Biotechnology Applications in Africa and the Caribbean," International Society of African Scientists, <www.monsantoafrica.com/reports/ISAS/ISAS.html>.

11 Personal Essays

The personal essay is a literary form. Like a poem, a play, or a story, it should feel meaningful to readers and relevant to their lives. A personal essay should speak in a distinctive voice and be both compelling and memorable.

11a Understand the assignment.

When you write a personal essay, you are exploring your experiences, clarifying your values, and composing a public self. The focus, however, does not need to be on you. You might write a personal

WRITING beyond COLLEGE

Personal Essays

Doctors, social workers, nutritionists—as well as novelists—publish memoirs and personal essays based on their life's work.

- Gloria Ladson-Billings, a teacher, reflects on her experience in the classroom to figure out what makes teachers successful.
- Oliver Sacks, a neurologist, writes about his experiences with people whose perceptual patterns are impaired and about what it means to be fully human.

essay about a tree in autumn, a trip to Senegal, an encounter with a stranger, or an athletic event. The real topic is how these objects and experiences have become meaningful to you.

When we read a personal essay, we expect to learn more than the details of the writer's experience; we expect to see the connections between that experience and our own. You may decide to intensify, clarify, or complicate the reader's sense of things. But no matter what you intend, your point is likely to be more effective if it is not stated directly. The details you emphasize, the words you choose, and the characters you create all communicate your point implicitly without turning it into "the moral of the story."

1. The personal essay as conversation

Personal essayists usually use the first person (*I* and *we*) to create a sense that the writer and reader are engaged in the open-ended give-and-take of conversation. How you appear in this conversation—shy, belligerent, or friendly, for example—will be determined by the details you include in your essay, as well as the connotations of the words you use. Consider how Meghan Daum represents herself in relation to both computer-literate and computer-phobic readers in the following excerpt from her personal essay "Virtual Love," which appeared in a 1997 issue of the *New Yorker*:

> The kindness pouring forth from my computer screen was bizarrely exhilarating, and I logged off and thought about it for a few hours before writing back to express how flattered and "touched"—this was probably the first time I had ever used that word in earnest—I was by his message.
>
> I am not what most people would call a computer person. I have no interest in chat rooms, news groups, or most Web sites. I derive a palpable thrill from sticking a letter in the United States mail.

213

TEXTCONNEX

Personal Writing and Social Networking Web Sites

In addition to the personal essays you write for class, you may use Web sites like *Facebook* and *MySpace* for personal expression and autobiographical writing. Remember that these sites are networked, so you do not always know who is reading your information. Strangers, including prospective employers, often view people's profiles and make judgments.

Besides Daum's conversational stance, notice the emotional effect of her remark on the word *touched* and her choice of words connoting excitement: *pouring forth, exhilarating,* and *palpable thrill.*

2. The personal essay as a link between one person's experience and a larger issue

To demonstrate the significance of a personal essay to its readers, writers usually connect their individual experience to a larger issue. Here, for example, are the closing lines of Daum's essay on "virtual love":

> The world had proved to be too cluttered and too fast for us, too polluted to allow the thing we'd attempted through technology ever to grow on the earth. PFSlider and I had joined the angry and exhausted living. Even if we met on the street, we wouldn't recognize each other, our particular version of intimacy now obscured by the branches and bodies and falling debris that make up the physical world.

Notice how Daum relates the disappointment of her failed Internet romance with "PFSlider" to a larger social issue: the general contrast between cyberspace and material realities. Her point, however, is quite surprising; most people do not think of cyberspace as more "intimate"—or touching—than their everyday, earthly world of "branches and bodies."

11b Approach writing a personal essay as a process.

Shaping your private personal writing into a personal essay for a public audience can be challenging. The following suggestions should help.

1. Keeping a journal or a writer's notebook where you can practice putting your experience into words
Record your observations about meaningful objects (houses, photographs, personal treasures), memorable incidents and experiences (an encounter with a stranger, coming to the United States, winning and losing), and distinctive situations (living arrangements, social cliques, neighborhood conflicts) in a journal.

2. Thinking about the broader meaning of your topic when planning the focus of your essay
Readers will appreciate the significance of your individual experience only if you connect it with something more social or general. For example, if you are writing about a turning point in your life, think of your experience as a metaphor for what we gain and what we lose as we grow and change.

3. Structuring your essay like a story
There are three common ways to narrate events and reflections:

▪ **Chronological sequence** uses an order determined by clock time; what happened first is presented first, followed by what happened second, then third, and so on.

▪ **Emphatic sequence** uses an order determined by the point you want to make; for emphasis, events and reflections are arranged from either least to most important or from most to least important.

▪ **Suspenseful sequence** uses an order determined by the emotional effect the writer wants the essay to have on the reader. To keep the reader hanging, the essay may begin in the middle of things with a puzzling event, then flash back or go forward to clear things up. Some essays may even begin with the end—with the insight achieved—and then flash back to recount how the writer came to that insight.

4. Letting details tell your story
The story takes shape through details. The details you emphasize, the words you choose, and the characters you create communicate the point of your essay.
Consider, for example, the following passage by Gloria Ladson-Billings:

> Mrs. Harris, my third-grade teacher, was quite a sharp dresser. She wore beautiful high-heeled shoes. Sometimes she switched to flats in the afternoon if her feet got tired, but every morning began with the click, click, click of her high heels as she greeted us up and down the rows. I wanted

215

to dress the way Mrs. Harris did. I didn't want to wear old-lady comforters like Mrs. Benn's and I certainly didn't want to wear worn-out loafers like those of my first-grade teacher, Miss Schwartz. I wanted to wear beautiful, shiny, high-heeled shoes like Mrs. Harris's. That was the way a teacher should look, I thought.

Ladson-Billings uses details to make her idea of a good teacher come alive for the reader. At one level—the literal—the "click, click, click" refers to the sound of Mrs. Harris's shoes. At another level, it represents the glamorous teacher. At the most figurative level, the "click, click, click" evokes the feminine kind of power that the narrator both longs for and admires.

5. Using the present tense strategically

When writers tell stories about themselves, they often use the *past tense,* as if the experience were over and done with ("once upon a time"). This choice makes sense, but the *present tense* creates a sense of immediacy and helps make an essay vivid and memorable. Notice how the student writer of the following passage puts the reader inside the young girl's head by purposefully changing from the past to the present tense:

> As I was learning the switchboard, I caught my Dad watching me out of the corner of his eye. Hmm, I hope he doesn't think that I'm going to give him the satisfaction of not doing a good job. Yes, he's deprived me of my beach days with Joey. But I am on display here. And the switchboard is so vital to this office!

If they have good reason to do so, writers of personal essays may also sometimes take liberties with certain other conventions of grammar and style. Be sure you understand any rules you may be stretching, however, and if you are writing a personal essay for a class assignment, be sure your instructor will accept the results. Some instructors, for example, might object to the shift from past to present tense in the paragraph above (*see Chapter 41: Confusing Shifts*). Some also might object to the last two sentences in the paragraph because they begin with coordinating conjunctions (*but* and *and*).

12 Essay Exams

If you spend some time now thinking about what you are expected to do in an essay exam, you may feel less stress the next time you are faced with one.

12a Prepare to take an essay exam.

As you prepare for the exam, consider the specific course as your writing context and the course's instructor as your audience. The best preparation for any exam is to learn the course material. Review your notes and readings. Think about how your instructor approached and presented the course material.

- What questions or problems did your instructor explicitly or implicitly address?
- What frameworks did your instructor use to analyze topics?
- What key terms did your instructor repeatedly use during lectures and discussions?

Essay exams are designed to test your knowledge, not just your memory. Make up some essay questions that require you to:

- **Explain** what you have learned in a clear, well-organized way. (*See question 1 in the box on p. 218.*)
- **Connect** what you know about one topic with what you know about another topic. (*See question 2 in the box on p. 218.*)
- **Apply** what you have learned to a new situation. (*See question 3 in the box on p. 218.*)
- **Interpret** the causes, effects, meanings, value, or potential of something. (*See question 4 in the box on p. 218.*)
- **Argue** for or against some controversial statement about what you have learned. (*See question 5 in the box on p. 218.*)

12b Approach essay exams strategically.

1. Planning your time
At the beginning of the exam period, quickly look through the whole exam, and determine how much time to spend on each part or question. You will want to move as quickly as possible through the questions that have lower point values and spend the bulk of your time responding to the questions that are worth the greatest number of points.

CHARTING the TERRITORY

Essay Exam Questions across the Curriculum

During finals week, you may be asked to respond to essay questions like the following:

1. Discuss the power of the contemporary presidency as well as the limits of that power. [*from a political science course*]

2. Compare and contrast the treatment of labor supply decisions in the economic models proposed by Greg Lewis and Gary Becker. [*from an economics course*]

3. Describe the observations that would be made in an alpha-particle scattering experiment if (a) the nucleus of an atom were negatively charged and the protons occupied the empty space outside the nucleus and (b) the electrons were embedded in a positively charged sphere. [*from a chemistry course*]

4. Examine the uses of caesura and enjambment in the following poem, and analyze their effect on the poem's rhythm. [*from a literature course*]

5. In 1800, was Thomas Jefferson a dangerous radical? Be sure to define your key terms and to support your position with evidence from specific events, documents, and so on. [*from an American history course*]

2. Responding to short-answer questions by showing the significance of the information

The most common type of short-answer question is the identification question: Who or what is X? In answering questions of this sort, present just enough information to show that you understand X's significance within the context of the course. For example, if you are asked to identify "Judith Loftus" on an American literature exam, don't just write "character who knows Huckleberry Finn is a boy." Instead, craft one or two sentences that identify Loftus as a character Huckleberry Finn encounters while he is disguised as a girl; by telling Huck how she knows that he is not a girl, Loftus complicates the reader's understanding of gender.

3. Responding to essay questions tactically

Keep in mind that essay questions usually ask you to do something specific with a topic. Begin by determining precisely what you are being asked to do.

Before you write anything, read the question—all of it—and circle the key words:

(Explain two) ways in which Picasso's *Guernica* evokes war's terrifying (destructiveness.)

To answer this question, focus on two of the painting's features, such as coloring and composition, not on Picasso's life.

4. Using the question itself to structure your response
Usually, you will be able to transform the question itself into the thesis of your answer. If you are asked to agree/disagree with the Federalists' characterization of Thomas Jefferson in the election of 1800, you might begin with the following thesis:

> In the election of 1800, the Federalists characterized Jefferson as a dangerous radical. Although Jefferson's ideas were radical for the times, they were not dangerous to the republic.

Take a minute or two to list evidence for each of your main points, and then write the essay.

5. Drafting the essay
As you write, observe the relevant discipline's conventions of form and style. Using your notes, state your thesis and develop a paragraph for each point in your list. Leave space between lines to make additions and corrections after your draft is complete. If you get stuck trying to think of a term or fact, briefly describe it and go on; the specific words may come to you later. Conclude by succinctly stating how you have supported your thesis.

6. Checking your work
Leave a few minutes to read quickly through your completed answer. Is your thesis consistent with what you ended up writing? Is each point well supported? Also look for words you might have omitted or key sentences that make no sense. You can usually cross out incorrect words and sentences and make corrections neatly above the original line of text. Above all, ensure the essay demonstrates your knowledge of the subject.

Sample essay test responses
A student's response to an essay question in an art appreciation course begins on the following page. Both the question (*below*) and the student's notes (*p. 220*) are provided.

QUESTION
Both of these buildings (Figure 1 and Figure 2) feature dome construction. Identify the buildings, and discuss the differences in the visual effects created by the different dome styles.

FIGURE 1   **FIGURE 2**

STUDENT'S NOTES

Fig 1: Pantheon. Plain outside—concrete, can barely see dome. Dramatic inside—dome opens up huge interior space. Oculus to sky: light, air, rain. Coffered ceiling.

Fig 2: Taj Mahal. Dramatic exterior—dome set high, marble, reflecting pool, exterior lines go up. Inside not meant to be visited.

STUDENT'S ANSWER

Answers identification question and states thesis.

Key points supported by details.

Uses specialized terms from course.

Sets up comparison.

Key point supported by details.

Overall comparison as a brief conclusion.

   The Pantheon (Figure 1) and the Taj Mahal (Figure 2) are famous for their dome construction. The styles of the domes are dramatically different, however, resulting in dramatically different visual effects.

   The Pantheon, which was built by the Romans as a temple to the gods, looks very plain on the exterior. The dome is barely visible from the outside, and it is made of a dull grey concrete. Inside the building, however, the dome produces an amazing effect. It opens up a huge space within the building, unobstructed by interior supports. The sides of the dome are coffered, and those recessed rectangles both lessen the weight of the dome and add to its visual beauty. Most dramatically, the top of the dome is open to the sky, which allows sun or rain to pour into the building. This opening is called the oculus, meaning "eye" (to or of Heaven).

   The Taj Mahal, which was built by a Muslim emperor of India as a tomb for his wife, is the complete opposite of the Pantheon—dazzling on the outside and plain on the inside. The large central dome is set up high on the base so that it can be seen from far away. It is made of white marble, which reflects light beautifully. The dome is surrounded by other structures that frame it and draw attention to its exterior—a long reflecting pond and four minarets. Arches and smaller domes on the outside of the building repeat the large dome's shape. Because the Taj Mahal's dome is tall and narrow, however, it does not produce the kind of vast interior space of the shorter, squatter Pantheon dome. Indeed, the inside of the Taj Mahal is not meant to be visited. Unlike the Pantheon, the dome of the Taj Mahal is intended to be admired from the outside.

13 Oral Presentations

Preparing an oral presentation, like preparing any text, is a process. Consider your audience and purpose as you choose the focus and level of your topic. Gather information, decide on the main idea of your presentation, think through the organization, and choose visuals that support your points.

13a Plan and shape your oral presentation.

1. Considering the interests, background knowledge, and attitudes of your audience

Find out as much as you can about your listeners before you prepare the speech. What does the audience already think about your topic? Do you want to intensify your listeners' commitment to what they already think, provide new and clarifying information, provoke more analysis and understanding of the issue, or change what they believe about something?

If you are addressing an unfamiliar audience, ask the people who invited you to fill you in on the audience's interests and expectations. It is also possible to adjust your speech once you get in front of your audience, making your language more or less technical, for instance, or adding more examples to illustrate points.

2. Working within the allotted time

Gauge how many words you speak a minute by reading a passage aloud at a conversational pace (about 120–150 words a minute is ideal). Be sure to time your presentation when you practice it.

 ## 13b Draft your presentation with the rhetorical situation in mind.

www.mhhe.com/
mhhb2
For more on crafting
introductions, go to

Writing >
Paragraph/Essay
Development >
Introductions

1. Making your opening interesting

A strong opening both puts the speaker at ease and gains the audience's attention and confidence. Try out several approaches to your introduction during rehearsal, to see which get the best reactions. Stories, brief quotations, striking statistics, and surprising statements are attention getters. Or craft an introduction that lets your listeners know what they have to gain from your presentation—for example, new information or new perspectives on a subject of common interest.

2. Making the focus and organization of your presentation explicit

Select two or three ideas that you most want your audience to hear—and to remember. Preview the content of your presentation in a statement such as "I intend to make three points about fraternities on campus," and then list the three points.

The phrase "to make three points" signals a topical organization. Other common organizational patterns include chronological organization (*at first, later, in the end*), causal organization (*because of that, then this follows*), and problem-solution organization (*given the situation, then this set of proposals*). A question-answer format also works well, either as an overall strategy or as part of another organizational pattern.

3. Being direct

What your audience hears and remembers has as much to do with how you say your message as it does with what you say. Use a direct, simple style.

- Choose basic sentence structures.
- Repeat key terms.
- Pay attention to the rhythm of your speech.
- Don't be afraid to use the pronouns *I, you,* and *we.*

Notice how applying these principles transforms the following written sentence into a group of sentences appropriate for oral presentation:

WRITTEN

Although the claim that the position of the stars can help people predict the future has yet to be substantiated by either an ample body or an exemplary piece of empirical research, advocates of astrology persist in pressing the claim.

ORAL

Your sign says a lot about you. So say advocates of astrology. But what evidence do we have that the position of the stars helps people predict the future? Do we have lots of empirical research or even one really good study? The answer is, "Not yet."

www.mhhe.com/ mhhb2

For an interactive tutorial on using PowerPoint, go to

Writing > PowerPoint Tutorial

4. Using visual aids: Posters and presentation software

Slides, posters, objects, video clips, and music help make your focus explicit. Avoid oversimplifying your ideas to fit them on a slide, and make sure the images, videos, or music fit your purpose and audience.

When preparing a poster presentation, keep the poster simple with a clear title, bullets listing your key points, and images that support your purpose. Ensure text can be read from several feet away. *(For more on design principles, see Chapter 6: Designing Academic Papers and Preparing Portfolios, pp. 105–12.)*

Presentation software such as PowerPoint can help you stay focused while you are speaking. The twelve PowerPoint slides in Figure 13.1 below and on page 224 offer advice on how to design

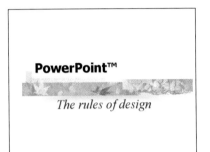
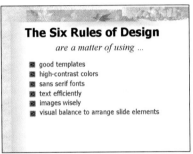

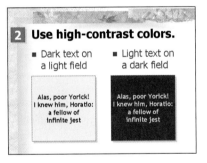
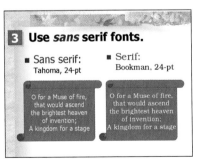
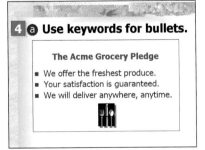

FIGURE 13.1 A sample PowerPoint presentation with advice on designing effective presentation slides.

223

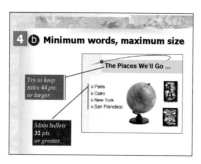

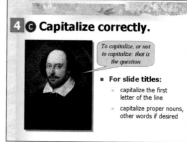

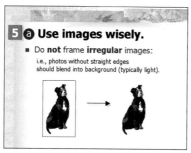

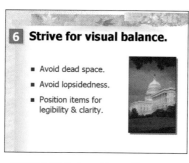

FIGURE 13.1 (*continued*)

effective slides for a presentation. (*For more on using presentation software see Chapter 14: Multimedia Writing, pp. 232–37*)

5. Concluding memorably

Try to make your ending truly memorable: return to that surprising opener, play with the words of your opening quotation, look at the initial image from another angle, or reflect on the story you have told. Use signal phrases such as "in conclusion" or "let me end by saying," if necessary. Keep your conclusion short to maintain the audience's attention.

TEXTCONNEX

Webcasts

Webcasts allow you to reach audiences anywhere in the world with an Internet connection. When you present a speech online, multimedia elements become even more important, particularly if your audience will not be able to see you. (*See Chapter 14: Multimedia Writing, pp. 232–37.*) Practice your presentation to ensure that you can access all necessary files easily. If your image will be broadcast, practice speaking into the camera or Webcam.

13c Prepare for your presentation.

1. Deciding whether to use notes or a written script

To be an effective speaker, make eye contact with your listeners; monitor their responses; and adjust what you say accordingly. For most occasions, it is inappropriate to write out everything you want to say and then read it word for word. Speak from an outline or notecards, and write out only those parts of your presentation where precise wording counts, such as quotations.

In some scholarly or formal settings, precise wording may be necessary, especially if your oral presentation is to be published or if your remarks will be quoted by others. Sometimes the setting for your presentation may be so formal or the audience may be so large that a script feels necessary. In such instances, do the following:

- Triple-space the typescript of your text.

- Avoid carrying sentences over from one page to another.

- Mark your manuscript for pauses, emphasis, and the pronunciation of proper names.

2. Rehearsing, revising, and polishing

Practice your presentation aloud. Adjust transitions that don't work, points that need further development, and sections that are too long.

After you have settled on the content of your speech and can project it comfortably, focus on polishing the style of your delivery. Video yourself or ask your friends to watch and listen to your rehearsal. Check that your body posture is straight but relaxed, that your voice is loud and clear, and that you are making eye contact around the room. Time your final rehearsals, adding or cutting as

225

necessary. If an on-site rehearsal is not possible, at least be sure to arrive at your presentation well in advance.

3. Accepting nervousness as normal

The adrenaline surge you feel before a presentation can invest your talk with positive energy. Practice and revise your presentation until it flows smoothly, and make sure that you have a strong opener to get you through the first, most difficult moments of a speech. Remember that other people cannot always tell that you are nervous.

14 Multimedia Writing

Multimedia writing combines words with images, video, or audio into a single composition. The most common form of multimedia writing—discussed in many chapters of this book—is a combination of words and still visuals such as photographs, maps, charts, or graphs. Another form is an oral presentation with any kind of visual support, from a diagram on a blackboard to a PowerPoint slide show (*see Chapter 13: Oral Presentations*). Digital technology also allows writers to create works that combine written words with sound, video, and animation. You probably have used social networking Web sites such as *Facebook* and *MySpace*, which let users integrate text, images, and other multimedia elements.

Like any form of composition, multimedia writing allows you to convey a message to a particular audience for a particular purpose: to inform, to interpret, or to persuade. A video or audio segment—like a photograph, map, or chart—must support the purpose of the writing in a way that is appropriate to the audience.

14a Learn about the tools for creating multimedia texts.

Multimedia writing can take a variety of forms and can be created with a variety of software tools. Here are a few options:

- Most word processors allow you to integrate still visuals with text in a single document, and many also make it possible to create a composition that permits readers to connect to various files—including audio, image, and video. (*See 14b and 14c.*)

- Most presentation software packages similarly allow you to accompany a presentation with audio and video files as well as still visuals. (*See 14d.*)

- A variety of programs and Web-based tools allow you to create your own **Web pages** and **Web sites,** which can include a wide range of multimedia features. (*See 14e.*)

- You can create a **weblog** (**blog**), on which, in addition to your written entries, you can post your multimedia files and links to files on other blogs and Web sites. You also can collaborate with other writers on a **Wiki**. (*See 14f.*)

☜ **14b** Combine text and images with a word-processing program to analyze images.

Two types of assignments you might be called on to write are image analyses and imaginary stories.

1. Composing image analyses

You may be called on to analyze a single image, such as a painting from a museum. In this case, your two tasks are to describe the picture as carefully as possible, using adjectives, comparisons, and words that help the reader focus on the picture and the details that compose it; and to analyze the *argument* the picture seems to be making.

Exercise 14.1 Image interpretations

1. In a local museum or on a museum Web site, find a painting created by an artist whose work is new to you. (Some examples of museum Web sites include http://www.moma.org/collection/ for the Museum of Modern Art (New York), http://www.artic.edu/ aic/ for the Art Institute of Chicago, and http://www.louvre.fr/ louvrea.htm for the Louvre in Paris.) Or you may wish to write about Breughel's *Fall of Icarus* on page 229.

    Take notes on your response to the painting, and write an initial analysis of it. As you do, consider the following:

   - Who or what is in the painting?
   - If there are people in the painting, are they active or passive? Rich or poor? Old or young?

- Are the people central to the painting, or are they peripheral? If peripheral, what is the painting's central focus?
- How does the artist represent the subjects of the painting—in other words, what does the artist's presentation of people, objects, buildings, or landscapes say about his or her attitude toward them?
- What in your own experience may be affecting your response? What personal associations do you make with the subject of the painting? How might your own position—for example, as a student, daughter or son, member of a political party—influence the way you interpret the painting?

Now read a short biography of the artist in a book or on the Web, and add that information to your analysis. Point out whether and how the biographical information either reinforces your interpretation or leads you to alter it.

2. Find an image in a current newspaper or magazine. First outline two possible arguments that the picture might be making. Then decide which is the more likely of the two arguments, and explain why.

2. Imagining stories

Sometimes a writer tries to imagine the story behind an evocative photograph. Often that story is as much an expression of the writer as it is a statement about the photograph.

Some photographs, like the one in Figure 14.1, taken on September 11, 2001, by photojournalist Thomas Hoepker, connect private life and public events. On the morning of the catastrophe, Hoepker drove across New York City's East River from Manhattan to Brooklyn, with the intention of shooting a panoramic view of the burning World Trade Center towers. He took this photo of five young people who, in the photographer's opinion, "didn't seem to care." When David Plotz, deputy editor of the online magazine *Slate*, saw the photo, he disagreed and called for a response from any of the people in the photograph <http://www.slate.com/id/2149508>. Walter Sipser, one of the photograph's subjects, wrote to *Slate*, saying, "We were in a profound state of shock" <http://www.slate.com/id/2149578>. What do you think?

If you have read W. H. Auden's poem "Musée des Beaux Arts" (*on p. 230*) or seen the painting described in the poem, Breughel's *Fall of Icarus* (*shown in Figure 14.2*), you may see a telling comparison between Hoepker's interpretation of the reaction of the photographic subjects to 9/11 and the response of those who observed "a boy falling

FIGURE 14.1 *New York City, September 11, 2001.* © Thomas Hoepker/ Magnum.

out of the sky." Compare the composition of Hoepker's photo with Breughel's painting (*Figure 14.2*). Hoepker himself wondered about "the devious lie of a snapshot" <http://slate.com/id/2149675>. In light of Sipser's remarks, what might Hoepker mean by that?

FIGURE 14.2 **Pieter Breughel's** *Fall of Icarus* **(ca 1554–1555).** Only Icarus's legs can be seen in the water between the closest boat and the shore.

229

Musée des Beaux Arts

W. H. Auden

About suffering they were never wrong,
The Old Masters; how well they understood
Its human position; how it takes place
While someone else is eating or opening a window or just walking dully
    along;
How, when the aged are reverently, passionately waiting
For the miraculous birth, there always must be
Children who did not specially want it to happen, skating
On a pond at the edge of the wood:
They never forgot
That even the dreadful martyrdom must run its course
Anyhow in a corner, some untidy spot
Where the dogs go on with their doggy life and the torturer's horse
Scratches its innocent behind on a tree.
In Breughel's Icarus, for instance: how everything turns away
Quite leisurely from the disaster; the ploughman may
Have heard the splash, the forsaken cry,
But for him it was not an important failure; the sun shone
As it had to on the white legs disappearing into the green
Water; and the expensive delicate ship that must have seen
Something amazing, a boy falling out of the sky,
Had somewhere to get to and sailed calmly on.

Exercise 14.2   Photographic stories

1. Find one photograph from at least fifty years ago in a magazine
   or book, on a Web site, or in a family collection. (The Library of
   Congress's online repository is an excellent source <http://www.
   loc.gov/rr/print/catalog.html>.) For the photograph, create two
   short, specific stories and one more general story. Explain the
   "logic" of each story using evidence from the photograph. As
   you look for stories, ask yourself these questions:

   ▪ Who or what is in the photograph?

   ▪ How is the photograph composed? What first draws your
     attention?

   ▪ If you think of the photograph as having a center, where
     would it be, and what would be in it?

   ▪ If you think of the photograph as being divided into quad-
     rants, what is in each one?

- What emotional reaction do you have to the photograph?
- If the photograph is in color, how is color used? What does it contribute to the photograph? If the photograph is in black and white, what effect does that have on you?
- What details in the picture evoke a mood?
- What is left out of the photograph and why? Can you imagine other items or people who, if included, would help tell a different story?
- Is the photograph about a short, specific story, a longer story, or both kinds of stories?
- How might your own position—for example, as a student, daughter or son, member of a political party—influence your view of the photo?

2. Take several photographs that allow for rich interpretations. Choose two of the photos and interpret them. Bring them to class, and ask two classmates to provide you with a story for each. Do their stories match yours? Do their stories seem more interesting than yours? Why or why not?

14c Use a word-processing program to create a hypertext essay.

Writers create **hypertext essays** using word-processing software, Web-development software, blogs, or wikis. **Links** in a document take the reader to other **files,** including text, image, audio, and video files. Links can take several forms:

- **Internal links** connect from one place to another in the same document, or to other files stored on the writer's computer or a storage device (CD, DVD, or flash drive).
- **External links** connect to Web sites or files on the Internet.

As with any evidence, however, a multimedia file must be relevant to the audience and purpose of the essay. It can either complement the essay's verbal claims or, like a good chart or graph, support the claims directly. For example, in a political science project on inaugural addresses, you might include links to video files of several presidents delivering their inaugural addresses. These links might simply complement your thesis, or they might provide direct evidence for an important point about, say, a particular president's style of delivery. However, unless your assignment includes specific directions to emphasize linked material as evidence, think of it as supplemental to your written claims.

If you have never created a hypertext essay, start small, with a limited set of links that all clearly serve your audience and purpose. Create internal links to the full information about works on your works-cited page, to any assignments that are related to your current topic, to tangential material that you collected while working on the essay and that provides additional context, or to a file in which you raise additional questions about your topic. Create external links to works on your topic written by your classmates or to background material on the Web.

> *Caution:* When you revise your hypertext essay, make sure all links are relevant and function correctly. Also, if your essay includes internal links to files on your computer, be sure to include those files with the essay file when you submit it to your instructor.

Exercise 14.3   Hypertext essays

1. Construct a hypertext essay in which you use links to create puns or jokes. In other words, compose the text; then insert links that let you talk back to your own points, as well as link to puns, jokes, and visuals on the Web.

2. Create a hypertext essay in which you use five links to connect your piece with some personal experience relevant to it or to connect it with relevant information about another assignment you are working on. For example, if you are writing about changes in agricultural societies, you might include links to your own experience with agriculture, from growing up on a farm to buying groceries in a store. You might also link to material you are studying in an economics class or an ancient history class.

ö **14d** Use presentation software to create multimedia presentations.

Presentation software makes it possible to incorporate audio, video, and animation into a talk. It can also be used to create multimedia compositions that viewers can go through on their own.

www.mhhe.com/
mhhb2

For an interactive
tutorial on using
PowerPoint, go to

Writing >
PowerPoint Tutorial

1. Using presentation software for an oral presentation
Presentation slides that accompany a talk should identify major points and display information in a visually effective way.

TEXTCONNEX

Using Storyboards

Artists, directors, and Web designers use storyboards—traditionally, comic-strip-like sketches of major changes in a scene sequence—to preview different sequences of visual elements.

Storyboarding can help you organize a hypertext essay (*14c*), a slide presentation (*14d*), a Web site (*14e*), or an electronic portfolio (*Chapter 6, pp. 114–17*). Sketch the elements of your document or presentation—some writers use an index card for each slide or screen—and rearrange them until you find a logical sequence. Consider how users will navigate based on the document's purpose (*see 14e, p. 237*). Your sketches should include the basic text and design for each slide or screen as well, including design elements that will be common to all slides or screens.

Remember that slides support your talk; they do not replace it. Limit the amount of information on each slide to no more than fifty words, and plan to show each slide for about one minute. Use bulleted lists and phrases rather than full sentences. Make fonts large enough to be seen by your audience: titles should be in 44-point type or larger, subheads in 32-point type or larger. High-contrast color schemes and sufficient blank space between slide elements will also increase the visibility of your presentation.

For a talk in a science course you might want to include only a single image and a set of key terms on each slide. For a talk about the writers Langston Hughes and Ralph Ellison you might use a slide like the one in Figure 14.3 (*p. 234*) to summarize their similarities and differences.

(*For more on preparing and presenting oral presentations, see Chapter 13: Oral Presentations, pp. 221–26.*)

233

Ralph Ellison and Langston Hughes

Similarities

- Were African American writers of the 20th century
- Lived in New York
- Experienced racism
- Were associated with radical political movements in 1930s
- Died of cancer

Differences

- Hughes was well traveled; Ellison rarely left home
- Hughes was prolific; Ellison completed only one novel and left another unfinished
- Ellison married; Hughes did not

FIGURE 14.3 **A slide for a presentation on Ralph Ellison and Langston Hughes.**

2. Using presentation software to create an independent composition

With presentation software, you can also create compositions that run on their own or at the prompting of the viewer. This capability is especially useful in distance learning settings, in which students attend class and share information electronically.

3. Preparing a slide presentation

The following guidelines apply.

Decide on a slide format You should begin thinking about slides while you plan what you are going to say. As you decide on the words for your talk or independent composition, you will think of visuals that support your points, and as you work out the visuals, you are likely to see additional points you can make—and adjust your presentation as a result. Every aspect of your slides—such as fonts, images, and animations—should support your purpose and appeal to your audience. Never use multimedia elements for mere decoration.

Before you create your slides, establish their basic appearance. What background color will they have? What typeface or typefaces? What design elements, such as borders and rules? Will the templates provided by the software suit your talk? Can you modify a template to suit your needs? The format you establish will be the canvas for all your slides—it needs to complement, not distract from, the images and text you intend to display.

FIGURE 14.4 The collapse of the Tacoma Narrows Bridge. The dramatic collapse of the bridge was captured on film, and some of the footage is available in video files.

Incorporate images into your presentation Include images when appropriate. To summarize quantitative information, you might use a chart or graph. To show geographical relationships, you would likely use a map. You can also add photographs that illustrate your points. In all cases, select appropriate, relevant images that support your purpose.

www.mhhe.com/
mhhb2
For more on
designing documents,
go to

Writing >
Writing Web
Links > Document
and Web Design

Incorporate relevant audio, video, and animation Slides can also include audio files, recording background information for each slide in an independent composition. Or for a presentation on music, you can insert audio files to show how a type of music has developed over time.

Slides can also include video files and animated drawings and diagrams. A video clip of the collapse of the Tacoma Narrows Bridge in violently high winds on November 7, 1940, for example (*see Figure 14.4*), might help illustrate a presentation on bridge construction. An animated diagram of the process of cell division could help illustrate a presentation on cellular biology. If you are using audio, video, or animation files that belong to others, cite the source. If you plan to make your presentation publicly available online, obtain permission to use these items from the copyright holder. (*For more on finding and citing multimedia, see Chapter 17, Finding and Creating Effective Visuals, pp. 281–89.*)

235

Incorporate hypertext links A presenter might use an internal link within a slide sequence to jump to another slide that illustrates or explains a particular point or issue. For instance, for a presentation on insects, you might include a hyperlink to a slide about insects specific to the part of the country in which you live, complete with an image of one of them. You can also create external links to resources on the Web. Be careful not to rely too much on external links, however, because they can undermine the coherence of a presentation. External links can also take a long time to load.

Caution: If you plan to make external links part of your presentation, make sure that you have a functioning Web browser on your computer and that a fast connection to the Internet is available where you will be giving the presentation. If possible, run through your presentation on site so your external links are cached.

---

4. Reviewing a slide presentation

Once you have the text of your presentation in final form and the multimedia elements in place, you should carefully review your slides to make sure they work together coherently.

- **Check how slides in your software's slide sorter window move one to the next.** Do you have an introductory slide? Do you need to add transitional effects that reveal the content of a slide gradually or point by point? Some transitions permit audio: would that support your purpose? Use transitional effects to support your rhetorical situation. Do you have a concluding slide?

- **Make sure that the slides are consistent with the script of the talk you plan to deliver.** If the slides are to function as an independent document, do they include enough introduction, an adequate explanation, and a clear conclusion?

- **Check the arrangement of your slides.** Try printing them and spreading them out over a large surface, rearranging them if necessary, before implementing needed changes on the computer.

- **Be sure the slides have a unified look.** For example, do all the slides have the same background? Do all use the same typefaces in the same way? Are headers and bullets consistent?

www.mhhe.com/
mhhb2

Exercise 14.4 Presentation slides

1. Choose three key terms related to multimedia, and define them in a three- to five-slide presentation for your class. In doing so, use any two of the features of presentation slides discussed in this section, and write a one-page reflection about why you chose those terms and those presentation features.

2. Draft a preview of a paper you are working on in an eight-slide presentation. Share this preview with your classmates in an eight-minute talk. Then ask them to tell you (a) what they think your main purpose is, (b) what worked well in the presentation, and (c) what you should consider changing when you write the paper.

 14e Create a Web site.

For more on designing Web sites, go to

Writing >
Writing Web
Links > Document
and Web Design

Thanks to Web editing software, it is now almost as easy to create a Web site and post it on the Internet as it is to write a paper using word-processing software. Many Web-based businesses like Google provide free server space for hosting sites and offer tools for creating Web pages. Many schools also make server space available for student Web sites.

To be effective, a Web site must be well designed and serve a well-defined purpose for its audience. In creating a Web site, plan the site, draft its content and select its visuals, and then revise and edit as you would for any other composition. (*See Chapters 3–5 in Part 1: Writing and Designing Texts, for more on these stages.*) The following sections offer guidelines for composing a Web site.

1. Planning a structure for your site

Like most paper documents, a Web site can have a linear structure, where one page leads to the next, and so on. Because of the hyperlinked nature of this medium, however, a site can also be organized in a hierarchy or with a number of pages that connect to a central page, or hub, like the spokes of a wheel. The diagrams in Figure 14.5 on page 239 illustrate the hierarchical and hub structures. To choose the structure that will work best for your site, consider how you expect visitors to use it. Visitors intrigued by the topic of Tyler County's historic buildings will probably want to explore. Visitors to a caregiver resources site will probably be looking to find specific information quickly. The structure of a site should accommodate its users' needs.

To determine your site's structure, try mapping the connections among its pages by arranging them in a storyboard. Represent each page with an index card and rearrange the pages on a flat surface, experimenting with possible configurations. Or use sticky notes on a whiteboard and draw arrows among them. How will readers navigate

237

CHECKLIST

Planning a Web Site

When you begin your Web composition, consider these questions:

☐ What is your purpose?

☐ Who are your viewers, and what are their needs? Will the site be limited by password to specific viewers, or will it have a broader audience?

☐ What design elements will appeal to your audience?

☐ What type of content will you include on your site: images, audio files, video files?

☐ Will you need to get permission to use any visuals or other files that you obtain from other sources?

☐ Given your technical knowledge, amount of content, and deadline, how much time should you allot to each stage of building your site?

☐ Will the site be updated, and if so, how frequently?

through the site? (*See the box on p. 233.*) Also begin planning the visual design of your site. For consistency, establish a template page, including background color and fonts. Choose a uniform location for material that will appear on each page, such as site title, page title, navigation links, and your contact information. (*See pp. 240–41 on designing a site with a unified look.*)

2. Gathering content for your site

The content for a Web site usually consists of written work along with links and graphics. Depending on your topic and purpose, you might also provide audio files, video files, and even animations.

There are some special requirements for written content that appears on a Web site:

■ Usually readers neither expect nor want lengthy text explanations. Instead, they want to find the link or information they are looking for within a few seconds.

■ Readers prefer short paragraphs ("chunks"), so the text for each topic or point should fit on one page. Avoid long passages that require readers to use the scroll bar.

Hierarchical Structure

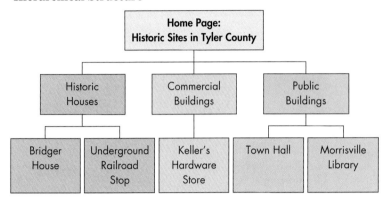

Hub Structure

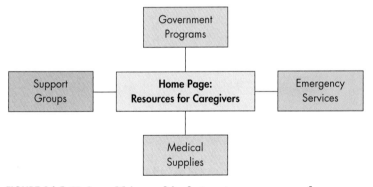

FIGURE 14.5 **Hub and hierarchical structures compared.**

- Use links to connect your interests with those of others and to provide extra sources of relevant and credible information. Make links part of your text and give them descriptive names, such as "Support Groups." Place links at the end of a paragraph so readers don't navigate away in the middle.

As you prepare your written text, gather any graphics, photographs, and audio and video files that you plan to include. Some sites allow you to download images; and some images, including many of the historical photographs available through the Library of Congress, are in the public domain. Another useful site for visual, audio, and video files is *Creative Commons* (http://search.creativecommons.org), which directs you to material licensed for specific types of use. Check the license of the material to see what is permitted.

Understanding Web Jargon

JPEG and **GIF:** Formats for photographs and other visuals that are recognized by browsers. Photographs that appear on a Web site should be saved in JPEG (pronounced "*jay-peg*") format, which stands for Joint Photographic Experts Group. The file extension is .jpg or .jpeg. Clip art should be saved as GIF files (Graphics Interchange Format, pronounced like *gift* without the *t*.)

HTML/XML: Hypertext markup language/extensible markup language. These languages tag or code text so that your browser can rebuild a document from the compressed files that travel through the Internet. It is not necessary to learn HTML or XML to publish on the Web. Programs such as FrontPage, PageMill, Dreamweaver, Nvue, and Mozilla provide a WYSIWYG (what you see is what you get) interface for creating Web pages. Most word-processing programs also have a "Save as HTML" option.

URL: Uniform resource locator or Web address. When you type or paste a URL into your Web browser, you are sending a request through your browser to another computer, asking it to transfer data to your computer.

Always cite material that you do not generate yourself. If your Web text will be public, request permission for use of any material not in the public domain unless the site says permission is not needed. Check for a credit in the source, and if the contact information of the creator is not apparent, e-mail the sponsor of the site and ask for it. (*For citation formats see Part 4: Documenting across the Curriculum.*)

3. Designing Web pages to capture and hold interest
On good Web sites, you will find such easy-to-follow links as "what you'll find here," FAQs (frequently asked questions), or "list of those involved." In planning the structure and content of your site, keep your readers' convenience in mind.

4. Designing a readable site with a unified look
The design of your site should suit its purpose and intended audience: a government site to inform users about copyright law will present an uncluttered design that focuses attention on the text. A university's **home page** might feature photographs of young people and sun-drenched lawns to entice prospective students. Readers generally appreciate a site with a unified look. "Sets" or "themes" are readily available at free graphics sites offering banners, navigation buttons, and other design

TEXTCONNEX

Web Resources for Site Design and Construction

- *Webmonkey* <http://www.webmonkey.com>
- *Web Guide: Designing a Web Page*
  <http://people.depauw.edu/djp/webguide/designwebpage.html>
- *American Council of the Blind*—information about creating Web pages for people with disabilities
  <http://acb.org/accessible-formats.html/>

elements. You can also create visuals with a graphics program or scan your personal art and photographs. Design your home page to complement your other pages, or your readers may lose track of where they are in the site—as well as their interest in staying.

- Use a design template (*see p. 238*) to keep elements of page layout consistent across the site.

- Align items such as text and images. (In Figure 14.8 on page 243, note that the heading "Library Highlights" lines up on the left with the icons below it.)

- Consider including a site map, a Web page that serves as a table of contents for your entire site. (*See Chapter 3, p. 51.*)

- Select elements such as buttons, signs, animations, sounds, and backgrounds with a consistent design suited to your purpose and audience.

- Use colors that provide adequate contrast, white space, and sans serif fonts that make text easy to read. Pages that are too busy are not visually compelling. (*For more on design, see Chapter 6: Designing Academic Papers and Preparing Portfolios, pp. 105–12.*)

- Limit the width of your text; readers find wide lines of text difficult to process.

- Leave time to find appropriate image, audio, and video files created by others, and to obtain permission to use them.

The two Web pages shown in Figure 14.6 (*on the following page*) illustrate some of these design considerations.

5. Designing a Web site that is easy to access and navigate

Help readers find their way to the areas of the site that they want to visit. Make it easy for them to take interesting side trips if they would like to without wasting their time or losing their way.

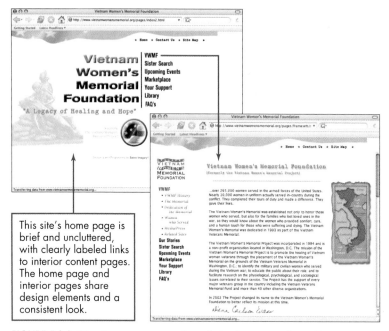

This site's home page is brief and uncluttered, with clearly labeled links to interior content pages. The home page and interior pages share design elements and a consistent look.

FIGURE 14.6 The home page and an interior page from the Web site of the Vietnam Women's Memorial Foundation.

- **Identify your Web site on each page, and provide a link to the home page.** Remember that people will not always enter your Web site through the home page. Give the title of the site on each page, and provide an easy-to-spot link to your home page.

- **Provide a navigation bar on each page.** A **navigation bar** can be a simple line of links that you copy and paste at the top or bottom of each page. For example, on the Web page from Governors State University shown in Figure 14.7, visitors can choose from three rows of links in the navigation bar at the top of the page.

- **Use graphics that load quickly.** Limit the size of your images to no more than 40 kilobytes, so that they will load quickly.

- **Use graphics judiciously.** Your Web site should not depend on graphics alone to make its message clear and interesting. Graphics should reinforce your purpose. For example, the designers of the Library of Congress Web site (*see Figure 14.8*) use icons, such as musical notation and a map, to help visitors navigate the site. Avoid clip art, which often looks unprofessional.

FIGURE 14.7 Governors State University home page.

FIGURE 14.8 The home page of the Library of Congress Web site.

243

■ **Be aware of the needs of visitors with disabilities.**
Provide alternate ways of accessing visual or auditory information. Include text descriptions of visuals, media files, and tables (for users of screen-reader software or text-only **browsers**). All audio files should have captions and full transcriptions. (*See Chapter 6, Designing Academic Papers and Preparing Portfolios, pp. 111–12.*)

6. Using peer feedback to revise your Web site

Before publishing your site on the Web to be read by anyone in the world, proofread your text carefully, and ask a few friends to look at your site and share their responses with you. Make sure your site reflects favorably on your abilities.

For MULTILINGUAL STUDENTS

Designing a Web Site Collaboratively

If you are asked to create a Web site as part of a class assignment, arrange to work with a partner or a small group. Periodically, you can invite peers to check over the writing you contribute and make suggestions. At the same time, you will be able to provide the project with the benefit of your multicultural viewpoint.

Exercise 14.5   Web site critique

Choose an example of a well-designed Web site and an example of one that is poorly designed. Compare and contrast aspects of the two designs.

Exercise 14.6   Web page creation

Convert the two hypertext essays you created for Exercise 14.3 into Web pages, using Web editing software to add visual elements.

14f Create and interact with Weblogs.

Weblogs (blogs) are part of Web 2.0, a term applied to Web sites that facilitate creativity and interaction among users. Blogs are Web sites that can be continually updated. Readers can often post comments on entries. Some blogs provide a space where a group of writers can discuss one another's work and ideas.

TEXTCONNEX

Blog Resources

Blogs 101—The New York Times—Directory of blogs by topic
<http://www.nytimes.com/ref/technology/blogs_101.html>
Technorati—Search engine for blogs <http://www.technorati.com>

In schools, classes have used blogs to discuss issues, organize work, compile portfolios, and gather and store material and commentary. Figure 14.9 depicts a blog for an English class at Queens College. Here, instructor Jason Tougow and his students discuss the title of their upcoming conference.

Blogs have become important vehicles for public discussion and commentary. For example, most presidential campaigns in 2008 maintained blogs on their Web sites, and many conventional news sources, like the *New York Times*, link to their own blogs on their Web sites. Compared to other types of publications and academic writing, blogs have an informal tone that combines information, entertainment, and personal opinion.

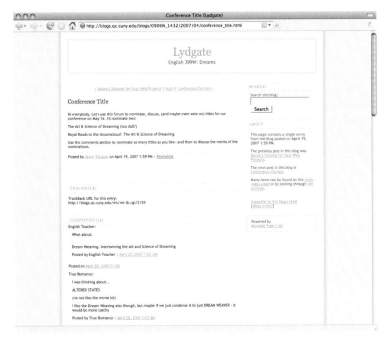

FIGURE 14.9 The blog for Jason Tougow's English course. Here, a student comments on the instructor's post.

CHECKLIST

Setting up a Blog

When you begin your blog, consider these questions:

☐ What is your purpose? How will your blog's visual design reflect that purpose?

☐ To whom will you give access? Should the blog be public or limited to a specific group of viewers?

☐ Do you want to allow others to post to your blog and/or comment on your posts?

☐ Do you want to set up a schedule of postings or a series of reminders that will cue you to post?

☐ Do you know others with blogs? Do you want to link to their sites? Should they link to yours and comment on it?

To begin blogging, set up a blog site with a server such as *Blogger* (blogger.com) or *Word Press* (wordpress.com). You may at first want to confine yourself to a very specific purpose before launching into wide-ranging commentary.

Some social networking sites such as *MySpace* also allow users to create blogs. These sites can sometimes be used to explore a topic or find an expert on a particular subject. For example, if school policy permits it you might informally survey your friends on a campus issue or set up a group to discuss the topic.

Caution: Blogs and profiles on social networking sites are more or less public depending on the level of access they allow. Do not post anything (including photographs and videos) that you would not want parents, teachers, and prospective employers to view.

14f

TEXTCONNEX

Wikis

A wiki is another kind of Web-interfaced database that can be updated easily. While a blog typically is managed by one person, a wiki allows multiple writers to post and edit content. Thus, wikis are useful spaces for collaborative authoring and research compilation.

One well-known wiki is the online encyclopedia *Wikipedia* (*see Chapter 18, p. 266*). Many instructors do not consider *Wikipedia* a credible source for papers because anyone can create or edit its content. Changes are not reviewed by experts before appearing on the site. Because the information provided isn't always correct, confirm it with another source. Some other wikis, such as *Citizendium*, rely on experts in a discipline to write and edit articles.

Exercise 14.7   Blogs

1. Examine a variety of blogs, and identify their purpose and audience. How do features of the visual design and the writing support the purpose?

2. Create your own blog with three of your classmates, and use it as a peer-review forum for your next paper assignment. How does this kind of peer review compare with a face-to-face review?

3. Choose a current-events blog to read for several days, and then post a comment on an issue. If the blog author or another reader responds to your comment, write in your print or electronic journal or blog about the resulting exchange.

4. Using the questions for previewing text and visuals in Chapter 7 (*pp. 122–24*), write a short rhetorical analysis of a blog.

Interplanetary probes help astronomers research the far reaches of the solar system. Voyager 2 sent this image of Saturn's rings to Earth.

PART

3

For all knowledge and wonder (which is the seed of knowledge) is an impression of pleasure in itself.
—FRANCIS BACON

Researching

15 Understanding Research

Your campus or neighborhood library provides valuable resources for almost any kind of research. These include not just books, magazines, and journals but access to specialized online databases and the expert guidance of a research librarian.

Doing research in the twenty-first century includes the library but is not limited to it. The Internet provides direct access in seconds to an abundance of information. This ease of access, however, can be treacherous. The results of Internet searches can sometimes provide an overwhelming flood of sources, many of them of questionable legitimacy.

The goal of Part 3 of this book is to help you learn about the research process. Chapters 15–22 provide tips for skillfully navigating today's research landscape, managing the information you discover within it, and using that information to write research papers.

15a Understand primary and secondary research.

Academic inquiry calls for both primary and secondary research. **Primary research** involves working in a laboratory, in the field, or with an archive of raw data, original documents, or authentic artifacts to

WRITING OUTCOMES

Part 3: Researching

This section will help you answer questions such as:

Rhetorical Knowledge

- What writing situation does my assignment specify? **(15c)**

Critical Thinking, Reading, and Writing

- What are primary and secondary research? **(15a, 19)**
- How can I tell if my sources are worth including? **(18)**
- How do I present my ideas along with those of my sources? **(21c–e)**

Processes

- How can I think of a topic for my research paper? **(15d)**
- How do I plan my research project? **(15e)**
- When and how should I use visuals in my research paper? **(17)**

Knowledge of Conventions

- What is an annotated bibliography, and how do I create one? **(21b)**
- When and how should I use paraphrases, summaries, and quotations? **(21c, e)**

make firsthand discoveries. (*For more information on primary research, see Chapter 19, pp. 299–306*). **Secondary research** involves looking at what other people have learned and written about a field or topic.

Your college research writing might require primary research, secondary research, or some combination of the two. For example, a research project for an education course might ask you to observe and document the behavior of children in a classroom and then to analyze your findings based on the work of child development specialists.

Knowing how to identify facts, interpretations, and evaluations is key to conducting good secondary research:

- **Facts** are objective. Like your body weight, facts can be measured, observed, or independently verified in some way.

- **Interpretations** spell out the implications of facts. Are you as thin as you are because of your genes—or because you exercise every day? The answer to this question is an interpretation.

- **Evaluations** are debatable judgments about a set of facts or a situation. Attributing a person's thinness to genes is an interpretation, but the assertion that "one can never be too rich or too thin" (credited to Wallis Simpson and Babe Paley) is an evaluation.

Once you are up-to-date on the facts, interpretations, and evaluations in a particular area, you will be able to design a research project that adds to this knowledge. Usually, what you will add is your *perspective* on the sources you found and read:

- Given all that you have learned about the topic, what strikes you as important or interesting?

- What patterns do you see, or what connections can you make between one person's work and another's?

- Where is the research going, and what problems still need to be explored?

TextConnex

Types of Sources

- *Research 101—The Basics* <http://www.lib.washington.edu/ uwill/research101/basic00.htm>: This page from the University of Washington site discusses the difference between primary and secondary research sources, as well as the difference between popular and scholarly periodicals.
- *Research Papers: Resources* <http://owl.english.purdue.edu/ workshops/hypertext/ResearchW/resource.html>: From The Purdue Online Writing Lab, offers guidelines for finding primary and secondary sources.

CHARTING the TERRITORY

Classic and Current Sources

Classic sources are well-known and respected older works that have made such an important contribution to a discipline or a particular area of research that contemporary researchers use them as touchstones for further research in that area. Current research is up to date but has not yet met the test of time. In many fields, sources published within the past five years are considered current. However, sources on topics related to medicine, recent scientific discoveries, or technological change must be much more recent to be considered current. Many disciplines also have key reference texts—discipline-specific encyclopedias and dictionaries, for example. These can usually direct you to classic sources.

15b Recognize the connection between research and college writing.

In one way or another, research informs all college writing. But some assignments require more rigorous and systematic research than others. These **research project** assignments offer you a chance to go beyond your course texts—to find and read both classic and current material on a specific issue. A research paper constitutes your contribution to the ongoing conversation about a specific issue.

When you are assigned to write a research paper for any of your college courses, the project may seem overwhelming at first. If you break the project into phases, however, and allow enough time for each phase, you should be able to manage your work and write a paper that contributes to the academic conversation.

15c Understand the research assignment.

Consider the rhetorical situation of the research project as you would any other piece of writing. Think about your paper's audience, purpose, and scope. (*See Chapter 2: Understanding Writing Assignments.*)

1. Audience
Although your *audience* will most likely include only your instructor and perhaps your fellow students, thinking critically about their needs and expectations will help you plan a research strategy and create a schedule for writing your paper.

Audience in Research Writing

Ask yourself the following questions about your audience. If your instructor approves, use your imagination to think about alternative audiences for your research—for example, a local school board for a paper about an education issue, the members of a state legislature for a paper about an environmental issue, or the readers of a newspaper's editorial page for a paper on a political issue.

- What does my audience already know about this subject? How much background information and context will I need to provide? (Your research should include *facts*.)
- Might my audience find my paper controversial or challenging? How should I accommodate and acknowledge different perspectives and viewpoints? (Your research should include *interpretations*, and you will need to balance opposing interpretations.)
- Do I expect my audience to take action based on my research? (Your research should include *evaluations*, carefully supported by facts and interpretations, that demonstrate clearly to members of your audience why they should adopt a particular course of action or point of view.)

2. Purpose

Your *purpose* for writing a research paper might be *informative*—to educate your audience about an unfamiliar subject or point of view (*see Chapter 8: Informative Reports, p. 137*). It might be *interpretive*—to reveal the meaning or significance of a work of art, a historic document, or a scientific study (*see Chapter 9: Interpretive Analyses, p. 157*). It might instead be *persuasive*—that is, to convince your audience, with logic and evidence, to accept your point of view on a contentious issue or to act on the information in your paper (*see Chapter 10: Arguments, p. 183*).

3. Scope

A project's scope includes the expected length, the deadline, and any other requirements such as number and type of sources. Most research assignments call for a mix of classic and current sources that address a range of viewpoints. Are primary sources appropriate? Should you include visuals, and is any type specified? Select a topic that will allow you to meet the assignment's scope. It might be difficult to find sufficient and appropriate sources if your topic is very current or specialized.

253

Tips

LEARNING in COLLEGE

Keywords Indicating Purpose in Research Assignments

Review your assignment for keywords that signal its purpose. Here are some examples.

- **Informative:** *explain, describe, compare, review*
- **Interpretive:** *analyze, compare, explain, interpret*
- **Persuasive:** *assess, justify, defend, refute, determine*

Sample Informative Research Assignments

- **History:** Describe the relationship between abolitionism and the women's suffrage movement prior to the Civil War.
- **Biology:** Explain the impact of zebra mussels on native fauna in a lake.

Sample Interpretive Research Assignments

- **History:** Interpret the *Declaration of Sentiments*—issued at the first women's rights convention in 1848—as a response to the *Declaration of Independence*.
- **Biology:** Analyze the results of recent studies of lakes infested with zebra mussels.

Sample Persuasive Research Assignments

- **History:** Defend or refute this statement: "The women's movement and the civil rights movement have long cooperated based on a historically rooted shared agenda."
- **Biology:** Determine the least invasive way to remove zebra mussels from a local ecosystem, and create an implementation plan for doing so.

www.mhhe.com/
mhhb2

For more on narrowing your topic, go to

Writing >
Paragraph/Essay
Development >
Thesis/Central
Idea

15d Choose an interesting research question for critical inquiry.

Approach your assignment in a spirit of critical inquiry. *Critical* in this sense does not mean "skeptical," "cynical," or even "urgent." Rather it refers to a receptive but reasonable and discerning frame of mind. Choosing a topic that interests you will help make the results of your inquiry meaningful to you and your readers.

1. Choosing a question with personal significance

Begin with the wording of the assignment, analyzing the project's required audience, purpose, and scope. (*See section 15c.*) Then browse through the course texts and your class notes, looking for a match between your interests and topics, issues, or problems in the subject area.

For example, suppose you have been assigned to write a seven- to ten-page report on some country's global economic prospects, for a business course. If you have recently visited Mexico, you might find it interesting to explore that country's prospects.

2. Making your question specific

The more specific your question, the more your research will have direction and focus. To make a question more specific, use the "five *w*'s and an *h*" strategy by asking about the *who, what, why, when, where,* and *how* of a topic (*see Chapter 3, pp. 36–37*).

After you have compiled a list of possible research questions, choose one that is relatively specific, or rewrite a broad one to make it more specific and therefore answerable within the scope of the assignment. For example, as Audrey Galeano developed a topic for a research paper on the impact of globalization for an anthropology course, she rewrote the following broad question to make it answerable:

TOO BROAD

How has globalization affected the Amazon River Basin?

ANSWERABLE

How has large-scale agriculture in the Amazon Basin affected the region's indigenous peoples?

(*Galeano's finished paper appears at the end of Chapter 24: APA Documentation Style, pp. 412–22*)

 CHARTING the TERRITORY

Typical Lines of Inquiry in Different Disciplines

Research topics and questions—even when related to a single broad issue—differ from one discipline to another. The following examples show the distinctions:

History: How did India's experience of British imperialism affect its response to globalization?

Marketing: How do corporations develop strategies for marketing their products to an international consumer audience?

Political Science: Why did many nations of Europe agree to unite, creating a common currency and an essentially "borderless" state called the European Union, or E.U.?

Anthropology: What is the impact of globalization on the world's indigenous cultures?

Try to rephrase a broad question as a statement, then add the word *because* or *by* at the end, and fill in the blank with possible answers. For example, if your broad question is "How has globalization affected the Amazon Basin?" restate it as "Globalization has affected the Amazon Basin by _____" and give a few precise reasons. Here are some examples Audrey Galeano considered:

Globalization has affected the Amazon Basin by _____

. . . overwhelming traditional forms of music, dress, and expression with global pop culture.
. . . encouraging the construction of roads that make the region more accessible.

3. Finding a challenging question

If a question can be answered with a simple yes or no, a dictionary-like definition, or a textbook presentation of information, you should choose another question or rework the simple one to make it more challenging and interesting.

NOT CHALLENGING	Has economic globalization contributed to the destruction of the Amazon rain forest?
CHALLENGING	How can agricultural interests and indigenous peoples in the Amazon region work together to preserve the environment while creating a sustainable economy?

4. Speculating about answers

Sometimes it can be useful to speculate on the answer to your research question so that you have a **hypothesis** to work with during the research process. Do not forget, however, that a hypothesis is a tentative answer that must be tested and revised against the evidence you turn up in your research. Be aware of the assumptions embedded in your hypothesis or research question. Consider, for example, the following hypothesis:

HYPOTHESIS	The global market for agricultural products will destroy the Amazon rain forest.

This hypothesis assumes that destructive farming practices are the only possible response in the Amazon to global demand. But assumptions are always open to question. Researchers must be willing to adjust their ideas as they learn more about a topic.

As the above example demonstrates, your research question must allow you to generate testable hypotheses. Assertions about your personal beliefs or feelings do not make testable hypotheses.

| **Exercise 15.1** | Answerable, challenging questions |

For each of the following broad topics, create at least three answerable, challenging questions.

1. Internet access is becoming as important as literacy in determining the livelihood of a nation's people.

2. Genetically modified organisms (GMOs) and biotechnology are controversial approaches to addressing the world's food problems.

3. The problem of terrorism requires a multilateral solution.

15e Create a research plan.

www.mhhe.com/
mhhb2

For resources to start
your research, go to

Research >
Discipline Specific
Resources

Your research will be more productive if you create both a general plan and a detailed schedule immediately after you receive your assignment. A general plan will ensure that you understand the full scope of your assignment. A detailed schedule will help you set priorities and meet your deadlines. To develop a general plan of research, answer the following questions:

- Do I understand exactly what my instructor expects?

- Is the purpose of my paper fundamentally informative, interpretive, or persuasive? Do I have a choice?

- If the topic is assigned: What do I already know about this topic?

- If the specific topic is open: What idea-generation techniques can I use to help me discover a topic?

- Will collaboration be allowed?

- Will I need to conduct primary as well as secondary research? If so, what general arrangements do I anticipate needing to make?

- How many and what kinds of sources am I expected to consult? (*See Chapters 16–18 for information on finding and evaluating sources.*)

- What citation style does my instructor want me to use? What are the expectations for the final presentation format of my research? (*See Part 4: Documenting across the Curriculum.*)

| **Exercise 15.2** | Research schedule |

Adapt this worksheet to create a research schedule whenever you have a research assignment. If you use a PDA, type in this schedule and set reminders or alarms for key dates (such as completing library

SOURCE SMART

Planning Your Search

Your research plan should include where you expect to find your sources. For example, you may have to visit the library to view print material that predates 1980; you will need to consult a subscription database online or at the library for recent scientific discoveries; historical documents may require archival research; and you may need to conduct field research, such as interviewing fellow students. Set priorities to increase your efficiency in each location (library, archive, online).

research, completing a first draft, or conferring with the campus writing center).

Task	Date
Phase I:	
Complete a general plan for research.	_____
Decide on a topic and a research question.	_____
Consult reference works and reference librarians.	_____
List relevant **keywords** for online searching (*see Chapter 16, pp. 266–67*).	_____
Compile a **working bibliography** (*see Chapter 21, pp. 314–18*).	_____
Sample some of the items in the bibliography.	_____
Make arrangements for primary research (if necessary).	_____
Phase II:	
Locate, read, and evaluate selected sources.	_____
Take notes; write summaries and paraphrases.	_____
Cross-check notes with working bibliography.	_____
Conduct primary research (if necessary).	_____
Find and create visuals.	_____
Confer with instructor or writing center (optional).	_____
Develop thesis and outline or plan organization of paper.	_____
Phase III:	
Write first draft.	_____
Decide which primary and secondary resource materials to include.	_____

Peer review (optional).   ———————

Revise draft.   ———————

Conference with instructor or writing center
(optional).   ———————

Perform final revision and editing.   ———————

Create in-text citations as well as
Works-Cited or References list.   ———————

Proofread and check spelling.   ———————

Due Date   ———————

16 Finding and Managing Print and Online Sources

The amount of information available in the library and on the Internet is vast. Usually, a search for useful sources entails three activities:

- Collecting keywords from reference works
- Using library databases
- Finding material in the library and on the Web

16a   Use the library in person and online.

Librarians know what is available at your library and how to get material from other libraries. They can also show you how to access the library's computerized book catalog, periodical databases, and electronic resources or how to use the Internet to find information relevant to your research project. At many schools, reference librarians are available for online chats at any time, and some take queries via text message. Your library's Web site may have links to subscription databases or important reference works available on the Internet, as shown in Figure 16.1 on the next page.

In addition, **help sheets** or online tutorials at most college libraries give the location of both general and discipline-specific periodicals and noncirculating reference books, along with information about the book catalog, special databases, indexes, Web resources, and library policies.

259

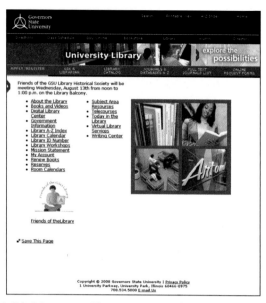

FIGURE 16.1 Linking to online resources from a college library's Web site. This page from the Web site of Governors State University Library provides links to a variety of Web-based reference sources.

www.mhhe.com/
mhhb2

For more information
on and links to library
resources, go to

Research >
Using the Library

16b Consult various kinds of sources.

You should always review more than one source, and usually more than one kind of source: general and specialized, books and articles, print and online. Chances are, you will consult more sources during your research than you will cite in your final project. Your assignment may specify how many print and electronic sources you

SOURCE SMART

Organizing Your Sources

List your sources alphabetically. For each, include citation information (*see p. 315*), key points, and relevance to your topic. Does the source support or detract from your claim? Is it an early source or a later one? Does it agree or disagree with other sources you have read? Do other sources reference this one? You might color-code your list to indicate related ideas across sources. Include useful quotations and their page numbers. (*For instructions on preparing a formal annotated bibliography and an example, see Chapter 21: Working with Sources and Avoiding Plagiarism, p. 319.*)

are expected to look at and cite. Some types of sources available to you are summarized in the following sections.

CHECKLIST

Finding Library Resources

Make it a point to tour your library when you begin college. Your library also may have online tutorials describing its resources. Be sure to do the following:

- ☐ Locate the reference desk and note its hours. (Reference books cannot be checked out, so you will need to schedule time to consult them while the library is open.) Collect any help sheets.

- ☐ Set up an account and a password to use the online catalog. Find out how to link to the catalog from a computer in your dorm or home. Also locate the library's card catalog if it has one.

- ☐ Locate the library's **stacks** (the shelves where it stores its collections of books). To get books from closed stacks, you have to request them and have them brought to you by a library employee.

- ☐ Learn your library's interlibrary loan policies.

- ☐ Learn about the library's **reserve service,** which lets professors set aside books and articles for students to consult for limited times, or post them electronically, ensuring their availability to everyone in the class.

- ☐ Locate your library's photocopying machines, computer terminals, printers, and other helpful devices.

- ☐ Locate and learn to use any online databases to which the library subscribes. These provide access to journal articles as well as newspapers and magazines often dating back to the 1980s. Older sources may be on microform or microfiche. Learn the location of the machines that allow you to read them.

- ☐ Find out about any multimedia resources or primary sources available online or at the library.

1. General reference works

General reference works provide overview information about a variety of topics. General encyclopedias (such as *Encyclopaedia Britannica*), for example, include entries for anything from the history of the alphabet to the science of zoology. Other general reference works include dictionaries, annuals, almanacs, biographical encyclopedias, and world atlases. They can introduce you to the basic concepts and vocabulary of a subject, giving you a source of **keywords** to use in online searches for more specialized sources. (*The basics of keyword searches are covered in section 16d.*)

2. Specialized reference works

Specialized reference works provide specific information relevant to particular disciplines. A discipline-specific encyclopedia of philosophy, for example, would have entries on important philosophers, major approaches to philosophy, and the meaning of significant philosophical terms. Other specialized reference works include discipline-specific biographical encyclopedias, almanacs, dictionaries, and bibliographies. These can also provide an overview of a topic as well as keywords.

3. Books

Most of the books you use will be in the library in printed form. Some books, however, are available online, including reports by think tanks, government agencies, and research groups. Some Web sites (such as Project Gutenberg, http://www.gutenberg.org/) provide the complete texts of classic works of literature that are no longer under copyright (*see Chapter 20, pp. 306–14*).

4. Periodical articles

Periodicals include newspapers and magazines from around the world, scholarly and technical journals (some of which may be available through online databases as well as in print), and Web-only publications.

5. Web sites

Many special-interest groups, government and academic organizations, and businesses maintain Web sites that provide information about policies, products, or particular points of view.

6. Other online sources

Online discussion groups, virtual environments, news groups, chat rooms, social networking sites, and blogs can sometimes provide access to people knowledgeable about a particular subject who can help guide your research. (Be careful, though; you can also encounter many unqualified people with suspect views in these environments.)

For MULTILINGUAL STUDENTS

Researching a Full Range of Sources

Your mastery of a language other than English can sometimes give you access to important sources. Even if you find researching in English challenging, it is important to broaden your search as soon as you can to include a range of print and Internet resources written in English.

7. Primary print sources

Primary print resources include government documents (the text of a law, for example); census data; pamphlets; maps; the original text of literary works; and the original manuscripts (or facsimiles) of literary works, letters, and personal journals, among many others. You can find these in your library, in special collections at other libraries, in government offices, and online.

8. Primary nonprint sources

In addition to written works, primary sources also include such nonprint items as works of art, video and audio recordings, sound archives, photographs, and the artifacts of everyday life.

9. Other primary sources

Other primary sources include a researcher's records from experiments or field research. These may include interviews, field notes, surveys, and the results of observation and laboratory experiments.

Exercise 16.1   Finding information at your library

Choose anyone born between 1900 and 1950 whose life and accomplishments interest you. You could select a politician, a film director, a rock star, a Nobel Prize–winning economist—*anyone*. At your library, find at least one of each of the following resources with information about or relevant to this person:

- A directory of biographies
- An article in a pre-1990 newspaper
- An article in a scholarly journal
- An audio or video recording, a photograph, or a work of art
- A printout of the search results of your library's electronic catalog
- A printout of an article obtained via a subscription database
- An obituary (if your subject has died)
- A list of your subject's accomplishments, including, for example, prizes received, books published, albums released, or movies made

LEARNING in COLLEGE

Popular or Scholarly?

The audience for and purpose of a source, especially a publication, determine whether it should be considered *scholarly* or *popular*. You may begin your inquiry into a research topic with popular sources, but to become fully informed, you need to delve into scholarly sources.

Popular sources:

- Are widely available on newsstands and in retail stores.
- Are printed on magazine paper with a color cover.
- Accept advertising for a wide range of popular consumer goods or are themselves advertised.
- Are published by a commercial publishing house or media company (such as Time Warner, Inc.).
- Include a wide range of topics in each issue, from international affairs to popular entertainment.
- Usually do not contain bibliographic information.
- If online, have a URL that likely ends in .com.

Scholarly sources:

- Are usually found in academic libraries, not on newsstands.
- List article titles and authors on the cover.
- Have few advertisements.
- Are published by scholarly or nonprofit organizations, often in association with a university press.
- Focus on discipline-specific topics.
- Include articles with extensive citations and bibliographies.
- Include articles mostly by authors who are affiliated with colleges, museums, or other scholarly institutions.
- Are **refereed** (which means, in the case of a scholarly journal, that each article has been reviewed, commented on, and accepted for publication by other scholars in the field).
- If online, have a URL that likely ends in .edu or .org.

16c Use printed and online reference works for general information.

Reference works provide an overview of a subject area and typically are less up to date than the specialized knowledge found in academic journals and scholarly books. If your instructor approves, you may start your research by consulting a general or discipline-specific

LEARNING in COLLEGE

Refining Keyword Searches

Although search engines vary, the following advice should work for many.

Group words together. Put quotation marks or parentheses around the phrase you are looking for—for example, "Dixieland jazz." This tells the search engine to find only sites with those two words in sequence.

Use Boolean operators.

AND (+)   Use AND or + when you need sites with both of two or more words: **Armstrong + Glaser.**

OR   Use OR if you want sites with either of two or more terms: **jazz OR "musical improvisation."**

NOT (–)   Use NOT or – in front of words that you do not want to appear together in your results: **Armstrong NOT Neil.**

Use truncation plus a "wildcard." For more results, combine part of a keyword with an asterisk (*) used as a wildcard: **music*** (for "music," "musician," "musical," and so forth).

Search the fields. Some search engines permit you to search within fields, such as the title field of Web pages or the author field of a library catalog. Thus **TITLE + "Louis Armstrong"** will give you all items that have "Louis Armstrong" in their title.

---

encyclopedia, but for college research you should explore your topic in greater depth. Often, the list of references at the end of an encyclopedia article can lead you to useful sources on your topic.

Reference books do not circulate, so plan to take notes or make photocopies of pages you may need to consult later. Check your college library's home page for access to online encyclopedias.

Here is a list of some other kinds of reference materials available in print, on the Internet, or both:

ALMANACS

■ *Almanac of American Politics*
■ *Information Please Almanac*
■ *World Almanac*

BIBLIOGRAPHIES

■ *Bibliographic Index*
■ *Bibliography of Asian Studies*

- *Books in Print*
- *MLA International Bibliography*

BIOGRAPHIES

- *African American Biographical Database*
- *American Men and Women of Science*
- *Dictionary of American Biography*
- *Dictionary of Literary Biography: Chicano Writers*
- *Dictionary of National Biography*
- *Webster's New Biographical Dictionary*
- *Who's Who*

DICTIONARIES

- *American Heritage Dictionary of the English Language*
- *Concise Oxford Dictionary of Literary Terms*
- *Dictionary of American History*
- *Dictionary of Philosophy*
- *Dictionary of the Social Sciences*
- *Oxford English Dictionary (OED)*

16d Understand keywords and keyword searches.

Most online research—whether in your library's catalog, in a specialized database, or on the Web—requires an understanding of **keyword searches.** In the context of online searching, a **keyword** is a term (or terms) you enter into a **search engine** (searching software) to find sources—books, journal articles, Web sites—that have information about a particular subject.

TEXTCONNEX

Wikipedia

The online encyclopedia *Wikipedia* offers information on almost any subject and can be a starting point for research. However, you should evaluate its content critically. Volunteers (who may or may not be experts) write *Wikipedia's* articles, and almost any user may edit any article. Although the site has some mechanisms to help it maintain accuracy, you should check any findings with another source (and cite that source, if you use the information).

To hone in on your subject, you often need to refine your initial search term. The "Learning in College" box on page 265 describes a variety of techniques for doing so that work in most search engines. Many search engines also have an advanced search feature that can help with the refining process.

16e Use print indexes and online databases to find articles in journals and other periodicals.

1. Periodicals

Newspapers, magazines, and scholarly journals that are published at regular intervals are classified as **periodicals.** The articles in scholarly and technical journals, written by experts and based on up-to-date research and information, are usually more detailed and reliable than articles in popular newspapers and magazines. Ask your instructor or librarian which periodicals are considered important in the discipline you are studying.

2. Indexes and Databases

Articles published in periodicals are cataloged in general and specialized **indexes.** Indexes are available on subscription-only online **databases,** as print volumes, and possibly on CD-ROMs. If you are searching for articles that are more than twenty years old, you may use print indexes or an appropriate electronic index. Print indexes can be searched by author, subject, or title. Electronic databases can also be searched by date and keyword and will provide you with a list of articles that meet your search criteria. (Some allow you to restrict your search to peer-reviewed scholarly journals.) Each entry in the list will include the information you need to find and cite the article. Depending on the database, you may also be able to see an abstract of each article, or even its full text. Once you find a relevant result, use its subject headings as keywords in future search queries. (*See the box "Learning in College: Formats for Database Information," on p. 274.*)

When selecting a database, consult its description on your library's site (often labeled "Info") to see the types of sources included, subjects covered, and number of periodicals included from each subject area. Would your topic be best served by a general database or one that is discipline specific? Should you focus on a particular type of periodical, such as newspapers? Also consider the time period each database spans.

Citation indexes, another type of database, indicate what other scholars have said about specific articles and books. They can help you assess a source's relevance, reliability, and position in current debates in the field.

The TextConnex box on pages 271–72 lists some of the major online databases and service providers, and Figures 16.2, 16.3, and 16.4 on pages 268–70 illustrate a search on one of them, ProQuest. Keep in mind that not all libraries subscribe to all databases.

Caution: When you refer to the full text of an article that you retrieved from a subscription database service, your citation must include the date on which you retrieved the article, the name of the database, and information about the publication in which the article appeared.

Name of the database service

Database to be searched

Advanced search options set to search the "document text" field for articles that mention both Louis Armstrong and Joe Glaser

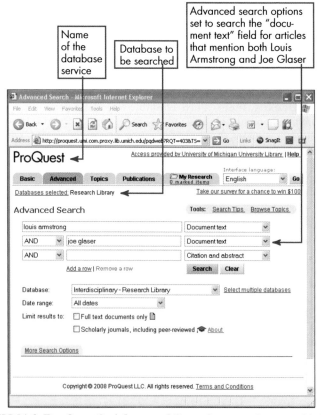

FIGURE 16.2 **ProQuest's Advanced Search page.** Image published with permission of ProQuest Information and Learning Company. Further reproduction is prohibited without permission.

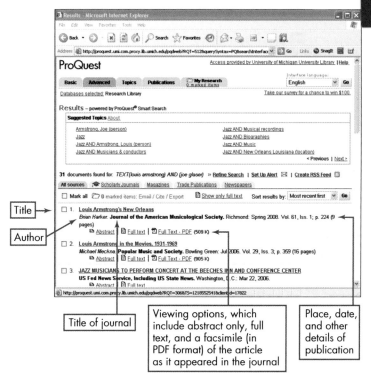

FIGURE 16.3 **Partial results of the search started in Figure 16.2.**
Image published with permission of ProQuest Information and Learning
Company. Further reproduction is prohibited without permission.

16f Use search engines and subject directories to find sources on the Internet.

To find information that has been published in Web pages, you will
need to use an Internet search engine. Because each searches the Web
in its own way, you will probably use more than one. Each search engine's home page provides a link to advice on using the search engine
efficiently as well as help with refining a search. Look for a link labeled "search help," "about us," or something similar.

Some Internet search engines provide for specialized searches—for
images, for example (*see Chapter 17*). *Google* offers *Google Book Search*,
which can help you find and view books on your topic. *Google Scholar*
locates only scholarly sources in response to a search term. At this point
it offers incomplete information, and you should not rely on it alone.

Many Internet search engines also include sponsored links—links
that a commercial enterprise has paid to have appear in response to
specific search terms. These are usually clearly identified.

www.mhhe.com/
mhhb2

For more information
on and links to
Internet resources,
go to

Research >
Using the Internet

269

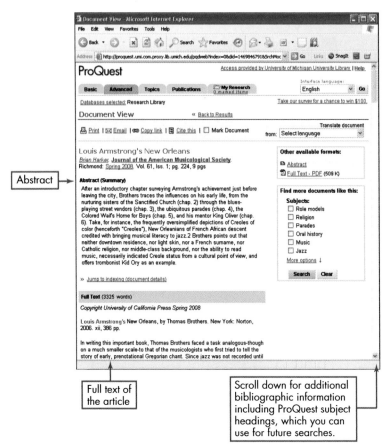

Abstract →

Full text of the article

Scroll down for additional bibliographic information including ProQuest subject headings, which you can use for future searches.

FIGURE 16.4 The abstract and the beginning of the full text of an article selected from results in Figure 16.3. Image published with permission of ProQuest Information and Learning Company. Further reproduction is prohibited without permission.

Internet keyword searches usually need to be carefully worded to provide relevant results. For example, a search of *Google* using the keywords *louis armstrong* (*Figure 16.5*) yields a list of more than 3,810,000 Web sites, a staggering number of links, or **hits.** Altering the keywords to make them more specific narrows the results significantly (*Figure 16.6 on p. 273*). (*See also the box on p. 265.*)

In addition to keyword searches, many Internet search engines offer a **subject directory,** a listing of broad categories. Clicking through this hierarchy of choices eventually brings you to a list of sites related to a specific topic.

(*Text continues on p. 272.*)

270

FIGURE 16.5 A keyword search in *Google.* An initial search using the keywords *louis armstrong* yields more than three million hits.

TEXTCONNEX

Some Online Subscription Databases

- **ABC-CLIO:** This service offers access to two history-related databases. *America: History and Life* covers the United States and Canada from prehistory to the present. *Historical Abstracts* addressess the rest of the world from 1450 to the present.

- **Lexis-Nexis Academic:** Updated daily, this online service provides full-text access to around 6,000 newspapers, professional publications, legal references, and congressional sources.

- **EBSCOhost:** This service's *Academic Search Premier* database provides full-text coverage for more than 8,000 scholarly publications and indexes articles in all academic subject areas.

- **ERIC:** This database lists publications in the area of education.

- **Factiva:** This database offers access to the Dow Jones and Reuters news agencies, including newspapers, magazines, journals, and Web sites.

- **General Science Index:** This index is general (rather than specialized). It lists articles by biologists, chemists, and other scientists.

- **GDCS:** Updated monthly, the *Government Documents Catalog Service* (*GDCS*) contains records of all publications printed by the United States Government Printing Office since 1976.

271

- **GPO Access:** This service of the U.S. Government Printing Office provides free electronic access to government documents.
- **Humanities Index:** This index lists articles from journals in language and literature, history, philosophy, and similar areas.
- **InfoTrac Web:** This Web-based service searches bibliographic and other databases such as the *General Reference Center Gold, General Business File ASAP,* and *Health Reference Center.*
- **JSTOR:** This archive provides full-text access to journals in the humanities, social sciences, and natural sciences.
- **MLA Bibliography:** Covering from 1963 to the present, the *MLA Bibliography* indexes journals, dissertations, and serials published worldwide in the fields of modern languages, literature, literary criticism, linguistics, and folklore.
- **PAIS International:** Produced by the Public Affairs Information Service, this database indexes literature on public policy, social policy, and the general social sciences from 1972 to the present.
- **Periodical Abstracts:** This database indexes more than 2,000 general and academic journals covering business, current affairs, economics, literature, religion, psychology, and women's studies from 1987 to the present.
- **ProQuest:** This service provide access to dissertations; many newspapers and journals, including many full-text articles back to 1996; information on sources in business, general reference, the social sciences, and humanities back to 1986; and a wealth of historical sources back to the nineteenth century.
- **PsycInfo:** Sponsored by the American Psychological Association (APA), this database indexes and abstracts books, scholarly articles, technical reports, and dissertations in the area of psychology and related disciplines.
- **Social Science Index:** This index lists articles from such fields as economics, psychology, political science, and sociology.
- **WorldCat:** This is a catalog of books and other resources available in libraries worldwide.

Some Web sites provide content-specific subject directories designed for research in a particular field. These sites are often reviewed or screened and are excellent starting points for academic research.

Other online tools can help you organize sources and keep track of your Web research. Save the URLs of promising sites to your browser's Bookmarks or Favorites. Your browser's history function can allow you to retrace your steps if you forget how to find a particular site. The box on page 279 includes additional online resources.

Number of hits

Revised search terms

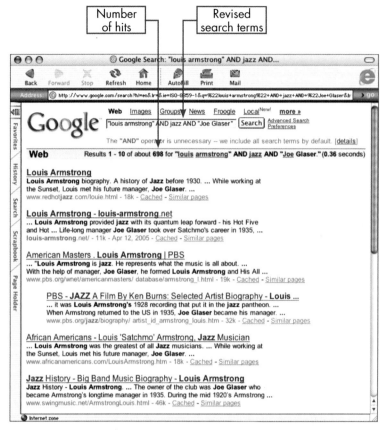

FIGURE 16.6 **Refining the search.** Putting quotes around *louis armstrong,* adding *jazz,* and adding *joe glaser* (Armstrong's longtime manager) reduces the number of hits to an almost manageable 698, as opposed to Figure 16.5's three million. (Note that the AND operator could have been omitted because *Google* treats terms by default as if they were joined by AND.)

Exercise 16.2 Finding information online

Look at the sample research topics listed in the "Charting the Territory" box on page 255, and conduct a keyword search for each on at least three search engines. Experiment with the phrasing of each keyword search, and compare your results with those of other classmates.

EXAMPLE   What is the impact of globalization on the world's indigenous cultures?

"indigenous culture" AND globalization

273

Tips | LEARNING in COLLEGE

Formats for Database Information

When searching a database, you may encounter both abstracts and the full texts of articles. Full-text articles may be available in either PDF or HTML format.

- **Abstract:** An **abstract** is a brief summary of a full-text article. Abstracts appear at the beginning of articles in some scholarly journals and are used in databases to summarize complete articles. If an abstract sounds useful, consult the full article.
- **Full text:** In a database search an article listed as "full text" comes with a link to the complete text of the article. However, it may not include accompanying photographs or other illustrations.
- **PDF** and **HTML:** Articles in databases and other online sources may be in either PDF or HTML format (or both). HTML (Hypertext Markup Language) documents have been formatted to read as Web pages. PDF (Portable Document Format) documents appear as a facsimile of the original page.

16g Use your library's online catalog or card catalog to find books.

In addition to searching library databases for periodicals and searching the Internet for relevant information, you will want to find books on your topic to explore it in depth. Books in most libraries are shelved by **call numbers,** a series of unique identifying numerals based on the Library of Congress classification system. In this system, books on the same topic have similar call numbers and are shelved together. Browsing the shelves near one source, therefore, can lead you to similar works. Some libraries use the Dewey Decimal system of call numbering, which classifies knowledge in divisions of 10 from 000 to 990. Whichever system your library uses, you will need the call number to locate the book on the library's shelves. When consulting a library catalog, be sure to jot down (or print out) the call numbers of books you want to consult. Some archives and specialized libraries use card catalogs. Cards usually are filed by author, title, and subject based on *Library of Congress Subject Headings* (*LCSH*).

You can conduct a keyword search of most online library catalogs by author, by title, or by subject (*Figure 16.7*). A search of the term *Louis Armstrong* by author would produce a list of works by Louis Armstrong; a search by title would produce a list of works with the words *Louis Armstrong* in the title; and a search by subject would

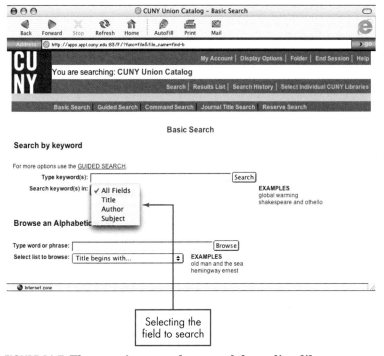

Courtesy of Libraries of The City University of New York. Microsoft® Internet Explorer screen shot reprinted with permission from Microsoft Corporation.

FIGURE 16.7 **The opening search page of the online library system of the City University of New York (CUNY).**

produce a list of works that are all or partly about Louis Armstrong. Subject terms appear in the *LCSH,* which provides a set of key terms that you can use in your search for sources. Keyword searches of many catalogs also include publisher, notes, and other fields.

The results of a keyword search of a library's online catalog will provide a list composed mostly of books. In the examples that follow of a search of the City University of New York Library's online catalog, notice that under the column "Format" other kinds of media that match a keyword subject search may be listed; you can alter the terms of a search to restrict the formats to a specific medium.

Figures 16.8 and 16.9 (*pp. 276–77*) show the results of experimenting with different keywords on the topic of jazz in general and Louis Armstrong in particular. Figure 16.8, a subject search using only the keyword *jazz,* resulted in too many hits to be practical. Figure 16.9, a subject search using the key term *Louis Armstrong,* produced a workable number.

In addition to searching the catalog, consult reference works to find books relevant to your topic. Bibliographies, such as the *MLA*

(*Text continues on p. 278.*)

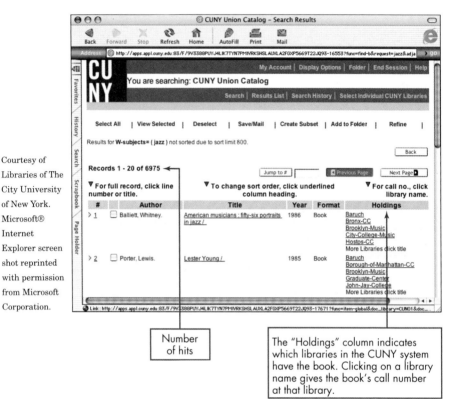

Courtesy of Libraries of The City University of New York. Microsoft® Internet Explorer screen shot reprinted with permission from Microsoft Corporation.

Number of hits

The "Holdings" column indicates which libraries in the CUNY system have the book. Clicking on a library name gives the book's call number at that library.

FIGURE 16.8 Searching an online catalog. Using the word *jazz* as a keyword in a subject search produces 6,975 sources.

LEARNING in COLLEGE

Cautions for Researching Online

In Chapter 18, we will consider ways to evaluate the usefulness and credibility of information you find on the Web. Here are some general cautions:

- The URL (Web address) is always subject to change.
- Topics are not usually covered in depth online. For depth and context, consult library databases for sources such as books and articles.
- Learn how to structure a keyword search to retrieve information relevant to you.

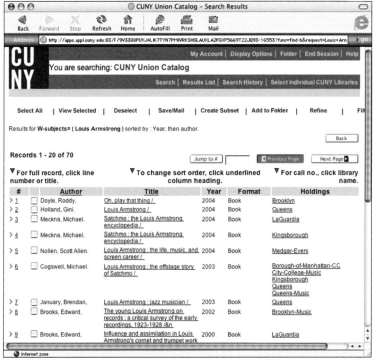

Courtesy of
Libraries of The
City University
of New York.
Microsoft®
Internet
Explorer screen
shot reprinted
with permission
from Microsoft
Corporation.

FIGURE 16.9 Changing a search term. A keyword search using the search term *Louis Armstrong* produces 70 results, a manageable number.

Bibliography, and review indexes, such as *Book Review Index*, can direct you to promising sources.

16h Take advantage of printed and online government documents.

The U.S. government publishes an enormous amount of information and research every year, most of which is available online. The *Monthly Catalog of U.S. Government Publications* and the *U.S. Government Periodicals Index* are available as online databases. The Government Printing Office's own Web site, *GPO Access* <http://www.gpoaccess. gov/>, is an excellent resource for identifying and locating federal government publications. Other online government resources include:

■ *FedWorld Information Network* (maintained by the National Technical Information Service) <http://www.fedworld.gov/>

TEXTCONNEX

Popular Internet Search Engines

General search engines: These sites allow for both category and keyword searches.

- *AltaVista* <http://www.altavista.com>
- *Google* <http://www.google.com>
- *Live Search (Microsoft)* <http://www.msn.com>
- *Vivisimo* <http://vivisimo.com>
- *Yahoo!* <http://www.yahoo.com>

Meta search engines: These sites search several different search engines at once.

- *Dogpile* <http://www.dogpile.com>
- *Internet Public Library* <http://www.ipl.org>
- *Ixquick* <http://www.ixquick.com>
- *Librarian's Index to the Internet* <http://lii.org>
- *Library of Congress* <http://loc.gov>
- *MetaCrawler* <http://www.metacrawler.com>
- *WebCrawler* <http://www.webcrawler.com>

Mediated search engines: These sites have been assembled and reviewed by people who sometimes provide annotations and commentary about topic areas and specific sites.

- *About.com* <http://www.about.com>
- *Looksmart* <http://search.looksmart.com/>

- *FirstGov* (the "U.S. Government's Official Web Portal") <http://firstgov.gov/>
- *The National Institutes of Health* <http://www.nih.gov>
- *U.S. Census Bureau* <http://www.census.gov>

16i Explore online communication.

The Internet provides access to communities with common interests and varying levels of expertise on different subjects. Carefully evaluate information from these sources (*see Chapter 18: Evaluating Sources, pp. 289–98*). Discussion lists (electronic mailing lists), Usenet news groups, blogs, and social networking sites are the most common communities. Various forums of synchronous communication in which people interact in real time exist as well. Before participating in any forums, observe the way members interact. Online forums can help you with research in the following ways:

- You can get an idea for a paper by finding out what topics interest and concern people and what people think about almost any topic.
- You can zero in on a very specific or current topic.
- You can query an expert in the field about your topic via e-mail or a social networking site.

Caution: The level of expertise among the people who participate in online forums and the scholarly seriousness of the forums themselves vary widely. Look for scholarly forums by way of your library or department Web site, and consider whether participants' claims appear reasonable. (*See also Chapter 18: Evaluating Sources, pp. 289–98.*)

Discussion lists (electronic mailing lists) are networked e-mail conversations on particular topics. Lists can be open (anyone can join) or closed (only certain people, such as members of a particular class or group, can join). If the list is open, you can subscribe by sending a message to a computer that has list-processing software installed on it.

Unlike lists, **Usenet news groups** are posted to a *news server,* a computer that hosts the news group and distributes postings to

TEXTCONNEX

Online Tools for Research

- ***Zotero*** <http://www.zotero.org>: Compatible with the Mozilla Firefox browser (version 2.0 and higher), this program automatically saves citation information for online text and images via your browser. It creates formatted references in multiple styles and helps you organize your sources by assigning tags (categories based on keywords) to them.
- ***Del.icio.us*** <http://www.del.icio.us>: This site allows you to create an online collection of Web links. You can access this list from any computer, and you can organize its entries by assigning tags.
- ***DiRT*** (*Digital Research Tools*) <http://digitalresearchtools. pbwiki.com/>: This site links to online tools that help researchers in the humanities and social sciences perform many tasks, such as collaborating with others, finding sources, and visualizing data.

participating servers. Postings are not automatically distributed by e-mail; you must subscribe to read them.

Podcasts are downloadable audio or video recordings, updated regularly. The Smithsonian provides reliable podcasts on many topics (http://www.si.edu/podcasts). **RSS** (Really Simple Syndication) **feeds** deliver the latest content from continually updated Web sites to your browser or home page. You can use RSS feeds to keep up with information on your topic, once you identify relevent Web sites.

Interactively structured Web sites provide another medium for online communication. **Social networking sites** help people form online communities. **Blogs** (*see Chapter 14*) can be designed to allow readers to post their own comments and queries. Blogs can convey the range of positions on a topic under debate. However, many blog postings consist of unsupported opinion, and they may not be monitored closely for accuracy. **Wikis,** sites designed for online collaboration, allow people both to comment on and to modify one another's contributions. When evaluating information from a wiki, check to see who can update content and whether experts review the changes. If content is not monitored by identified experts, it is safest to check your findings with another source. (*See the box on* Wikipedia *on p. 266.*).

Synchronous communication includes **chat rooms** organized by topic, where people can carry on real-time discussions. **Instant messaging (IM)** links only people who have agreed to form a conversing group. Other formats include virtual worlds such as *Second Life*, multiuser dimensions (MUDs), and object-oriented multiuser dimensions (MOOs). These can be used for collaborative projects.

TEXTCONNEX

Discussion Lists and News Groups

Check the following Web sites for more information about discussion lists and news groups:

- *Tile.net: The Reference to Internet Discussion and Information Lists* <http://tile.net/lists>: Allows you to search for discussion lists by name, description, or domain.

- *Google Groups* <http://www.google.com>: Allows you to access, create, and search news groups.

- *Newsreaders.com* <http://www.newsreaders.com/guide/news.html>: Explains why you would want a newsreader and how to use one.

- *Harley Hahn's Master List of Usenet Newsgroups* <http://www.harley.com/usenet>: A master list of Usenet news groups with descriptions. Search by category or keyword.

17 Finding and Creating Effective Visuals

Visuals often serve as support for a writer's thesis, sometimes to enhance an argument and other times to constitute the complete argument. A relief organization, for example, might post a series of compelling visuals on its Web site to persuade potential donors to contribute money following a catastrophic event.

For some writing situations, you will be able to prepare or provide your own visuals. You may, for example, provide your own sketch of an experiment, or, as the authors of the lab report in Chapter 8 have done, create bar graphs from data that you have collected (*see section 8f, p. 153*). In other situations, however, you may decide to create a visual from data that you have found in a source, or you may search in your library or on the Internet for a visual to use.

Caution: Whether you are using data from a source to create an image or incorporating an image created by someone else into your project, you must give credit to the source of the data or image. Furthermore, if you plan to publish a visual you have selected from a source on a Web site or in another medium, you must obtain permission to use it from the copyright holder, unless the source specifically states that such use is allowed.

17a Find quantitative data and display the data visually.

Research writing in many disciplines—especially in the sciences, social sciences, business, math, engineering, and other technical fields—often requires reference to quantitative information. That information generally has more impact when it is displayed visually in a chart, graph, or map than as raw numbers alone. Pie charts, for instance, show percentages of a whole. Bar graphs are often used to compare groups over time. Line graphs also show trends over time, such as the impact of wars on immigration rates and population movements. These ways of showing information are also tools of analysis. (*For examples of graphs and charts and situations in which to use them, see pp. 52–53 in Chapter 3, the box on p. 286, and pp. 69–70 in Chapter 4.*)

1. Finding existing graphs, charts, and maps

As you search for print and online sources (*see Chapter 16*), take notes on useful graphs, charts, or maps that you can incorporate (with proper acknowledgment) into your paper. Some you may find

www.mhhe.com/
mhhb2

For resources to begin your search, go to

Research >
Discipline Specific
Resources

www.mhhe.com/
mhhb2

For an interactive tutorial, go to

Writing >
Visual Rhetoric

CHECKLIST

Deciding When to Use an Image in Your Paper

Consider these questions as you look for visuals:

☐ What contribution will each image make to the text?

☐ What contribution will the set of images make to the text?

☐ How many images will you need?

☐ Where will each image appear in the text?

☐ Does the audience have enough background information to interpret the image in the way you intend?

☐ If not, is their additional information you should include in the text?

☐ What information needs to be in the caption?

☐ Have you reviewed your own text (and perhaps asked a colleague to review it, as well) to see how well the image is "working"—in terms of appropriateness, location, and context?

in online sources. If an image is available in print only, you may be able to use a scanner to print and digitize it. The graph in Figure 17.1 comes from the National Hurricane Center Web site. It shows the position of Hurricane Jeanne on September 23, 2004, and Jeanne's predicted path for the next five days, along with predicted wind speed and intensity.

SOURCE SMART

Citing Data

Make citations of data specific. Indicate the report and page number or Web address(es) where you found the information, as well as any other elements required by your documentation style. If you analyze the data, refer to any analysis in the source before presenting your own interpretation.

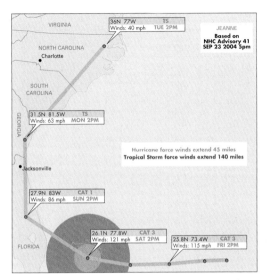

FIGURE 17.1 **A map showing the projected path and intensity of Hurricane Jeanne.**

2. Creating visuals from quantitative data

Sometimes you may find data presented in writing or in tables that would be effective in your paper as a chart or graph. You can use the data to create a visual using the graphics tools available in spreadsheet or other software.

For example, suppose you were writing a paper on population trends in the United States in the nineteenth century and wanted to illustrate the country's population growth during that period with a line graph. For population data, you might go to the Web site of the U.S. Census Bureau, which provides a wealth of quantitative historical information about the United States, all of it in the public domain. Most Census data, however, appears in tables like the one at the top of Figure 17.2 on the next page. As the figure shows, if you transfer data from such a table to a spreadsheet program or some word-processing programs, you can use the program to create a graph.

3. Displaying the data accurately

Display data in a way that is consistent with your purpose and not misleading to viewers. For example, scholar Nancy Kaplan has pointed out distortions in a graph from a National Endowment for the Arts report on reading practices (*Figure 17.3 on p. 285*). The NEA graph presents the years 1988 to 2004, showing a sharp decline in reading. However, the source for the graph, the National Center for Educational Statistics (NCES), presents a less alarming picture in Figure 17.4. (*See p. 285 to compare these two graphs.*)

283

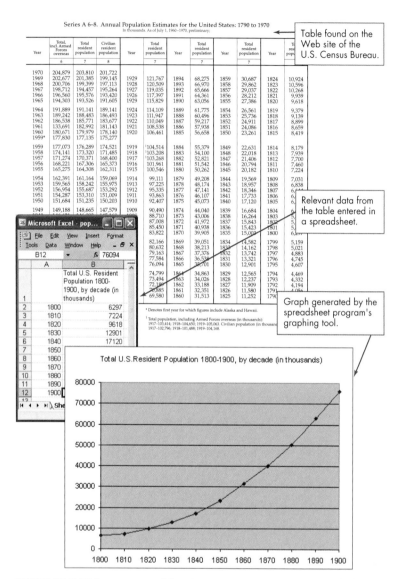

FIGURE 17.2 **Using a spreadsheet program to create a graph from data in a table.**

The NCES graph indicates that reading levels have fluctuated little from 1971 to 2004. In addition, the NEA graph is not consistent in its units: the period 1984 to 1988 takes up the same amount of space as 1988 to 1990. In selectively displaying and distorting data, the NEA graph stacks the deck to argue for the existence of a reading crisis.

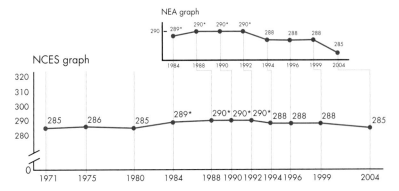

FIGURE 17.3 **NEA graph: A distorted display of reading practices indicates a decline.**

FIGURE 17.4 **NCES graph: An accurate display of reading practices shows only mild fluctuations.**

Avoid intentionally or unintentionally distorting data. Do not use photo-editing software to alter photographs. Plot the axes of line and bar graphs so that they do not misrepresent data. (*See Chapter 5, pp. 91–93.*)

👁 **17b** Search for appropriate images in online and print sources.

Photographs, pictures of artwork, drawings, diagrams, and maps can provide visual support for many kinds of papers, particularly in the humanities (English and other languages, philosophy, music, theater, and other performing arts). As with a display of quantitative data, you might choose an image from a source to use in your paper, or you might create one. If you were preparing a report comparing the way corporations are organized, for example, you might use organization charts that appear in corporate reports. Alternatively, you might use your word processor's drawing features to create your own organization charts based on information you find in the corporate reports. When using an image from another source, be sure to cite it correctly. If the image will appear on a public Web site, ask the copyright holder for permission.

1. Search online image collections and subscription databases

Several libraries and other archival institutions maintain collections of images online. The Library of Congress, for example, is a rich source of images (most in the public domain) relating to American history. Follow the guidelines for usage posted on these sites. Your library also may subscribe to an image database such as the *AP Multimedia Archive. (See the "TextConnex" box on page 288 for the URLs of these image collections.)*

www.mhhe.com/
mhhb2

For a selection of
search engines, go to
Research >
Additional Links
on Research

2. Using a search engine to conduct a keyword search for images on the Internet

Many search engines have the ability to search the Web for images alone. Suppose you were writing a paper on the northern frontier of Roman Britain. You might include a map of England separated from Scotland by Hadrian's Wall. Such an image would help the reader understand the relationship between these different territories. To find an appropriate image you could conduct an image search on

CHECKLIST

What Kind of Chart or Graph Should I Use?

In deciding on the kind of chart or graph to use, consider these questions:

☐   What information do you want to show, and why?

☐   What options do you have for displaying the information?

☐   How much context do you want to include, and why?

☐   How many charts or graphs might you need?

☐   How detailed should each one be, and why?

☐   Will your visual serve to analyze the future, or will it report on the past?

☐   How dynamic does the chart or graph need to be?

☐   What information will you leave out or minimize, and how important is that loss?

☐   What other information—an introduction, an explanation, a summary, an interpretation—will your readers need to make sense of the chart or graph?

(See also Chapter 3, pp. 52–53.)

FIGURE 17.5 An image search on *Google*. A search using the term *Hadrian's Wall* brings up pictures of the wall itself, as well as maps of its location and other images, some relevant and some not.

Google by clicking on the Images option, and entering the keyword *Hadrian's Wall,* as shown in Figure 17.5.

Image- and media-sharing sites such as *Flickr* and *YouTube* can provide sources for multimedia projects. Read the information on the site carefully to see what uses are permitted.

The *Creative Commons* site (www.creativecommons.org) lets you search for material with a *Creative Commons* license. Such a license, shown in Figure 17.6 on the next page, states permitted uses of the content. The material shown can be reproduced or altered for noncommercial purposes, as long as it is cited.

Assume that copyright applies to material on the Web unless the site says otherwise. If your project will be published or placed on a public Web site, you must obtain permission to use this material. (*See Chapter 20: Plagiarism, Copyright, and Intellectual Property,* pp. 306–14).

> *Caution:* The results of Internet image searches need to be carefully evaluated for relevance and reliability. (*See Chapter 18: Evaluating Sources, pp. 290–98.*) Make sure you record proper source information as well.

FIGURE 17.6 Creative Commons license. This page shows the terms of use for a particular online work.

TEXTCONNEX

Some Online Image Collections

Art Institute of Chicago <http://www.artic.edu/aic/index.html>: Selected works from the museum's collection

Library of Congress <http://www.loc.gov/>

National Archives Digital Classroom <http://www.archives.gov/digital_classroom/index.html>: Documents and photographs from American history

National Aeronautics and Space Administration <http://www.nasa.gov/vision/universe/features/index.html>: Images and multimedia features on space exploration

National Park Service Digital Image Archive <http://photo.itc.nps.gov/storage/images/index.html>: Thousands of public-domain photographs of U.S. national parks

New York Public Library <www.nypl.org/digital/>

Schomburg Center for Research in Black Culture <www.nypl.org/research/sc/sc.html>

VRoma: A Virtual Community for Teaching and Learning Classics <http://www.vroma.org/>: Images and other resources related to ancient Rome

3. Scanning images from a book or journal

You can use a scanner to scan some images from books and journals into a composition, but as always, only if you are sure your use is within fair use guidelines. (*See Chapter 20: Plagiarism, Copyright, and Intellectual Property, pp. 313–14.*) Credit the source of the image as well as the publication in which you found it.

18 Evaluating Sources

Digital technologies may grant fast access to a tremendous variety of sources, but it is up to you to evaluate each potential source to determine whether it is both *relevant* and *reliable*. A source is relevant if it pertains to your research topic. A source is reliable if it provides trustworthy information.

Evaluating sources requires you to think critically and make judgments about which sources will be useful for answering your research question. This process helps you manage your research and focus your time on those sources that deserve close scrutiny.

18a Question print sources.

Just because something is in print does not make it relevant or true. How can you determine whether a print source is likely to be both reliable and useful? Before assessing a source's reliability, make sure it is relevant to your topic. The box on the following pages provides some questions to ask about any source you are considering.

Relevance can be a tricky matter. Your sociology instructor will expect you to give special preference to sociological sources in a project on the organization of the workplace. Your business management

For MULTILINGUAL WRITERS

Questioning Sources

Although some cultures emphasize respect for established authors, the intellectual tradition of U.S. universities values careful questioning. Consider the pertinence and reliability of all sources.

Relevance and Reliabilty of Sources

1. Judging relevance

☐ **Do the source's title and subtitle indicate that it addresses your specific research question?** Is the level and degree of detail appropriate?

☐ **What is the publication date?** Is the material up-to-date, classic, or historic? The concept of "up to date" depends on discipline and topic. Ask your instructor how recent your sources need to be.

☐ **Does the table of contents of a book indicate that it contains useful information?**

☐ **If the source is a book, does it have an index?** Scan the index for keywords related to your topic.

☐ **Does the abstract at the beginning or summary at the end of an article suggest it will be useful?** An abstract or a summary presents the main points made in an article.

☐ **Does the work contain subheadings?** Skim the headings to see whether they indicate that the source covers useful information.

2. Judging reliability

☐ **What information can you find about the writer's credentials?** Consult biographical information about the writer in the source itself, in a biographical dictionary, or with an Internet search of the writer's name. Is the writer affiliated with a research institution? Is the writer an expert on the topic? Is the writer cited frequently in other sources about the topic?

☐ **Who is the publisher?** University presses and academic publishers are considered more scholarly than the popular press. Ask your instructor which publishers are most prominent in a specific discipline.

☐ **Does the work include a bibliography of works consulted or cited?** Trustworthy writers cite a variety of sources and document their citations properly. Does this source do so? Does the source include a variety of citations?

☐ **Does the work argue reasonably for its position and treat other views fairly?** What kind of tone does the author use? Is the work objective or subjective? Are the writer's arguments clear and logical? What is the author's point of view? Does he or she present opposing views fairly? (*For more on evaluating arguments, see Chapter 10: Arguments, pp. 184–93.*)

instructor will expect you to use material from that field in a project on the same topic. Be prepared to find that some promising sources turn out to be less relevant than you first thought.

18b Question Internet sources.

www.mhhe.com/ mhhb2

For an interactive tutorial on using the CARS checklist, go to

Research > CARS Source Evaluation Tutor

Although the questions in the Checklist box on pages 290–91 should be applied to online sources, Web resources also require additional methods of assuring the credibility of information presented. Most of the material in the library has been evaluated to some extent for credibility. Editors and publishers have reviewed the content of books, magazines, journals, and newspapers. Some presses and publications are more reputable than others. Subscription databases generally compile articles that originally appeared in print, and librarians try to purchase the most reliable databases. While you should still

SOURCE SMART

Evaluating Citations

When you look for sources using a database or library catalog, save yourself time by eliminating inappropriate search results. Based on the citation alone, you can judge:

■ The author's level of expertise (with a simple Web, catalog, or database search).
■ The title's relevance to your research question.
■ The source's currency.
■ The publisher's or publication's reputation.

evaluate all sources, you can have some confidence that most of the material you find in the library is credible.

In contrast, anyone can create a Web site that looks attractive but contains nonsense. Similarly, the people who post to blogs, discussion lists, and news groups may not be experts or even marginally well informed. So even though information on the Web may be valuable and timely, you must assess its credibility carefully. Consult the CARS (Credibility, Accuracy, Reasonableness, Support) Checklist box on pages 297–98 and consider the following questions when determining whether online information is reliable:

1. Who is hosting the site? Is the site hosted by a university or by a government agency (like the National Science Foundation or the National Endowment for the Humanities)? In general, sites hosted by institutions devoted to advancing knowledge are more likely to be trustworthy. However, they remain open to critical inquiry (as demonstrated by the NEA graph on p. 285).

2. Who is speaking on the site? A nationally recognized biologist is likely to be more credible on biological topics than a graduate student in biology. If you cannot identify the author, who is the editor or compiler? If you cannot identify an author, editor, or compiler, it is prudent not to use the source.

3. What links does the site provide? If it is networked to sites with obviously unreasonable or inaccurate content, you must question the credibility of the original site.

4. Is the information on the site supported with documentation from scholarly or otherwise reliable sources? Reliable sources of information could include government reports, for example. Do other sources cite this one?

Consider the following factors as well.

1. Assessing authority and credibility

Are the author (or editor) and sponsor of the Web site identifiable? Is the author's biographical information included? What does a Web search of the author's name reveal? Is there any indication that the author has relevant expertise on the subject? The following extensions in the Web address, or uniform resource locator (URL), can help you determine the type of site (which often tells you something about its purpose):

.com commercial (business)	**.edu** educational	**.mil** military
.org nonprofit organization	**.gov** U.S. government	**.net** network

TEXTCONNEX

Evaluating Sources

"Evaluating Web Pages: Techniques to Apply & Questions to Ask" <http://www.lib.berkeley.edu/TeachingLib/Guides/Internet/Evaluate.html>: This site from the UC Berkeley Library provides a step-by-step guide to evaluating online sources.

"Evaluating Sources of Information" <http://owl.english.purdue.edu/handouts/research/r_evalsource.html>: From the Purdue Online Writing Lab, this page provides guidelines for evaluating print and online sources.

A tilde (~) followed by a name in a URL usually means the site is a personal home page not affiliated with any organization.

2. Evaluating audience and purpose

How does the appearance of the site work with the tone of any written material to suggest an audience? (For example, a commercial site such as *Nike.com* uses music, graphics, and streaming technology to appeal to a certain kind of consumer.)

As Figures 18.1, 18.2, and 18.3 on the following pages suggest, a site's purpose influences the way it presents information and the reliability of that information. Is the site's main purpose to advocate a cause, raise money, advertise a product or service, provide factual information, present research results, provide news, share personal information, or offer entertainment? Sites focused on scholarship, with well-documented evidence, will be most useful to you.

Always try to view a site's home page so that you can best evaluate its audience and purpose. To find the home page, you may need to delete everything after the first slash in the URL.

3. Judging objectivity and bias

Look carefully at the purpose and tone of the text. Is there evidence of obvious bias? Nearly all sources express a point of view or bias either explicitly or implicitly. You should consult sources that represent a range of opinions on your topic. However, unreasonable sources have no place in academic debate. Clues that indicate a lack of reasonableness include an intemperate tone, broad claims, exaggerated statements of significance, conflicts of interest, no recognition of opposing views, and strident attacks on opposing views. (*For more on evaluating arguments, see Chapter 10: Arguments, pp. 184–93.*)

293

4. Weighing relevance and timeliness

In what ways does the information from the online source specifically address your topic or thesis? Are the site's intended audience and purpose similar to yours? Does the site indicate how recently it was updated, and are most of its links still working?

5. Context

How does the source fit with other information you have found or already know about the subject? If the source is a blog or a post on a discussion list, do others' comments or posts make the writer appear more credible?

Consider a student writing a paper on the reintroduction of gray wolves in the western United States following their near extinction. Many environmentalists have favored this program, while farmers and ranchers have worried about its impact on livestock. Recent debate has centered on whether wolf populations have recovered sufficiently to no longer need protection.

The student conducts a keyword search using an online search engine and finds the site in Figure 18.1, from the U.S. Fish and Wildlife Service. This site focuses on the gray wolf population in

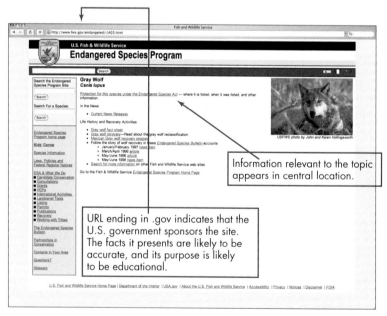

Information relevant to the topic appears in central location.

URL ending in .gov indicates that the U.S. government sponsors the site. The facts it presents are likely to be accurate, and its purpose is likely to be educational.

FIGURE 18.1 U.S. Fish & Wildlife Service Endangered Species Program site on the gray wolf. This government site provides information on the efforts to preserve and rebuild the gray wolf population in the United States.

America and its status under the Endangered Species Act. The site has a reasonable, somewhat objective stance. As the site of a U.S. government agency, its data is likely to be accurate, although such sites are not immune from politics or bias. For example, the U.S. Fish & Wildlife Service conducted the wolf reintroduction program and probably approves of it (whether or not it endorses continued protection for wolves). Information on the site appears in a simple, easy-to-follow format, indicating an educational purpose. It links to other government sites, such as the Department of the Interior site. Scrolling down, the student sees the site has been updated recently. This site's apparent authority, credibility, and purpose make it a good source for facts about the wolf reintroduction program.

Next the student finds the site in Figure 18.2. Following the link that says "About us," the student learns that the site is sponsored by the WWF (originally World Wildlife Fund), a nonprofit organization that advocates for environmental conservation. The site's purpose appears to be educational and persuasive: it includes information about wolves and a call to action on their behalf. It includes policy papers with clearly documented sources for the data, suggesting the

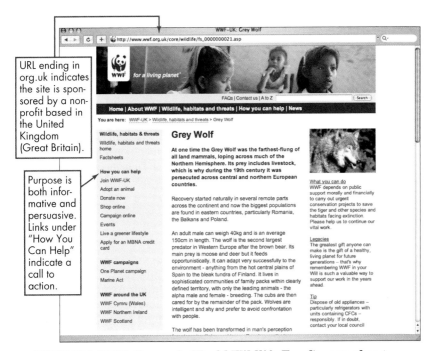

FIGURE 18.2 **WWF (formerly World Wildlife Fund) page about Europe's grey wolf.** This advocacy site describes efforts to preserve a wolf population in Europe.

295

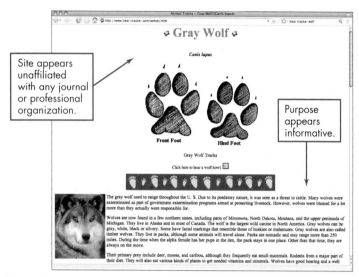

FIGURE 18.3 This site's information appears to be accurate, but it does not document its sources or present its author's credentials.

site's reliability. However, the student should note that the site deals only with the reintroduction of wolves in Europe, not the United States. It would be a relevant source if the student used the European reintroduction program as an example.

After further research, the student reaches the site in Figure 18.3. This site gives apparently accurate information about wolves in an impartial way. Scrolling down, the student sees that the site also features advertisements, which do not appear in most scholarly sources. The site does not state the author's credentials, nor does it include documentation for its information. For these reasons, the student should confirm its statements with another source before using them in an academic paper.

18c Evaluate a source's arguments.

As you read the sources you have selected, you should continue to assess their reliability. Look for arguments that are qualified, supported with evidence, and well documented. Avoid relying on sources that appeal solely to emotions instead of rational thought or that promote one-sided agendas instead of inquiry and discussion.

A fair-minded researcher needs to read and evaluate sources on many sides of an issue. Doing so includes consulting relevant primary sources if they exist.

CHECKLIST

Using the CARS Checklist to Evaluate Web Sites

A Web site that is credible, accurate, reasonable, and supported (CARS) should meet the following criteria.

Credibility

☐ The source is trustworthy; you would consider a print version to be authoritative (for example, an online edition of a respected newspaper or major news magazine).

☐ The argument and use of evidence are clear and logical.

☐ The author's or sponsor's credentials are available (visit the home page and look for a link that says "About Us").

☐ Quality control is evident (spelling and grammar are correct; links are functional).

☐ The source is a known or respected authority; it has organizational support (such as a university, a research institution, or a major news publication).

Accuracy

☐ The site is updated frequently, if not daily (and includes "last-updated" information).

☐ The site is factual, not speculative, and provides evidence for its assertions.

☐ The site is detailed; text appears in full paragraphs.

☐ The site is comprehensive, including archives, links, and additional resources. A search feature and table of contents or tabs allow users to quickly find the information they need.

☐ The site's purpose includes completeness and accuracy.

Reasonableness

☐ The site is fair, balanced, and objective. (Look at comments on a blog or related messages on a news group.)

(continued)

☐ The site makes its purpose clear (is it selling something? prompting site visitors to sign a petition? promoting a new film?).

☐ The site contains no conflicts of interest.

☐ The site content does not include fallacies or a slanted tone (*for more on fallacies, see Chapter 10: Arguments, pp. 188–91*).

Support

☐ The site lists sources for its information, providing links where appropriate.

☐ The site clarifies which content it is responsible for and which links are created by unrelated authors or sponsors.

☐ The site provides contact information for its authors and/or sponsors.

☐ If the site is an academic resource, it follows the conventions of a specific citation style (for example, MLA, APA).

Exercise 18.1   Web site evaluation

Working alone or in groups, choose one of the following topics:

1. The cost of prescription drugs in the United States
2. Alternative energy sources
3. Immigration
4. Global warming
5. The role of private and charter schools in a democracy

For your topic, find at least three Web sites and analyze them according to the CARS checklist. Describe and rate each site's credibility, accuracy, reasonablenes, and support. Be prepared to share example Web pages with your class (either print them out, or use a projection screen) and to point out how they demonstrate the characteristics you have identified.

19 Doing Research in the Archive, Field, and Lab

Research involves more than finding answers to questions in books, journal articles, and other print and online resources (**secondary research**). (*See Chapter 15: Understanding Research, pp. 250–59.*) When you conduct **primary research**—looking up old maps, consulting census records, polling community members, interviewing participants in a campus protest, observing the natural world—you participate in the discovery of knowledge.

The three kinds of primary research discussed in this chapter are archival research, field research, and laboratory research:

- **Archival research:** An **archive** is a cataloged collection of documents, manuscripts, or other materials, possibly including receipts, wills, photographs, sound recordings, or other kinds of media. Usually, an archive is organized around one key person, movement, circumstance, or phenomenon.

- **Field research:** Field research takes you out into the world to gather and record information.

- **Laboratory research:** Most science courses you take will include a laboratory component. In the laboratory, you work individually or on a team to record each step of an experiment. Eventually, you will create your own experiments.

19a Adhere to ethical principles when doing primary research.

In the archive, field, or lab, you work directly with something precious and immediate: an original record, a group of people, or special

---

CHARTING the TERRITORY

Research in the Disciplines

Different forms of primary research are characteristic of different disciplines. Here are some examples:

- **Archival research:** Languages and literature; education; music and the performing arts; visual arts; media and popular culture; social sciences
- **Field research:** Social sciences; marketing and advertising; media and communication
- **Laboratory research:** Life sciences; physical sciences; computer science; engineering

materials. An ethical researcher shows respect for materials, experimental subjects, fellow researchers, and readers. Here are some guidelines for ethical research:

- Handle original documents and materials with great care, always leaving sources and data available for other researchers.
- Report your sources and results accurately.
- Follow proper procedures when working with human participants.

Research with human participants should also adhere to the following basic principles:

- **Confidentiality:** People who fill out surveys, participate in focus groups, or respond to interviews should be assured that their names will not be used without their permission.
- **Informed consent:** Before participating in an experiment, all participants must sign a statement affirming that they understand the general purpose of the research.
- **Minimal risk:** Participants in experiments should not incur any risks greater than they do in everyday life.
- **Protection of vulnerable groups:** Researchers must be held strictly accountable for research done with the physically disabled, prisoners, those who are mentally incompetent, minors, the elderly, and pregnant women.

Be fair when you refute the primary research or the views of others. Even if your purpose is to prove fellow researchers wrong, review their work and state their viewpoints in words that they themselves would recognize as accurate.

19b Prepare yourself for archival research.

Archives are found in libraries, museums, other institutions, private collections, and on video- and audiotape. Some archival collections are accessible through the Internet. Your own attic may contain family archives—letters, diaries, and photograph collections that could have value to a researcher. The more you know ahead of time about your area of study, the more likely you will be to see the significance of an item in an archival collection.

Archives generally require that you telephone or e-mail to arrange a time for your visit. Some archives may be restricted; call or e-mail well in advance to find out whether you will need references, a letter of introduction, or other qualifying papers.

Archives also generally require you to present a photo identification, and to leave personal items at a locker or coat check. They will also have strict policies about reproducing materials and rarely if ever allow anything to leave the premises. The more you know about the archive's policies and procedures before you visit, the more productive your visit will be.

19c Plan your field research carefully.

Field research involves recording observations, conducting interviews, and administering surveys. If your research plans include visiting a place of business, a house of worship, a school or hospital, or nearly any other building, call first and obtain permission. Explain the nature of your project, the date and time you would like to visit, how much time you think you will need, and exactly what it is you will be doing (observing? interviewing people? taking photographs?). Ask for a confirming letter or e-mail. If you need to cancel or reschedule your visit, be sure to give ample notice. Always write a thank-you note after you have concluded your research.

If you are denied permission to do your field research at a particular place, do not take it personally. Do *not* attempt to conduct your research without first obtaining permission. To do so is unethical and may constitute illegal trespassing.

1. Observing and writing field notes

When you use direct observation, keep careful records in order to retain the information you gather (*see Figure 19.1 on p. 303*). Here are some guidelines to follow:

- Be systematic in your observations, but be alert to unexpected behavior.
- Record what you see and hear as objectively as possible.
- Take more notes than you think you will need.
- When appropriate, categorize the types of behavior you are looking for, and devise a system for counting instances of each type.
- When you have recorded data over a significant period of time, group your observations into categories for more careful study.

(*For advice on conducting direct observations for a case study, see Chapter 9: Interpretive Analyses, pp. 175–78.*)

2. Conducting interviews

Interviews may be conducted in person, by phone, or online. To be useful as research tools, they require systematic preparation and implementation.

TEXTCONNEX

Online Information about Archives

Here are some Internet sites that will help you find and understand a wide range of archival sources:

- **American Memory** <http://memory.loc.gov/ammem>: This site offers access to more than 9 million digital items from over 100 collections of material on U.S. history and culture.

- **ArchivesUSA** <http://archives.chadwyck.com>: This subscription service is available through ProQuest. It provides information about 150,000 collections of primary source material and more than 5,000 other manuscript repositories.

- **Radio Program Archive** <http://umdrive.memphis.edu/ mbensman/public>: This site lists radio archives available from the University of Memphis and explains how to obtain audio cassettes of significant radio programs.

- **Repositories of Primary Sources** <www.uidaho.edu/ special-collections/OtherRepositories.html>: This site lists more than 5,000 Web sites internationally, including holdings of manuscripts, rare books, historical photographs, and other archival materials.

- **Television News Archive** <http://tvnews.vanderbilt.edu>: This site provides summaries of television news broadcasts and information on how to order videocassettes.

- **U.S. National Archives and Records Administration** (NARA) <http://www.nara.gov>: Learn how to use the National Archives in this site's research room, and then search the site for the documents you want.

- **Virtual Library Museums Page** <http://www.icom.org/vlmp>: This site lists online museums throughout the world.

- **Women Writers Project** <http://www.wwp.brown.edu/texts/ wwoentry.html>: This site lists archived texts—by pre-Victorian women writers—that are available through the project.

- Identify appropriate people for your interviews based on your purpose.

- Do background research, and plan a list of open-ended questions.

- Take careful notes, and if possible make a recording of the interview (but only if you have obtained your subject's permission beforehand). Verify quotations.

- Follow up on vague responses with questions that ask for specific information. Do not rush your interviewees.

FIGURE 19.1 Observing and taking notes. Systematic, purposeful observation and careful note taking are crucial to the success of all field work. Archeologist Anna Roosevelt takes notes during the excavation of a site in the Amazon region of South America.

- Politely probe inconsistencies and contradictions.
- Write thank-you notes to interviewees, and later send them copies of your report.

You might identify appropriate subjects on your campus through a relevant academic department. For example, if your research paper is on the effects of globalization on manufacturing jobs in the United States, you might visit the home pages of your campus business and political science departments to see whether anyone on the faculty is studying that issue.

Group interviews, called *focus groups,* serve in a number of fields, including marketing, education, and psychology. To find subjects for

SOURCE SMART

Quoting from Interviews

Before an interview, obtain permission to quote the interviewee. If the interview is not being recorded (or captured on a transcript if online), use oversized quotation marks to enclose direct quotations in your notes. Record the interviewee's name and the location and date of the interview in your research notebook. Afterward, verify quotations with your interviewee.

a focus group, consider posting flyers around campus or advertising in your campus newspaper.

3. Taking surveys

Conducted either orally or in writing, **surveys** are made up of structured questions. Written surveys are called **questionnaires.**

The surveys and polls used by political campaigns and the news media are designed with the help of statisticians and tabulated according to complex mathematical equations. For many college research projects, an informal survey (one not designed to be statistically accurate) may be adequate. Try to approximate a random sampling of a large group.

 LEARNING in COLLEGE

Conducting a Survey

Student Lara Delforest wanted to know if students would support a plan to provide more shuttle-bus service from existing parking garages.

She asked these questions to qualify a potential respondent:

1. Are you a student on this campus?
2. Do you currently drive to campus?
3. If you do drive, where do you park?
4. If you don't drive, how do you get to campus?

Lara thanked but did not ask further questions of respondents who were not regularly on campus or who did not drive or take public transportation. She asked these additional questions of the rest:

5. Is the availability of parking on or near campus a factor in your decision to drive or not to drive?
6. If you drive to campus, are you aware of other options? If so, what are those options?
7. For each of the options you just mentioned, explain what would make you consider or reject each one.
8. Are you in favor of creating more parking spaces on campus? Why or why not?
9. Would you be in favor of adding additional campus shuttle buses from existing off-campus parking? Why or why not?

Lara asked the respondents their full names (but accepted just first names) so that she could accurately identify them. To keep her notes organized, Lara turned to a new page of her notebook for each respondent.

The following suggestions will help you prepare informal surveys:

- **Define your purpose and your target population.** Are you trying to gauge attitudes, learn about typical behaviors, or both?
- **Write clear directions and questions.** For example, if you are asking multiple-choice questions, make sure that you cover all possible options and that your options do not overlap.
- **Use neutral language.** Make sure your questions do not suggest a preference for one answer over another.
- **Make the survey brief and easy to complete.** Most informal surveys should be no longer than one page (front and back).

Many colleges have offices that must review and approve student surveys. Check to see what guidelines your school may have.

19d Keep a notebook when doing lab research.

To provide a complete and accurate account of your laboratory work, keep careful records in a notebook. The following guidelines will help you take accurate notes on your research:

1. **Record immediate, on-the-spot, accurate notes on what happens in the lab.** Write down as much detail as possible. Measure precisely; do not estimate. Identify major pieces of apparatus, unusual chemicals, and laboratory animals in enough detail that a reader can determine, for example, the size or type of equipment you used. Use drawings, when appropriate, to illustrate complicated equipment setups. Include tables, when useful, to present results.

2. **Follow a basic format.** Present your results in a format that allows you to communicate all the major features of an experiment. The five basic sections you need are title, purpose, materials and methods, results, and conclusions. (*See Chapter 8: Informative Reports, pp. 147–54.*)

3. **Write in complete sentences.** Resist the temptation to use shorthand to record your notes. Later, the complete sentences will provide a clear record of your procedures and results. Highlight connections within and between sentences by using the following transitions: *then, next, consequently, because,* and *therefore.* Cause-effect relationships should be clear.

4. Revise and correct your laboratory notebook in visible ways when necessary. If you make mistakes in recording laboratory results, correct them as clearly as possible, either by erasing or by crossing out and rewriting on the original sheet. If you make an uncorrectable mistake in your lab notebook, simply fold the sheet lengthwise and mark "omit" on the face side.

Unanticipated results often occur in the lab, and you may find yourself jotting down notes on a convenient piece of scrap paper. Attach these notes to your notebook.

20 Plagiarism, Copyright, and Intellectual Property

Integrity and honesty require us to acknowledge others, especially when we use their words or ideas. Researchers who fail to acknowledge their sources—either intentionally or unintentionally—commit plagiarism. Buying a term paper from an online paper mill or "borrowing" a friend's completed assignment are obvious forms of plagiarism. But plagiarism also involves paraphrasing or summarizing others' material without properly citing the source of the idea or information. (*See Chapter 21: Working with Sources and Avoiding Plagiarism, pp. 322–32, for more on paraphrasing and summarizing.*)

www.mhhe.com/
mhhb2
For more information, go to

Research >
Avoiding
Plagiarism >
What Is Plagiarism?

Journalists who are caught plagiarizing are publicly exposed and often fired by the publications they write for. Scholars who fail to acknowledge the words and ideas of others lose their professional credibility, and often their jobs. Students who plagiarize may receive a failing grade for the assignment or course and face other disciplinary action—including expulsion. Your campus probably has a written policy regarding plagiarism and its consequences.

The Internet has made many types of sources available, and it can be unclear what, when, and how to cite. For example, bloggers and other Web authors often reproduce material from other sites, while some musicians make their music available for free download. Although the line between "original" and "borrowed" appears to be blurring, there are guidelines to help you credit sources appropriately.

20a   Understand how plagiarism relates to copyright and intellectual property.

Related to plagiarism are copyright and intellectual property, which apply to *published* use of someone else's work. **Copyright** is the legal right to control the reproduction of any original work—a piece of writing, a musical composition, a play, a movie, a computer program, a photograph, a work of art. A copyrighted work is the **intellectual property** of the copyright holder, whether that entity is a publisher, a record company, an entertainment conglomerate, or the individual creator of the work. This section provides additional information on these important legal concepts.

1. Copyright

A copyrighted text—such as a novel, a short story in a magazine, or an article in an academic journal—cannot be reproduced (in print or online) without the written permission of the copyright holder. The copyright protects the right of authors and publishers to make money from their productions. The legal efforts of some musicians and recording companies to stop the free downloading of music from the Internet are based on copyright law. The musicians and companies claim—and the

SOURCE SMART

Determining What Is "Common Knowledge"

Information that an audience could be expected to know from many sources is considered common knowledge. You do not need to cite common knowledge if you use your own wording and sentence structure. Common knowledge can take various forms, including at least these four:

- Folktales with no particular author (for example, Johnny Appleseed spread apple trees across the United States)
- Common sense (for example, property values in an area will fall if crime rises)
- Historical facts and dates (for example, the United States entered World War II in 1941)
- Information found in many general reference works (for example, the heart drives the body's circulation system)

Maps, charts, graphs, and other visual displays of information are not considered common knowledge. Even though everyone knows that Paris is the capital of France, if you reproduce a map of France in your paper, you must credit the map's creator.

courts have so far agreed—that downloaders are stealing their intellectual property. Even when artists like Prince and Radiohead make their songs available online for free, they still control copyright. You could not sample one of these songs in a new work that you plan to sell without the artist's consent.

2. Fair use

www.mhhe.com/ mhhb2

For information on material that does not need citing, go to

Research > Avoiding Plagiarism > Common Knowledge

Most academic uses of copyrighted sources are protected under the **fair use** provision of copyright law. Under this provision, you can legally quote a brief passage from a copyrighted text in a paper without infringing on the copyright. Of course, to avoid plagiarism, you must identify the passage as a quotation and cite it properly. (*For details, see pp. 313–14 and 328–31.*)

3. Intellectual property

In addition to works protected by copyright, intellectual property includes patented inventions, trademarks, industrial designs, and similar intellectual creations that are protected by other laws.

SOURCE SMART

What Must Be Acknowledged?

You **do not** have to acknowledge:

- Common knowledge expressed in your words and sentence structure (*see the box on p. 307*)
- Your independent thinking
- Your original field observations, surveys, or experimental results

You **must** acknowledge:

- Any concepts you learned from a source, whether or not you copy the source's language
- Interviews other than surveys
- Abstracts
- Visuals
- Statistics, including those you use to create your own visuals (*see Chapter 17, pp. 281–83*)
- Your own work for another assignment (use *only* with your instructor's permission)

Acknowledge the source each time you cite from the material, regardless of the length of the selection. If you use multiple sources in a paragraph, make clear which sentences are from which sources.

20b Avoid plagiarism.

Under pressure, we tend to make poor choices. Inadvertent plagiarism occurs when busy students take notes carelessly, forgetting to jot down the source of a paraphrase or accidentally inserting material downloaded from a Web site into a paper. Deliberate plagiarism occurs when students wait until the last minute and then "borrow" a paper from a friend or copy and paste large portions of an online article into their own work. No matter how tired or pressured you may be, nothing can justify plagiarism.

To avoid plagiarism, adhere to these guidelines:

- When you receive your research assignment, write down your thoughts and questions before you begin looking at sources. Use this record to keep track of changes in your ideas.

- As you proceed with your research, distinguish your additional ideas from those of others by using a different color or font.

- Do not rely too much on one source, or you may easily slip into using that person's thoughts as your own.

- Keep accurate records while doing research and taking notes. If you do not know where you got an idea or a piece of information, do not use it in your paper until you find out.

- When you take notes, be sure to put quotation marks around words, phrases, or sentences taken verbatim from a source, and note the page number. If you use any of those words, phrases, or sentences when summarizing or paraphrasing the source, make sure to put them in quotation marks. Changing a word here and there while keeping a source's sentence structure or phrasing constitutes plagiarism, even if you credit the source for the ideas. (*For more on paraphrase, summary, and quotation, see Chapter 21: Working with Sources and Avoiding Plagiarism, pp. 322–28.*)

- Cite the sources of all ideas, opinions, facts, and statistics that are not common knowledge. (*See the box on p. 307.*)

- Choose an appropriate documentation style, and use it consistently and properly. (*See Part 4: Documenting across the Curriculum.*)

When working with electronic sources, keep in mind the following guidelines:

- Print out or save to your computer any online source you consult. Note the date on which you viewed the source. Keep the complete URL in case you need to view the source again. Some documentation styles require you to include the URL in your citation. (*See Chapter 21: Working*

309

TEXTCONNEX

Learning More about Plagiarism,
Copyright and Fair Use, and Intellectual Property

Plagiarism

- For more information about plagiarism, see the Council of Writing Program Administrators' "Defining and Avoiding Plagiarism: The WPA Statement on Best Practices" <www.wpacouncil.org/positions/plagiarism.html>.
- Educators at Indiana University offer tips on avoiding plagiarism at <www.Indiana.edu/~frick/plagiarism.html>.
- Georgetown University's Honor Council offers an example of a campus honor code pertaining to plagiarism and academic ethics at <gervaseprograms.georgetown.edu/hc/plagiarism.html>.

Copyright and Fair Use

- For information on and a discussion of fair use, see *Copyright and Fair Use* at <fairuse.stanford.edu>, and the U.S. Copyright Office at <www.copyright.gov>.
- The University of Texas posts guidelines for fair use and multimedia projects at <www.utsystem.edu/OGC/IntellectualProperty/mmfruse.htm>.

Intellectual Property

- For information about what constitutes intellectual property and related issues, see the World Intellectual Property Organization Web site at <www.wipo.int>.
- For a legal perspective, the American Intellectual Property Law Association offers information and overviews of recent cases at <www.aipla.org>.

with Sources and Avoiding Plagiarism, pp. 315–16 for other information to note about your sources.)

- If you copy and paste a passage from a Web site into a word-processing file, use a different font to identify that material as well as the URL and your access date.
- Acknowledge all sites you use as sources, including those you access via links on another site.
- As a courtesy, request permission before quoting from blogs, news group postings, or e-mails.
- Acknowledge any audio, video, or illustrated material that has informed your research.

CHECKLIST

Avoiding Plagiarism

Sources

☐ Is my thesis my own idea, not something I found in one of my sources?

☐ Have I used a variety of sources, not just one or two?

☐ Have I identified each source clearly?

☐ Do I fully understand and explain all words, phrases, and ideas in my paper?

☐ Have I acknowledged all ideas that are neither based on my original thinking nor common knowledge?

Quotations

☐ Have I enclosed in quotation marks any uncommon terms, distinctive phrases, or direct quotations from a source?

☐ Have I checked all quotations against the original source?

☐ Do I include ellipsis marks and brackets where I have altered the original wording and capitalization of quotations?

Paraphrases

☐ Have I used my own words and sentence structure for all paraphrases?

☐ Have I maintained the original meaning?

Summaries

☐ Do all my summaries include my own wording and sentence structure? Are they shorter than the original text?

☐ Do they accurately represent the content of the original?

Documentation

☐ Have I indicated my source for all quotations, paraphrases, summaries, statistics, and visuals either within the text or in a parenthetical citation?

☐ Have I included citations for all visuals from other sources (or visuals based on data from other sources)?

☐ Have I included page numbers as required for all quotations, paraphrases, and summaries?

☐ Does every in-text citation have a corresponding entry in the list of works cited or references?

Permission

☐ If I am composing a public online text, have I received all needed permissions?

 For MULTILINGUAL STUDENTS

Cultural Assumptions and
Misunderstandings about Plagiarism

Respect for ownership of ideas is a core value in the United States. Your culture may consider the knowledge in classic texts a national heritage and, therefore, common property. As a result, you may have been encouraged to incorporate words and information from those texts into your writing without citing their source. In the United States, academic culture requires you to identify any use you make of someone else's original work and to cite the work properly in an appropriate documentation style (*see Part 4: Documenting across the Curriculum, which begins on p. 341*). You must similarly credit the source of ideas that are not considered common knowledge. You should accept these rules as nonnegotiable and apply them conscientiously to avoid plagiarism and its serious consequences. When in doubt about citation rules, ask your instructor.

TEXTCONNEX

Plagiarism and Online Sources

When you use material from a Web site, you might inadvertently be quoting material that has itself been plagiarized from another source. How can you be certain that material in an online source is being used fairly? Follow the guidelines in Chapter 18: Evaluating Sources to evaluate a Web site's reliability. You can also choose a sentence from the suspect material and enter it into a search engine. If you get a hit, investigate further to see if one site is copying from the other—or both are copying from some other source. Ask your instructor for further advice.

Although it is easy to copy and paste material from the Internet without acknowledgment, it is ill-advised to do so. Instructors can just as easily detect such plagiarism by taking the copied text and using a search engine to locate the original.

Posting material on a publicly accessible Web site is usually considered the legal equivalent of publishing it in print format. (Password-protected sites generally are exempt.) When writing a composition to be posted online and accessible to the general public, seek copyright permission from all your sources. (*See the guidelines for fair use below and the box on p. 310.*)

20c Use copyrighted materials fairly.

www.mhhe.com/
mhhb2

For more information
and interactive
exercises, go to

Research >
Avoiding
Plagiarism >
Using Copyrighted
Materials

All original works, including student papers, graphics, videos, and e-mail, are covered by copyright, even if they do not bear an official copyright symbol. A copyright grants its owner—often the creator—exclusive rights to the use of a protected work, including reproducing, distributing, and displaying the work. The popularity of the Web as a venue of publication has led to increased concerns about the fair use of copyrighted material. Before you publish your paper on the Web or produce a multimedia presentation that includes audio, video, and graphic elements copied from a Web site, make sure that you have used copyrighted material fairly by considering these four questions:

▪ **What is the purpose of the use?** Educational, nonprofit, and personal uses are more likely to be considered fair than commercial use.

- **What is the nature of the work being used?** In most cases, imaginative and unpublished materials can be used only if you have the permission of the copyright holder.

- **What effect would this use have on the market for the original?** The use of a work is usually considered unfair if it would hurt sales of the original.

- **How much of the copyrighted work is being used?** The use of a small portion of a text is more likely to be considered fair than copying a whole work.

While no clear legal definition of "a small portion of text" exists, one conservative guideline is that you can quote up to fifty words from an article (print or online) and three hundred words from a book. It is safest to ask permission to republish an entire work or a substantial portion of a text (be cautious with poems, plays, and songs). Images and multimedia clips are considered entire works. Also, you may need permission to link your Web site to another.

When in doubt, always ask permission.

21 Working with Sources and Avoiding Plagiarism

Once you have a research question to answer, an idea about what the library and Internet have to offer, and some reliable, appropriate materials in hand, you are ready to begin working with your sources. Attention to detail and keeping careful records at this stage will help you stay organized, save time, and avoid plagiarism later.

21a Maintain a working bibliography.

As you research, compile a **working bibliography**—a list of those books, articles, pamphlets, Web sites, and other sources that seem most likely to help you answer your research question. Maintain an accurate and complete record of all sources you consult, so that you will be able to find any source again and cite all your sources accurately.

Although the exact bibliographic information you will need depends on your documentation style, the following list includes the major elements of most systems. (*See Part 4: Documenting across the Curriculum, pp. 341–450, for the requirements of specific documentation styles.*)

Book:

- Call number (so you can find the source again; not required for documentation)
- All authors, editors, and translators
- Title of chapter
- Title and subtitle of book
- Edition (if not the first), volume number (if applicable)
- Publication information (city, publisher, date)
- Medium (print)

Periodical article:

- Authors
- Title and subtitle of article
- Title and subtitle of periodical
- Date, edition or volume number, issue number
- Page numbers
- Medium (print)

Article from database (in addition to the above):

- Name of database
- Date you retrieved source
- URL of database's home page (if online)
- Page numbers (if any, as with a PDF)
- Medium (Web, CD-ROM, or DVD-ROM)

Internet source (including visual, audio, video):

- All authors, editors, or creators
- Title and subtitle of source
- Title of site, project, or database
- Version or edition, if any
- Publication information, if available, including any about a version in another medium (such as print, radio, or film)
- Date of electronic publication or latest update, if available
- Sponsor of site
- Date you accessed site
- URL of site
- Any other identifying numbers, such as a Digital Object Identifier (DOI)

Other sources:

- Author or creator
- Title
- Format (for example, photograph or lecture)
- Title of publication, if any

(*continued on p. 316*) **315**

Other sources (*continued*)
- Publisher, sponsor, or institution housing the source

- Date of creation or publication
- Any identifying numbers

(*See the foldouts at the beginning of Chapters 23 and 24 for examples of these elements.*)

You can record bibliographic information on note cards or in a word-processing file; you can print out or e-mail to yourself bibliographic information from the results of online searches in databases and library catalogs; or you can record bibliographic information directly on photocopies or printouts of source material. You can also save most Web pages and other online sources to your computer.

1. Using note cards or a word processor

Before computers became widely available, most researchers used 3-by-5-inch or 4-by-6-inch note cards to compile the working bibliography, with each potential source getting a separate card as in Figure 21.1. This method is still useful. Besides not requiring a computer, it allows you to rearrange information when you are deciding how to organize your paper. You can use the cards to include all information necessary for documentation, to record brief quotations, and to note your own comments (carefully marked as yours).

Instead of handwriting on cards, you can record bibliographic information in a word-processor file. You can also combine the two methods, recording bibliographic information in a word-processing file, then printing it, cutting it out, and taping it on a note card.

SOURCE SMART

The Uses and Limits of Bibliographic Software

Programs like *Microsoft Word 2007* allow you to store source data, automatically insert citations in common documentation styles, and generate a list of references. These programs often do not incorporate the most recent updates to documentation styles. Nor do they accommodate all types of sources. Talk to your instructor before using bibliographic software, and check your citations carefully against the models in *Part 4: Documenting across the Curriculum (pp. 341–450).* Also double-check references that a database creates for you.

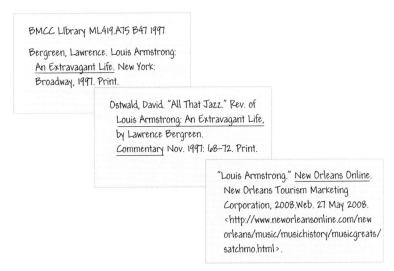

BMCC Library ML419.A75 B47 1997

Bergreen, Lawrence. Louis Armstrong:
An Extravagant Life. New York:
Broadway, 1997. Print.

Ostwald, David. "All That Jazz." Rev. of
Louis Armstrong: An Extravagant Life,
by Lawrence Bergreen.
Commentary Nov. 1997: 68–72. Print.

"Louis Armstrong." New Orleans Online.
New Orleans Tourism Marketing
Corporation, 2008.Web. 27 May 2008.
< http://www.neworleansonline.com/new
orleans/music/musichistory/musicgreats/
satchmo.html >.

FIGURE 21.1 Three sample bibliography note cards (in MLA style)—one for a book (*top*), one for a journal article (*middle*), and one for a Web site (*bottom*). (If typed, titles would be italicized instead of underlined. MLA style does not require call numbers or (usually) URLs, but it is useful to note this information while doing research.)

2. Printing the results of online searches in databases and library catalogs

Search results in online indexes and databases usually include complete bibliographic information about the sources they list. (*See Figure 16.3, p. 269, as well as the foldouts preceding Chapters 23 and 24 for illustrations showing where to find this information.*) You can print these results directly from your browser or, in some cases, save them on disk and transfer them to a word-processing file. Be sure to record also the name and URL of the database and the date of your search. (If you download the full text of an article from a database and refer to it in your paper, your citation must include information about the database if your documentation style requires it, as well as bibliographic information about the article itself.) If you rely on search-result printouts to compile your working bibliography, you may want to use a highlighter to indicate those sources you plan to consult.

You can similarly print out or save bibliographic information from the results of searches of online library catalogs. Some college libraries make it possible to compile a list of sources and e-mail it to yourself as in Figure 21.2 on the next page.

317

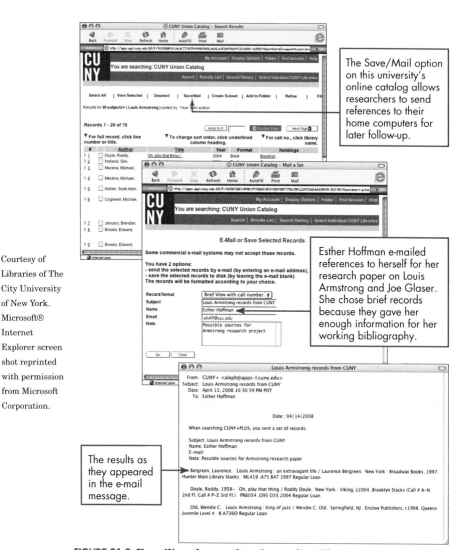

Courtesy of
Libraries of The
City University
of New York.
Microsoft®
Internet
Explorer screen
shot reprinted
with permission
from Microsoft
Corporation.

The Save/Mail option on this university's online catalog allows researchers to send references to their home computers for later follow-up.

Esther Hoffman e-mailed references to herself for her research paper on Louis Armstrong and Joe Glaser. She chose brief records because they gave her enough information for her working bibliography.

The results as they appeared in the e-mail message.

FIGURE 21.2 E-mailing the results of an online library catalog search.

3. Using photocopies and printouts from Web sites

If you photocopy articles, essays, or pages of reference works from a print or microfilm source, take time to note the bibliographic information on the photocopy. Spending a few extra minutes to do so can save you lots of time later. Similarly, if you print out a source you find on a Web site or copy it to your computer, be sure to note the site's author, sponsor, date of publication or last update, complete URL, and the date you visited it.

Bergreen, Laurence. *Louis Armstrong: An Extravagant Life.* New York: Broadway, 1997. Print.
Aimed at a popular audience, Bergreen's book provides a detailed history of Armstrong's life as well as its social context. Bergreen also presents Armstrong's relationship with manager Glaser throughout the years and Glaser's own colorful background. Essentially the partnership provided benefits to both performer and manager. (Ostwald notes a few errors.)

Collier, James Lincoln. *Louis Armstrong: An American Genius.* New York: Oxford UP, 1983. Print.
This scholarly study of Armstrong's life and work presents his formative influence on American music. Collier includes numerous telling details that support my ideas about Armstrong and Glaser's relationship, such as the fact that Glaser paid Armstrong's personal expenses while acting as his manager.

FIGURE 21.3 Sample annotated bibliography. A section of Esther Hoffman's annotated bibliography.

21b Create an annotated bibliography.

An annotated bibliography can be very useful to you in your research. The bibliography includes full citation details, correctly formatted, which you will need for your paper. The annotation provides a summary of major points for each source, including your own reactions and ideas about where this material might fit in your paper (*see Figure 21.3*). Also record your evaluation of the source's relevance and reliability (*see Chapter 18: Evaluating Sources, pp. 289–98*). As you conduct research, you will find that an annotated bibliography helps you remember what you have found in your search, as well as helping you organize your findings.

21c Take notes on your sources.

Taking notes helps you think through your research question. Having a research question in mind helps you read more systematically. Use a source heading or table of contents to look for the most relevant sections. As you work, you can take notes on the information you find in sources by annotating photocopies of the source material or by noting useful ideas and quotations on paper, on cards, or in a computer file. See if categories emerge that can help you organize your paper.

www.mhhe.com/
mhhb2

For more information
and interactive
exercises, go to

Research >
Research
Techniques

1. Annotating
One way to take notes is to annotate photocopied articles and printouts from online information services or Web sites, as in Figure 21.4

319

(*on p. 321*). (You also can do this for sources you save to your computer by using the Comments feature in your word processor (*see Chapter 5, pp. 80–81*).) As you read, write the following notes directly on the page or in the electronic file:

- On the first page, write down complete bibliographic information for the source.
- As you read, record your questions, reactions, and ideas. Note any potential new directions for your research.
- Comment on ideas that agree with or differ from those you have already thought about.
- Put important and difficult passages into your own words by paraphrasing or summarizing them. (*For help with paraphrasing and summarizing, see pp. 322–27.*)
- Highlight statements that you may want to quote because they are key to your readers' understanding of the issue or are especially well expressed.

2. Taking notes in a research journal or log

A **research journal** or **research log** is a tool for keeping track of your research. It can be a spiral or loose-leaf notebook, a box of note cards, a word-processing document on a laptop computer, or a blog—whatever you are most comfortable with. Use the journal to write down leads for sources to consult and to record ideas and observations about your topic as they occur to you. If you use a blog, you can link to potential sources.

When you have finished annotating a photocopy, printout, or electronic version of an article, use your research journal to explore some of the comments, connections, and questions you recorded. If you do not have a copy of the material to annotate, take notes directly in your journal. Writing down each idea on a separate card, notebook page, word-processing page, or blog entry (with appropriate tags) will make it easier to organize the material later. Whatever method you use, be sure to record the source's bibliographic information as well as the specific page number for each idea.

Enclose in quotation marks any exact words from a source. If you think you may forget that the phrasing, as well as the idea, came from someone else, label the passage a quotation and note the page number, as Esther Hoffman did in the following excerpt from her research journal:

Notes on Dan Morgenstern. "Louis Armstrong and the Development and Diffusion of Jazz." Louis Armstrong: A Cultural Legacy. Ed. Marc H. Miller. Seattle: U of Washington P and Queens Museum of Art, 1994. 94–145. Print.
- Armstrong having trouble with managers. Fires Johnny Collins in London, 1933. Collins blocks Armstrong from playing with Chick Webb's band (pp. 124–25).

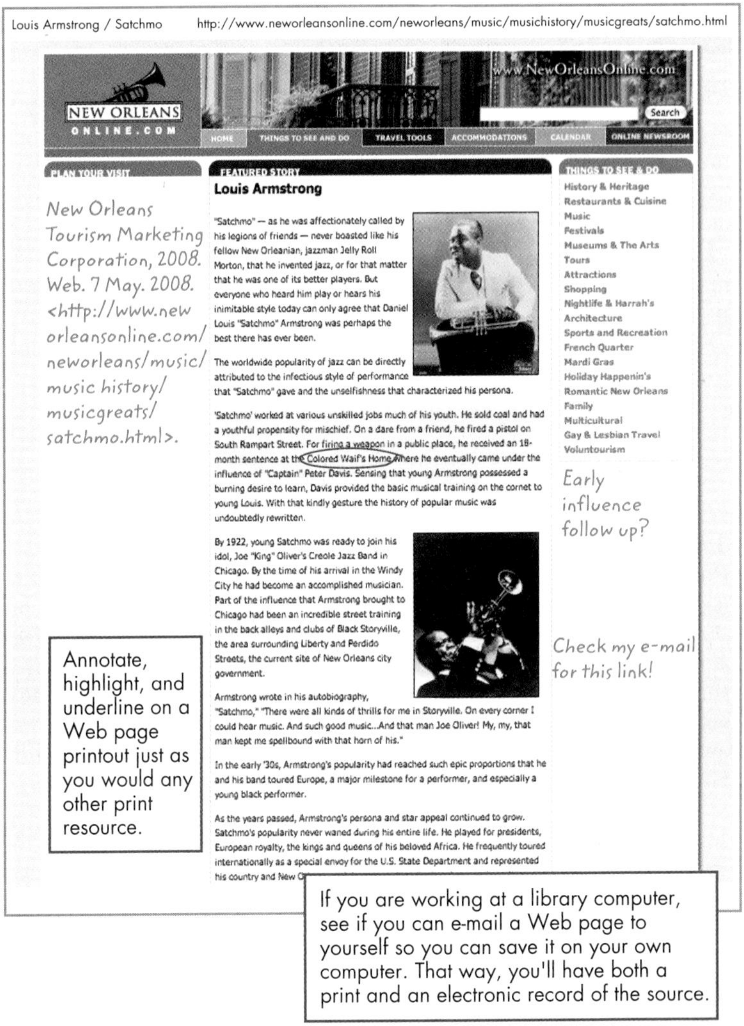
Louis Armstrong / Satchmo http://www.neworleansonline.com/neworleans/music/musichistory/musicgreats/satchmo.html
NEW ORLEANS ONLINE.COM
www.NewOrleansOnline.com
Search
HOME
THINGS TO SEE AND DO
TRAVEL TOOLS
ACCOMMODATIONS
CALENDAR
ONLINE NEWSROOM
PLAN YOUR VISIT
FEATURED STORY
Louis Armstrong
"Satchmo" — as he was affectionately called by his legions of friends — never boasted like his fellow New Orleanian, jazzman Jelly Roll Morton, that he invented jazz, or for that matter that he was one of its better players. But everyone who heard him play or hears his inimitable style today can only agree that Daniel Louis "Satchmo" Armstrong was perhaps the best there has ever been.
The worldwide popularity of jazz can be directly attributed to the infectious style of performance that "Satchmo" gave and the unselfishness that characterized his persona.
'Satchmo' worked at various unskilled jobs much of his youth. He sold coal and had a youthful propensity for mischief. On a dare from a friend, he fired a pistol on South Rampart Street. For firing a weapon in a public place, he received an 18-month sentence at the Colored Waif's Home where he eventually came under the influence of "Captain" Peter Davis. Sensing that young Armstrong possessed a burning desire to learn, Davis provided the basic musical training on the cornet to young Louis. With that kindly gesture the history of popular music was undoubtedly rewritten.
By 1922, young Satchmo was ready to join his idol, Joe "King" Oliver's Creole Jazz Band in Chicago. By the time of his arrival in the Windy City he had become an accomplished musician. Part of the influence that Armstrong brought to Chicago had been an incredible street training in the back alleys and clubs of Black Storyville, the area surrounding Liberty and Perdido Streets, the current site of New Orleans city government.
Armstrong wrote in his autobiography, "Satchmo," "There were all kinds of thrills for me in Storyville. On every corner I could hear music. And such good music...And that man Joe Oliver! My, my, that man kept me spellbound with that horn of his."
In the early '30s, Armstrong's popularity had reached such epic proportions that he and his band toured Europe, a major milestone for a performer, and especially a young black performer.
As the years passed, Armstrong's persona and star appeal continued to grow. Satchmo's popularity never waned during his entire life. He played for presidents, European royalty, the kings and queens of his beloved Africa. He frequently toured internationally as a special envoy for the U.S. State Department and represented his country and New O
THINGS TO SEE & DO
History & Heritage
Restaurants & Cuisine
Music
Festivals
Museums & The Arts
Tours
Attractions
Shopping
Nightlife & Harrah's
Architecture
Sports and Recreation
French Quarter
Mardi Gras
Holiday Happenin's
Romantic New Orleans
Family
Multicultural
Gay & Lesbian Travel
Voluntourism
New Orleans Tourism Marketing Corporation, 2008. Web. 7 May. 2008. <http://www.neworleansonline.com/neworleans/music/music history/musicgreats/satchmo.html>.
Early influence follow up?
Check my e-mail for this link!
Annotate, highlight, and underline on a Web page printout just as you would any other print resource.
If you are working at a library computer, see if you can e-mail a Web page to yourself so you can save it on your own computer. That way, you'll have both a print and an electronic record of the source.

FIGURE 21.4 An annotated Web page printout.

- *Armstrong turned to Glaser, an old Chicago acquaintance. Quote: "Joe Glaser … proved to be the right man at the right time" (p. 128).*

Unless you think you might use a quotation in your paper, it is usually better to express the author's ideas in your own words in your notes. To do this you need to understand paraphrasing and summarizing.

SOURCE SMART

Deciding to Quote, Paraphrase, or Summarize

Point is eloquently, memorably, or uniquely stated	→	Quote
Details important but not uniquely or eloquently expressed	→	Paraphrase
Long section of material (with many points), main ideas important, details not important	→	Summarize
Part of longer passage is uniquely stated	→	Use quotation inside para- phrased or summarized passage

3. Paraphrasing

Paraphrase when a passage's details are important to your topic but its exact words are not memorable. When you paraphrase, you put someone else's statements into your words and sentence structures. A paraphrase should be about the same length and level of detail as the original. Paraphrase when you need to reorder a source's ideas or clarify complicated information. Cite the original writer and put quotation marks around any exact phrasing from the source. See the Source Smart box on page 323 for advice on approaching the task.

Tips

LEARNING in COLLEGE

Using Sources to Establish Your Credibility

As noted in Chapter 10, effective writers appeal to their audience by demonstrating that they are *reasonable, ethical,* and *empathetic (see pp. 197–98).* When you present relevant evidence from reliable sources, you demonstrate that you are reasonable. When you take care to put other writers' ideas into your own words and indicate the sources of all ideas and quotations that are not your own and that are not common knowledge, you demonstrate that you are ethical, and therefore trustworthy. When you carefully follow the citation formats required by the discipline that you are writing in, you demonstrate your consideration, or empathy, for your readers by making it easier for them to consult your sources if they wish to.

SOURCE SMART

Guidelines for Writing a Paraphrase

- **Read the passage carefully.** Focus on the sequence of ideas and important details.
- **Be sure you understand the material.** Look up any unfamiliar words.
- **Imagine addressing an audience that has not read the material.**
- **Without looking at the original passage, write down its main ideas and key details.**
- **Use clear, direct language.** Express complicated ideas as a series of simple ones.
- **Check your paraphrase against the original.** Make sure your text conveys the source's ideas accurately without copying its words or sentence structures. Add quotes around any phrases from the source or rewrite them.
- **Note the citation information.** List author and page number after every important point.

In the first unacceptable paraphrase that follows, the writer has done a word-for-word translation, using synonyms for some terms but retaining the phrases from the original (highlighted) and failing to enclose them in quotation marks ("nonsense syllables," "free invention of rhythm, melody, and syllables"). Notice also how close the sentence structures in the first faulty paraphrase are to the original.

SOURCE

Scat singing. A technique of jazz singing in which onomatopoeic or nonsense syllables are sung to improvised melodies. Some writers have traced scat singing back to the practice, common in West African musics, of translating percussion patterns into vocal lines by assigning syllables to characteristic rhythms. However, since this allows little scope for melodic improvisation and the earliest recorded examples of jazz scat singing involved the free invention of rhythm, melody, and syllables, it is more likely that the technique began in the USA as singers imitated the sounds of jazz instrumentalists.

—J. Bradford Robinson, *The New Grove Dictionary of Jazz* "Scat Singing" from *New Grove Dictionary of Jazz* 2e (OUP 2002), edited by Kernfield, B. Reproduced by permission of Oxford University Press, Inc.

UNACCEPTABLE PARAPHRASE: PLAGIARISM

Scat is a way of singing that uses nonsense syllables and extemporaneous melodies. Some people think that scat goes back to the custom in West African music of turning drum rhythms into vocal lines. But that does not explain the free invention of rhythm, melody, and syllables of the first recorded instances of scat singing. It is more likely that scat was started in the U.S. by singers imitating the way instrumental jazz sounded (Robinson 425).

In the second example of a faulty paraphrase (below), the writer has merely substituted synonyms (such as "meaningless vocalization" instead of "nonsense syllables") for the original author's words and kept the source's sentence structure. Because it relies on the sentence structure of the original source, the paraphrase constitutes plagiarism.

UNACCEPTABLE PARAPHRASE (SENTENCE STRUCTURE OF SOURCE): PLAGIARISM

Scat is a way of singing that uses meaningless vocalization and extemporaneous melodies. One theory is that scat originated from the West African custom of turning drum rhythms into singing. But that doesn't explain the loose improvisation of pulse, pitch, and sound of the first recorded instances of scat singing. Scat more probably was started in the United States by singers imitating the way instrumental jazz sounded (Robinson 425).

The third unacceptable paraphrase (below) alters the sentence structure of the source but plagiarizes by using some of the original wording (highlighted below) without quotation marks.

UNACCEPTABLE PARAPHRASE (WORDING FROM SOURCE): PLAGIARISM

Scat, a highly inventive type of jazz singing, combines onomatopoeic or nonsense syllables with improvised melodies (Robinson 425).

By contrast, the acceptable paraphrase expresses all ideas from the original using different wording and phrasing. Although it quotes a few words from the source, the writer has used quotation marks and expressed the definition in a new way. The author's name indicates where the paraphrase begins.

ACCEPTABLE PARAPHRASE

According to Robinson, scat is a highly inventive type of jazz singing that combines "nonsense syllables [with] improvised melodies." Although syllabic singing of drum rhythms occurs in West Africa, scat probably owes more to the early attempts of American singers to mimic both the sound and the inventive musical style of instrumental jazz (Robinson 425).

Note that an acceptable paraphrase that does not include a direct quotation still requires a citation.

In the following two paraphrases of a podcast, note that the unacceptable paraphrase copies words and phrasing from the source.

SOURCE

Two of the greatest all-time performers in the history of popular music are coupled on this exciting and entertaining album. The Groaner and Satchmo team up for a great bash that has been arranged for and constructed by the talented Billy May.

— Fresh Sounds, "Bing Crosby Meets Louis Armstrong."
Jazzarific: Jazz Vinyl Podcast.

UNACCEPTABLE PARAPHRASE: PLAGIARISM

The Groaner and Satchmo collaborate on this exciting album that the talented Billy May has arranged.

ACCEPTABLE PARAPHRASE

The Fresh Sounds podcast describes this thrilling album that brings together two consummate performers, Bing Crosby and Louis Armstrong, with arrangements by Billy May (Fresh Sounds).

Exercise 21.1 Paraphrase

Read the following passage, annotating as necessary. Write a paraphrase of the passage, and then compare your paraphrase with those of your classmates. What are the similarities and differences among your paraphrases? How can you tell if a paraphrase is acceptable or unacceptable?

SOURCE

The origins of jazz, an urban music, stemmed from the countryside of the South as well as the streets of America's cities. It resulted from two distinct musical traditions, those of West Africa and Europe. West Africa gave jazz its incessant rhythmic drive, the need to move and the emotional urgency that has served the music so well. The European ingredients had more to do with classical qualities pertaining to harmony and melody.

The blending of these two traditions resulted in a music that played around with meter and reinterpreted the use of notes in new combinations, creating blue notes that expressed feelings both sad and joyous. The field hollers of Southern sharecropping slaves combined with the more urban, stylized sounds of musicians from New Orleans, creating a new music.

325

Gospel music from the church melded with what became known in the 20th century as the blues offered a vocal ingredient that translated well to instruments.

—JOHN EPHLAND, "Down Beat's Jazz 101: The Very Beginning" (from downbeat.com)

www.mhhe.com/
mhhb2
For more information
and interactive
exercises, go to
Research >
Avoiding Plagiarism
> Summarize/
Paraphrase

4. Summarizing

When you **summarize,** you state the main point of a piece, condensing paragraphs into sentences, pages into paragraphs, or a book into a few pages. As you work with sources, you will summarize more frequently than you quote or paraphrase. Summarizing works best

SOURCE SMART

Guidelines for Writing a Summary

- **Read the material carefully.** Determine which parts are relevant to your paper.
- **Be sure you understand the material.** Look up unfamiliar words.
- **Imagine addressing an audience that has not read the material.**
- **Identify the main point of the source, in your words.** Compose a sentence that names the text, the writer, what the writer does (reports, analyzes, argues), and the most important point.
- **Note any other points that relate to your topic.** State each one (in your words) in one sentence or less. Simplify complex language.
- **If the text is longer than a few paragraphs, divide it into sections, and in one or two sentences sum up each section.** Writers move between subtopics or from the statement of an idea to the supporting evidence. Compose a topic sentence for each of these sections. If possible, annotate the text to mark the different portions and highlight key sentences in each.
- **Combine your sentence stating the writer's main point with your sentences about secondary points or those summarizing the text's sections.**
- **Check your summary against the original** to see if it makes sense, expresses the source's meaning, and does not copy any wording or sentence structure.
- **Note all the citation information for the source.**

for very long passages or when the central idea of a passage is important but the details are not. See the Source Smart box on the previous page for advice on approaching the task.

Here are two summaries of the passage by John Ephland in Exercise 21.1. The unacceptable summary is simply a restatement of Ephland's thesis using much of his phrasing (highlighted).

UNACCEPTABLE SUMMARY: PLAGIARISM

The origins of jazz are two distinct musical traditions, those of West Africa and Europe. New meters and new note combinations capable of expressing both sad and joyous feelings resulted from the blending of these two traditions.

The acceptable summary states Ephland's main point in the writer's own words. Note that the acceptable summary still requires a citation.

ACCEPTABLE SUMMARY

According to Ephland, jazz has its roots in the musical traditions of both West Africa and Europe. It combines rhythmic, harmonic, and melodic features of both traditions in new and emotionally expressive ways (Ephland).

(For a summary of a longer passage, see Chapter 7: Reading, Thinking, Writing: The Critical Connection, p. 133.)

Exercise 21.2 Summary

Read the following passage and write a summary of it. Compare your summary with those of your classmates. What are the similarities and differences among your summaries? How does writing a paraphrase compare with writing a summary? Which task was more difficult, and why?

SOURCE

Male musicians dominated the jazz scene when the music first surfaced, making it difficult for women to enter their ranks. The fraternity of jazzmen also frowned upon women wind instrumentalists. However, some African American women, in the late 19th century, played the instruments that were barred from the "opposite sex". . . . Many of their names have been lost in history, but, a few have survived. For example, Mattie Simpson, a cornetist, performed 'on principal and prominent streets of each city' (10) in Indianapolis, in 1895; Nettie Goff, a trombonist, was a member of The Mahara Minstrels, and Mrs. Laurie Johnson, a trumpeter, had a career that spanned 30 years. They all broke instrumental taboos.

—MARIO A. CHARLES, "The Age of a Jazzwoman:
Valaida Snow, 1900–1956"

www.mhhe.com/
mhhb2
For more information
and interactive
exercises, go to
Research >
Avoiding
Plagiarism >
Using Quotations

5. Quoting directly

Sometimes the writer of a source will say something so eloquently and perceptively that you will want to include that writer's words as a **direct quotation** in your paper.

In general, quote:

- Primary sources (for example, in a paper about Louis Armstrong, a direct quotation from Armstrong or an associate)
- Literary sources, when you analyze the wording
- Sources containing very technical language that cannot be paraphrased
- An authority in the field whose words support your thesis
- Debaters explaining their different positions on an issue

To avoid inadvertent plagiarism, be careful to indicate that the content is a direct quotation when you copy it into your note cards or your research notebook. Place quotation marks around the direct quotation. You might also use a special color to indicate direct quotations or deliberately make quotation marks oversized.

When referring to most secondary sources, paraphrase or summarize instead of quoting. Your readers will have difficulty following a paper with too many quotations, and they may think you lack original ideas. Try to keep quotations short.

In some instances you may use paraphrase, summary, and quotation together. You might summarize a long passage, paraphrase an important section of it, and directly quote a short part of that section.

Note: If you have used more than one quotation or substantial paraphrase every paragraph or two, revise your work to include more of your own reflections on the topic.

21d Synthesize: Take stock of what you have learned.

When you take stock, you assess the research you have done. You also synthesize what you have learned from the sources you have consulted. Think about how the sources you have read relate to one another. Ask yourself when, how, and why your sources agree or disagree, and consider where you stand on the issues they raise. Did anything you read surprise or disturb you? Writing down your responses to such questions can help you clarify what you have learned from working with sources.

In college writing, the credibility of your work depends on the relevance and reliability of your sources as well as the scope and depth of your reading and observation. College research projects usually require multiple viewpoints. A paper on Louis Armstrong, for example, is unlikely to be credible if it relies on only one source of information. A paper about an issue in the social sciences will not be taken seriously if it cites research on only one side of the debate.

As the context and kind of writing change, so too do the requirements for types and numbers of sources. As a general rule, however, you should consult more than two sources and use only sources that are both reliable and respected by people working in the field. To determine whether you have located appropriate and sufficient sources, ask yourself the following questions:

- Are your sources trustworthy? (*See Chapter 18: Evaluating Sources.*)

- If you have started to develop a tentative answer to your research question, have your sources provided you with a sufficient number of facts, examples, and ideas to support that answer?

- Have you used sources that examine the issue from several different perspectives?

21e Integrate quotations, paraphrases, and summaries properly and effectively.

www.mhhe.com/
mhhb2
For more information
and interactive
exercises, go to
Research >
Avoiding
Plagiarism >
Using Sources
Accurately

Ultimately you will use some of the paraphrases, summaries, and quotations you have collected during the course of your research to support and develop the ideas you present in your research paper. Here are some guidelines for integrating them properly and effectively. (Examples in this section represent MLA style for in-text and block quotations.)

1. Integrating quotations

Short quotations should be enclosed in quotation marks and well integrated into your sentence structure. Set off longer quotations in blocks (*see p. 331*). The following example from Esther Hoffman's paper on Louis Armstrong and Joe Glaser shows the use of a short quotation:

> In his dedication to the unpublished manuscript "Louis Armstrong and the Jewish Family in New Orleans, the Year of 1907," Armstrong calls Glaser "the best friend that I ever had," while in a letter to Max Jones, he writes, "I did not get really happy until I got with my man—my dearest friend—Joe Glaser" (qtd. in Jones and Chilton 16).

The following poorly integrated quotation uses the wrong verb tense and distorts the meaning of the original: "Armstrong writes that he 'get really happy until I got with my man—my dearest friend—Joe Glaser.'" Always make sure a quotation works grammatically and logically in your writing.

When you are integrating someone else's words into your writing, use a **signal phrase** that indicates whom you are quoting. The signal phrases "Armstrong calls Glaser," and "he writes" identify Armstrong as the source of the two quotations in the passage on page 329.

A signal phrase indicates where your words end and the source's words begin. The first time you quote a source, include the author's full name. Often you will want to add the author's credentials (or authority to describe a topic): for example, "literary scholar Jacob Miller" or "Armstrong's wife, Lucille." You may also include the title of the work for context: "In *Louis Armstrong: An Extravagant Life,* biographer Laurence Bergreen argues . . . ."

Instead of introducing a quotation, the signal phrase can follow or interrupt it:

FOLLOWS   "I did not get really happy until I got with my man—my dearest friend—Joe Glaser," writes Armstrong.

INTERRUPTS   "I did not get really happy," writes Armstrong, "until I got with my man— my dearest friend— Joe Glaser."

The verb you use in a signal phrase should show the reader how you are using the quotation in your paper. If your source provides an example that strengthens your argument, you could say, "Mann *supports* this line of reasoning." (*See the box on p. 331.*)

MLA style places signal phrase verbs in the present or present prefect tenses (*Johnson writes; Gonzalez has written*); APA style uses the past and past perfect tenses (*Johnson wrote; Gonzalez has found*). (*See Chapter 22, pp. 337–38 for more on these documentation styles.*) When a quotation, paraphrase, or summary in MLA or APA style begins with a signal phrase, the ending citation includes the page number (unless the work lacks page numbers). You can quote without a signal phrase if you give the author's name in the parenthetical citation.

Brackets within quotations   Sentences that include quotations must make sense grammatically. Sometimes you may have to adjust a quotation to make it fit properly into your sentence. Use brackets to indicate any minor adjustments you have made in wording, capitalization, or verb tense (*see 55i, pp. 772–73*). For example, *my* has been changed to *his* to make the quotation fit in the following sentence:

Armstrong confided to a friend that Glaser's death "broke [his] heart" (Bergreen 490).

Ellipses within quotations   Use ellipses to indicate that words have been omitted from the body of a quotation, but be sure that what you omit does not significantly alter the source's meaning. (*For more on using ellipses, see Chapter 54: Quotation Marks and 55j, pp. 774–77.*)

> As Morgenstern puts it, "Joe Glaser . . . proved to be the right man at the right time" (128).

Quotations in block format Quotations longer than four lines should be used rarely, because they tend to break up your text and make readers impatient. Research papers should consist primarily of your own analysis of sources. Always tell your readers why you want them to read a long quotation, and afterward, comment on it.

If you use a verse quotation longer than three lines or a prose quotation longer than four typed lines, set the quotation off on a new line and indent each line one inch (ten spaces) from the left margin. Indent the first line of each new paragraph in the quotation by another quarter inch. (*This is MLA style; for APA style, see Chapter 54, p. 758.*) Double-space above and below the quotation. If the quotation is more than one paragraph, indent the first line of each new paragraph a quarter inch. Do not use quotation marks with a block quotation. Writers often introduce a block quotation with a sentence ending in a colon. (*For examples of block quotations, see Chapter 54: Quotation Marks, p. 759.*)

Tips LEARNING in COLLEGE

Varying Signal Phrases

To keep your work interesting, to show the original writer's purpose (*Martinez describes* or *Lin argues*), and to connect the quotation to your reasoning (*Johnson refutes . . .*), use appropriate signal phrases such as following:

acknowledges	concedes	holds	refutes
adds	concludes	implies	rejects
admits	considers	insists	remarks
argues	contends	interprets	reports
asks	denies	maintains	responds
asserts	describes	notes	shows
charges	emphasizes	observes	speculates
claims	explains	points out	states
comments	expresses	proposes	suggests
complains	finds	proves	warns

Some single phrases, such as *considers*, make a claim more defensible. It is more difficult to support a more absolute claim about a source, such as *proves*. In general you should avoid ascribing emotion or tone to a written source unless that emotion is very clear. Avoid verbs like *smirks, huffs, retorts,* and *cries,* as well as adverbs such as *angrily, knowingly,* and *coyly.*

331

2. Integrating paraphrases and summaries

The principles for integrating paraphrases and summaries into your text are similar to those for including direct quotations. You want a smooth transition between a source's point and your own voice, and you want to accurately attribute the information to its source. Although you do not need to use ellipses or the block format for paraphrases and summaries (because they are in your own words), you will want to use signal phrases and citations.

Besides crediting others for their work, signal phrases can make ideas more interesting by giving them a human face. Here are some examples:

> *As biographer Laurence Bergreen points out,* Armstrong easily reached difficult high notes, the F's and G's that stymied other trumpeters (248).

In this passage, Esther Hoffman uses the signal phrase *As biographer Louis Bergreen points out* to identify Bergreen as the source of the paraphrased information about Louis Armstrong's extraordinary technical abilities.

> According to Howard Mandel in his blog entry "International Jazz at IAJE," young people today listen not only to pop music but also to jazz, especially its current eclectic styles.

This passage in a paper by Roger Hart uses the signal phrase *According to Howard Mandel* to lead into a summary of Mandel's blog entry. No citation is needed because the signal phrase names the author and the source lacks page numbers.

> A 1960 letter from Glaser to Lucille Armstrong corroborates Gold's account; it shows that Glaser assumed responsibility for buying the musician and his wife a new car as well as for filing the paperwork needed to retain the old license plate number.

In this passage, Esther Hoffman uses the word *corroborates* to signal her paraphrase of an original letter she found in the Louis Armstrong archives. She directly names the source (the author of the letter), so she does not need additional parenthetical documentation.

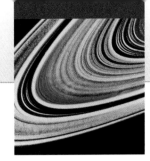

22 Writing the Paper

You have chosen a challenging research question and have located, read, and evaluated a variety of sources. Now you need a thesis that will allow you to share what you have learned as well as your perspective on the issue.

22a Plan and draft your paper.

Begin planning by recalling the context and purpose of your paper. If you have an assignment sheet, review it to see if the paper is supposed to be primarily informative, interpretive, or argumentative. Consider how much your audience is likely to know about your topic. Keep your purpose, audience, and context in mind as you decide on a thesis to support and develop.

1. Deciding on a thesis

Consider the question that guided your research as well as others provoked by what you have learned during your research. Revise the wording of these questions and summarize them in a central question that is interesting and relevant to your audience (*see Chapter 15: Understanding Research, pp. 254–57*). After you write down this question, compose an answer that you can use as your working thesis, as Esther Hoffman does in the following example:

www.mhhe.com/
mhhb2
For help with
developing a
thesis, go to
Writing >
Paragraph/Essay
Development >
Thesis/Central
Idea

HOFFMAN'S FOCAL QUESTION

What kind of relationship did Louis Armstrong and Joe Glaser have?

HOFFMAN'S WORKING THESIS

Armstrong and Glaser enjoyed not only a successful business partnership but also a complex friendship based on mutual respect and caring.

(*For more on devising a thesis, see Chapter 3: Planning and Shaping the Whole Essay, pp. 42–46.*)

2. Outlining a plan for supporting and developing your thesis

Guided by your tentative thesis, outline a plan that uses your sources in a purposeful way. Decide on the organization you will use to support your thesis—chronological, problem-solution, or thematic—and develop your support by choosing facts, examples, and ideas drawn from a variety of sources. A chronological organization presents examples from earliest to most recent, and a problem-solution structure introduces an issue and a means of addressing it. A thematic

www.mhhe.com/
mhhb2
For interactive help
with outlines, go to
Writing >
Outlining Tutor

organization orders examples from simple to complex, specific to general, or in another logical way. (*See Chapter 3: Planning and Shaping the Whole Essay, p. 46, for more on these organizational structures.*)

For her interpretive paper on Armstrong and Glaser, Hoffman decided on a thematic organization, an approach structured around raising and answering a central question:

- State the question: What kind of relationship did Louis Armstrong have with his longtime manager, Joe Glaser? Did Glaser dominate Armstrong?
- State the thesis: Armstrong and Glaser enjoyed a mutual business and personal relationship.
- Offer background information on the Jazz Age.
- Introduce Armstrong as a great musician who was once a poor waif.
- Introduce Glaser, Armstrong's manager for thirty-four years.
- Discuss Glaser as Armstrong's business manager and support for the idea that Glaser made Armstrong a star.
- Discuss Armstrong's resistance to being controlled by Glaser.
- Conclude: Armstrong and Glaser worked well together as friends who respected and cared for each other.

To develop this outline, Hoffman would need to list supporting facts, examples, or ideas for each point as well as indicate the sources of this information. Each section should center on her original thinking, backed by her analysis of sources. (*For more on developing an outline, see Chapter 3: Planning and Shaping the Whole Essay, pp. 47–51.*)

3. Organizing and evaluating your information
Your note-taking strategies will determine how you collect and organize your information. If you have taken notes on index cards, group them according to topic and subtopic, using your paper's formal or informal outline as a guide. For example, Esther Hoffman could have used the following categories to organize her notes:

Biography – Armstrong
Biography – Glaser
Glaser as manager
Conflict – A & G
Armstrong – media image
Jazz – general info

Sorting index cards into stacks corresponding to topics and subtopics allows you to see what you have gathered. A small stack of cards for a particular topic might mean that the topic is not as important to your thesis as you had originally thought—or that you may need to do additional research on that specific subtopic.

If your notes are primarily on your computer, you can create a new folder or page for each topic and subtopic, and then copy and paste to move information to the appropriate category.

As with all writing, the process of planning a research paper usually does not unfold in distinct steps. While outlining, you may revise your thesis. As you look for support for your outline in your research and notes, you may decide to adjust the outline or the thesis.

4. Writing a draft that you can revise, share, and edit
When you have a tentative thesis and a plan, you are ready to write a draft. Many writers find that they can present their thesis or focal question at the end of an introductory paragraph or two. The introduction should interest readers.

As you write beyond the introduction, be prepared to reexamine and refine your thesis and outline. When you draw on ideas from your sources, be sure to quote and paraphrase effectively and properly. Take care to integrate quotations, paraphrases, and summaries accurately (*see Chapter 21, pp. 329–32*). Include source citations in all your drafts. (*For advice on quoting and paraphrasing, see Chapter 21: Working with Sources and Avoiding Plagiarism, pp. 322–28, and section 22c of this chapter.*)

Make your conclusion as memorable as possible. You may need to review the paper as a whole before writing the conclusion. In the final version of Hoffman's paper, on pages 378–90, note how she uses a visual and a play on words—"more than meets the eye"—to end her paper. In doing so, she enhances her concluding point—that Armstrong and Glaser were different, yet complementary, and that their relationship was complex. Hoffman did not come up with the last line of her paper until she revised and edited her first draft. It is not uncommon for writers to come up with fresh ideas for their introduction, body paragraphs, or conclusion at this stage—one reason why it is important to spend time revising and editing your paper. (*For more on revising, see Chapter 5: Revising and Editing, pp. 76–103.*)

5. Integrating visuals
Well-chosen visuals like photographs, drawings, charts, graphs, and maps can sometimes help illustrate your argument. In some cases, a visual might itself be a subject of your analysis. Esther Hoffman found two pictures in her archival research about Louis Armstrong. She describes both of them in her paper and was able to include a reproduction of one in her work.

There are two additional components to consider when integrating visuals into your paper: figure numbers and captions.

www.mhhe.com/
mhhb2
For more
information
and interactive
excercises,
go to
Writing >
Paragraph/Essay
Development >
Drafting and
Revising

335

CHECKLIST

Revising and Editing a Research Paper

Consider these questions as you read your draft and gather feedback from your instructor and peers (*see also the Checklist box, "Avoiding Plagiarism," Chapter 20, pp. 311–12*):

Thesis and structure

☐ How does my paper address the topic and purpose given in the assignment?

☐ How does my thesis fit my evidence and reasoning?

☐ Is the central idea of each section based on my own thinking and backed with evidence from my sources?

☐ What strategies have I used to deal with the most likely critiques of my thesis? How might I address any that remain?

☐ Are the order of sections and the transitions between sections logical?

☐ What evidence do I have to support each point? Is it sufficient?

Editing: Use of sources

☐ Do my paraphrases and summaries alter the wording and sentence structure, but not the meaning, of the original text?

☐ Have I checked all quotations for accuracy and used ellipses or brackets where necessary?

☐ Do signal phrases set off and establish context for quotations, paraphrases, and summaries?

☐ Have I provided adequate in-text citation for each source? Do my in-text citations match my Works-Cited or References page?

☐ Do all of my illustrations have complete and accurate captions?

(*See also the Checklists "Revising Your Draft for Content and Organization," p. 82, "Revising Visuals," p. 93, "Editing Sentences and Words," pp. 94–95, and "Proofreading," p. 99.*)

- **Figure numbers:** Both MLA and APA styles require writers to number each image in a research paper. In MLA style, the word *figure* is abbreviated to *Fig.* In APA style, the full word *Figure* is written out.

- **Captions:** Each visual that you include in your paper must be followed by a caption that includes the title of the visual (if it has one; otherwise, a brief description will do) and its source. In MLA style, each caption begins with the figure number and a period after the number (Fig. 1.); in APA style, use italics for the figure number (*Figure 1*) and no period.

22b Revise your draft.

After you have completed a draft of your research paper, you may be asked to share it with other members of your class for peer review and feedback. If not, you still can use the checklist on page 336 to review your own work.

You may prefer to revise a hard copy of your draft by hand, or you might find it easier to use the Track Changes feature in your word-processing program. Either way, be sure to keep previous versions of your essay drafts. Even if your instructor does not require you to hand in preliminary drafts, it is useful to have a record of how your paper evolved—especially if you need to track down a particular source or want to reincorporate something that you had removed earlier in the process.

22c Document your sources.

www.mhhe.com/
mhhb2
For help with
documenting sources,
go to
Research >
Avoiding
Plagiarism >
Citing Sources

Whenever you use information, ideas, or words from someone else's work, you must acknowledge that person. As noted in the box on page 307, the only exception to this principle is when you use information that is common knowledge, such as the chemical composition of water or the names of the thirteen original states. When you tell readers what sources you have consulted, they can more readily understand your paper as well as the conversation you are participating in by writing it.

How sources are documented varies by field and discipline. Choose a documentation style that is appropriate for the particular course you are taking, and use it properly and consistently.

Specific documentation styles meet the needs of different disciplines. Literature, foreign languages, and some other humanities disciplines use MLA style. Researchers in these disciplines use many historic texts including multiple editions of certain sources. The author's name and the page number, but not the year, appear in the in-text citation. The edition of the source appears in the Works-Cited list. The author's full

CHARTING the TERRITORY

Documentation Styles Explained in This Text

TYPE OF COURSE	DOCUMENTATION STYLE MOST COMMONLY USED	WHERE TO FIND THIS STYLE IN THE HANDBOOK
Humanities (English, religion, music, art, philosophy, history)	MLA (Modern Language Association) or Chicago (*Chicago Manual of Style*)	MLA: *pp. 342–90* Chicago: *pp. 423–41*
Social sciences (anthropology, psychology, sociology, education, and business)	APA (American Psychological Association)	APA: *pp. 391–422*
Sciences (mathematics, natural sciences, engineering, physical therapy, computer science)	CSE (Council of Science Editors)	CSE: *pp. 442–50*

name appears at the first mention of the work, and sources are referred to in present tense (because writing exists in the present).

APA style, used by practitioners of the social sciences, places the date of a work in the in-text citation because the currency of sources matters to these disciplines. References to past research appear in the past tense, and researchers are referred to only by last name in the text.

Chicago, or CMS, style, used by other humanities disciplines, has two forms. The first minimizes the in-text references to sources by using footnotes or endnotes indicated by superscript numerals. Disciplines that draw on it, such as history, tend to use many sources. An alternative form of Chicago style resembles APA style.

CSE style, used by the sciences, also has different forms. Name-year style shares important features with APA style, whereas citation-sequence and citation-name styles use endnotes with a number assigned to each source. The prevalence of abbreviations in CSE style indicates that researchers are expected to know the major texts in their fields.

If you are not sure which of the styles covered in this handbook to use, ask your instructor. If you are required to use an alternative, discipline-specific documentation style, consult the list of manuals on page 339.

CHARTING the TERRITORY

Style Manuals for Specific Disciplines

SPECIFIC DISCIPLINE	POSSIBLE STYLE MANUAL
Chemistry	Coghill, Anne M., and Lorrin R. Garson, eds. *The ACS Style Guide: A Manual for Authors and Editors.* 3rd ed. Washington: American Chemical Society, 2006.
Geology	Bates, Robert L., Rex Buchanan, and Marla Adkins-Heljeson, eds. *Geowriting: A Guide to Writing, Editing, and Printing in Earth Science.* 5th ed. Alexandria: American Geological Institute, 1995.
Government and Law	Garner, Diane L., and Diane H. Smith, eds. *The Complete Guide to Citing Government Information Resources: A Manual for Writers and Librarians.* Rev. ed. Bethesda: Congressional Information Service, 1993.
	Harvard Law Review et al. *The Bluebook: A Uniform System of Citation.* 18th ed. Cambridge: Harvard Law Review Assn., 2005.
Journalism	Goldstein, Norm, ed. *Associated Press Stylebook 2008.* New York: Associated Press, 2008.
Linguistics	Linguistic Society of America. "LSA Style Sheet." *LSA Bulletin.* Published annually in the December issue.
Mathematics	American Mathematical Society. *AMS Author Handbook: General Instructions for Preparing Manuscripts.* Providence: AMS, 2007.
Medicine	Iverson, Cheryl, ed. *American Medical Association Manual of Style: A Guide for Authors and Editors.* 10th ed. New York: Oxford University Press, 2007.
Political Science	American Political Science Association. *Style Manual for Political Science.* Rev. ed. Washington: APSA, 2001.

339

For her paper on Louis Armstrong and Joe Glaser, Esther Hoffman used the MLA documentation style. (*The final draft of the paper appears at the end of Chapter 23: MLA Documentation Style, on pp. 378–90.*)

22d Present and publish your work.

There are many ways to share the results of your research. New technologies make it possible to create sophisticated audio and video presentations and Web sites. In both your academic and your professional career, you will likely be called upon to present your ideas, information, and research using presentation software such as PowerPoint or through visual tools such as iDVD. You might use desktop publishing software to prepare a research manuscript for interoffice or interdepartmental publication, or for publication in a newspaper or journal. Make the presentation of your research suit your audience and your purpose.

(*For more information on oral presentations, see Chapter 13: Oral Presentations, pp. 221–26. To learn more about presentation software and other multimedia tools, see Chapter 14: Multimedia Writing, pp. 226–47. For a discussion of document design, see Chapter 6: Designing Academic Papers and Preparing Portfolios, pp. 104–17.*)

The Library of Congress houses the largest collection of books and documents in the world, and all U.S. libraries use its cataloging systems. The Library's architectural design suggests the Italian Renaissance; its interior features work by American artists.

Nothing gives an author so much pleasure as to find his works respectfully quoted by other learned authors.

—BENJAMIN FRANKLIN

Documenting across the Curriculum

23 MLA Documentation Style

The documentation style developed by the Modern Language Association (MLA) is used by many researchers in the arts and humanities, especially by those who write about language and literature. The guidelines presented here are based on the seventh edition of the *MLA Handbook for Writers of Research Papers* (New York: MLA, 2009).

www.mhhe.com/
mhhb2

For links to Web sites
for documentation
styles used in various
disciplines, go to

Research > Links
to Documentation
Sites

23a The elements of MLA documentation style

College papers include information, ideas, and quotations from sources that must be accurately documented. Documentation allows others to see the path you have taken in researching and writing your paper. (*For more on what to document, see Chapter 22: Writing the Paper, pp. 333–40.*)

MLA style requires writers to list their sources in a works-cited list at the end of a paper. Answering the questions in the foldout charts that follow will help you find the appropriate model works-cited entry for your source. The reverse side of the foldout indicates where to find the information you need for a citation. (*See also the directory on pages 351–53.*)

WRITING OUTCOMES

Part 4: Documenting across the Curriculum

This section will help you answer questions such as:

Rhetorical Knowledge

- Which disciplines use MLA, APA, Chicago, and CSE styles? **(23–26)**

Critical Thinking, Reading, and Writing

- Why do I need to document my sources? **(23a, 24b–c, 25a, 26)**

Processes

- How should I label visuals in MLA **(23e)** and APA **(24d)** styles?

Knowledge of Conventions

- How do I cite sources in the text of my paper or in notes? (MLA: **23b**, APA: **24b**, Chicago: **25a**, CSE: **26a**)
- How and when do I create a listing of sources at the end of my paper in MLA **(23c)**, APA **(24c)**, and CSE **(26c)** styles?

Self-Assessment: *Take an online quiz at www.mhhe.com / mhhb2 to test your familiarity with the topics covered in Chapters 23–24. Pay special attention to the sections in these chapters that correspond to any questions you answer incorrectly.*

Identifying and Documenting Sources in MLA Style

Resources for Writers

Works-Cited List: ...ooks

...YOUR SOURCE A COMPLETE BOOK?

...ES | **Go to this entry** *on page*

...A COMPLETE BOOK WITH ONE NAMED AUTHOR?	
t the only book by this author that you are citing?	1 *350*
...e you citing more than one book by this author?	2 *353*
...es it also have an editor, translator, or illustrator?	7, 16, 24 *354, 356, 358*
t a published doctoral dissertation?	39 *361*
...A COMPLETE BOOK WITH TWO OR THREE NAMED AUTHORS?	3 *353*
...A COMPLETE BOOK WITH MORE THAN THREE NAMED AUTHORS?	4 *353*
...A COMPLETE BOOK WITHOUT A NAMED AUTHOR?	
...he author an organization?	5 *353*
...he author anonymous or unknown?	23 *358*
...A COMPLETE BOOK WITH AN EDITOR OR A TRANSLATOR?	
...here an editor instead of an author?	6 *354*
...es it have both an editor and an author?	7 *354*
...it an anthology?	13 *356*
...it a translation?	16 *356*
...it the published proceedings of an academic conference?	38 *360*
...A COMPLETE BOOK WITH A VOLUME OR AN EDITION NUMBER?	
...it part of a multivolume work (e.g., Volume 3)?	19 *357*
...it one in a series?	20 *357*
...es it have an edition number (e.g., Second Edition)?	17 *357*
...A COMPLETE BOOK BUT NOT THE ONLY VERSION?	
...your book a republished work (e.g., a classic novel)?	21 *357*
...your book a religious text (e.g., the Bible)?	18 *357*
...HE BOOK FROM A PUBLISHER'S IMPRINT?	14 *356*
...ES THE BOOK'S TITLE INCLUDE THE TITLE OF ANOTHER BOOK?	22 *357*
...A GRAPHIC NOVEL OR COMIC BOOK?	25 *358*

...YOUR SOURCE PART OF A BOOK?

...ES | **Go to this entry** *on page*

...T FROM AN EDITED BOOK?	
...it a work in an anthology?	8 *354*
...it a chapter in an edited book?	8 *354*
...e you citing two or more items from the same anthology?	9 *354*
...it an article from a collection of reprinted articles?	12 *356*
...it a published letter (e.g., part of a published collection)?	47 *362*
...T FROM A REFERENCE WORK (e.g., AN ENCYCLOPEDIA)?	
...it an article with an author?	10 *354*
...it an article without a named author?	11 *356*
...T A PREFACE, AN INTRODUCTION, A FOREWORD, OR AN AFTERWORD?	15 *356*
...T A REPRODUCTION OF A WORK OF ART?	45 *362*

...he next panel or the directory on pages 351–53
...lt your instructor.

Entries in a Works-Cited List: Print **Periodicals** or Other Print Sources

❓ IS YOUR SOURCE FROM A JOURNAL, A MAGAZINE, OR A NEWSPAPER?

NO   YES | **Go to this entry** *on page*

IS IT FROM AN ACADEMIC JOURNAL?	
Does the journal have a volume number?	26 *358*
Does the journal have an issue number but no volume number?	27 *359*
Is your source an abstract (a brief summary) of an article?	34 *360*
IS IT FROM A MAGAZINE?	
Is the magazine published monthly?	28 *359*
Is the magazine published weekly?	29 *359*
Is your source a letter to the editor?	35 *360*
Is it a review (e.g., a review of a book or film)?	32 *359*
Is it an interview?	42 *361*
Is it stored on microfiche, microform, or microfilm?	119 *375*
IS IT FROM A NEWSPAPER?	
Is it an article?	30 *359*
Is it an interview?	42 *361*
Is it an editorial?	33 *360*
Is it a letter to the editor?	35 *360*
Is it a review (e.g., a review of a book or film)?	32 *359*
Is it stored on microfiche, microform, or microfilm?	119 *375*
IS THE AUTHOR UNKNOWN?	31 *359*

❓ IS IT A PRINT SOURCE BUT NOT A BOOK, A PART OF A BOOK, OR AN ARTICLE IN AN ACADEMIC JOURNAL, A MAGAZINE, OR A NEWSPAPER?

NO   YES | **Go to this entry** *on page*

IS IT PUBLISHED BY THE GOVERNMENT OR A NONGOVERNMENT ORGANIZATION?	
Is it a pamphlet or other type of document?	36, 37 *360*
Is it a court case or other legal document?	50 *363*
Is it from the *Congressional Record*?	75 *368*
IS IT AN ACADEMIC WORK?	
Is it an unpublished dissertation?	40 *361*
Is it an abstract of a dissertation?	41 *361*
Is it an unpublished essay?	49 *362*
IS IT A PERSONAL LETTER OR A LETTER FROM AN ARCHIVE?	48, 49 *362*
IS IT A VISUAL TEXT OR AN ADVERTISEMENT?	
Is it a map or chart?	43 *361*
Is it a cartoon?	44 *362*
Is it a reproduction of a work of visual art?	45 *362*
Is it an advertisement?	46 *362*
IS IT STORED IN AN ARCHIVE?	49 *362*
IS IT PUBLISHED IN MORE THAN ONE MEDIUM (e.g., A BOOK AND A CD-ROM)?	120 *376*

Check the directory on pages 351–53 or consult your instructor.

Entries in a Works-Cited List: **Electronic** or Other Nonprint Sources

❓ DID YOU FIND YOUR NONPRINT SOURCE ONLINE?

NO   YES | **Go to this entry** *on page*

DID YOU FIND YOUR SOURCE USING AN ONLINE DATABASE (e.g., INFOTRAC)?	
Is it an article from a scholarly journal?	94 *371*
Is it an abstract (a brief summary of an article from a scholarly journal)?	95 *371*
Is it a newspaper article?	92 *371*
Is it a magazine article?	93 *371*
IS IT FROM AN ONLINE SCHOLARLY JOURNAL?	
Is it an article?	88 *370*
Is it a review (e.g., a book review)?	89 *371*
Is it an editorial?	90 *371*
Is it a letter to the editor?	91 *371*
IS IT FROM AN ONLINE MAGAZINE OR NEWSPAPER?	
Is it an article?	59, 60 *364, 365*
Is it an editorial or a letter to the editor?	61, 62 *365*
Is it a review?	63 *365*
Is it an interview?	64 *365*
DOES YOUR ONLINE SOURCE ALSO EXIST IN PRINT OR ANOTHER MEDIUM?	
Is it a book or part of a book?	76, 77 *368*
Is it a doctoral dissertation?	78 *369*
Is it a pamphlet or brochure?	79 *369*
Is it a map or chart?	80 *369*
Is it a cartoon?	81 *369*
Is it a work of art (e.g., painting, drawing, photograph)?	82 *369*
Is it an online broadcast interview?	86 *370*
Is it an online radio or TV program?	84, 85 *370*
Is it an online video?	83 *369*
IS YOUR SOURCE SPONSORED BY OR RELATED TO THE GOVERNMENT?	74, 75 *368*
DOES YOUR SOURCE EXIST ONLY ONLINE?	
Is it an entire Web site or independent work?	
Is it a personal Web site?	53 *364*
Is it an entire blog?	57 *364*
Is it a home page for a course or an academic department?	54, 55 *364*
Is it a page on a social networking site?	56 *364*
Is it another independent Web site or source?	51 *363*
Is it part of a larger online work?	
Is it a blog entry?	58 *364*
Is it part of a wiki or another reference work?	65, 66 *366, 367*
Is it a map?	67 *367*
Is it an audio or video podcast?	68, 69 *367*
Is it an online video?	70 *367*
Is it another short work from a Web site?	52 *364*
Is it an online communication?	
Is it a posting to a news group, online forum, or discussion list?	71, 72 *367*
Is it a synchronous (real-time) communication?	73 *367*
Is it an e-mail communication?	97 *372*
Is it an e-mail interview?	116 *375*

Go to next panel.

❓ IS IT A COMPUTER-BASED SOURCE NOT FOUND ONLINE?

NO   YES | **Go to this entry** *on page*

IS IT A DIGITAL FILE STORED ON YOUR COMPUTER?	
Is it a text file?	98 *372*
Is it a PDF file?	99 *372*
Is it an audio file (e.g., an MP3)?	100 *372*
Is it an image?	101 *372*
Is it another type of file?	102 *372*
IS IT A CD-ROM OR DVD-ROM?	103–05 *373*
IS IT COMPUTER SOFTWARE?	106 *373*

❓ IS IT ANOTHER NONPRINT SOURCE?

NO   YES | **Go to this entry** *on page*

IS IT A FILM, DVD, OR VIDEOTAPE?	107, 108 *373*
IS IT A PERSONAL OR AN ARCHIVAL VIDEO OR AUDIO RECORDING?	109 *374*
IS IT A BROADCAST INTERVIEW?	112 *374*
IS IT A RADIO OR TV PROGRAM?	110, 111 *374*
IS IT A PERSONAL OR TELEPHONE INTERVIEW?	116 *375*
IS IT A SOUND RECORDING, MUSICAL COMPOSITION, OR WORK OF ART?	113-15 *374–75*
IS IT A LECTURE, SPEECH, OR PERFORMANCE?	117, 118 *375*
IS IT MICROFICHE/MICROFORM/MICROFILM?	119 *375*
DO ITS COMPONENTS INCLUDE MULTIPLE MEDIA (e.g., A BOOK WITH A CD-ROM)?	120 *376*

Check the directory on pages 351–53 or consult your instructor.

Resources for Writers

Finding Source Information for MLA Style

The Elements of an MLA Works-Cited Entry: Book

Author — Bergreen, Laurence. — Book title *Louis Armstrong: An Extravagant Life.*

New York: Broadway, 1997. Print. ← Medium

Place of publication · Publisher · Date of publication

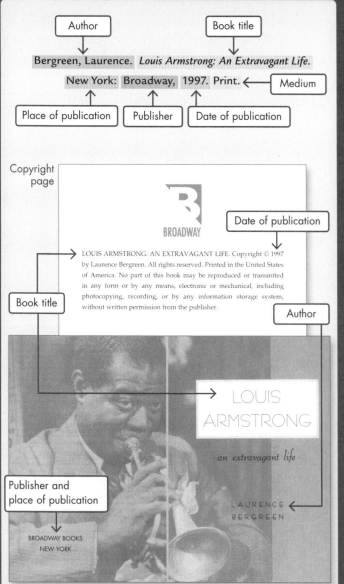

Copyright page

Book title

Author

Publisher and place of publication

Title page (in this case, two pages)

Information for a book citation can be found on the book's title and copyright pages.

The Elements of an MLA Works-Cited Entry: Journal Article

Author — Article title
Edwards, Brent Hayes. "Louis Armstrong and the Syntax of Scat."

Critical Inquiry 28.3 (2002): 618-49. Print. ← Medium

Journal title · Volume number · Year of publication · Page numbers

Issue number

Author and article title

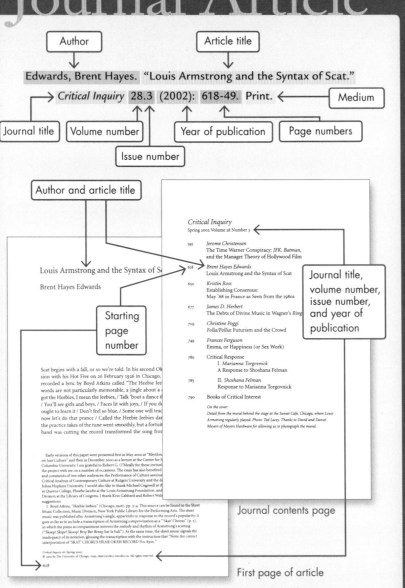

Journal title, volume number, issue number, and year of publication

Starting page number

Journal contents page

First page of article

Some academic journals, like this one, provide most of the information needed for a citation on the first page of an article as well as, like others, on the cover or contents page. You will need to look at the article's last page for the last page number.

The Elements of an MLA Works-Cited Entry: Journal Article from an Online Database

Journal title · Author · Article title · Medium
Edwards, Brent Hayes. "Louis Armstrong and the Syntax of Scat."

Critical Inquiry 28.3 (2002): 618-49. *ProQuest Research Library.* Web.

5 May 2008.

Date of access · Issue number · Page numbers · Database title

Volume number · Year of publication

Database title

Author

Article title

Journal title, year of publication, volume and issue number, and page range information

A citation for an article obtained from an online database includes information about the database, the medium, and the date of access in addition to information about the print version of the article. Information about the date of access comes from the researcher's notes.

The Elements of an MLA Works-Cited Entry: Short Work on a Web Site

Author · Title of short work · Title of
Dunham, Will. "Companies Seek Alternatives to Plastic Chemical."
Reuters, 17 Sept. 2008. Web. 18 Sept. 2008.

Sponsor or publisher · Date of publication or most recent update · Medium · Date of access

Title of Web site

Date of publication or most recent update · Author · Title of short

If you cannot find the source's author or sponsor, look for a link that "About us" or "Contact us." If the source has an edition or version place it after the site title. See page 370 for online scholarly journals 368 for works existing online and in another medium (e.g., print o

The MLA documentation style has three parts:

- In-text citations
- List of works cited
- Explanatory notes and acknowledgments

In-text citations and a list of works cited are mandatory; explanatory notes are optional.

23b MLA style: In-text citations

In-text citations let readers know that they can find full bibliographical information about your sources in the list of works cited at the end of your paper.

1. Author named in sentence In your first reference, give the author's full name as the source presents it. Afterward, use the last name only, unless two or more of your sources have the same last name (*see no. 6*) or unless two or more works by the same author appear in your works-cited list (*no. 3*).

signal phrase
As Thomas J. Hennessey explains, record deals were usually negotiated by "white

middlemen" (127).

The parenthetical page citation comes after the closing quotation mark but before the period.

2. Author named in parentheses If you do not name the source's author in your sentence, then you must provide the name in the parentheses. (Give the full name if the author of another source has the same last name.)

Armstrong easily reached difficult high notes, the F's and G's that stymied other
no comma after author's name
trumpeters (Bergreen 248).

There is no comma between the author's name and the page number. If you cite two or more distinct pages, however, separate the numbers with a comma: (Bergreen 450, 457).

3. Two or more works by the same author If you use two or more works by the same author, you must identify which work you are citing, either in your sentence or in an abbreviated form in parentheses: (Collier, *Louis Armstrong* 330).

book title is italicized
In *Louis Armstrong: An American Genius*, James Lincoln Collier reports that Glaser

paid Armstrong's mortgage, taxes, and basic living expenses (330).

343

(See pp. 350–76 for works-cited examples.)

1. Author named in sentence 343
2. Author named in parentheses 343
3. Two or more works by the same author 343
4. Two or three authors 344
5. More than three authors 344
6. Authors with the same last name 345
7. Organization as author 345
8. Unknown author 345
9. Entire work 346
10. Paraphrased or summarized source 346
11. Source of a long quotation 346
12. Source of a short quotation 346
13. One-page source 347
14. Government publication 347
15. Photograph, map, graph, chart, or other visual 347
16. Web site or other online electronic source 347
17. Work with numbered paragraphs or sections instead of pages 348
18. Work with no page or paragraph numbers 348
19. Multivolume work 348
20. Literary work 348
21. Religious text 349
22. Historical document 349
23. Indirect source 349
24. Two or more sources in one citation 349
25. Two or more sources in one sentence 350
26. Work in an anthology 350
27. E-mail, letter, personal interview 350

4. Two or three authors of the same work   If a source has up to three authors, you should name them all either in your text, as the next example shows, or in parentheses: (Jones and Chilton 160, 220).

> According to Max Jones and John Chilton, Glaser's responsibilities included
>
> booking appearances, making travel arrangements, and paying the band members'
>
> salaries (160, 220).

5. More than three authors   If a source has more than three authors, either list all the authors or give the first author's last name followed by "et al.," meaning "and others." Do the same in your works-cited list.

> Changes in social regulations are bound to produce new forms of subjectivity
>
> (Henriques et al. 275).

MLA IN-TEXT CITATIONS

- Name the author, either in a signal phrase such as "Laurence Bergreen maintains" or in a parenthetical citation.
- Include a page reference in parentheses. No "p." precedes the page number, and if the author is named in the parentheses, there is no punctuation between the author's name and the page number.
- Place the citation as close to the material being cited as possible and before any punctuation marks that divide or end the sentence except in a block quotation, where the citation comes one space after the period or final punctuation mark. See no. 12 for quotations ending with a question mark or an exclamation point.
- Italicize the titles of books, magazines, and plays. Place quotation marks around the titles of articles and short poems.
- For Internet sources, follow the same general guidelines as for print sources. Keep the parenthetical citation simple, providing enough information for your reader to find the full citation in your works-cited list. Cite either the author's name or the title of the site or article. Begin the parenthetical citation with the first word of the corresponding works-cited list entry.
- For works without page or paragraph numbers, give the author or title only. Often it is best to mention them in your sentence, in which case no parenthetical citation is needed.

6. Authors with the same last name   If the authors of two or more of your sources have the same last name, include the first initial of the author you are citing (R. Campbell 63); if the first initial is also shared, use the full first name, as shown below.

> In the late nineteenth century, the sale of sheet music spread rapidly in a
>
> Manhattan area along Broadway known as Tin Pan Alley (Richard Campbell 63).

7. Organization as author   Treat the organization as the author. If the name is long, put it in a signal phrase.

> The Centre for Contemporary Cultural Studies claims that "there is nothing
>
> inherently concrete about historiography" (10).

8. Unknown author   When no author is given, cite a work by its title, using either the full title in a signal phrase or an abbreviated version in the parentheses. When abbreviating the title, begin with the word by which it is alphabetized in your works-cited list.

title of article

"Squaresville, USA vs. Beatsville" makes the Midwestern small-town home seem

boring compared with the West Coast artist's "pad" (31).

The Midwestern small-town home seems boring compared with the West Coast

artist's "pad" ("Squaresville" 31).

9. Entire work   Acknowledge an entire work in your text, not in a parenthetical citation. Include the work in your list of works cited and include in the text the word by which the entry is alphabetized.

Sidney J. Furie's film *Lady Sings the Blues* presents Billie Holiday as a beautiful

woman in pain rather than as the great jazz artist she was.

10. Paraphrased or summarized source   If you include the author's name in your paraphrase or summary, include only the page number or numbers in your parenthetical citation. Signal phrases clarify that you are paraphrasing or summarizing.

signal phrase

Bergreen recounts how in Southern states, where blacks were prohibited from

entering many stores, Glaser sometimes had to shop for the band's food and other

supplies (378, 381).

11. Source of a long quotation   For a quotation of more than four typed lines of prose or three of poetry, do not use quotation marks. Instead, indent the material you are quoting by one inch. Following the final punctuation mark of the quotation, allow one space before the parenthetical information.

Glaser managed the Sunset Café, a club where Armstrong often performed:

> There was a pronounced gangster element at the Sunset, but Louis,
>
> accustomed to being employed and protected by mobsters, didn't think
>
> twice about that. Mr. Capone's men ensured the flow of alcohol, and their
>
> presence reassured many whites. (Bergreen 279)

12. Source of a short quotation   Close the quotation before the parenthetical citation. If the quotation concludes with an exclamation point or a question mark, place the closing quotation mark after that punctuation mark and place the sentence period after the parenthetical citation.

His innovative singing style also featured "scat," a technique that combines

brackets enclose a word that substitutes for omitted text

"nonsense syllables [with] improvised melodies" (Robinson 515).

Shakespeare's Sonnet XVIII asks, "Shall I compare thee to a summer's day?" (line 1).

13. One-page source You need not include a page number in the parenthetical citation for a one-page printed source.

14. Government publication To avoid an overly long parenthetical citation, name within your text the government agency that published the source.

According to a report issued by the Bureau of National Affairs, many employers in 1964 needed guidance to apply new workplace rules that ensured fairness and complied with the Civil Rights Act of 1964 (32).

15. Photograph, map, graph, chart, or other visual

VISUAL APPEARS IN YOUR PAPER

An aerial photograph of Manhattan (Fig. 3), taken by the United States Geographical Survey, demonstrates how creative city planning can introduce parks and green spaces within even the most densely populated urban areas.

If the caption you write for the image includes all the information found in a works-cited list entry, you need not include it in your list. (*See p. 386 for an example.*)

VISUAL DOES NOT APPEAR IN YOUR PAPER

An aerial photograph of Manhattan taken by the United States Geographical Survey demonstrates how creative city planning can introduce parks and green spaces within even the most densely populated urban areas (TerraServer-USA).

Provide a parenthetical citation that directs your reader to information about the source of the image in your works-cited list.

16. Web site or other online electronic source If you cannot find the author of an online source, then identify the source by title, either in your text or in a parenthetical citation. Because most online sources do not have set page, section, or paragraph numbers, they must usually be cited as entire works.

"Peter Davis gave [Armstrong] "basic musical training on the cornet" ("Louis Armstrong").

17. Work with numbered paragraphs or sections instead of pages Give the paragraph or section number(s) after the author's name and a comma. To distinguish them from page numbers, use the abbreviation *par(s)*. or the type of division such as *section(s)*.

> Rothstein suggests that many German Romantic musical techniques may have
>
> originated in Italian opera (par. 9).

18. Work with no page or paragraph numbers When citing an online or print source without page, paragraph, or other reference numbers, try to include the author's name in your text instead of in a parenthetical citation.

> author's name
> Crouch argues that Armstrong remains a driving force in present-day music, from
>
> country and western music to the chanted doggerel of rap.

19. Multivolume work When citing more than one volume of a multivolume work in your paper, include with each citation the volume number, followed by a colon, a space, and the page number.

> Schuller argues that even though jazz's traditional framework appears European,
>
> its musical essence is African (1: 62).

If you consult only one volume of a multivolume work, then specify that volume in the works-cited list (*see p. 390*), but not in the parenthetical citation.

20. Literary work
Novels and literary nonfiction books Include the relevant page number, followed by a semicolon, a space, and the chapter number.

> Louis Armstrong figures throughout Ellison's *Invisible Man*, including in the
>
> narrator's penultimate decision to become a "yes" man who "undermine[s] them
>
> with grins" (384; ch. 23).

If the author is not named in your sentence, add the name in front of the page number: (Ellison 384; ch. 23).

Poems Use line numbers, not page numbers.

> In "Trumpet Player," Hughes says that the music "Is honey / Mixed with liquid fire"
>
> (lines 19-20). This image returns at the end of the poem, when Hughes concludes
>
> that "Trouble / Mellows to a golden note" (43-44).

Note that the word *lines* (not italicized), rather than *l.* or *ll.*, is used in the first citation to establish what the numbers in parentheses refer to; subsequent citations need not use the word *lines* (again, not italicized).

Plays and long, multisection poems Use division (act, scene, canto, book, part) and lines, not page numbers. In the following example, notice that arabic numerals are used for act and scene divisions as well as for line numbers: (*Ham.* 2.3.22-27). The same is true for canto, verse, and lines in the following citation of Byron's *Don Juan*: (*DJ* 1.37.4-8). (The *MLA Handbook* lists abbreviations for titles of certain literary works.)

21. Religious text Cite material in the Bible, Upanishads, or Koran by book, chapter, and verse, using an appropriate abbreviation when the name of the book is in the parentheses rather than in your sentence. Name the edition from which you are citing.

As the Bible says, "The wise man knows there will be a time of judgment"

(*Holy Bible, Rev. Stand. Vers.*, Eccles. 8.5).

Note that titles of biblical books are not italicized.

22. Historical document For familiar documents such as the Constitution and the Declaration of Independence, provide the document's name and the numbers of the parts you are citing.

Judges are allowed to remain in office "during good behavior," a vague standard

that has had various interpretations (US Const., art. 3, sec. 1).

23. Indirect source When you quote or paraphrase a quotation you found in someone else's work, put *qtd. in* (not italicized, meaning "quoted in") before the name of your source.

Armstrong confided to a friend that Glaser's death "broke [his] heart" (qtd. in

Bergreen 490).

In your list of works cited, list only the work you consulted, in this case the indirect source by Bergreen.

24. Two or more sources in one citation When you credit two or more sources, use a semicolon to separate the citations.

Giving up his other business ventures, Glaser now became Armstrong's exclusive

agent (Bergreen 376-78; Collier 273-76; Morgenstern 124-28).

25. Two or more sources in one sentence Include a parenthetical reference after each idea or quotation you have borrowed.

> Ironically, Americans lavish more money each year on their pets than they spend on
>
> children's toys (Merkins 21), but the feral cat population—consisting of abandoned
>
> pets and their offspring—is at an estimated 70 million and growing (Mott).

26. Work in an anthology When citing a work in a collection, give the name of the specific work's author, not the name of the editor of the whole collection.

> When Dexter Gordon threatened to quit, Armstrong offered him a raise—without
>
> consulting with Glaser (Morgenstern 132).

Here, Morgenstern is cited as the source even though his work appears in a collection edited by Marc Miller. Note that the list of works cited must include an entry for Morgenstern (*see p. 390*).

27. E-mail, letter, or personal interview Cite by name the person you communicated with, using either a signal phrase or parentheses.

> Much to Glaser's surprise, both "Hello, Dolly" and "What a Wonderful World"
>
> became big hits after the rights had been sold (Jacobs).

In the works-cited list, after giving the person's last name you will need to identify the kind of communication and its date (*see pp. 362, 372, and 375*).

23c MLA style: List of works cited

MLA documentation style requires a works-cited page with full bibliographic information about your sources. The list of works cited should appear at the end of your paper, beginning on a new page entitled "Works Cited." Include only those sources you cite in your paper, unless your instructor tells you to prepare a "Works Consulted" list.

Books

1. Book with one author Italicize the book's title. Generally only the city, not the state, is included in the publication data. Conclude with the medium (print). Notice that in the example the publisher's name, *Wayne State University Press,* is abbreviated to *Wayne State UP.*

> Hennessey, Thomas J. *From Jazz to Swing: African-Americans and Their Music*
>
> *1890-1935.* Detroit: Wayne State UP, 1984. Print.

MLA WORKS-CITED ENTRIES: DIRECTORY to SAMPLE TYPES

(See pp. 343–50 for examples of in-text citations.)

2. Two or more works by the same author(s) Give the author's name in the first entry only. For subsequent works authored by that person, replace the name with three hyphens and a period. Alphabetize by title.

Collier, James Lincoln. *Jazz: The American Theme Song.* New York: Oxford UP, 1993. Print.

---. *Louis Armstrong: An American Genius.* New York: Oxford UP, 1983. Print.

3. Book with two or three authors Name the two or three authors in the order in which they appear on the title page, putting the last name first for the first author only.

Davis, Miles, and Quincy Troupe. *Miles: The Autobiography.* New York: Simon, 1989. Print.

4. Book with four or more authors When a work has more than three authors, you may list them all or use the abbreviation *et al.* (meaning "and others") to replace the names of all authors except the first.

Henriques, Julian, et al. *Changing the Subject: Psychology, Social Regulation, and Subjectivity.* New York: Methuen, 1984. Print.

5. Organization as author Consider as an organization any group, commission, association, or corporation whose members are not identified on the title page.

Centre for Contemporary Cultural Studies. *Making Histories: Studies in History*

Writing and Politics*. London: Hutchinson, 1982. Print.

6. Book by an editor or editors   If the title page lists an editor instead of an author, begin with the editor's name followed by the abbreviation *ed.* (not italicized). Use *eds.* when more than one editor is listed. Only the first editor's name should appear in reverse order.

Miller, Paul Eduard, ed. *Esquire's Jazz Book*. New York: Smith, 1944. Print.

7. Book with an author and an editor   Put the author and title first, followed by the abbreviation *Ed.* (not italicized, for "edited by") and the name of the editor. However, if you cited something written by the editor see no. 15.

editor's name not in reverse order

Armstrong, Louis. *Louis Armstrong: A Self-Portrait*. Ed. Richard Meryman. New York:

Eakins, 1971. Print.

8. Work in an anthology or chapter in an edited book   List the author and title of the selection, followed by the title of the anthology, *Ed.* and the editor's name, publication data, page numbers of the selection, and medium.

Smith, Hale. "Here I Stand." *Readings in Black American Music*. Ed. Eileen Southern.

New York: Norton, 1971. 286-89. Print.

9. Two or more items from one anthology   Include a complete entry for the anthology beginning with the name of the editor(s). Each selection should have its own entry in the alphabetical list that includes only the author, title of the selection, editor, and page numbers.

entry for a selection from the anthology
Johnson, Hall. "Notes on the Negro Spiritual." Southern 268-75.

entry for the anthology
Southern, Eileen, ed. *Readings in Black American Music*. New York: Norton, 1971. Print.

entry for a selection from the anthology
Still, William Grant. "The Structure of Music." Southern 276-79.

10. Signed article in an encyclopedia or another reference work   Cite the author's name, title of the entry (in quotation marks), title of the reference work (italicized), editor, publication information, and medium. Omit page numbers if entries appear in alphabetical order.

MLA LIST of WORKS CITED

- Begin on a new page with the centered title "Works Cited."
- Include an entry for every source cited in your text.
- Include author, title, publication data, and medium (such as print, Web, radio) for each entry, if available. Use a period to set off each of these elements from the others. Leave one space after the periods.
- Do not number the entries.
- Put entries in alphabetical order by author's or editor's last name. If the work has more than one author, see nos. 3 and 4 (*p. 353*). (If the author is unknown, use the first word of the title, excluding the articles *a, an,* or *the*).
- Italicize titles of books, periodicals, long poems, and plays. Put quotation marks around titles of articles, short stories, and short poems.
- Capitalize the first and last and all important words in all titles and subtitles. Do not capitalize articles, prepositions, coordinating conjunctions, and the *to* in infinitives unless they appear first or last in the title. Place a colon between title and subtitle unless the title ends in a question mark or an exclamation point.
- In the publication data, abbreviate months and publishers' names (Dec. rather than December; Oxford UP instead of Oxford University Press), and include the name of the city in which the publisher is located but not the state (unless the city is obscure or ambiguous): Ithaca: Cornell UP. Use n.p. in place of publisher or location information if none is available. If the date of publication is not given, provide the approximate date, enclosed in brackets: [c. 1975]. If you cannot approximate the date, write n.d. for "no date."
- Do not use p., pp., or page(s). Use n. pag. if the source lacks page or paragraph numbers or other divisions. When page spans over 100 have the same first digit, do not repeat it for the second number: 243–47.
- Abbreviate all months except May, June, and July.
- For articles and other print sources that skip pages, provide the page number for the beginning of the article followed by a plus (+) sign.
- Use a hanging indent: Start the first line of each entry at the left margin, and indent all subsequent lines of the entry five spaces (or one-half inch on the computer).
- Double-space within entries and between them.

Robinson, J. Bradford. "Scat Singing." *The New Grove Dictionary of Jazz*. Ed. Barry

Kernfeld. Vol. 3. London: Macmillan, 2002. Print.

11. Unsigned entry in an encyclopedia or another reference work
Start the entry with the title. For well-known reference works, omit the place and publisher.

"Scat." *Merriam-Webster's Collegiate Dictionary*. 11th ed. 2003. Print.

12. Article from a collection of reprinted articles

Haney-Peritz, Janice. "Monumental Feminism and Literature's Ancestral House:

Another Look at 'The Yellow Wallpaper.'" *Women's Studies* 12.2 (1986): 113-28.
abbreviation for "reprinted"
Rpt. in *The Captive Imagination: A Casebook on "The Yellow Wallpaper."* Ed.

Catherine Golden. New York: Feminist, 1992. 261-76. Print.

13. Anthology

Eggers, Dave, ed. *The Best American Nonrequired Reading 2007*. Boston: Houghton,

2007. Print.

14. Publisher's imprint
For books published by a division within a publishing company, known as an "imprint," put a hyphen between the imprint and publisher.

title in title, see no. 22
Wells, Ken, ed. *Floating Off the Page: The Best Stories from* The Wall Street Journal's

"Middle Column." New York: Wall Street Journal-Simon, 2002. Print.

15. Preface, foreword, introduction, or afterword
When the writer of the part is different from the author of the book, use the word *By* after the book's title and cite the author's full name. If the book's sole author wrote the part and the book has an editor, use only the author's last name after *By*. If there is no editor and the author wrote the part, cite the complete book.

name of part of book
Crawford, Richard. Foreword. *The Jazz Tradition*. By Martin Williams. New York:

Oxford UP, 1993. v-xiii. Print.

16. Translation
The translator's name goes after the title, with the abbreviation *Trans.*

Goffin, Robert. *Horn of Plenty: The Story of Louis Armstrong*. Trans. James F. Bezov.

New York: Da Capo, 1977. Print.

356

17. Edition other than the first Include the number of the edition: *2nd ed., 3rd ed.* (not italicized) and so on. Place the number after the title, or if there is an editor, after that person's name.

> Panassie, Hugues. *Louis Armstrong*. 2nd ed. New York: Da Capo, 1980. Print.

18. Religious text Give the version, italicized; the editor's or translator's name (if any); and the publication information including medium.

> *New American Standard Bible*. La Habra: Lockman Foundation, 1995. Print.

> *The Upanishads*. Trans. Eknath Easwaran. Tomales, CA: Nilgiri, 1987. Print.

19. Multivolume work The first example indicates that the researcher used more than one volume of the work; the second shows that only the second volume was used.

> Lissauer, Robert. *Lissauer's Encyclopedia of Popular Music in America*. 3 vols. New
>
> York: Facts on File, 1996. Print.

> Lissauer, Robert. *Lissauer's Encyclopedia of Popular Music in America*. Vol. 2. New
>
> York: Facts on File, 1996. Print.

20. Book in a series After the medium, put the name of the series and, if available on the title page, the number of the work.

> Floyd, Samuel A., Jr., ed. *Black Music in the Harlem Renaissance*. New York: Greenwood,
>
> Name of series not italicized
>
> 1990. Print. Contributions in Afro-American and African Studies 128.

21. Republished book Put the original date of publication, followed by a period, before the current publication data.

> original publication date
>
> Cuney-Hare, Maud. *Negro Musicians and Their Music*. 1936. New York: Da Capo,
>
> 1974. Print.

22. Title in a title When a book's title contains the title of another book, do not italicize the second title. For the novel *Invisible Man*:

> O'Meally, Robert, ed. *New Essays on* Invisible Man. Cambridge: Cambridge UP,
>
> 1988. Print.

23. Unknown author   The citation begins with the title. In the list of works cited, alphabetize the citation by the first important word, excluding the articles *A, An,* and *The.*

> Webster's College Dictionary. New York: Random; New York: McGraw, 1991. Print.

Note that this entry includes both of the publishers listed on the dictionary's title page; they are separated by a semicolon.

24. Book with illustrator   List the illustrator after the title with the abbreviation *illus.* (not italicized). If you refer primarily to the illustrator, put that name before the title instead of the author's.

> Carroll, Lewis. *Alice's Adventures in Wonderland and through the Looking-Glass.*
>
>   Illus. John Tenniel. New York: Modern Library-Random, 2002. Print.

> Tenniel, John, illus. *Alice's Adventures in Wonderland and through the Looking-Glass.*
>
>   By Lewis Carroll. New York: Modern Library-Random, 2002. Print.

25. Graphic novel or comic book   Cite graphic narratives created by one person as you would any other book or multivolume work. For collaborations, begin with the person whose work you refer to most and list others in the order in which they appear on the title page. Indicate each person's contribution. (*For part of a series, see no. 20.*)

> Satrapi, Marjane. *Persepolis.* 2 vols. New York: Pantheon-Random, 2004-05. Print.

> Moore, Alan, writer. *Watchmen.* Illus. David Gibbons. Color by John Higgins. New
>
>   York: DC Comics, 1995. Print.

Periodicals

Periodicals are published at set intervals, usually four times a year for scholarly journals, monthly or weekly for magazines, and daily or weekly for newspapers. Between the author and the publication data are two titles: the title of the article, in quotation marks, and the title of the periodical, italicized. (*For online versions of print periodicals and periodicals published only online, see pp. 364–65 and 370–71.*)

26. Article in a journal with volume numbers   Most journals have a volume number corresponding to the year and an issue number for each publication that year. The issue may be indicated by a month or season. Put the volume number after the title. Follow it with a period and the issue number. Give the year of publication in parentheses, followed by a colon, a space, and the page numbers of the article. End with the medium.

Tirro, Frank. "Constructive Elements in Jazz Improvisation." *Journal of the American*

Musicological Society 27.2 (1974): 285-305. Print.

27. Article in a journal with issue numbers only   Give only the issue number.

Lousley, Cheryl. "Knowledge, Power and Place." *Canadian Literature* 195 (2007): 11-

30. Print.

28. Article in a monthly magazine   Provide the month and year, abbreviating all months except May, June, and July.

Walker, Malcolm. "Discography: Bill Evans." *Jazz Monthly* June 1965: 20-22. Print.

29. Article in a weekly magazine   Include the complete date of publication: day, month, and year.

Taylor, J. R. "Jazz History: The Incompleted Past." *Village Voice* 3 July 1978: 65-67.

Print.

30. Article in a newspaper   Provide the day, month, and year. If an edition is named on the top of the first page, specify the edition—*natl. ed.* or *late ed.* (without italics), for example—after the date. If the section letter is part of the page number, see the first example. Give the title of an unnumbered section with *sec* (not italicized). If the article appears on nonconsecutive pages, put a plus (+) sign after the first page number.

Blumenthal, Ralph. "Satchmo with His Tape Recorder Running." *New York Times*

3 Aug. 1999, natl. ed.: E1+. Print.

Just, Julie. "Children's Bookshelf." *New York Times* 15 Mar. 2009, natl. ed., Book

Review sec.:13. Print.

31. Unsigned article   The citation begins with the title and is alphabetized by the first word, excluding articles such as *A, An,* or *The.*

"Squaresville, USA vs. Beatsville." *Life* 21 Sept. 1959: 31. Print.

32. Review   Begin with the name of the reviewer and, if there is one, the title of the review. Add *Rev. of* (without italics, meaning "review of") and the title plus the author or performer of the work being reviewed.

Ostwald, David. "All That Jazz." Rev. of *Louis Armstrong: An Extravagant Life,* by

Laurence Bergreen. *Commentary* Nov. 1997: 68-72. Print.

359

33. Editorial   Treat editorials as articles, but add the word *Editorial* (not italicized) after the title. If the editorial is unsigned, begin with the title.

> Shaw, Theodore M. "The Debate over Race Needs Minority Students' Voices."
>
> Editorial. *Chronicle of Higher Education* 25 Feb. 2000: A72. Print.

34. Abstract of a journal article   Collections of abstracts from journals can be found in the library's reference section. Include the publication information for the original article, followed by the title of the publication that provides the abstract, the volume, the year in parentheses, and the item or page number.

> Theiler, Anne M., and Louise G. Lippman. "Effects of Mental Practice and Modeling
>
> on Guitar and Vocal Performance." *Journal of General Psychology* 122.4 (1995):
>
> 329-43. *Psychological Abstracts* 83.1 (1996): item 30039. Print.

35. Letter to the editor

> Tyler, Steve. Letter. *National Geographic Adventure* Apr. 2004: 11. Print.

Other Print Sources

36. Government document   Either the name of the government and agency or the name of the document's author comes first. If the government and agency name come first, follow the title of the document with the word *By* for a writer, *Ed.* for an editor, or *Comp.* for a compiler (if any), and give the name. Publication information and medium come last.

> United States. Bureau of Natl. Affairs. *The Civil Rights Act of 1964: Text, Analysis,*
>
> *Legislative History; What It Means to Employers, Businessmen, Unions,*
>
> *Employees, Minority Groups.* Washington: BNA, 1964. Print.

For the format to use when citing the *Congressional Record,* see no. 75.

37. Pamphlet or brochure   Treat as a book. If the pamphlet or brochure has an author, list his or her name first; otherwise, begin with the title.

> *All Music Guide to Jazz.* 2nd ed. San Francisco: Miller Freeman, 1996. Print.

38. Conference proceedings   Cite as you would a book, but include information about the conference if it is not in the title.

Mendel, Arthur, Gustave Reese, and Gilbert Chase, eds. *Papers Read at the International*

Congress of Musicology Held at New York September 11th to 16th, 1939. New York:

Music Educators' Natl. Conf. for the American Musicological Soc., 1944. Print.

39. Published dissertation Cite as you would a book. After the title, add *Diss.* (not italicized) for "dissertation," the name of the institution, the year the dissertation was written, and the medium.

Fraser, Wilmot Alfred. *Jazzology: A Study of the Tradition in Which Jazz Musicians*

Learn to Improvise. Diss. U of Pennsylvania, 1983. Ann Arbor: UMI, 1987. Print.

40. Unpublished dissertation Begin with the author's name, followed by the title in quotation marks, the abbreviation *Diss.* (not italicized), the name of the institution, the year the dissertation was written, and the medium.

Reyes-Schramm, Adelaida. "The Role of Music in the Interaction of Black Americans

and Hispanos in New York City's East Harlem." Diss. Columbia U, 1975. Print.

41. Abstract of a dissertation Use the format for an unpublished dissertation. After the dissertation date, give the abbreviation *DA* or *DAI* (for *Dissertation Abstracts* or *Dissertation Abstracts International*), then the volume number, the issue number, the date of publication, the page number, and the medium.

Quinn, Richard Allen. "Playing Together: Improvisation in Postwar American

Literature and Culture." Diss. U of Iowa, 2000. *DAI* 61.6 (2001): 2305A. Print.

42. Published interview Name the person interviewed and give the title of the interview or the descriptive term *Interview* (not italicized), the name of the interviewer (if known and relevant), the publication information, and the medium.

Armstrong, Louis. Interview by Richard Meryman. "Authentic American Genius." *Life*

15 Apr. 1966: 92-102. Print.

43. Map or chart Cite as you would a book with an unknown author. Italicize the title of the map or chart, and add the word *Map* or *Chart* (not italicized) following the title.

Let's Go Map Guide to New Orleans. Map. New York: St. Martin's, 1997. Print.

44. Cartoon Include the cartoonist's name, the title of the cartoon (if any) in quotation marks, the word *Cartoon* (not italicized), the publication information, and the medium.

> Myller, Jorgen. "Louis Armstrong's First Lesson." Cartoon. *Melody Maker* Mar.
>
> 1931: 12. Print.

45. Reproduction of artwork Treat a photograph of a work of art in another source like a work in an anthology (*no. 8*). Italicize the titles of both the artwork and the source, and include the institution or collection and city where the work can be found prior to information about the source in which it appears.

> Da Vinci, Leonardo. *Mona Lisa.* N.d. Louvre, Paris. *Gardner's Art Through the Ages:*
>
> *A Concise History of Western Art.* By Fred S. Kleiner and Christin J. Mamiya.
>
> Belmont, CA: Thomson, 2008. 253. Print.

46. Advertisement Name the item or organization being advertised, include the word *Advertisement* (not italicized), and indicate where the ad appeared.

> Hartwick College Summer Music Festival and Institute. Advertisement. *New York*
>
> *Times Magazine* 3 Jan. 1999: 54. Print.

47. Published letter Treat like a work in an anthology, but include the date. Include the number, if one was assigned by the editor. If you use more than one letter from a published collection, follow the instructions for cross-referencing in no. 9.

> Hughes, Langston. "To Arna Bontemps." 17 Jan. 1938. *Arna Bontemps—Langston Hughes*
>
> *Letters 1925-1967.* Ed. Charles H. Nichols. New York: Dodd, 1980. 27-28. Print.

48. Personal letter To cite a letter you received, start with the writer's name, followed by the descriptive phrase *Letter to the author* (not italicized), the date, and MS (manuscript).

> Cogswell, Michael. Letter to the author. 15 Mar. 2008. MS.

To cite someone else's unpublished personal letter, see no. 49.

49. Manuscripts, typescripts, and material in archives Give the author, a title or description (*Letter, Notebook*), the form (*MS.* if handwritten, *TS.* if typed), any identifying number, and the name and location of the institution housing the material. (Do not italicize any part of the citation.)

Glaser, Joe. Letter to Lucille Armstrong. 28 Sept. 1960. MS. Box 3. Louis Armstrong

Archives. Queens College City U of New York, Flushing.

Pollack, Bracha. "A Man ahead of His Time." 1997. TS.

50. Legal source (print or online)   To cite a specific act, give its name, Public Law number, its Statutes at Large number, page range, the date it was enacted, and the medium.

Energy Policy Act of 2005. Pub. L. 109-58. 119 Stat. 594-1143. 8 Aug. 2005. Print.

To cite a law case, provide the name of the plaintiff and defendant, the case number, the court that decided the case, the date of the decision, and the medium.

PRINT

Ashcroft v. the Free Speech Coalition. 535 US 234-73. Supreme Court of the US.

2002. Print.

WEB

Ashcroft v. the Free Speech Coalition. 535 US 234-73. Supreme Court of the US.

2002. *Supreme Court Collection*. Legal Information Inst., Cornell U Law School, n.d.

Web. 20 May 2008.

For more information about citing legal documents or from case law, MLA recommends consulting *The Bluebook: A Uniform System of Citation,* published by the Harvard Law Review Association.

Online Sources

The examples that follow are based on guidelines for the citation of electronic sources in the seventh edition of the *MLA Handbook for Writers of Research Papers* (2009).

For scholarly journals published online, see no. 88. For periodical articles from an online database, see no. 92. Cite most other Web sources according to nos. 51–52. For works that also exist in another medium (e.g. print), the MLA recommends including information about the other version in your citation. See nos. 76–87.

Basic Web sources

51. Web site or independent online work   Begin with the author, editor (*ed.*), compiler (*comp.*), director (*dir.*), performer (*perf.*), or translator (*trans.*), if any. Give the title (italicized), the version or edition (if any), the publisher or sponsor (or *n.p.*), publication date (or last update, or *n.d.*), medium, and your access date. (Use italics for the title only.) Citations 51–74 follow this format.

> Raeburn, Bruce Boyd, ed. *William Ransom Hogan Archive of New Orleans Jazz.* Tulane
>
> U, 13 Apr. 2006. Web. 11 May 2008.

52. Part of a Web site or larger online work   Give the title of the part in quotation marks.

> Oliver, Rachel. "All About: Forests and Carbon Trading." *CNN.com.* Cable News
>
> Network, 11 Feb. 2008. Web. 14 Mar. 2008.

53. Personal Web site   If no title is available, use a descriptive term such as "Home page."

> no publisher
> Henson, Keith. *The Keith Henson Jazzpage.* N.p., 1996. Web. 11 May 2008.

54. Home page for a course   After the instructor's name, list the site title, then the department and school names.

> Web site title
> Hea, Kimme. *Spatial and Visual Rhetorics.* Dept. of English, U of Arizona, 4 Jan. 2003.
>
> Web. 11 May 2008.

55. Home page for an academic department

> *Department of English.* U of Arizona, 14 May 2008. Web. 19 May 2008.

56. Personal page on a social networking site

> Xiu Xiu. "Xiu Xiu." *MySpace.com.* MySpace, 26 Apr. 2008. Web. 11 May 2008.

57. Entire blog

> McLennan, Doug. *Diacritical.* ArtsJournal, 20 Feb. 2008. Web. 11 May 2008.

58. Blog entry

> McLennan, Doug. "The Rise of Arts Culture." *Diacritical.* ArtsJournal, 21 Nov. 2007.
>
> Web. 11 May 2008.

59. Article in an online magazine

> Borushko, Matthew. "The Reinvention of Jazz." *The Atlantic.com.* Atlantic Monthly
>
> Group, 18 Apr. 2007. Web. 13 May 2008.

TEXTCONNEX

Web Addresses in MLA Citations

Only include the URL (Web address) of an online source in a citation if your reader would be unable to find the source without it (via a search engine). For example, basic citation information might not sufficiently identify your source if multiple versions of a document exist online without version numbers. Place a URL at the end of your citation in angle brackets and end with a period.

> Raeburn, Bruce Boyd, ed. *William Ransom Hogan Archive of New Orleans Jazz.*
>
> Tulane U, 13 Apr. 2006. Web. 11 May 2008. <http://www.tulane
>
> .edu/~lmiller/JazzHome.html>.

If you need to divide a URL between lines, do so after a slash and do not insert a hyphen. If the URL is long (more than one line of your text), give the URL of the site's search page. Do not make the URL a hyperlink.

60. Article in an online newspaper

> Howard, Hilary. "A Cruise for Jazz Fans with a Soft Side." *New York Times*. New York
> sponsor
>
> Times, 11 May 2008. Web. 11 May 2008.

61. Editorial in an online newspaper
Include the word *Editorial* (not italicized) after the published title of the editorial.

> "Schwarzenegger's Bad-News Budget." Editorial. *SFGate*. San Francisco Chronicle,
> sponsor
>
> 14 Jan. 2008. Web. 12 May 2008.

62. Letter to the editor in an online newspaper
Include the name of the letter writer, as well as the word *Letter* (not italicized).

> Dow, Roger. Letter. *SFGate*. San Francisco Chronicle, 10 Jan. 2008. Web. 12 May 2008.
> sponsor

63. Online review

> Kot, Greg. "The Roots Fuel Their Rage into 'Rising Down.'" Rev. of *Rising Down*, by the
> sponsor
>
> Roots. *chicagotribune.com*. Chicago Tribune, 11 May 2008. Web. 12 May 2008.

64. Online interview
See no. 42 for a print interview.

- Begin with the name of the writer, editor, compiler, translator, director, or performer.
- Put the title of a short work in quotation marks.
- If there is no title, use a descriptive term such as *editorial* or *comment* (not italicized).
- Italicize the name of the publication or Web site. The online versions of some print magazines and newspapers have different titles than the print versions.
- Cite the date of publication or last update.
- For an online magazine or newspaper article or a Web original source, give the source (in quotation marks), the site title (italicized), version (if any), publisher or sponsor, date of publication, medium (*Web*), and access date. (*See p. 364.*)
- You may cite online sources that also appear in another medium with information about the other version (*see pp. 368–70*). (Do not cite online versions of print newspapers and magazines in this way.)
- For a journal article, include the article title (in quotation marks), periodical title (italicized), volume and issue numbers, and inclusive page numbers or *n. pag.* (not italicized). Conclude with the medium (Web) and access date. (*See pp. 370–71.*)
- To cite a periodical article from an online database, provide the print publication information, the database title (italicized), the medium, and your access date.
- If the source is not divided into sections or pages, include *n. pag.* (not italicized) for "no pagination." Give the medium (Web).
- Include your most recent date of access to the specific source (not the general site).
- Conclude the citation with a URL only if readers may have difficulty finding the source without it (*see the box on p. 365*).

Haddon, Mark. Interview by Dave Weich. *Powells.com*. Powell's Books, 24 June 2003.

Web. 15 May 2008.

65. Article in an online encyclopedia or another reference work Begin with the author's name if any is given.

"Louis Armstrong." *Encyclopaedia Britannica Online*. Encyclopaedia Britannica, 2008.

Web. 12 May 2008.

66. Entry in a wiki   List the title of the entry, the wiki name, the sponsor, the date of latest update, the medium, and your access date. Check with your instructor before using a wiki as a source.

> "Symphony." *Citizendium*. Citizendium Foundation, 1 Nov. 2007. Web. 12 May 2008.

67. Online map (Web only)   Include the descriptive word *Map*.

> "Denver, Colorado." Map. *Google Maps*. Google, 12 May 2008. Web. 12 May 2008.

68. Audio podcast

> no publisher
> Fresh Sounds. "Jazzarific: Bing Crosby Meets Louis Armstrong." *JazzVinyl.com*. N.p., 26 Dec. 2007. Web. 12 May 2008.

69. Video podcast

> Mahr, Krista. "Saving China's Grasslands." *Time.com*. Time, Inc., 10 Oct. 2007. Web. 12 May 2008.

70. Online video (Web original)   For material posted online from a film, TV series, or other non-Web source, see nos. 83 and 85.

> Wesch, Michael. "The Machine Is Us/ing Us." *Digital Ethnography*. Kansas State U, 31 Jan. 2007. Web. 12 May 2008.

71. Posting to a news group or an electronic forum   Treat an archived posting as a Web source. Use the subject line as the title of the posting and give the name of the Web site. If there is no subject, substitute *Online posting* (not italicized).

> Pomeroy, Leslie K., Jr. "Racing with the Moon." *rec.music.bluenote*. N.p., 4 May 2008. Web. 12 May 2008.

72. Posting to an e-mail discussion list   Include the author and use the subject line as the title.

> Harbin, David. "Furtwangler's Beethoven 9 Bayreuth." *Opera-L Archives*. City U of New York, 3 Jan. 2008. Web. 12 May 2008.

73. Synchronous (real-time) communication   Cite the online transcript of a synchronous communication as you would a Web site. Include a description, the title of the forum, the date of the event, the medium, and the date of access. If relevant, the speaker's name can begin the citation.

Curran, Stuart, and Harry Rusche. "Discussion: Plenary Log 6. Third Annual Graduate

Student Conference in Romanticism." *Prometheus Unplugged: Emory MOO.*

Emory U, 20 Apr. 1996. Web. 4 Jan. 1999.

74. Online government publication except the *Congressional Record*   Begin with the name of the country, followed by the name of the sponsoring department, the title of the document, and the names (if listed) of the authors.

United States. National Commission on Terrorist Attacks upon the United States. *The*

9/11 Commission Report. By Thomas H. Kean, et al. 5 Aug. 2004. Web. 12 May. 2008.

75. *Congressional Record* (online or print)   The *Congressional Record* has its own citation format, which is the same for print and online (apart from the medium). Abbreviate the title and include the date and page numbers. Give the medium (print or Web).

Cong. Rec. 28 Apr. 2005: D419-D428. Web. 12 May 2008.

Web sources also available in another medium

If an online work also appears in another medium (e.g., print), the MLA recommends (but does not require) that your citation include information about the other version of the work. (Information about the editor or sponsor of the Web site or database is optional in this model.) If the facts about the other version of the source are not available, cite as a basic Web source (*see nos. 51–52*). (Articles on the Web sites of newspapers and magazines are never cited with print publication information. *For academic journals, see nos. 88–91.*)

76. Online book   Cite as a print book (*no. 1*). Instead of ending with *Print* (not italicized), give the Web site or database, the medium (Web), and your access date. Optional information about the site's sponsor, publisher, or editor follows the site name.

Arter, Jared Maurice. *Echoes from a Pioneer Life.* Atlanta: Caldwell, 1922. *Documenting*
          optional name and location of Web publisher
the American South. U of North Carolina, Chapel Hill. Web. 21 May 2008.

77. Selection from an online book   Add the title of the selection after the author. If the online version of the work lacks page numbers, use *n. pag.* instead. (Capitalize the *n* in *n. pag.* when it follows a period.)

Sandburg, Carl. "Chicago." *Chicago Poems.* New York, Holt, 1916. N. pag.

Bartleby.com. Web. 12 May 2008.

78. Online dissertation   Give the Web site or database, the medium (Web), and your access date. Or cite as a basic Web source (*see nos. 51–52*).

> Kosiba, Sara A. "A Successful Revolt? The Redefinition of Midwestern Literary Culture
>
> in the 1920s and 1930s." Diss. Kent State U, 2007. *OhioLINK*. Web. 12 May 2008.

79. Online pamphlet or brochure (also in print)   Cite as a book. Give the title of the Web site or database, the medium (Web), and your access date. Or cite as a basic Web source (*see no. 51*).

> United States. Securities and Exchange Commission. Division of Corporate Finance.
>
> *International Investing: Get the Facts.* Washington: GPO, 1999. *US Securities and*
>
> *Exchange Commission.* Web. 12 May 2008.

80. Online map or chart (also in print)   See no. 43 for a print map. Remove the medium; add the title of the database or Web site, the medium (Web), and your access date. (See no. 67 for a Web-only map.) Or cite as a basic Web source (*see nos. 51–52*).

> *MTA New York City Subway.* New York: Metropolitan Transit Authority, 2008. *MTA*
>
> *New York City Transit.* Web. 12 May 2008.

81. Online cartoon (also in print)   See no. 44 for a cartoon. Remove the medium; add the database or site, the medium (Web), and your access date. Or cite as a basic Web source (*see nos. 51–52*).

> Ziegler, Jack. "A Viking Funeral for My Goldfish." *New Yorker* 19 May 2008: 65.
>
> *Cartoonbank.com.* Web. 20 May 2008.

82. Online rendering of visual artwork   Cite as you would the original (*no. 115*). Remove the medium; add the database or Web site, the medium (Web), and your access date. Or cite as a basic Web source (*see nos. 51–52*).

> Seurat, Georges-Pierre. *Evening, Honfleur.* 1886. Museum of Mod. Art, New York.
>
> *MoMA.org.* Web. 8 May 2008.

83. Online video/film (also on film, DVD, or videocassette)   See nos. 107–08 for a film or video. Remove the medium; add the database or site, the medium (Web), and your access date. Or cite as a basic Web source (*see nos. 51–52*).

Night of the Living Dead. Dir. George A. Romero. Image Ten, 1968. *Internet Archive.*

Web. 12 May 2008.

84. Online radio program   See no. 110 for a radio program. Remove the medium; add the database or site, the medium (Web), and your access date. Or cite as a basic Web source (*see nos. 51–52*).

"Bill Evans: 'Piano Impressionism.'" *Jazz Profiles.* Narr. Nancy Wilson. Natl. Public

Radio. WGBH, Boston, 27 Feb. 2008. *NPR.org.* Web. 16 Mar. 2008

85. Online TV program   See no. 111 for a TV program. Remove the medium; add the database or site, the medium (Web), and your access date. Or cite as a basic Web source (*see nos. 51–52*).

                  director of episode
  episode   (not series)   series performer in series
"Local Ad." Dir. Jason Reitman. *The Office.* Perf. Steve Carrell. NBC. WNBC, New York,

12 Dec. 2007. *NBC.com.* Web. 12 May 2008.

86. Online broadcast interview   See no. 112 for a broadcast interview. Remove the medium; add the database or site and the medium (Web), and give your access date. Or cite as a basic Web source (*see nos. 51–52*).

Jones, Sharon. Interview by Terry Gross. *Fresh Air.* Natl. Public Radio. WNYC, New

York, 28 Nov. 2007. *NPR.org.* Web. 12 May 2008.

87. Online archival material   Provide the information for the original. Add the Web site or database, the medium (Web), and your access date. Otherwise, cite as a basic Web source (*see nos. 51–52*).

                          date uncertain
Whitman, Walt. "After the Argument." [c. 1890]. The Charles E. Feinberg Collection

of the Papers of Walt Whitman, Lib. of Cong. *The Walt Whitman Archive.* Web.

13 May 2008.

Works in online scholarly journals

Use the same format for all online journals, including those with print editions.

88. Article in an online journal   Give the author, the article title (in quotation marks) or a term such as *Editorial* (not italicized), the journal title (italicized), the volume number, issue number, date, and the inclusive page range (or *n. pag.*—not italicized—if the source lacks page numbers). Conclude with the medium (Web) and your access date.

Parla, Jale. "The Wounded Tongue: Turkey's Language Reform and the Canonicity of the Novel." *PMLA* 123.1 (2008): 27-40. Web. 7 May 2008.

89. Review in an online journal

Friedman, Edward H. Rev. of *Transnational Cervantes*, by William Childers. *Cervantes: Bulletin of the Cervantes Society of America* 27.2 (2007): 41-43. Web. 13 May 2008.

90. Editorial in an online journal

Heitmeyer, Wilhelm, et al. "Letter from the Editors." Editorial. *International Journal of Conflict and Violence* 1.1 (2007): n. pag. Web. 14 May 2008.

91. Letter to the editor in an online journal

Destaillats, Frédéric, Julie Moulin, and Jean-Baptiste Bezelgues. Letter. *Nutrition & Metabolism* 4.10 (2007): n. pag. Web. 14 May 2008.

Works from online databases

In addition to information about the print version of the source, provide the title of the database (in italics), the medium (Web), and your access date.

92. Newspaper article from an online database

Blumenfeld, Larry. "House of Blues." *New York Times* 11 Nov. 2007: A33. *Academic Universe*. Web. 31 Dec. 2007.

93. Magazine article from an online database

Farley, Christopher John. "Music Goes Global." *Time* 15 Sept. 2001: 4+. *General OneFile*. Web. 31 Dec. 2007.

94. Journal article from an online database

Nielson, Aldon Lynn. "A Hard Rain." *Callaloo* 25.1 (2002): 135-45. *Academic Search Premier*. Web. 17 Mar. 2008.

95. Journal abstract from an online database

Dempsey, Nicholas P. "Hook-Ups and Train Wrecks: Contextual Parameters and the Coordination of Jazz Interactions." *Symbolic Interaction* 31.1 (2008): 57-75. Abstract. *Academic Search Premier*. Web. 17 Mar. 2008.

96. Work from a subscription service   Cite the database but not the library subscription service (e.g., EBSCO, InfoTrac) or the subscribing library. Follow the format of nos. 92–95.

In the past, America Online offered personal database subscriptions. However, it has stopped doing so, and most subscription databases can be accessed at the library.

97. E-mail   Include the author, the subject line (if any) in quotation marks, the descriptive term *Message to* (not italicized), and the name of the recipient, the date of the message, and the medium.

> Hoffman, Esther. "Re: My Louis Armstrong Paper." Message to J. Peritz. 14 Apr. 2008.
>
> E-mail.

Other Electronic (Non-Web) Sources

98. A text file stored on your computer   Cite local word-processor documents as manuscripts (*see no. 49*) and note the date last modified if you wish to cite a specific version. Record the file format as the medium.

> McNutt, Lea. "The Origination of Avian Flight." 2008. *Microsoft Word* file.
>
> Hoffman, Esther. "Louis Armstrong and Joe Glaser: More Than Meets the Eye." File
>
> last modified on 9 May 2008. *Microsoft Word* file.

99. A PDF file   Treat local PDF files as published and follow the closest print model.

> United States. US Copyright Office. *Report on Orphan Works*. Washington: US
>
> Copyright Office, 2006. PDF file.

100. An audio file   Use the format for a sound recording (*see no. 113*). Record the file format as the medium.

> Holiday, Billie. "God Bless the Child." *God Bless the Child*. Columbia, 1936. MP3 file.

101. A visual file   Cite local image files as works of visual art (*see no. 115*). Record the file format as the medium.

> Gursky, Andreas. *Times Square, New York*. 1997. Museum of Mod. Art, New York.
>
> JPEG file.

102. Other digital files   Record the file format as the medium (for example, *XML file*). If the format is unclear, use the designation *Digital *file.* Do not italicize the medium. Use the citation format of the most closely related print or nonprint source.

103. CD-ROM or DVD-ROM published periodically   If a CD-ROM or DVD-ROM is revised on a regular basis, include in its citation the author, title of the work, any print publication information, medium, title of the CD-ROM or DVD-ROM (if different from the original title), vendor, and date of electronic publication.

> Ross, Alex. "Separate Worlds, Linked Electronically." *New York Times* 29 Apr. 1996,
>
> late ed.: A22. CD-ROM. *New York Times Ondisc.* UMI-ProQuest. Dec. 1996.

104. CD-ROM or DVD-ROM not published periodically   Works on CD-ROM or DVD-ROM are usually cited like books or parts of books if they are not revised periodically. The medium and the name of the vendor (if different from the publisher) appear after the publication data. For a work that also exists in print, give the print publication information (as in the example) followed by the medium, electronic publisher, and date of electronic publication.

> print publisher omitted for pre-1900 work
>
> Jones, Owen. *The Grammar of Ornament.* London, 1856. CD-ROM. Octavo, 1998.

105. CD-ROM or DVD-ROM with multiple discs   List the total number of discs at the end of the entry, or give the number of the disc you reviewed if you used only one.

> American Educational Research Association. *AERA Journals Collection.* Washington:
>
> AERA, 2007. CD-ROM. 10 discs.

106. Computer software   Include the title, version, publisher, and date in your text or in an explanatory note. Do not include an entry in your works-cited list.

Audiovisual and Other Nonprint Sources

107. Film   Begin with the title (italicized) unless you want to highlight a particular contributor. For a film, cite the director and the featured performer(s) or narrator (*Perf.* or *Narr.*, neither italicized), followed by the distributor and year. Conclude with the medium.

> *Artists and Models.* Dir. Raoul Walsh. Perf. Jack Benny, Ida Lupino, and Alan
>
> Townsend. Paramount, 1937. Film.

108. DVD or videotape   See no. 107. Include the original film's release date if relevant. Conclude with the medium (*DVD* or *Videocassette*). Do not italicize the medium.

373

Casablanca. Dir. Michael Curtiz. Perf. Humphrey Bogart and Ingrid Bergman. 1942.

Warner Home Video, 2000. DVD.

109. Personal/archival video or audio recording Give the date recorded and the location of the recording.

Adderley, Nat. Interview by Jimmy Owens. Rec. 2 Apr. 1993. Videocassette.

Schomburg Center for Research in Black Culture, New York Public Lib.

110. Radio program Give the episode title (in quotation marks), the program title (italicized), the name of the series (if any), the network (call letters), the city, the broadcast date, and the medium. Name individuals if relevant.

"Legends Play 'Jazz in our Time.'" *Jazz Set.* Narr. Dee Dee Bridgewater. WBGO-FM,

New York, 17 Jan. 2008. Radio.

111. TV program Cite as you would a radio program (*see no. 110*), but give *Television* as the medium.

episode director of episode series performer in series
"Local Ad." Dir. Jason Reitman. *The Office.* Perf. Steve Carrell. NBC. WNBC, New York,

12 Dec. 2007. Television.

112. Broadcast interview Give the name of the person interviewed, followed by the word *Interview* (not italicized) and the name of the interviewer if you know it. End with information about the broadcast and the medium.

Knox, Shelby. Interview by David Brancaccio. *NOW.* PBS. WNET, New York, 17 June

2005. Television.

113. Sound recording Start with the composer, conductor, or performer, depending on your focus. Include the following information: the work's title (italicized); the artist(s), if not already mentioned; the manufacturer; the date of release; and the medium.

Armstrong, Louis. *Town Hall Concert Plus.* RCA Victor, 1957. LP.

114. Musical composition Include only the composer and title, unless you are referring to a published score. Published scores are treated like books except that the date of composition appears after the title. Titles of instrumental pieces are not italicized when known only by form and number, unless the reference is to a published score.

Ellington, Duke. *Satin Doll.*

Haydn, Franz Josef. Symphony No. 94 in G Major.

reference to a published score
Haydn, Franz Josef. *Symphony No. 94 in G Major.* 1791. Ed. H. C. Robbins Landon.

Salzburg: Haydn-Mozart, 1965. Print.

115. Artwork Provide the artist's name, the title of the artwork (italicized), the date (if unknown, write *n.d.*), the medium, and the institution or private collection and city (or *n.p.*) in which the artwork can be found. For anonymous collectors, write *Private collection* and omit city (do not write *n.p.*).

Leonard, Herman. *Louis Armstrong: Birdland 1949.* 1949. Photograph. Barbara

Gillman Gallery, Miami.

116. Personal, telephone, or e-mail interview Begin with the person interviewed, followed by *Personal interview, Telephone interview,* or *E-mail interview* (not italicized) and the date of the interview. (*See no. 42 for a published interview.*)

Jacobs, Phoebe. Personal interview. 5 May 2008.

117. Lecture or speech Give the speaker, the title (in quotation marks), the name of the forum or sponsor, the location, and the date. Conclude with *Address* or *Lecture* (not italicized).

Taylor, Billy. "What Is Jazz?" John F. Kennedy Center for the Performing Arts,

Washington. 14 Feb. 1995. Lecture.

118. Live performance To cite a play, opera, dance performance, or concert, begin with the title; followed by the authors (*By*); information such as the director (*Dir.*) and major performers; the site; the city; the performance date; and the word *Performance* (not italicized).

Ragtime. By Terrence McNally, Lynn Athrens, and Stephen Flaherty. Dir. Frank

Galati. Ford Performing Arts Center, New York. 11 Nov. 1998. Performance.

119. Microfiche/microform/microfilm Cite as you would the print version. Include the medium, followed by the name of the microform and any identifying numbers.

Johnson, Charles S. "A Southern Negro's View of the South." *Journal of Negro*

Education 26.1 (1957): 4-9. Microform. *The Schomburg Collection of the New*

York Public Library 167 (1970): 101405.

120. Publication in more than one medium   If you are citing a publication that consists of several different media, list alphabetically all of the media you consulted. Follow the citation format of the medium you used primarily (which is print in the example).

> Sadker, David M., and Karen Zittleman. *Teachers, Schools, and Society: A Brief*
>
> *Introduction to Education.* New York: McGraw, 2007. CD-ROM, print, Web.

23d   MLA style: Explanatory notes and acknowledgments

Explanatory notes are used to cite multiple sources for borrowed material or to give readers supplemental information. You can also use explanatory notes to acknowledge people who helped you with research and writing. Acknowledgments are a courteous gesture. If you acknowledge someone's assistance in your explanatory notes, be sure to send that person a copy of your paper.

TEXT

One answer to these questions is suggested by a large (24-by-36-inch) painting

discovered in Armstrong's house.[2]

NOTE

[2]I want to thank George Arevalo of the Louis Armstrong Archives for his help on

this project. George showed me the two pictures I describe in this paper. Seeing

those pictures helped me figure out what I wanted to say—and why I wanted to

say it. For introducing me to archival research and to the art of Louis Armstrong,

TEXTCONNEX

Electronic Submission of Papers

Some instructors may request that you submit your paper electronically. Keep these tips in mind:

- Confirm the appropriate procedure for submission.
- Find out in advance the preferred format for the submission of documents. *Always ask permission before sending an attached document to anyone.*
- If you are asked to send a document as an attachment, save your document as a "rich text format" (.rtf) file or in PDF format.
- As a courtesy, run a virus scan on your file before sending it electronically or submitting it on a disk or CD-ROM.

I also want to thank the head of the Louis Armstrong Archives, Michael Cogswell, and my English teacher, Professor Amy Tucker.

👁 **23e** MLA style: Paper format

The following guidelines will help you prepare your research paper in the format recommended by the seventh edition of the *MLA Handbook for Writers of Research Papers*. For an example of a research paper that has been prepared using MLA style, see pages 379–90.

Materials   Back up your final draft on a flash drive, CD, or DVD. Use a high-quality printer and high-quality, white 8½-by-11-inch paper. Put the printed pages together with a paper clip.

Heading and title   Include a separate title page if your instructor requires one (see Figure 23.1). In the upper left-hand corner of the first page of the paper, one inch from the top and side, type on separate, double-spaced lines your name, your instructor's name, the

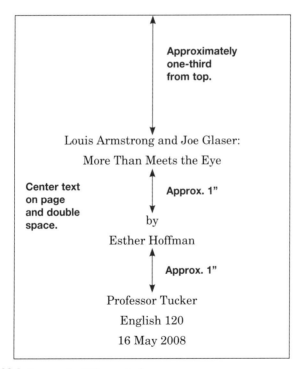

Approximately one-third from top.

Louis Armstrong and Joe Glaser:
More Than Meets the Eye

Center text on page and double space.

Approx. 1"

by
Esther Hoffman

Approx. 1"

Professor Tucker
English 120
16 May 2008

FIGURE 23.1 **A sample title page for a paper.**

course number, and the date. Double-space between the date and the paper's title and between the title and the first line of text, as well as throughout your paper. The title should be centered and properly capitalized (*see p. 379*). Do not italicize the title or put it in quotation marks or bold type.

If your instructor requires a title page, prepare it according to his or her instructions or like the example in Figure 23.1 on page 377. If your instructor requires a final outline, place it between the title page and the first page of the paper.

Margins and spacing Use one-inch margins all around, except for the top right-hand corner, where the page number goes. Your right margin should be ragged (not "justified," or even).

Double-space lines throughout the paper, including in quotations, notes, and the works-cited list. Indent the first word of each paragraph one-half inch (or five spaces) from the left margin. For block quotations, indent one inch (or ten spaces) from the left.

Page numbers Put your last name and the page number in the upper right-hand corner of the page, one-half inch from the top and flush with the right margin.

Visuals Place visuals (tables, charts, graphs, and images) close to the place in your text where you refer to them. Label and number tables consecutively (*Table 1, Table 2*) and give each one an explanatory caption; put this information above the table. The term *Figure* (abbreviated *Fig.*) is used to label all other kinds of visuals, except for musical illustrations, which are labeled *Example* (abbreviated *Ex.*). Place figure or example captions below the visual. Below all visuals, cite the source of the material and provide explanatory notes as needed. *(For more on using visuals effectively, see Part 1: Writing and Designing Texts.)*

23f Student paper in MLA style

As a first-year college student, Esther Hoffman wrote the following paper for her composition course. She knew little about Louis Armstrong and jazz before her instructor took the class to visit the Louis Armstrong Archives. Esther did archival research based on what she learned from consulting online and print sources.

Hoffman 1

Esther Hoffman

Professor Tucker

English 120

16 May 2008

Louis Armstrong and Joe Glaser:

More Than Meets the Eye

Louis Armstrong's biography reads like a classic American success story. From humble beginnings Armstrong rose to become an international superstar, a so-called King of Jazz, and a familiar figure forty years after his death in 1971. Less well known is Joe Glaser, Armstrong's longtime manager. Yet Armstrong once credited his accomplishments to Glaser, saying, "Anything that I have done musically since I signed up with Joe Glaser at the Sunset, it was his suggestions" (qtd. in Jones and Chilton 175). Was Glaser really as central to Armstrong's work and life as this comment makes him seem? Did he dominate his famous client? On the contrary, the two appear to have enjoyed a remarkably equitable and successful partnership. However, to truly understand their relationship, it is necessary to consider the context of the Jazz Age and each man's background.

In the 1920s, jazz music was at its height in creativity and popularity. Chicago had become one of the jazz capitals of America, and its clubs showcased the premier talents of the time, performers like Jelly Roll Morton and Joe Oliver. Eager for fame and fortune, many young black musicians who had honed their craft in New Orleans "were drawn to Chicago, New York, Los Angeles, and other cities by the chance to make a career and . . . a living" (James).

On every page: writer's last name and page number.

Title centered, not italicized.

Double-spaced throughout.

Indirect source.

Poses key questions that thesis will answer.

Thesis statement.

Background scene sketched.

Web source cited by author.

379

Hoffman 2

Paragraph indent 5 spaces or ½".

Topic introduced.

MLA in-text citation: author (Bergreen) named in signal phrase.

MLA in-text citation: author named in parentheses.

Development by narration (see p. 63).

Web source cited by title.

Among these émigrés was Louis Armstrong, a gifted musician who developed into "perhaps the best [jazz musician] that has ever been" ("Louis Armstrong"). Armstrong played the trumpet and sang with unusual improvisational ability as well as technical mastery. As biographer Laurence Bergreen points out, Armstrong easily reached difficult high notes, the F's and G's that stymied other trumpeters (248). His innovative singing style also featured "scat," a technique that "place[s] emphasis on the human voice as an additionally important component in jazz music" (Anderson 329). According to one popular anecdote, Armstrong invented scat during a recording session; mid-song, he dropped his lyrics sheet and--not wanting to disrupt a great take--began to improvise (Edwards 619). Eventually Armstrong's innovations became the standard, as more and more jazz musicians took their cue from his style.

Armstrong's beginnings give no hint of the greatness that he would achieve. In New Orleans, he was born into poverty and received little formal education. As a youngster, Armstrong had to take odd jobs like delivering coal and selling newspapers so that he could earn money to help his family. At the age of twelve, Armstrong was placed in the Colored Waifs' Home to serve an eighteen-month sentence for firing a gun in a public place. There "Captain" Peter Davis gave him "basic musical training on the cornet" ("Louis Armstrong"). Older, more established musicians soon noticed Armstrong's talent and offered him opportunities to play with them. In 1922, Joe Oliver invited Armstrong to join his band in Chicago, and the twenty-one-year-old trumpeter headed north.

Hoffman 3

It was in Chicago that Armstrong met Joe Glaser. According to Bergreen, Glaser had a reputation for being a tough but trustworthy guy who could handle any situation. He was raised in a middle-class home by parents who were Jewish immigrants from Russia. As a young man, Glaser got caught up in the Chicago underworld and soon had a rap sheet that included indictments for running a brothel as well as for statutory rape.[1] Glaser's mob connections also led to his involvement in Chicago's club scene, a business almost completely controlled by gangsters like Al Capone. During the era of Prohibition, Glaser managed the Sunset Cafe, a club where Armstrong often performed:

> There was a pronounced gangster element at the Sunset, but Louis, accustomed to being employed and protected by mobsters, didn't think twice about that. Mr. Capone's men ensured the flow of alcohol, and their presence reassured many whites. (Bergreen 279)

By the early thirties, Armstrong had become one of the most popular musicians in the world. He attracted thousands of fans during his 1930 European tour, and his "Hot Five" and "Hot Seven" recordings were considered some of the best jazz ever played. Financially, Armstrong should have been doing very well, but instead he was having business difficulties. He owed money to Johnny Collins, his former manager, and Lil' Hardin, his ex-wife, was suing him for a share of the royalties on the song "Struttin' with Some Barbecue." At this point, Armstrong asked Glaser to be his business manager. Glaser quickly paid off Collins and settled with Lil' Hardin. Giving up his other business ventures, Glaser now became Armstrong's exclusive agent (Morgenstern 124-28; Collier 273-76; Bergreen 376-78). For

Focus introduced.

Superscript number indicating an explanatory note.

Block quotation indented 10 spaces or 1".

Summary of material from a number of sources.

Citation of multiple sources.

381

Hoffman 4

the next thirty-four years, his responsibilities included booking appearances, organizing the bands, making travel arrange-ments, and paying the band members' salaries (Jones and Chilton 160, 220).

Use of information from two separate pages in one source.

Some might posit that Glaser controlled all aspects of Armstrong's work and life. This view is suggested by a large (24-by-36-inch) oil painting discovered in Armstrong's house.[2] Joe Glaser is pictured in the middle of the canvas. Four black-and-white quadrants surround the central image of Glaser. One quadrant depicts a city scene, the scene in which Glaser thrived. The bottom two quadrants picture dogs, a reminder that Glaser raised show dogs. The remaining quadrant presents an image of Louis Armstrong. By placing Glaser in the center and Armstrong off in a corner, the unknown artist seems to suggest that even though Armstrong was the star, it was Glaser who made him one.

Development by description (see p. 64).

In fact, Glaser did advance Armstrong's career in numerous important ways. In 1935, he negotiated the lucrative record contract with Decca that led to the production of hits like "I'm in the Mood for Love" and "You Are My Lucky Star" (Bergreen 380). Glaser also decided when to sell the rights to Armstrong's songs. Determined to make as much money as possible, he sometimes sold the rights to a song as soon as it was released, especially when he thought the song might not turn out to be a big hit. However, in at least two instances, this money-making strategy backfired: much to Glaser's surprise, both "Hello, Dolly" and "What a Wonderful World" became big hits after the rights had been sold (Jacobs).

Presents a claim plus supporting evidence.

To expand Armstrong's popularity, Glaser increased his exposure to white audiences in the United States. In 1935, articles on Armstrong appeared in *Vanity Fair* and *Esquire*, two

Development by illustration (see p.62).

magazines with a predominantly white readership (Bergreen 385). Glaser also promoted Armstrong's movie career. At a time when only a handful of black performers were accepted in Hollywood, Armstrong had roles in a number of films, including *Pennies from Heaven* (1936) with Bing Crosby. Moreover, "Jeepers Creepers," a song Armstrong sang in *Going Places* (1938), received an Academy Award nomination (Bogle 149, 157). Of course, more exposure sometimes meant more discomfort, if not danger, especially when Armstrong and his band members were touring in the South. Bergreen recounts how in Southern states, where blacks were prohibited from entering many stores, Glaser sometimes had to shop for the band's food and other supplies (378, 381).

Note use of transitional expressions (see pp. 88–89).

As Armstrong's manager, Glaser also exerted some control over the musician's personal finances and habits. According to Dave Gold, an accountant who worked for Associated Booking, it was Glaser who paid Armstrong's mortgage, taxes, and basic living expenses (Collier 330). A 1960 letter from Glaser to Lucille Armstrong corroborates Gold's account; it shows that Glaser assumed responsibility for buying the musician and his wife a new car as well as for filing the paperwork needed to retain the old license plate number. More personal were Glaser's attempts to control Armstrong's habitual use of marijuana. In 1931, Armstrong received a suspended sentence after his arrest for marijuana possession. He continued to use the drug, however, especially during performances, and told Glaser that he wanted to write a book about marijuana's positive effects. Glaser flatly rejected the book idea and, fearful of a scandal, also forbade Armstrong's smoking any marijuana while on tour in Europe (Pollack).

Support by expert opinion (see p. 187).

Support by key fact (see p. 187).

Support by anecdote (see p. 187).

Restatement
of thesis.

Clearly, Glaser was in a position to affect powerfully Armstrong's career and his life. However, Armstrong seemed to recognize that he gave Glaser whatever power over him the manager enjoyed. When he wanted to, Armstrong could and did resist Glaser's control, and that may be one reason why he liked and trusted Glaser as much as he did.

After Glaser became his manager, Armstrong no longer had to worry about the behind-the-scenes details of his career. He was free to concentrate on creating music and making the most of the opportunities his manager worked out for him. Glaser booked Armstrong into engagements with legendary performers like Benny Goodman, Ella Fitzgerald, and Duke Ellington. He also worked with the record companies to ensure that Armstrong would make the best and most profitable recordings possible (Bergreen 457). During the thirty-four years they worked together, both Armstrong and Glaser made lots of money. More important, their relationship freed Armstrong to make extraordinary music.

If Armstrong acquiesced to most of Glaser's business decisions, it may have been because he had no reason to resist them. However, when he deemed it necessary, Armstrong acted on his own. For example, in 1944 a talented band member named Dexter Gordon threatened to quit, so Armstrong offered him a raise--without consulting first with Glaser (Morgenstern 132). In 1957, when Armstrong wanted to put a stop to backstage crowding, he not only directed Glaser to make a sign prohibiting guests from going backstage but also told him exactly what to say on the sign (Armstrong, "Backstage Instructions"). As these incidents suggest, when Armstrong was displeased with the way his career was being handled, he acted to amend the situation.

Source cited:
archival
material.

Armstrong also knew how to resist Glaser's attempts to control the more personal aspects of his life. In a recent interview, Phoebe Jacobs, formerly one of Glaser's employees, sheds new light on the relationship between the manager and the musician. Armstrong's legendary generosity was tough on his pocketbook. It was well known that if someone needed money, Armstrong would readily hand over some bills. At one point, Glaser asked Jacobs to give Armstrong smaller denominations so that he would not give away so much money. The trumpeter soon figured out what was going on and admonished Jacobs for following Glaser's orders about money that belonged to him, not Glaser. On another occasion, Armstrong declined an invitation to join Glaser for dinner at a Chinese restaurant, saying, "I want to eat what I want to eat" (qtd. by Jacobs).

Source cited: personal interview.

Even though he sometimes pushed Glaser away, Armstrong obviously loved and trusted his manager. In all the years of their association, the two men signed only one contract and, in the musician's words, "after that we didn't bother" (qtd. in Jones and Chilton 240). A picture of Joe Glaser in one of Armstrong's scrapbooks bears the following label in the star's handwriting: "the greatest." In his dedication to the un-published manuscript "Louis Armstrong and the Jewish Family in New Orleans, the Year of 1907," Armstrong calls Glaser "the best friend that I ever had," while in a letter to Max Jones, he writes, "I did not get really happy until I got with my man--my dearest friend--Joe Glaser" (qtd. in Jones and Chilton 16). In 1969, Joe Glaser died. Referring to him again as "the greatest," Armstrong confided to a friend that Glaser's death "broke [his] heart" (qtd. in Bergreen 490).

Authoritative quotation (see p. 196).

Memorable quotation (see pp. 329–31).

Wording of quotation adjusted (see p. 330).

Hoffman 8

FIG. 1. An anonymous watercolor caricature of Armstrong with his manager, Joe Glaser, c. 1950. Louis Armstrong Archives, Queens College, City U of New York, Flushing.

Effective visual.

Concludes with qualified version of thesis.

Memorable illustration.

Although there are hints of a struggle for the upper hand, the relationship between Louis Armstrong and Joe Glaser seems to have been genuinely friendly and trusting. Armstrong gave Glaser a good deal of authority over his career, and Glaser used that authority to make Armstrong a musical and monetary success. Armstrong was happy to take the opportunities that Glaser provided for him, but he was not submissive. This equitable and friendly relationship is depicted by another picture found in Armstrong's house. Although the 25-by-21-inch picture, shown in fig. 1., is a caricature that may seen jarring to contemporary viewers, when understood in its historical context it implies a mutual relationship between Armstrong and Glaser. The pair stand side by side, and Glaser has his hand on Armstrong's shoulder. Armstrong, who is dressed for a performance, looks and smiles at us as if he were facing an audience. But Glaser looks only at

Armstrong, the musician who was his main concern from 1935 to the day he died. In appearance alone, the men are clearly different. But seen in their longstanding partnership, the two make up a whole--one picture that offers us more than meets the eye.

Hoffman 10

Notes

New page,
title centered.

¹Bergreen 372-76. Even though Ostwald points out a
few mistakes in Bergreen's *Louis Armstrong: An Extravagant Life*,
I think the book's new information about Glaser is useful and
trustworthy.

Gives
supplemental
information
about key
source.

²I want to thank George Arevalo of the Louis Armstrong
Archives for his help on this project. George showed me the two
pictures I describe in this paper. Seeing those pictures helped
me figure out what I wanted to say--and why I wanted to say it.
For introducing me to archival research and to the art of
Louis Armstrong, I also want to thank the head of the Louis
Armstrong Archives, Michael Cogswell, and my English teacher,
Professor Amy Tucker.

Indent first
line 5 spaces
or ½".

Acknowledges
others who
helped.

Hoffman 11

Works Cited

Anderson, T. J. "Body and Soul: Bob Kaufman's *Golden Sardine.*" *African American Review* 34.2 (2000): 329-46. *Academic Search Complete.* Web. 11 Apr. 2008.

Armstrong, Louis. "Backstage Instructions to Glaser." Apr. 1957. MS. Accessions 1997-26. Louis Armstrong Archives. Queens College City U of New York, Flushing.

---. "Louis Armstrong and the Jewish Family in New Orleans, the Year of 1907" 31 Mar. 1969. MS. Box 1. Louis Armstrong Archives. Queens College City U of New York, Flushing.

Bergreen, Laurence. *Louis Armstrong: An Extravagant Life.* New York: Broadway, 1997. Print.

Bogle, Donald. "Louis Armstrong: The Films." Miller 147-79.

Collier, James Lincoln. *Louis Armstrong: An American Genius.* New York: Oxford UP, 1983. Print.

Edwards, Brent Hayes. "Louis Armstrong and the Syntax of Scat." *Critical Inquiry* 28.3 (2002): 618-49. Print.

Glaser, Joe. Letter to Lucille Armstrong. 28 Sept. 1960. MS. Box 3. Louis Armstrong Archives. Queens College City U of New York, Flushing.

Jacobs, Phoebe. Personal interview. 5 May 2008.

James, Gregory N. *The Southern Diaspora: How the Great Migrations of Black and White Southerners Transformed America.* Chapel Hill: U of North Carolina P, 2007. N. pag. *Blues, Jazz, and the Great Migration.* Web. 7 May 2008.

Jones, Max, and John Chilton. *Louis: The Louis Armstrong Story, 1900-1971.* Boston: Little, 1971. Print.

"Louis Armstrong." *New Orleans Online.* New Orleans Tourism Marketing Corporation, 2008. Web. 7 May 2008.

New page, title centered.

Source: journal article in on-line database

Source: archival material.

3 hyphens used instead of repeat-ing author's name.

Source: whole book.

Source: journal.

Source: personal interview.

Entries in alphabetical order.

389

Miller, Marc, ed. *Louis Armstrong: A Cultural Legacy*. Seattle: U of
    Washington P and Queens Museum of Art, 1994. Print.

Morgenstern, Dan. "Louis Armstrong and the Development
    and Diffusion of Jazz." Miller 95-145.

Ostwald, David. "All That Jazz." Rev. of *Louis Armstrong:
    An Extravagant Life*, by Laurence Bergreen. *Commentary*
    Nov. 1997: 68-72. Print.

Pollack, Bracha. "A Man ahead of His Time." 1997. TS.

Robinson, J. Bradford. "Scat Singing." *The New Grove Dictionary
    of Jazz*. Ed. Barry Kernfeld. Vol. 3. London: Macmillan,
    2002. 515-16. Print.

Source: work
in edited
book cross-
referenced to
Miller

Source:
review in
a monthly
magazine.

Hanging in-
dent 5 spaces
or ½".

24 APA Documentation Style

Many researchers in behavioral and social sciences like psychology, sociology, and political science as well as in communications, education, and business use the documentation style developed by the American Psychological Association (APA). The guidelines presented here are based on the sixth edition of its *Publication Manual* (Washington: APA, 2010). For updates to the APA documentation system, check the APA-sponsored Web site at <http://www.apastyle.org>.

24a The elements of APA documentation style

APA documentation style emphasizes the author and year of publication, making it easy for readers to tell if the sources cited are current. It has two mandatory parts:

- In-text citations
- List of references

APA style requires writers to list their sources in a list of references at the end of a paper. Answering the questions in the foldout charts that follow will help you find the appropriate model reference entry for your source. The reverse side of the foldout indicates where to find the information you need for a citation. (*See also the directory on pages 397–98.*)

www.mhhe.com/
mhhb2
For links to Web sites for documentation styles used in various disciplines, go to

Research > Links to Documentation Sites

24b APA style: In-text citations

In-text citations let readers know that they can find full information about an idea you have paraphrased or summarized or the source of a quotation in the list of references at the end of your paper.

1. Author named in sentence   Follow the author's name with the year of publication (in parentheses).

signal phrase
According to Brookfield (2001), nearly 12 percent of the Amazonian rain forest in Brazil

has been shaped or influenced by thousands of years of indigenous human culture.

2. Author named in parentheses   If you do not name the source's author in your sentence, then you must include the name in the parentheses, followed by the date and, if you are giving a quotation or a specific piece of information, the page number. Separate the name, date, and page number with commas.

391

The Organization of Indigenous Peoples of the Colombian Amazon attempted in 2001

to take legal action to ban such fumigation over indigenous lands. Their efforts were not
ampersand used within parentheses
supported by the Colombian government (Lloyd & Soltani, 2001, p. 5).

3. Two to five authors If a source has five or fewer authors, name
all of them the first time you cite the source.

As Kaimowitz, Mertens, Wunder, and Pacheco (2004) report in "Hamburger Connection

Fuels Amazon Destruction," there are three key factors behind the burgeoning demand

for Brazilian beef and the resulting burning of the Amazon rain forest for pasture.

If you put the names of the authors in parentheses, use an ampersand
(&) instead of *and*.

There are three key factors behind the burgeoning demand for Brazilian beef and

the resulting burning of the Amazon rain forest for pasture (Kaimowitz, Mertens,

Wunder, & Pacheco, 2004, p. 3).

After the first time you cite a work by three or more authors, use
the first author's name plus *et al.* Always use both names when citing
a work by two authors.

Another key factor is concern over livestock diseases in other countries (Kaimowitz

et al., 2004, p. 4).

APA IN-TEXT CITATIONS: DIRECTORY to SAMPLE TYPES

(See pp. 396–410 for examples of references entries.)

Identifying and Documenting Sources in APA Style

Resources for Writers

st of References: ooks or Other Print Sources

IS YOUR SOURCE A COMPLETE BOOK?

ES — Go to this entry *on page*

T A COMPLETE BOOK WITH ONE NAMED AUTHOR?	
it the only book by this author that you are citing?	1 *396*
e you citing more than one book by this author?	4 *396*
oes it also have an editor or translator?	5, 8 *396, 398*
T A COMPLETE BOOK WITH MORE THAN ONE MED AUTHOR?	2 *396*
T A COMPLETE BOOK WITHOUT A NAMED AUTHOR EDITOR?	
the author an organization?	3 *396*
the author anonymous or unknown?	11 *399*
T A COMPLETE BOOK WITH AN EDITOR OR TRANSLATOR?	
there an editor instead of an author?	5 *396*
it a translation?	8 *398*
T AN ENTIRE REFERENCE WORK?	10 *399*
T A COMPLETE BOOK WITH A VOLUME OR AN EDITION NUMBER?	
it part of a multivolume work (e.g., Volume 3)?	13 *400*
oes it have an edition number (e.g., Second Edition)?	12 *400*
T A REPUBLISHED WORK (e.g., A CLASSIC STUDY)?	14 *400*

S YOUR SOURCE PART OF A BOOK?

ES — Go to this entry *on page*

T A WORK FROM AN ANTHOLOGY OR A CHAPTER IN AN ITED BOOK?	6 *396*
T AN ARTICLE IN A REFERENCE WORK (e.g., AN ENCYCLOPEDIA)?	9 *398*
T A PUBLISHED PRESENTATION FROM A CONFERENCE?	26 *402*
T AN INTRODUCTION, PREFACE, FOREWORD, OR AFTERWORD?	7 *398*

he next panel or the directory on pages 397–98 ult your instructor.

Entries in a List of References: Print Periodicals or Other Print Sources

? IS YOUR SOURCE FROM AN ACADEMIC JOURNAL, A MAGAZINE, OR A NEWSPAPER?

NO   YES — Go to this entry *on page*

IS IT FROM AN ACADEMIC JOURNAL?	
Are the page numbers continued from one issue of the journal to the next?	15 *400*
Do the page numbers in each issue of the journal start with 1?	16 *400*
Is it an abstract (a brief summary) of a journal article?	17 *400*
Is it a review (e.g., a review of a book)?	23 *401*
Is it a published presentation from a conference?	26 *402*
IS IT FROM A MONTHLY OR WEEKLY MAGAZINE?	
Is it an article?	19 *401*
Is it a letter to the editor?	21 *401*
Is it a review (e.g., a review of a book)?	23 *401*
IS IT FROM A NEWSPAPER?	
Is it an article?	20 *401*
Is it an editorial or a letter to the editor?	21 *401*
Is it a review (e.g., a review of a book)?	23 *401*
IS THE AUTHOR UNKNOWN?	22 *401*
ARE YOU CITING TWO OR MORE ARTICLES PUBLISHED IN THE SAME YEAR BY THE SAME AUTHOR?	18 *401*

? IS IT A PRINT SOURCE BUT NOT A BOOK, A PART OF A BOOK, OR AN ARTICLE IN AN ACADEMIC JOURNAL, A MAGAZINE, OR A NEWSPAPER?

NO   YES — Go to this entry *on page*

IS IT PUBLISHED BY THE GOVERNMENT OR A NONGOVERNMENT ORGANIZATION?	
Is it a government document?	24 *402*
Is it a report or a working paper?	25 *402*
Is it a brochure, pamphlet, fact sheet, or press release?	28 *403*
Is it from the *Congressional Record*?	57 *408*
IS IT AN UNPUBLISHED CONFERENCE PRESENTATION?	26 *402*
IS IT A DISSERTATION OR DISSERTATION ABSTRACT?	27 *402*

Check the directory on pages 397–98 or consult your instructor.

Entries in a List of References: Electronic or Other Nonprint Sources

? DID YOU FIND YOUR NONPRINT SOURCE ONLINE?

NO   YES — Go to this entry *on page*

IS IT FROM AN ONLINE SCHOLARLY JOURNAL?	
Is it an article with a Digital Object Identifier (DOI)?	41 *405*
Is it an article without a DOI?	42 *405*
Is it an article from a database?	43 *406*
Is it an abstract (a brief summary) of an article) from a collection of abstracts?	44 *406*
IS IT A DISSERTATION?	45 *406*
IS IT A NEWSPAPER ARTICLE?	
Is it an article from a database?	46 *406*
Is it an article from an online newspaper?	47 *406*
IS IT A MAGAZINE ARTICLE?	
Is it an article from a database?	46 *406*
Is it from a magazine published only online?	48 *406*
Is it an article that was also published in print?	48 *406*
Is it online exclusive material from a magazine with a print edition?	49 *407*
IS IT A NEWSLETTER ARTICLE?	50 *407*
IS IT A BLOG POSTING?	61 *409*
IS IT FROM AN ONLINE REFERENCE WORK?	59 *408*
IS IT PART OF A WIKI?	60 *409*
IS IT FROM A PERSONAL OR ORGANIZATIONAL WEB SITE?	
Is it a document or report from a Web site?	51 *407*
Is it a visual from a Web site?	52 *407*
Is it on a university's Web site?	53 *407*
IS IT AN ELECTRONIC BOOK?	
Is it an electronic edition of a print book?	54 *407*
Is it an electronic book with no print version?	55 *408*
IS IT A POSTING TO AN ONLINE NEWSGROUP?	62 *409*
IS IT A POSTING TO AN ELECTRONIC MAILING LIST?	63 *409*
IS IT A PERSONAL E-MAIL OR INSTANT MESSAGE?	64 *409*
IS IT A GOVERNMENT PUBLICATION?	
Is it from the *Congressional Record*?	57 *408*
Is it another government document available online?	56 *408*
IS IT AN ONLINE DOCUMENT WITHOUT A DATE OR AN AUTHOR?	58 *408*
IS IT AN MP3 OR AUDIO PODCAST?	65, 66 *409, 410*
IS IT AN ONLINE VIDEO?	68 *410*
IS IT A PODCAST TV SERIES EPISODE?	67 *410*

Go to next panel.

? IS YOUR SOURCE A NONPRINT SOURCE THAT IS NOT PUBLISHED ONLINE?

NO   YES — Go to this entry *on page*

IS IT COMPUTER SOFTWARE?	69 *410*
IS IT A FILM, DVD, OR VIDEOTAPE?	29 *403*
IS IT A TV SERIES OR EPISODE?	32, 33 *403, 404*
IS IT A RADIO BROADCAST?	31 *403*
IS IT A CD OR AUDIO RECORDING?	30 *403*
IS IT A LIVE PERFORMANCE?	37 *404*
IS IT A MUSICAL COMPOSITION?	38 *404*
IS IT A SPEECH OR LECTURE?	39 *404*
IS IT AN IMAGE, MAP, OR VISUAL?	35, 36 *404*
IS IT AN ADVERTISEMENT?	34 *404*

Check the directory on pages 397–98 or consult your instructor.

Finding Source Information for APA Style

The Elements of an APA References Entry: Book

Author · Date of publication · Book title

Brookfield, H. (2001). *Exploring agrodiversity*. New York, NY: Columbia University Press.

Publisher · Place of publication

Date of publication

Publisher and place of publication

> Columbia University Press.
> Publishers since 1893
> New York Chichester, West Sussex
>
> Copyright © 2001 Columbia University Press
> All rights reserved
>
> Library of Congress Cataloging-in-Publication Data
>
> Brookfield, H.
>   Exploring agrodiversity / Harold Brookfield
>   p. cm. — (Issues, cases, and methods in
>   biodiversity conservation series)
>   Includes bibliographical references (p.   )
>   ISBN 0-231-10232-1 (cloth : alk. paper) —
>   ISBN 0-231-10233-X (pbk : alk paper)
>   1. Agrodiversity. I. Title II. Series
> S494.5.A43 B76 2000
> 306.3'49—dc21   00-045175
>
> Casebound editions of Columbia University Press books
> are printed on permanent and durable acid-free paper.
> Printed in the United States of America
> c 10 9 8 7 6 5 4 3 2 1
> p 10 9 8 7 6 5 4 3 2 1

Exploring **Agrodiversity**

Harold Brookfield

Book title and author

Copyright page

COLUMBIA UNIVERSITY PRESS   NEW YORK

Title page

Information for a book citation can be found on the book's title and copyright pages.

The Elements of an APA References Entry: Journal Article

Author · Year of publication · Article title · Journal title

Epstein, J. (2002). A voice in the wilderness. *Latin Trade*, 10(12), 26.

Volume · Issue number · Page number

Journal title

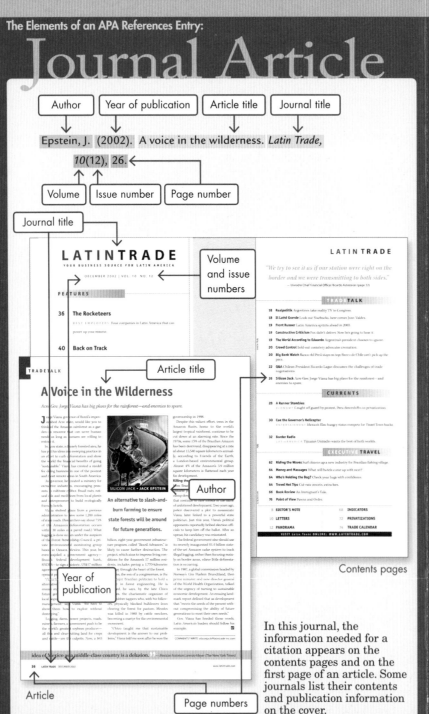

Volume and issue numbers

Article title

Year of publication

Author

Page numbers

Article

Contents pages

In this journal, the information needed for a citation appears on the contents pages and on the first page of an article. Some journals list their contents and publication information on the cover.

The Elements of an APA References Entry: Online Journal Article with DOI Assigned

Article title · Authors · Year of publication

Soares-Filho, B., Alencar, A., Nepstad, D., Cerqueira, G., del Carmen Vera Diaz, M., Rivero, S., . . . Voll, E. (2004). Simulating the response of land-cover changes to road paving and governance along a major Amazon highway: The Santarém-Cuiabá corridor. *Global Change Biology, 10*, 745–764. doi:10.1111/j.1529-8817.2003.00769.x

Volume · Page numbers · DOI · Journal title

Volume (and issue) number · Journal title · Year of publication

Authors

Article title

DOI

Page numbers

From Soares-Filho et al., *Global Change Biology, 10*, 745–764, May 2004, Blackwell Synergy. Reprinted with permission.

If the article has a DOI (Digital Object Identifier), the citation does not require a URL. This article lists the DOI beneath the journal and citation information. For journals paginated by issue, include the issue number in parentheses after the volume number.

The Elements of an APA References Entry: Short Work on a Web Si[te]

Organizations as authors · Date of publication or last update

U'wa Defense Project, & Amazon Watch. (October 23, 2006). *The U[...] consultation process and Ecopetrol's oil project on their reserve in Co[...]* [Press release]. Retrieved from http://amazonwatch.org/news /view_news.php?id=1240

Identify the document type for specific documents, such as fact sheets and press releases.

URL

Document type · URL · Sponsor

Newsroom
Press Release

Title · Date of publication or last update · Authors

The above citation derives from the APA model for an online repor[t]. [You] may need to search on a site to find author, date, and other inform[ation]. List an individual author's last name first. If no date is given, us[e] *n.d.* Supplemental information about format may follow the title. [When] the author is also the Web site sponsor (Amazon Watch). When the [...] author is not the sponsor, name the sponsor after "Retrieved from [...] *no. 51 on p. 407*). Include the home page URL for magazine, news[...] and journal articles (lacking a DOI). Give the full URL for other [...]

APA IN-TEXT CITATIONS

- Identify the author(s) of the source, either in the sentence or in a parenthetical citation.
- Indicate the year of publication of the source following the author's name, either in parentheses if the author's name is part of the sentence or, if the author is not named in the sentence, after the author's name and a comma in the parenthetical citation.
- Include a page reference for a quotation or specific piece of information. Put "p." before the page number. If the author is named in the text, the page number appears in the parenthetical citation following the borrowed material. Page numbers are not necessary when you are summarizing the source as a whole or paraphrasing an idea found throughout a work. (*For more on summary, paraphrase, and quotation, see Chapter 21: Working with Sources and Avoiding Plagiarism, pp. 322–32.*)
- If the source does not have page numbers (as with many online sources), do your best to direct readers. If the source has no page or paragraph numbering or easily identifiable headings, just use the name and date. (*See no. 13 and note on p. 395.*)

4. Six or more authors   For in-text citations of a work by six or more authors, always give the first author's name plus *et al.* In the reference list, however, list up to seven author names. For more than seven authors, list the first six authors' names, followed by three ellipses and the last author's name.

As Barbre et al. (1989) have argued, using personal narratives enables researchers

to connect the individual and the social.

5. Organization as author   Treat the organization as the author, and spell out its name the first time the source is cited. If the organization is well known, you may use an abbreviation thereafter.

According to a report issued by the Inter-American Association for Environmental

Defense (2004), a significant proportion of Colombia's indigenous peoples live

within these protected parklands.

Public service announcements were used to inform parents of these findings

(National Institute of Mental Health [NIMH], 1991).

In subsequent citations, only the abbreviation and the date need to be given: (*NIMH, 1991*).

6. Unknown author Give the first one or two important words of the title. Use quotation marks for titles of articles, chapters, or Web pages and italics for titles of books, periodicals, or reports.

> The transformation of women's lives has been hailed as "the single most important change of the past 1,000 years" ("Reflections," 1999, p. 77).

7. Two or more authors with the same last name If the authors of two or more sources have the same last name, always include their first initial, even if the year of publication differs.

> M. Smith (1988) showed how globalization has restructured both cities and states.

8. Two or more works by the same author in the same year Alphabetize the works by their titles in your reference list and assign a letter in alphabetical order (for example, *2006a*, *2006b*). Use that same year-letter designation in your in-text citation.

> J. P. Agarwal (1996b) described the relationship between trade and foreign direct investment (FDI).

9. Two or more sources cited at one time Cite the authors in the order in which they appear in the list of references, separated by a semicolon.

> Other years see greater destruction from large-scale economic and industrial initiatives, such as logging (Geographical, 2000; Kaimowitz et al., 2004, p. 2).

10. E-mail, letters, conversations To cite information received from unpublished forms of personal communication—such as conversations, letters, notes, and e-mail messages—give the source's initials and last name, and provide as precise a date as possible. Because readers do not have access to them, do not include personal communications in your reference list.

> According to ethnobotanist G. Freid (personal communication, May 4, 2008), the work of research scientists in the Brazilian Amazon has been greatly impeded within the past 10 years because of the destruction of potentially unrecorded plant species.

11. Specific part of a source Include the chapter (*Chapter*), page (*p.*), figure, or table number.

> Despite the new law, the state saw no drop in car fatalities involving drivers ages 16–21 (Johnson, 2006, Chapter 4).

12. Indirect source When referring to a source that you know only from reading another source, use the phrase *as cited in,* followed by the author of the source you actually read and its year of publication.

> According to the Center for International Forestry Research, an Indonesia-based NGO (as cited in Prugh, 2004), an area of land the size of Uruguay was deforested in the years 2002 and 2003 alone.

The work by Prugh would be included in the references list, but the work by the Center for International Forestry Research would not.

13. Electronic source Cite the author's last name and the publication date. If the document is a PDF (portable document format) file with stable page numbers, cite the page number. If the source has paragraph numbers instead of page numbers, use *para.* instead of *p.* (*see no. 14*).

> Applications of herbicides have caused widespread damage to biodiversity, livestock, and crops and have caused "thousands" of peasants and indigenous peoples to flee these lands (Amazon Alliance, 2004).

Note: If the specific part lacks page or paragraph numbering, cite the heading and the number of the paragraph under that heading where the information can be found. If the heading is long, use a short version in quotation marks. If you cannot determine the date, use the abbreviation "n.d." in its place: (*Wilson, n.d.*).

14. Two or more sources in one sentence Include a parenthetical reference after each fact, idea, or quotation you have borrowed.

> By one estimate, nearly 12 percent of the Amazonian rain forest in Brazil has been shaped or influenced by thousands of years of indigenous human culture (Brookfield, 2001); the evidence is as basic as the *terra preta do Indio*, or "Indian Black Earth" (Glick, 2007, para. 4), for which the Brazilian region of Santarem is known.

15. Sacred or classical text Cite within your text only, and include the version you consulted as well as any standard book, part, or section numbers.

> The famous song sets forth a series of opposites, culminating in "a time to love, and a time to hate; a time of war, and a time of peace" (Eccles. 3:8, King James Bible).

395

24c APA style: References

APA documentation style requires a list of references where readers can find complete bibliographical information about the sources referred to in your paper. The list should appear at the end of your paper, beginning on a new page titled "References."

Books

1. Book with one author

> Brookfield, H. (2001). *Exploring agrodiversity*. New York, NY: Columbia University
>
> Press.

2. Book with two or more authors
For more than seven authors, list the first six, three ellipses, and the final author.

> Goulding, M., Mahar, D., & Smith, N. (1996). *Floods of fortune: Ecology and economy*
>
> *along the Amazon*. New York, NY: Columbia University Press.

3. Organization as author
When the publisher is the author, use *Author* instead of repeating the organization's name as the publisher.

> Deutsche Bank, Economics Department. (1991). *Rebuilding Eastern Europe*. Frankfurt,
>
> Germany: Author.

4. Two or more works by the same author
List the works in publication order, with the earliest one first. If a university publisher's name includes the state, do not repeat it.

> Wilson, S. (Ed.). (1997). *The indigenous people of the Caribbean*. Gainesville:
>
> University Press of Florida.

> Wilson, S. (1999). *The emperor's giraffe and other stories of cultures in contact*.
>
> Boulder, CO: Westview Press.

If the works were published in the same year, put them in alphabetical order by title and add a letter *(a, b, c)* to the year to distinguish each entry in your in-text citations *(see no. 18)*.

5. Book with editor(s)
Add *(Ed.)* or *(Eds.)* after the name. If a book lists an author and an editor, treat the editor like a translator *(see no. 8)*.

> Lifton, K. (Ed.). (1998). *The greening of sovereignty in world politics*. Cambridge: The
>
> Massachusetts Institute of Technology Press.

6. Selection in an edited book or anthology
The selection's author, year of publication, and title come first, followed by the word

APA REFERENCE ENTRIES: DIRECTORY to SAMPLE TYPES

In and information about the edited book. The page numbers of the selection go in parentheses after the book's title.

Wilmer, F. (1998). Taking indigenous critiques seriously: The enemy 'r' us. In K. Lifton

(Ed.), *The greening of sovereignty in world politics* (pp. 55–60). Cambridge: The

Massachusetts Institute of Technology Press.

7. Introduction, preface, foreword, or afterword   List the author and the section cited. If the book has a different author, next write *In*, followed by the book's author and the title.

Bellow, S. (1987). Foreword. In A. Bloom, *The closing of the American mind: How*

higher education has failed democracy and impoverished the souls of today's

students. New York, NY: Simon & Schuster.

8. Translation   After the title of the translation, put the name(s) of the translator(s) in parentheses, followed by the abbreviation *Trans.*

Jarausch, K. H., & Gransow, V. (1994). *Uniting Germany: Documents and debates,*

1944–1993 (A. Brown & B. Cooper, Trans.). Providence, RI: Berg.

9. Article in an encyclopedia or another reference work   Begin with the author of the selection, if given. If no author is given, begin with the selection's title.

title of the selection
Arawak. (2000). In *The Columbia encyclopedia* (6th ed., p. 2533). New York, NY:

Columbia University Press.

10. Entire dictionary or reference work Unless an author or editor is indicated on the title page, list dictionaries by title, with the edition number in parentheses. (The in-text citation should include the title or a portion of the title.) (*See no. 9 on citing an article in a reference book and no. 11 on alphabetizing a work listed by title.*)

The American Heritage dictionary of the English language (4th ed.). (2000). Boston, MA: Houghton Mifflin.

Hinson, M. (2004). *The pianist's dictionary.* Bloomington: Indiana University Press.

11. Unknown author or editor Start with the title. When alphabetizing, use the first important word of the title (excluding articles such as *The, A,* or *An*).

Give me liberty. (1969). New York, NY: World.

APA LIST of REFERENCES

- Begin on a new page with the centered title "References."
- Include a reference for every in-text citation except personal communications and sacred or classical texts (*see in-text citations no. 10 on p. 394 and no. 15 on p. 395*).
- Put references in alphabetical order by author's last name.
- Give the last name and first or both initials for each author. If the work has more than one author, see no. 2 (*p. 396*).
- Put the publication year in parentheses following the author or authors' names.
- Capitalize only the first word and proper nouns in titles. Also capitalize the first word following the colon in a subtitle.
- Use italics for titles of books but not articles. Do not enclose titles of articles in quotation marks.
- Include the city and publisher for books. Give the state or country. If a university publisher's name includes the state, do not repeat it.
- Include the periodical name and volume number (both in italics) as well as the page numbers for a periodical article.
- End with the DOI, if any (*see no. 15 and the box on p. 405*).
- Separate the author's or authors' name(s), date (in parentheses), title, and publication information with periods.
- Use a hanging indent: Begin the first line of each entry at the left margin, and indent all subsequent lines of an entry (five spaces).
- Double-space within and between entries.

12. Edition other than the first

Smyser, W. R. (1993). *The German economy: Colossus at crossroads* (2nd ed.). New

York, NY: St. Martin's Press.

13. One volume of a multivolume work   If the volume has its own title, put it before the title of the whole work. No period separates the title and parenthetical volume number.

Handl, G. (1990). The Mesoamerican biodiversity legal project. In *Yearbook of*

international environmental law (Vol. 4). London, England: Graham & Trotman.

14. Republished book   In-text citations should give both years: "As Le Bon (1895/1960) pointed out. . . ."

Le Bon, G. (1960). *The crowd: A study of the popular mind.* New York, NY: Viking.

(Original work published 1895)

Periodicals

15. Article in a journal paginated by volume   Italicize the periodical title and the volume number. A DOI ends the entry if available (*see no. 41*).

Nasir, N. S., & Cooks, J. (2009). Becoming a hurdler: How learning settings afford

identities. *Anthropology & Education Quarterly, 40,* 41–61. doi:10.1111/j.1548

-1492.2009.01027.x

16. Article in a journal paginated by issue   Include the issue number (in parentheses after the volume number). The issue number is not italicized. A DOI ends the entry if available (not shown). (*See no. 15.*)

Epstein, J. (2002). A voice in the wilderness. *Latin Trade, 10*(12), 26.

17. Abstract   For an abstract that appears in the original source, add the word *Abstract* in brackets after the title. If the abstract appears in a printed source that is different from the original publication, first give the original publication information for the article, followed by the publication information for the source of the abstract. If the dates of the publications differ, cite them both, with a slash between them, in the in-text citation: *Murphy (2003/2004).*

Burnby, J. G. L. (1985, June). Pharmaceutical connections: The Maw's family

[Abstract]. *Pharmaceutical Historian, 15*(2), 9–11.

Murphy, M. (2003). Getting carbon out of thin air. *Chemistry & Industry, 6,* 14–16.

Abstract retrieved from *Fuel & Energy Abstracts,* 2004, *45,* 389.

18. Two or more works in one year by the same author Alphabetize by title, and attach a letter to each entry's year of publication, beginning with *a*. In-text citations must use the letter as well as the year.

Agarwal, J. P. (1996a). *Does foreign direct investment contribute to unemployment in home countries? An empirical survey* (Discussion Paper No. 765). Kiel, Germany: Institute of World Economics.

Agarwal, J. P. (1996b). Impact of Europe agreements on FDI in developing countries. *International Journal of Social Economics, 23*(10/11), 150–163.

19. Article in a magazine After the year, add the month for magazines published monthly or the month and day for magazines published weekly. Note that the volume and issue numbers are also included.

Gross, P. (2001, February). Exorcising sociobiology. *New Criterion, 19*(6), 24.

20. Article in a newspaper Use *p.* or *pp.* with the section and page number. List all page numbers, separated by commas, if the article appears on discontinuous pages: *pp. C1, C4, C6.* If there is no identified author, begin with the title of the article.

Smith, T. (2003, October 8). Grass is green for Amazon farmers. *The New York Times,* p. W1.

21. Editorial or letter to the editor

Editorial: Financing health care reform [Editorial]. (2009, July 7). *The New York Times,* p. A22.

Deren, C. (2005, May 5). The last days of LI potatoes? [Letter to the editor]. *Newsday,* p. A49.

22. Unsigned article Begin the entry with the title, and alphabetize it by the first important word (excluding articles such as *The, A,* or *An*).

Reflection on a thousand years: Introduction. (1999, April 18). *The New York Times Magazine,* p. 77.

23. Review If the review is untitled, use the bracketed description in place of a title.

Kaimowitz, D. (2002). Amazon deforestation revisited [Review of the book *Brazil, forests in the balance: Challenges of conservation with development,* by U. Lele, V. Viana, A. Verissimo, S. Vosti, K. Perkins, & S. A. Husain]. *Latin American Research Review, 37,* 221–236.

401

Scott, A. O. (2002, May 10). Kicking up cosmic dust [Review of the motion picture

Star wars: Episode II—Attack of the clones, produced by 20th Century Fox,

2002], 2007. *The New York Times*, p. B1.

Other Print and Audiovisual Sources

24. Government document   When no author is listed, use the government agency as the author.

U.S. Bureau of the Census. (1976). *Historical statistics of the United States: Colonial*

times to 1970. Washington, DC: Government Printing Office.

For an enacted resolution or piece of legislation, see no. 57.

25. Report or working paper   If the issuing agency numbered the report, include that number in parentheses after the title.

Agarwal, J. P. (1996a). *Does foreign direct investment contribute to unemployment in*

home countries? An empirical survey (Discussion Paper No. 765). Kiel, Germany:

Institute of World Economics.

26. Conference presentation   Treat published conference presentations as a selection in a book (*no. 6*), as a periodical article (*no. 15* or *no. 16*), or as a report (*no. 25*), whichever applies. For unpublished conference presentations, provide the author, the year and month of the conference, the title of the presentation, and the presentation's form, forum, and place.

Markusen, J. (1998, June). *The role of multinationals in global economic analysis.*

Paper presented at the First Annual Conference in Global Economic Analysis,

West Lafayette, IN.

Desantis, R. (1998, June). *Optimal export taxes, welfare, industry concentration and*

firm size: A general equilibrium analysis. Poster session presented at the First

Annual Conference in Global Economic Analysis, West Lafayette, IN.

27. Dissertation or dissertation abstract   Use this format for an unpublished dissertation. For a dissertation accessed via a database, see no. 45.

Luster, L. (1992). *Schooling, survival and struggle: Black women and the GED*

(Unpublished doctoral dissertation). Stanford University, Palo Alto, CA.

If you used an abstract from *Dissertation Abstracts International,* treat the entry like a periodical article.

Weinbaum, A. E. (1998). Genealogies of "race" and reproduction in transatlantic

modern thought. *Dissertation Abstracts International, 58,* 229.

28. Brochure, pamphlet, fact sheet, press release   If there is no date of publication, put *n.d.* in place of the date. If the publisher is an organization, list it first, and name the publisher as *Author.*

United States Postal Service. (1995). *A consumer's guide to postal services and*

products [Brochure]. Washington, DC: Author.

Union College. (n.d.). *The Nott Memorial: A national historic landmark at Union*

College [Pamphlet]. Schenectady, NY: Author.

29. Film, DVD, videotape   Begin with the cited person's name and, if appropriate, a parenthetical notation of his or her role. After the title, identify the medium, followed by the country and name of the distributor. (*For online video, see no. 68.*)

Rowling, J. K., Kloves, S. (Writers), Yates, D. (Director), & Barron, D. (Producer).

(2009). *Harry Potter and the half-blood prince* [Motion picture]. United States:

Warner Brothers Pictures.

30. CD, audio recording   See no. 65 for an MP3 or no. 66 for an audio podcast.

title of piece   title of album
Corigliano, J. (2007). Red violin concerto [Recorded by J. Bell]. On *Red violin*

concerto [CD]. New York, NY: Sony Classics.

31. Radio broadcast   See no. 66 for an audio podcast.

Adamski, G., & Conti, K. (Hosts). (2007, January 16). *Legally speaking* [Radio

broadcast]. Chicago, IL: WGN Radio.

32. TV series   For an entire TV series or specific news broadcast, treat the producer as author.

Simon, D., & Noble, N. K. (Producers). (2002). *The wire* [Television series]. New York,

NY: HBO.

33. Episode from a TV series Treat the writer as the author and the producer as the editor of the series. See no. 67 for a podcast TV series episode.

> Burns, E., Simon, D. (Writers), & Johnson, C. (Director). (2002). The target [Television
>
> series episode]. In D. Simon & N. K. Noble (Producers), *The wire*. New York, NY:
>
> HBO.

34. Advertisement

> Geek Squad. (2007, December 10). [Advertisement]. Minneapolis/St. Paul, MN: WCCO-TV.

35. Image, photograph, work of art If you have reproduced a visual, give the source information with the caption. See no. 51 for online visuals.

> Smith, W. E. (1950). *Guardia Civil, Spain* [Photograph]. Minneapolis, MN:
>
> Minneapolis Institute of Arts.

36. Map or chart If you have reproduced a visual, give the source information with the caption (*for an example, see p. 422*). See no. 51 for online visuals.

> *Colonial Virginia* [Map]. (1960). Chapel Hill, VA: Virginia Historical Society.

37. Live performance

> Ibsen, H. (Author), Bly, R. (Translator), & Carroll, T. (Director). (2008, January 12). *Peer*
>
> *Gynt* [Theatrical performance]. Guthrie Theater, Minneapolis, MN.

38. Musical composition

> Rachmaninoff, S. (1900). *Piano concerto no. 2, opus 18* [Musical composition].

39. Lecture, speech, address List the speaker; the year, month, and date (if available); and the title of the presentation (in italics). Include location information when available. (For online versions, add "Retrieved from," the Web site sponsor, and the URL.)

> Cicerone, R. (2007, September 22). *Climate change in the U.S.* George S. Benton
>
> Lecture given at Johns Hopkins University, Baltimore, MD.

40. Personal interview Like other unpublished personal communications, personal interviews are not included in the reference list. See in-text citation entry no. 10 (*p. 394*).

- Many print and online books and articles have a Digital Object Identifier (DOI), a unique alphanumeric string. Citations of online documents with DOIs do not require the URL.
- Include a retrieval date only for items that probably will change (such as a wiki).
- Do not include information about a database or library subscription service in the citation unless the work is difficult to find elsewhere (e.g., archival material).
- Include the URL of the home page for journal, magazine, and newspaper articles lacking a DOI.
- Include the full URL for all other items lacking a DOI.
- For nonperiodicals, name the site sponsor in the retrieval statement unless the author is the sponsor (*see no. 51*). This format derives from the APA model for an online report.

author
Butler, R. A. (2008, July 31). *Future threats to the Amazon rain forest.* Retrieved
Web site sponsor
from Mongabay.com website: http://news.mongabay.com/2009

/0601-brazil_politics.html

author as Web site sponsor
Sisters in Islam. (2007). *Mission.* Retrieved from http://sistersinislam.org.my

/mission.html

Electronic Sources

41. Online journal article with a Digital Object Identifier (DOI) If your source has a DOI, include it at the end of the entry; URL and access date are not needed.

Ray, R., Wilhelm, F., & Gross, J. (2008). All in the mind's eye? Anger rumination

and reappraisal. *Journal of Personality and Social Psychology, 94,* 133–145.

doi:10.1037/0022-3514.94.1.133

42. Online journal article without a DOI Include the URL of the journal's home page.

Chan, L. (2004). Supporting and enhancing scholarship in the digital age:

The role of open access institutional repository. *Canadian Journal of*

Communication, 29, 277–300. Retrieved from http://www.cjc-online.ca

43. Journal article from an online, subscription, or library database   Include database information only if the article is rare or found in just a few databases. (*Otherwise, see nos. 41 and 42.*) Give the URL of the database's home page.

> Gore, W. C. (1916). Memory, concept, judgment, logic (theory). *Psychological*
>
> > *Bulletin, 13,* 355–358. Retrieved from PsycARTICLES database: http://
> >
> > psycnet.apa.org

44. Abstract from database as original source

> O'Leary, A., & Wolitski, R. J. (2009). Moral agency and the sexual transmission of
>
> > HIV. *Psychological Bulletin, 135,* 478–494. Abstract retrieved from PsycINFO
> >
> > database: http://psycnet.apa.org

45. Published dissertation from a database   Include the dissertation file number at the end of the entry.

> Gorski, A. (2007). *The environmental aesthetic appreciation of cultural landscapes*
>
> > *(Doctoral dissertation).* Available from ProQuest Dissertations and Theses
> >
> > database. (UMI No. 1443335)

46. Newspaper or magazine article from a database   Include database information for archival material not easily found elsewhere. Give the URL of the database's home page. (*Otherwise, see no. 47 for a newspaper article or no. 48 for a magazine article.*)

> Culnan, J. (1927, November 20). Madison to celebrate arrival of first air mail
>
> > plane. *Wisconsin State Journal,* p. A1. Retrieved from Wisconsin Historical
> >
> > Society database: http://www.wisconsinhistory.org/WLHBA

47. Article in an online newspaper

> Rohter, L. (2004, December 12). South America seeks to fill the world's table. *The*
>
> > *New York Times.* Retrieved from http://www.nytimes.com

48. Article in an online magazine   Include the volume and issue numbers after the magazine title.

> Biello, D. (2007, December 5). Thunder, hail, fire: What does climate change mean
>
> > for the U.S.? *Scientific American, 297*(6). Retrieved from http://www.sciam.com

49. Online exclusive magazine content

Francis, A. (2006, March 24). Fighting for the rainforest [Online exclusive].

Newsweek. Retrieved from http://www.newsweek.com

50. Article in an online newsletter   Give the full URL.

Gray, L. (2008, February). Corn gluten meal. *Shenandoah Chapter Newsletter, Virginia*

Native Plant Society. Retrieved from http://www.vnps.org/chapters

/shenandoah/Feb2008.pdf

51. Document or report on a Web site   Include the Web site sponsor in the retrieval statement unless the author of the work is also the sponsor. Here, the author is the World Health Organization and the sponsor is BPD Sanctuary.

World Health Organization. (1992). *ICD-10 criteria for borderline personality disorder.*

Retrieved from BPD Sanctuary website: http://www.mhsanctuary.com

/borderline/icd10.htm

52. Visual on a Web site   If you have used a graph, chart, map, or image, give the source information following the figure caption (*for an example, see p. 422*).

Seattle [Map]. (2008). Retrieved from http://www.mapquest.com

53. Document on a university's Web site   Include relevant information about the university and department in the retrieval statement.

Tugal, C. (2002). Islamism in Turkey: Beyond instrument and meaning. *Economy*

and Society, 31, 85–111. Retrieved from University of California–Berkeley,

Department of Sociology website: http://sociology.berkeley.edu

/public_sociology_pdf/tugal.pps05.pdf

54. Electronic version of a print book

Mill, J. S. (1869). *On liberty.* (4th ed.). Retrieved from http://books.google.com/books

Richards, G. (1997). *"Race," racism, and psychology* [Adobe Reader version].

Retrieved from http://www.ebookstore.tandf.co.uk/html/index.asp

55. Online book, no print edition

Stevens, K. (n.d.). *The dreamer and the beast.* Retrieved from http://www

.onlineoriginals.com/showitem.asp?itemID=321

56. Online government document except the *Congressional Record*

National Commission on Terrorist Attacks Upon the United States. (2004).

The 9/11 Commission report. Retrieved from Government Printing Office

website: http://www.gpoaccess.gov/911/index.html

57. *Congressional Record* (online or in print)   For enacted resolutions or legislation, give the number of the congress after the number of the resolution or legislation, the *Congressional Record* volume number, the page number(s), and year, followed by *(enacted)*.

H. Res. 2408, 108th Cong., 150 Cong. Rec. 1331–1332 (2004) (enacted).

Give the full name of the resolution or legislation when citing it within your sentence, but abbreviate the name when it appears in a parenthetical in-text citation: *(H. Res. 2408, 2004)*.

58. Online document lacking either a date or an author   Place the title before the date if no author is given. Use the abbreviation *n.d.* (no date) for any undated document.

Center for Science in the Public Interest. (n.d.). *Food additives to avoid.* Retrieved

from Mindfully.org website: http://www.mindfully.org/Food/Food-Additives

-Avoid.htm

59. Article in an online reference work   Begin with the author's name, if given, followed by the publication date. If no author is given, place the title before the date. Include the full URL.

Attribution theory. (2009). In *Encarta.* Retrieved from http://encarta.msn.com

/encyclopedia_761586848/Attribution_Theory.html

60. Wiki article   Wikis are collaboratively written Web sites. Most are updated regularly, so include the access date in your citation. Check with your instructor before using a wiki article as a source.

Demographic transition. (2007, October 8). Retrieved March 3, 2008, from

Citizendium website: http://en.citizendium.org/wiki/Demographic_transition

61. Blog posting

Eggers, A. (2009, May 20). Debates on goverment transparency websites [Web log

message]. Retrieved from Social Science Statistics Blog website: http://www

.iq.harvard.edu/blog/sss

62. Post to a newsgroup or discussion forum   Provide the message's author, its date, and its subject line as the title. Give the identifying information *Online forum comment* in brackets.

Jones, D. (2001, February 3). California solar power [Online forum comment]. Retrieved

from http://yarchive.net/space/politics/california_power.html

63. Post to an electronic mailing list   Provide the message's author, its date, and its subject line as the title. After the phrase *Electronic mailing list message*, give the address of the archived message.

Glick, D. (2007, February 10). Bio-char sequestration in terrestrial ecosystems—

A review [Electronic mailing list message]. Retrieved from http://

bioenergylists.org/newsgroup-archive/terrapreta_bioenergylists.org

/2007-February/000023.html

64. E-mail or instant message (IM)   E-mail, instant messages, or other nonarchived personal communication should be cited in the body of your paper but not given in the references list (*see in-text citation entry no. 10, on p. 394*).

65. MP3

Hansard, G., & Irglova, M. (2006). Falling slowly. On *The swell season* [MP3]. Chicago,

IL: Overcoat Recordings.

66. Audio podcast

Glass, I. (Host). (2008, June 30). Social engineering. *This American life* [Audio

podcast]. Retrieved from This American Life website: http://www

.thisamericanlife.org

67. Podcast TV series episode

Reitman, J. (Director), & Novak, B. J. (Writer). (2007). Local ad [Television series

episode]. In S. Carrell, M. Kaling, L. Eisenberg, & G. Stupnitsky (Producers),

The office [Video podcast]. Retrieved from NBC website: http://www.nbc

.com/the_office/video/episodes.shtml

68. Online video   For an online speech, see no. 39.

Wesch, M. (2007, March 8). The machine is us/ing us [Video file]. Retrieved from

mediatedcultures.net/ksudigg/?p=84

69. Computer software   Cite only specialized software.

Buscemi, S. (2003). AllWrite! 2.1 with online handbook [Computer software].

New York, NY: McGraw-Hill.

👁 **24d** APA style: Paper format

The following guidelines are recommended by the *Publication Manual of the American Psychological Association,* sixth edition. For an example of a research paper that has been prepared using APA style, see pages 412–22.

Materials.   Back up your final draft. Use a high-quality printer and high-quality white 8½-by-11-inch paper. Do not justify your text or hyphenate words at the right margin; it should be ragged.

Title page.   The first page of your paper should be a title page. Center the title between the left and right margins in the upper half of the page, and put your name a few lines below the title. Most instructors will also want you to include the course number and title, the instructor's name, and the date. *(See p. 412 for an example.)*

Margins and spacing.   Use one-inch margins all around, except for the upper right-hand corner, where the page number goes, and the upper left-hand corner, where the running head goes.

Double-space lines throughout the paper, including in the abstract, within any notes, and in the list of references. Indent the first word of each paragraph one-half inch (or five spaces). Place two spaces after a period at the end of a sentence.

For quotations of more than forty words, use block format and indent five spaces from the left margin. Double-space the quoted lines.

Page numbers and abbreviated titles.   All pages, including the title page, should have the words "Running head" and a short version of your title in uppercase letters. Put this information in the upper left-hand corner of each page, about one-half inch from the top. Put the page number in the upper right-hand corner.

Abstract.   Instructors sometimes require an abstract—a summary of your paper's thesis, major points or lines of development, and conclusions. The abstract appears on its own numbered page, entitled "Abstract," right after the title page. It should not exceed 150 to 250 words.

Headings.   Primary headings should be boldfaced and centered. All key words in the heading should be capitalized.

Secondary headings should be boldfaced and appear flush against the left-hand margin. Do not use a heading for your introduction, however. (*For more on headings, see Chapter 6: Designing Academic Papers and Preparing Portfolios, pp. 110–11.*)

Visuals.   Place each visual (table, chart, graph, or image) on its own page following the reference list and any content notes. Tables precede figures. Label each visual as a table or a figure, and number each kind consecutively (Table 1, Table 2). Provide an informative caption for each visual. Cite the source of the material, and provide explanatory notes as needed. (*For more on using visuals effectively, see Chapter 4: Drafting Paragraphs and Visuals, pp. 62–72.*)

24e   Student paper in APA style

Audrey Galeano researched and wrote a report on the indigenous peoples of the Amazon for her anthropology course, Indigenous Peoples and Globalization. Her sources included books, journal articles, and Web documents.

411

Running head: SAVING THE AMAZON   1

Saving the Amazon:

Globalization and Deforestation

Audrey Galeano

Anthropology 314: Indigenous Peoples and Globalization

Professor Mura

May 3, 2008

Abstract

The impact of globalization on fragile ecosystems is a complex problem. In the Amazon River basin, globalization has led to massive deforestation as multinational corporations exploit the rain forest's natural resources. In particular, large-scale industrial agriculture has caused significant damage to the local environment. In an effort to resist the loss of this ecosystem, indigenous peoples in the Amazon basin are reaching out to each other, to nongovernmental organizations (NGOs), and to other interest groups to combat industrial agriculture and promote sustainable regional agriculture. Although these efforts have had mixed success, it is hoped that the native peoples of this region can continue to live on their homelands without feeling intense pressure to acquiesce to industrialization or to relocate.

Abstract appears on a new page after the title page. First line is not indented.

Essay concisely and objectively summarized—key points included, but not details or statistics.

Paragraph should not exceed 150 to 250 words.

413

1" 3 ½"

Saving the Amazon:

Globalization and Deforestation

For thousands of years, the indigenous peoples of the Amazon River basin have practiced forms of sustainable agriculture. These peoples developed ways of farming and hunting that enabled them to provide food and trade goods for their communities with minimal impact on the environment. These methods have endured despite colonization and industrialization. Today, the greatest threat to indigenous peoples in the Amazon River basin is posed by the massive deforestation caused by industrial-scale farming and ranching, as revealed in satellite images taken since 1988 by Brazil's National Institute of Space Research. (See graph in Figure 1.) Because of the injury to ecosystems and native ways of life, indigenous peoples and antiglobalization activists have joined forces to promote sustainable agriculture and the rights of native peoples throughout the Amazon River basin.

Sustainable Lifeways, Endangered Lives

Recent work in historical ecology has altered our understanding of how humans have shaped what is romantically called "virgin forest." As anthropologist Anna Roosevelt (as cited in Society for California Archaeology, 2000) observes, "People adapt to environments but they also change them. There are no virgin environments on earth in areas where people lived." By one estimate, nearly 12 percent of the Amazonian rain forest in Brazil has been shaped or influenced by thousands of years of indigenous human culture (Brookfield, 2001); the evidence is as basic as the *terra preta do Indio,* or "Indian Black Earth" (Glick, 2007, para. 4), for which the Brazilian region of Santarem is known.

Full title repeated on first page only.

Figure appears at end of paper.

Thesis statement.

Primary heading, centered and boldfaced, subtly reveals writer's stance.

Parenthetical citation of source with organization as author.

Information from two sources combined in one sentence.

The previous thousands of years of human influence on the Amazon is slight, however, compared with the modern-day destruction of rain forests around the globe, and in the Amazon River basin in particular. The sources of this destruction vary from country to country and year to year, with certain years affected more by climate change and other years seeing greater destruction from human initiatives, such as logging (Walker, Moran, & Anselin, 2000). According to the Center for International Forestry Research, an Indonesia-based nongovernmental organization (NGO), an area of land the size of Uruguay was deforested in the years 2002 and 2003 alone. Nearly all of this land was cleared for industrial agriculture and cattle ranching (Prugh, 2004).

Globalization and Agricultural Destruction

Large-scale industrial agriculture seeks out the least expensive ways to produce the highest number of crops. Perhaps the largest cash crop of the late 20th and early 21st centuries is soy, which has numerous uses and is among the least expensive crops to produce. According to Roberto Smeraldi, director of the environmental action group Friends of the Earth, "soybeans are the single biggest driver for deforestation" in the Brazilian Amazon; in the 12 months ending in August 2003, 9,169 square miles of rain forest had been cleared by soy farmers, ranchers, and loggers in Brazil (as cited in Stewart, 2004, paras. 4–5). Although Brazilian officials have attempted to regulate depredations of the rain forest by multinational soy producers, Stewart notes that, in 2003, soybean production brought nearly $8 billion to the Brazilian economy, forcing indigenous and small-scale farmers off their lands and damaging local climate.

Support by key facts (see p. 187).

Paragraph expands on introductory paragraph.

Details introduced and linked to broader issue of globalization.

An Associated Press (AP) report reprinted on the Organic Consumer's Association website describes the impact of soy production on Brazil's Xingu National Park, a protected rain forest reserve that is home to 14 indigenous tribes. "The soy is arriving very fast. Every time I leave the reservation I don't recognize anything anymore because the forest keeps disappearing," a director of the Xingu Indian Land Association is quoted as observing (AP, 2003, para. 11). Although the industrial soy farms have not crossed the borders of the Xingu National Park, they surround the protected lands and have raised fears that chemical pesticides and deforestation will dry up rivers and kill fish. "Our Xingu is not just what's here. It's a very long thread, and when it rains the soy brings venom down the same river that passes by our door," says Capivara chief Jywapan Kayabi (para. 24).

Cattle ranching has also led to the deforestation of the Amazon. The cattle population of the Amazon nations increased from 26 million in 1990 to 57 million in 2002 (Prugh, 2004). Attention to the destruction caused by industrial cattle-ranching began in the late 1980s. Barrett (2001) points out that ranchers were using lands already depleted of fertility and biodiversity by logging, road building, and colonization of the Brazilian Amazon in the 1960s and 1970s. Ranching, Barrett observes, "doesn't require nutrient-rich soil" and therefore "took the place vacated by other activities, along with the blame for soil erosion and loss of biodiversity" (p. 1).

Indigenous Peoples and Regional Activism

Depopulation of these lands as a result of colonization meant that traditional agricultural practices were no longer sustained. In recent years, antiglobalization NGOs, the

Abbreviation given at first mention of organization.

First main cause of deforestation discussed.

Abbreviation for organization used in parenthetical citation.

Second main cause of deforestation discussed.

Page number given for quotation.

international movement for indigenous peoples' rights, and
increased understanding of the consequences of deforestation
are helping native peoples reclaim lands and reestablish
traditional agricultural practices. However, some kinds of
alliances and interventions are not as productive as others.

A contributing factor in the problem of deforestation shows the complexity of the situation.

Anthropologists da Cunha and de Almeida ask a
provocative question: "Can traditional peoples be described as
'cultural conservationists'?" (2000, p. 315). Although as many
as 50 indigenous groups in Amazonia still have no contact with
the outside world, other indigenous peoples have secured their
land rights through international efforts over the past 20 years.
Some of these efforts, da Cunha and de Almeida argue, are
influenced by romantic ideas about "noble savages" and
fail to acknowledge the ways in which indigenous peoples in
contemporary Brazil make a living from rain forest resources.

Barham and Coomes (1997) also note that a better
understanding of how indigenous peoples live is necessary if the
efforts of international groups such as Amazon Alliance are to
succeed. Indigenous peoples need to see some material benefit
from conservationist practices. After all, as da Cunha and de
Almeida write, "Traditional peoples are neither outside the central
economy nor any longer simply in the periphery of the world
system" (2000, p. 315).

Local culture, history, and economics shown to be linked to global systems.

Franke Wilmer (1998) suggests that "human action
and its impact in the world are directed by a view that is
dangerously out of touch with natural laws which, according
to indigenous peoples, govern all life on this planet" (p. 57).
For instance, although the Kayapo people of south-central
Amazonia have been devastated by colonization, they still "used
their knowledge to manipulate ecosystems in remarkable

Running head: SAVING THE AMAZON   7

ways . . . to maximize biological diversity" (Brookfield, 2001, p. 141). Among the Kayapo's sustainable practices are crop rotation, the use of ash to fertilize fields, and the transition of older fields back to secondary forest (Brookfield, 2001).

Some socially conscious global corporations have attempted to help indigenous Amazonian farmers develop sustainable, profitable crops. Two of the best-known efforts, described in a 2003 *New York Times* article by Tony Smith, provide a cautionary tale. In the 1990s, the British multinational "green" cosmetics company The Body Shop and American ice cream manufacturer Ben and Jerry's both developed "eco-friendly" products from the Amazon. Ben and Jerry's Rainforest Crunch ice cream used Brazil nuts that were harvested in a sustainable fashion by an Amazonian cooperative, and The Body Shop used the oils from Brazil nuts in some of its cosmetics.

But Rainforest Crunch proved so popular that the cooperative could not meet the demand, and Ben and Jerry's had to turn to other suppliers, "some notorious for their antilabor practices" (Smith, 2003, p. W1). The Body Shop wound up being sued by a chief of the Kayapo tribe, whose image was used in Body Shop advertising without permission (Smith).

The best solution might be for Brazilian businesses, developers, government officials, and indigenous peoples to work together. One new initiative described in the *Times* article is the cultivation of the sweet-scented native Amazon grass called

priprioca, on which the Sao Paulo cosmetics company Natura is basing a new fragrance. Farmer Jose Mateus, who has grown watermelons and manioc on his small farm near the Amazon city of Belem, has agreed to grow priprioca instead—and he expects to get twice the price for the grass that he would for his usual crop

(Smith, 2003). Eduardo Luppi, director of innovation for Natura, comments, "We do have the advantage that we are Brazilian and we are in Brazil. If you are in England or America and want to manage something like this in the Amazon by remote control, you can forget it" (as cited in Smith, 2003, p. W1).

Although indigenous peoples face extraordinary obstacles in their quest for environmental justice, some political officials support their struggles. In the Acre state of Brazil, Governor Jorge Viana was inspired by the example of martyred environmental activist Chico Mendes to secure financing from Brazil's federal development bank for sustainable development in his impoverished Amazonian state (Epstein, 2002). Viana, who holds a degree in forest engineering, told the journal *Latin Trade* that "we want to bring local populations into the policy of forest management. . . . We have to show them how to exploit without destroying" (as cited in Epstein, p. 26).

Conclusion

The social, economic, climate-related, and political pressures on the Amazonian ecosystem may prove insurmountable; report after report describes the enormous annual loss of rain forest habitat. The best hope for saving the rain forest is public pressure on multinational agricultural corporations to practice accountable, safe, and sustainable methods. In addition, it is important to encourage indigenous peoples to practice their age-old sustainable agriculture and land-management strategies while guaranteeing their rights and safety. Much in the Amazon has been ruined, but cooperative efforts like those discussed in this paper can nurture and sustain what remains for future generations.

Essay concludes on a concerned yet optimistic note, balancing writer's and sources' concerns.

419

References

Associated Press. (2003, December 18). *Soybeans: The new threat to Brazilian rainforest.* Retrieved from Organic Consumers Association website: http://www.organicconsumers.org /corp/soy121903.cfm

Barham, B. L., & Coomes, O. T. (1997). Rain forest extraction and conservation in Amazonia. *The Geographical Journal, 163,* 180.

Barrett, J. R. (2001). Livestock farming: Eating up the environment? *Environmental Health Perspectives, 109,* A312.

Brookfield, H. (2001). *Exploring agrodiversity.* New York, NY: Columbia University Press.

da Cunha, M. C., & de Almeida, M. (2000). Indigenous people, traditional people and conservation in the Amazon. *Daedalus, 129,* 315.

Epstein, J. (2002). A voice in the wilderness. *Latin Trade, 10*(12), 26.

Glick, D. (2007, February 10). Bio-char sequestration in terrestrial ecosystems—A review [Electronic mailing list message]. Retrieved from http://bioenergylists.org/newsgroup-archive /terrapreta_bioenergylists.org/2007-February/000023.html

Prugh, T. (2004). Ranching accelerates Amazon deforestation. *World Watch, 17*(4), 8.

Smith, T. (2003, October 8). Grass is green for Amazon farmers. *The New York Times,* p. W1.

Society for California Archaeology. (2000). *Interview with Anna C. Roosevelt.* Retrieved from http://www.scahome .org/about_ca_archaeology/2000_Roosevelt.html

New page, heading centered.

Entries in alphabetical order and double-spaced.

Hanging indent 5 spaces or $\frac{1}{2}''$.

Stewart, A. (2004, July 14). Brazil's soy success brings environmental challenges. *Dow Jones*. Retrieved from Amazonia website: http://www.amazonia.org.br/English /noticias/noticia.cfm?id=116059

Walker, R., Moran, E., & Anselin, L. (2000). Deforestation and cattle ranching in the Brazilian Amazon: External capital and household processes. *World Development, 28,* 683–699.

Wilmer, F. (1998). Taking indigenous critiques seriously: The enemy 'r' us. In K. Lifton (Ed.), *The greening of sovereignty in world politics* (pp. 55–60). Cambridge: The Massachusetts Institute of Technology Press.

Running head: SAVING THE AMAZON   11

Graph
presents
statistics in
visual form
for readers.

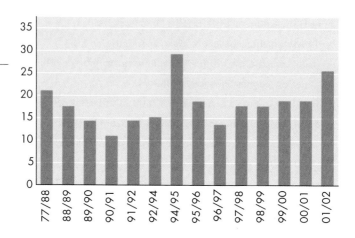

Figure 1. Annual deforestation rates in the Brazilian Amazon,
1977–2002 (thousands of square kilometers). Bars represent-
ing multiple years show the mean for those years. Data from

Informative
caption
and source
note appear
below the
figure.

National Institute of Space Research, Brazil (2002). Graph adapted
from *Hamburger connection fuels Amazon destruction: Cattle ranching and deforestation in Brazil's Amazon* (p. 2), by D. Kaimowitz,
B. Mertens, S. Wunder, and P. Pacheco, 2004, retrieved from
Center for International Forestry Research website: http://www
.cifor.cgiar.org/publications/pdf_files/media/Amazon.pdf

25 Chicago Documentation Style

There are many documentation styles besides those developed by the Modern Language Association (*see Chapter 23*) and the American Psychological Association (*see Chapter 24*). In this chapter, we cover the *Chicago Manual* style. To learn about other style types, consult the list of style manuals on page 338. If you are not sure which style to use, ask your instructor.

The note and bibliography style presented in the fifteenth edition of *The Chicago Manual of Style* (Chicago: University of Chicago Press, 2003) is used in many disciplines, including history, art, philosophy, business, and communications. This style has three parts:

- Numbered in-text citations
- Numbered footnotes or endnotes
- A bibliography of works consulted

www.mhhe.com/
mhhb2
For links to Web sites
for documentation
styles in various
disciplines, go to

Research > Links
to Documentation
Sites

The first two parts are necessary; the third is optional, unless your instructor requires it. (Chicago also has an alternative author-date system that is similar to APA style.) For more information on this style, consult the *Chicago Manual of Style*. For updates and answers to frequently asked questions about this style, go to the *Chicago Manual*'s Web site at <http://www.press.uchicago.edu> and click on "*Chicago Manual of Style* Web site."

25a Chicago style: In-text citations and notes.

Whenever you use information or ideas from a source, you need to indicate what you have borrowed by putting a superscript number in the text ([1]) at the end of the borrowed material. These superscript numbers are placed after all punctuation marks except for the dash.

As biographer Laurence Bergreen points out, Armstrong easily reached difficult

high notes, the F's and G's that stymied other trumpeters.[3]

If a quotation is fairly long, you can set it off as a block quotation. Indent it five spaces or one-half inch from the left margin, and double-space the quotation, leaving an extra space above and below it. Place the superscript number after the period that ends the quotation. (*See p. 439 for an example.*)

Each in-text superscript number must have a corresponding note either at the foot of the page or at the end of the text. Indent the first line of each footnote like a paragraph. Footnotes begin with the number and are single-spaced, with a double space between notes.

If you are using endnotes instead of footnotes, they should begin after the last page of your text on a new numbered page titled "Notes." Single-space within and double-space between endnotes.

The first time you cite a source in either a footnote or an endnote, you should include a full citation. Subsequent citations require less information.

FIRST REFERENCE TO SOURCE

3. Laurence Bergreen, *Louis Armstrong: An Extravagant Life* (New York: Broadway Books, 1997), 248.

ENTRY FOR SOURCE ALREADY CITED

6. Bergreen, 370.

If several pages pass between references to the same title, include a brief version of the title to clarify the reference.

ENTRY FOR SOURCE ALREADY CITED IN LONGER PAPER

7. Bergreen, *Louis Armstrong*, 370.

If you quote from the same work immediately after providing a full footnote, use the abbreviation *Ibid.* (Latin for "in the same place"), followed by the page number.

8. Ibid., 370.

25b Chicago style: Bibliography.

Some instructors require a separate list of works cited or of works consulted. If you are asked to provide a works-cited list, do so on a separate, numbered page titled "Works Cited." If the list should include all works you consulted, title it "Bibliography." Here is a sample entry:

Bergreen, Laurence. *Louis Armstrong: An Extravagant Life.* New York: Broadway Books, 1997.

25c Sample Chicago-style notes and bibliography entries.

CHICAGO STYLE: DIRECTORY to SAMPLE TYPES

Books

1. Book with one author

NOTE

1. James Lincoln Collier, *Louis Armstrong: An American Genius* (New York: Oxford University Press, 1983), 82.

BIBLIOGRAPHY ENTRY

Collier, James Lincoln. *Louis Armstrong: An American Genius*. New York: Oxford University Press, 1983.

2. Multiple works by the same author After providing complete information in the first footnote, include only a shortened version of the title with the author's last name and the page number in any subsequent footnotes. In the bibliography, list entries either in

425

BIBLIOGRAPHY or WORKS-CITED LIST in CHICAGO STYLE

- Begin on a new page.
- Begin with the centered title "Works Cited" if you are including only works referred to in your paper. Use the title "Bibliography" if you are including every work you consulted.
- List sources alphabetically by author's (or editor's) last name.
- Capitalize the first and last words in titles as well as all important words and words that follow colons.
- Indent all lines except the first of each entry five spaces, using your word processor's hanging indent feature.
- Use periods between author and title as well as between title and publication data.
- Single-space each entry; double-space between entries.

alphabetical order by title or from earliest to most recent. After the first listing, replace the author's name with a "3-em" dash (type three hyphens in a row).

NOTES

7. Collier, *Jazz,* 154.

12. Collier, *Louis Armstrong,* 32.

BIBLIOGRAPHY ENTRIES

Collier, James Lincoln. *Jazz: The American Theme Song.* New York: Oxford University Press, 1993.

———. *Louis Armstrong: An American Genius.* New York: Oxford University Press, 1983.

3. Book with two or more authors   In notes, you can name up to three authors. When there are three authors, put a comma after the first name and a comma plus *and* after the second.

NOTE

2. Miles Davis and Quincy Troupe, *Miles: The Autobiography* (New York: Simon & Schuster, 1989), 15.

BIBLIOGRAPHY ENTRY

Davis, Miles, and Quincy Troupe. *Miles: The Autobiography.* New York: Simon & Schuster, 1989.

When more than three authors are listed on the title page, use *and others* or *et al.* after the first author's name in the note.

NOTE

3. Julian Henriques and others, *Changing the Subject: Psychology, Social Regulation and Subjectivity* (New York: Methuen, 1984), 275.

BIBLIOGRAPHY ENTRY

Henriques, Julian, Wendy Holloway, Cathy Urwin, Couze Venn, and Valerie Walkerdine. *Changing the Subject: Psychology, Social Regulation and Subjectivity.* New York: Methuen, 1984.

Give all author names in bibliography entries.

4. Book with an author and an editor or a translator   Put the author's name first and add the editor's (*ed.*) or translator's (*trans.*) name after the title. Spell out *Edited* or *Translated* in the bibliography entry.

NOTE

4. Louis Armstrong, *Louis Armstrong: A Self-Portrait,* ed. Richard Meryman (New York: Eakins Press, 1971), 54.

BIBLIOGRAPHY ENTRIES

Armstrong, Louis. *Louis Armstrong: A Self-Portrait.* Edited by Richard Meryman. New York: Eakins Press, 1971.

Goffin, Robert. *Horn of Plenty: The Story of Louis Armstrong.* Translated by James F. Bezov. New York: Da Capo Press, 1977.

5. Book with editor(s)

NOTE

5. Paul Eduard Miller, ed., *Esquire's Jazz Book* (New York: Smith & Durrell, 1944), 31.

BIBLIOGRAPHY ENTRY

Miller, Paul Eduard, ed. *Esquire's Jazz Book.* New York: Smith & Durrell, 1944.

6. Organization as author

NOTE

6. Centre for Contemporary Cultural Studies, *Making Histories: Studies in History Writing and Politics* (London: Hutchinson, 1982), 10.

BIBLIOGRAPHY ENTRY

Centre for Contemporary Cultural Studies. *Making Histories: Studies in History Writing and Politics.* London: Hutchinson, 1982.

7. Work in an anthology or part of an edited book   Begin with the author and title of the specific work or part.

NOTES

7. Hale Smith, "Here I Stand," in *Readings in Black American Music,* ed. Eileen Southern (New York: Norton, 1971), 287.

8. Richard Crawford, foreword to *The Jazz Tradition,* by Martin Williams (New York: Oxford University Press, 1993).

BIBLIOGRAPHY ENTRIES

Smith, Hale. "Here I Stand." In *Readings in Black American Music*, edited by Eileen Southern, 286–89. New York: Norton, 1971.

Crawford, Richard. Foreword to *The Jazz Tradition,* by Martin Williams. New York: Oxford University Press, 1993.

In notes, descriptive terms such as *foreword* are not capitalized. In bibliography entries, these descriptive terms are capitalized.

8. Article in an encyclopedia or a dictionary   For well-known reference works, publication data can be omitted from a note, but the edition or copyright date should be included. There is no need to include page numbers for entries in reference works that are arranged alphabetically; the abbreviation *s.v.* (meaning "under the word") plus the entry's title can be used instead.

NOTES

9. J. Bradford Robinson, "Scat Singing," in *The New Grove Dictionary of Jazz* (2002).

10. *Encyclopaedia Britannica,* 15th ed., s.v. "Jazz."

Reference works are not listed in the bibliography unless they are unusual or crucial to your paper.

BIBLIOGRAPHY ENTRY

Robinson, J. Bradford. "Scat Singing." In *The New Grove Dictionary of Jazz.* Edited by Barry Kernfeld. Vol. 3. London: Macmillan, 2002.

9. The Bible Abbreviate the name of the book, and use arabic numerals for chapter and verse, separated by a colon. Name the version of the Bible cited, and do not include the Bible in your bibliography.

NOTE

11. Eccles. 8:5 (Jerusalem Bible).

10. Edition other than the first Include the number of the edition after the title or, if there is an editor, after that person's name.

NOTE

12. Hugues Panassie, *Louis Armstrong,* 2d ed. (New York: Da Capo Press, 1980), 12.

BIBLIOGRAPHY ENTRY

Panassie, Hugues. *Louis Armstrong.* 2d ed. New York: Da Capo Press, 1980.

11. Multivolume work Put the volume number in arabic numerals followed by a colon, before the page number.

NOTE

13. Robert Lissauer, *Lissauer's Encyclopedia of Popular Music in America* (New York: Facts on File, 1996), 2:33–34.

BIBLIOGRAPHY ENTRY

Lissauer, Robert. *Lissauer's Encyclopedia of Popular Music in America.* Vol. 2. New York: Facts on File, 1996.

12. Work in a series Include the name of the series as well as the book's series number. The series name should not be italicized or underlined.

NOTE

14. Samuel A. Floyd, ed., *Black Music in the Harlem Renaissance,* Contributions in Afro-American and African Studies, no. 128 (New York: Greenwood Press, 1990), 2.

BIBLIOGRAPHY ENTRY

Floyd, Samuel A., ed. *Black Music in the Harlem Renaissance.* Contributions in Afro-American and African Studies, no. 128. New York: Greenwood Press, 1990.

13. Unknown author   Cite anonymous works by title, and alphabetize them by the first word, ignoring *A*, *An*, or *The*.

NOTE

> 15. *The British Album* (London: John Bell, 1790), 2:43–47.

BIBLIOGRAPHY ENTRY

The British Album. Vol. 2. London: John Bell, 1790.

14. Source quoted in another source   Quote a source within a source only if you are unable to find the original source. List both sources in the entry.

NOTE

> 16. Peter Gay, *Modernism: The Lure of Heresy* (New York: Norton, 2007), 262, quoted in Terry Teachout, "The Cult of the Difficult," *Commentary* 124, no. 5 (2007): 66–69.

BIBLIOGRAPHY ENTRY

Gay, Peter. *Modernism: The Lure of Heresy.* New York: Norton, 2007. Quoted in Terry Teachout. "The Cult of the Difficult." *Commentary* 124, no. 5 (2007): 66–69.

Periodicals

15. Article in a journal paginated by volume   When journals are paginated by yearly volume, your citation should include the following: author, title of article in quotation marks, title of journal, volume number and year, and page number(s).

NOTE

> 17. Frank Tirro, "Constructive Elements in Jazz Improvisation," *Journal of the American Musicological Society* 27 (1974): 300.

BIBLIOGRAPHY ENTRY

Tirro, Frank. "Constructive Elements in Jazz Improvisation." *Journal of the American Musicological Society* 27 (1974): 285–305.

16. Article in a journal paginated by issue   If the periodical is paginated by issue rather than by volume, add the issue number, preceded by the abbreviation *no.*

NOTE

> 18. Sarah Appleton Aguiar, "'Everywhere and Nowhere': Beloved's 'Wild' Legacy in Toni Morrison's *Jazz*," *Notes on Contemporary Literature* 25, no. 4 (1995): 11.

BIBLIOGRAPHY ENTRY

Aguiar, Sarah Appleton. "'Everywhere and Nowhere': Beloved's 'Wild' Legacy in Toni Morrison's *Jazz.*" *Notes on Contemporary Literature* 25, no. 4 (1995): 11–12.

17. Article in a magazine
Identify magazines by week (if available) and month of publication. In the note, give only the specific page cited; in the bibliography, give the full range of pages.

NOTE

19. Malcolm Walker, "Discography: Bill Evans," *Jazz Monthly,* June 1965, 22.

BIBLIOGRAPHY ENTRY

Walker, Malcolm. "Discography: Bill Evans." *Jazz Monthly,* June 1965, 20–22.

If the article cited does not appear on consecutive pages, do not put any page numbers in the bibliography entry. You can, however, give specific pages in the note. In Chicago style, the month precedes the date, and months are not abbreviated.

NOTE

20. J. R. Taylor, "Jazz History: The Incompleted Past," *Village Voice,* July 3, 1978, 65.

BIBLIOGRAPHY ENTRY

Taylor, J. R. "Jazz History: The Incompleted Past." *Village Voice,* July 3, 1978.

18. Article in a newspaper
Provide the author's name (if known), the title of the article, the name of the newspaper, and the date of publication. Do not give a page number. Instead, give the section number or title if it is indicated. If applicable, indicate the edition (for example, *national edition*) before the section number.

NOTE

21. Ralph Blumenthal, "Satchmo with His Tape Recorder Running." *New York Times,* August 3, 1999, sec. E.

Newspaper articles cited in the text of your paper do not need to be included in a bibliography or reference list. However, if you are asked to include newspaper articles in the bibliography or reference list, or if you did not provide full citation information in the essay or the note, format the entry as follows.

BIBLIOGRAPHY ENTRY

Blumenthal, Ralph. "Satchmo with His Tape Recorder Running." *New York Times,* August 3, 1999, sec. E.

19. Unsigned article or editorial in a newspaper   Begin the note and the bibliography or reference list entry with the name of the newspaper.

NOTE

22. *New York Times,* "A Promising Cloning Proposal," October 15, 2004.

BIBLIOGRAPHY ENTRY

New York Times, "A Promising Cloning Proposal," October 15, 2004.

Other Sources

20. Review   If the review is untitled, start with the author's name (if any) and *review of* for a note or *Review of* for a bibliography entry.

NOTE

23. David Ostwald, "All That Jazz," review of *Louis Armstrong: An Extravagant Life,* by Laurence Bergreen, *Commentary,* November 1997, 72.

BIBLIOGRAPHY ENTRY

Ostwald, David. "All That Jazz." Review of *Louis Armstrong: An Extravagant Life,* by Laurence Bergreen. *Commentary,* November 1997, 68–72.

21. Interview   Start with the name of the person interviewed. If a record of an unpublished interview exists, note the medium and where it may be found. Only interviews accessible to your readers are listed in the bibliography. Treat published interviews like articles.

NOTES

24. Louis Armstrong, "Authentic American Genius," interview by Richard Meryman, *Life,* April 15, 1966, 92.

25. Michael Cogswell, interview by author, May 3, 2008, tape recording, Louis Armstrong Archives, Queens College CUNY, Flushing, NY.

BIBLIOGRAPHY ENTRY

Armstrong, Louis. "Authentic American Genius." Interview by Richard Meryman. *Life,* April 15, 1966, 92–102.

22. Personal letter or e-mail   Do not list in your bibliography.

NOTES

26. Jorge Ramados, letter to author, November 30, 2007.

27. Goerge Hermanson, e-mail message to author, November 15, 2007.

23. Government document   If it is not already obvious in your text, name the country first.

NOTE

28. Bureau of National Affairs, *The Civil Rights Act of 1964: Text, Analysis, Legislative History; What It Means to Employers, Businessmen, Unions, Employees, Minority Groups* (Washington, DC: BNA, 1964), 22–23.

BIBLIOGRAPHY ENTRY

U.S. Bureau of National Affairs. *The Civil Rights Act of 1964: Text, Analysis, Legislative History; What It Means to Employers, Businessmen, Unions, Employees, Minority Groups.* Washington, DC: BNA, 1964.

24. Unpublished dissertation or document   Include a description of the document as well as information about where it is available. If more than one item from an archive is cited, include only one entry for the archive in your bibliography (*see p. 441*).

NOTES

29. Adelaida Reyes-Schramm, "The Role of Music in the Interaction of Black Americans and Hispanos in New York City's East Harlem" (Ph.D. diss., Columbia University, 1975), 34–37.

30. Joe Glaser to Lucille Armstrong, September 28, 1960, Louis Armstrong Archives, Rosenthal Library, Queens College CUNY, Flushing, NY.

BIBLIOGRAPHY ENTRIES

Reyes-Schramm, Adelaida. "The Role of Music in the Interaction of Black Americans and Hispanos in New York City's East Harlem." Ph.D. diss., Columbia University, 1975.

Glaser, Joe. Letter to Lucille Armstrong. Louis Armstrong Archives. Rosenthal Library, Queens College CUNY, Flushing, NY.

25. DVD or videocassette   Include the original release date before the publication information if it differs from the release date for the DVD or videocassette.

NOTE

31. *Wit,* DVD, directed by Mike Nichols (New York: HBO Home Video, 2001).

BIBLIOGRAPHY

Wit. DVD. Directed by Mike Nichols. New York: HBO Home Video, 2001.

26. Sound recording   Begin with the composer or other person responsible for the content.

NOTE

32. Louis Armstrong, *Town Hall Concert Plus,* RCA INTS 5070.

BIBLIOGRAPHY ENTRY

Armstrong, Louis. *Town Hall Concert Plus.* RCA INTS 5070.

27. Artwork   Begin with the artist's name, and include both the name and the location of the institution holding the work. Works of art are usually not included in the bibliography.

NOTE

33. Herman Leonard, *Louis Armstrong: Birdland 1949,* black-and-white photograph, 1949, Barbara Gillman Gallery, Miami.

28. CD-ROM or other electronic non-Internet source   Indicate the format after the publication information.

NOTE

34. *Microsoft Encarta Multimedia Encyclopedia,* s.v. "Armstrong, (Daniel) Louis 'Satchmo'" (Redmond, WA: Microsoft, 1994), CD-ROM.

BIBLIOGRAPHY ENTRY

Microsoft Encarta Multimedia Encyclopedia. "Armstrong, (Daniel) Louis 'Satchmo.'" Redmond, WA: Microsoft, 1994. CD-ROM.

Online Sources

The fifteenth edition of *The Chicago Manual of Style* specifically addresses the documentation of electronic and online sources. In general, citations for electronic sources include all of the information required for print sources, in addition to a URL and, in some cases, the date of access. There are three key differences between Chicago- and MLA-style online citations:

- Chicago requires URLs for all online sources. They should not be enclosed in angle brackets.
- Months are not abbreviated, and the date is usually given in the following order: month, day, year (September 13, 2008).
- Dates of access are necessary only for sites that are frequently updated (such as news media sites or blogs) and for books.

29. Online book   Include the date of access in parentheses.

NOTE

> 35. Carl Sandburg, *Chicago Poems* (New York: Henry Holt, 1916), http://www.bartleby.com/165/index.html (accessed March 18, 2008).

BIBLIOGRAPHY ENTRY

> Sandburg, Carl. *Chicago Poems*. New York: Henry Holt, 1916. http://www.bartleby.com/165/index.html (accessed March 18, 2008).

30. Partial or entire Web site   Identify as many of the following as you can: author (if any), title of short work or page (if applicable), title or sponsor of site, and URL.

NOTES

> 36. Bruce Boyd Raeburn, "An Introduction to New Orleans Jazz," *William Ransom Hogan Archive of New Orleans Jazz*, http://www.tulane.edu/~lmiller/BeginnersIntro.html.

> 37. Tulane University, *William Ransom Hogan Archive of New Orleans Jazz*, http://www.tulane.edu/~lmiller/JazzHome.html.

BIBLIOGRAPHY ENTRIES

> Raeburn, Bruce Boyd. "An Introduction to New Orleans Jazz." *William Ransom Hogan Archive of New Orleans Jazz*. http://www.tulane.edu/~lmiller/BeginnersIntro.html.

> Tulane University. *William Ransom Hogan Archive of New Orleans Jazz*. http://www.tulane.edu/~lmiller/JazzHome.html.

31. Article from an online journal, magazine, or newspaper
Include the date of access if required or if the material is time sensitive.

435

NOTES

38. Janet Schmalfeldt, "On Keeping the Score," *Music Theory Online* 4, no. 2 (1998), http://www.societymusictheory.org/mto/issues/mto.98.4.2/mto.98.4.2.schmalfeldt_frames.html.

39. Michael E. Ross, "The New Sultans of Swing," *Salon,* April 18, 1996, http://www.salon.com/weekly/music1.html.

40. Don Heckman, "Jazz, Pop in Spirited Harmony," *Los Angeles Times,* August 10, 2005, http://articles.latimes.com/2005/08/10/calendar/et-hancock10 (accessed August 12, 2008).

BIBLIOGRAPHY ENTRIES

Schmalfeldt, Janet. "On Keeping the Score." *Music Theory Online* 4, no. 2 (1998). http://www.societymusictheory.org/mto/issues/mto.98.4.2/mto.98.4.2.schmalfeldt_frames.html.

Ross, Michael E. "The New Sultans of Swing." *Salon,* April 18, 1996. http://www.salon.com/weekly/music1.html.

Heckman, Don. "Jazz, Pop in Spirited Harmony." *Los Angeles Times,* August 10, 2005. http://articles.latimes.com/2005/08/10/calendar/et-hancock10 (accessed August 12, 2008).

32. Journal, magazine, or newspaper article from a library subscription database   Give the home page URL. Access date is optional.

41. T. J. Anderson, "Body and Soul: Bob Kaufman's *Golden Sardine,"* *African American Review* 34, no. 2 (Summer 2000): 329–46, http://www.ebsco.com (accessed April 11, 2008).

BIBLIOGRAPHY ENTRY

Anderson, T. J. "Body and Soul: Bob Kaufman's *Golden Sardine." African American Review* 34, no. 2 (Summer 2000): 329–46. http://www.ebsco.com (accessed April 11, 2008).

33. Blog posting

NOTE

42. Rich Copley, "Major Universities Can Have a Major Impact on Local Arts," *Flyover,* March 15, 2008, http://www.artsjournal.com/flyover/2008/03/major_universities_can_have_a.html (accessed March 18, 2008).

BIBLIOGRAPHY ENTRY

Copley, Rich. "Major Universities Can Have a Major Impact on Local Arts." *Flyover.*
March 15, 2008. http://www.artsjournal.com/flyover/2008/03/major_
universities_can_have_a.html (accessed March 18, 2008).

34. E-mail to discussion list   Give the URL if the posting is archived.
Do not create a bibliography entry.

NOTE

43. Roland Kayser, e-mail to Opera-L mailing list, January 3, 2008, http://
listserv.bccls.org/cgi-bin/wa?A2=ind0801A&L=OPERA-L&D=0&P=57634.

35. Podcast

NOTE

44. Fresh Sounds [pseud.], "Bing Crosby Meets Louis Armstrong," *Jazzarific:
Jazz Vinyl Podcast*, http://jazzvinyl.podomatic.com/entry/2006-12-26T10_29_
06-08_00.

BIBLIOGRAPHY ENTRY

Fresh Sounds [pseud.]. "Bing Crosby Meets Louis Armstrong." *Jazzarific: Jazz Vinyl
Podcast.* http://jazzvinyl.podomatic.com/entry/2006-12-26T10_29_06-08_00.

25d Sample from a student paper in Chicago style.

The following excerpt from Esther Hoffman's paper on Louis
Armstrong has been adapted and put into Chicago style so that you
can see how citation numbers, endnotes, and bibliography work
together. (*Hoffman's entire paper, in MLA style, can be found on
pages 379–90.*)

Chicago style allows you the option of including a title page. If
you do provide a title page, count it as page 1, but do not include
the number on the page. Put page numbers in the upper right-hand
corner of the remaining pages, except for the pages with the titles
"Notes" and "Bibliography" or "Works Cited"; on these pages, the
number should be centered at the bottom of the page.

www.mhhe.com/
mhhb2

For a complete
sample paper in
Chicago style, go to

Research > sample
Research papers >
CMS Style

2

Louis Armstrong's life seems like a classic American success story. From humble beginnings Armstrong rose to become an international superstar, a so-called King of Jazz, and a familiar figure forty years after his death in 1971. Less well known is Joe Glaser, Armstrong's longtime manager. Yet Armstrong once credited his accomplishments to Glaser, saying, "Anything that I have done musically since I signed up with Joe Glaser at the Sunset, it was his suggestions."[1] Was Glaser really as central to Armstrong's work and life as this comment makes him seem? Did he dominate his famous client? Considered in the context of the Jazz Age and each man's background, the relationship between Armstrong and Glaser actually appears to have been a remarkably equitable and successful partnership.

In the 1920s, jazz music was at its height in creativity and popularity. Chicago had become one of the jazz capitals of America, and its clubs showcased the premier talents of the time, performers like Jelly Roll Morton and Joe Oliver. Eager for fame and fortune, many young black musicians who had honed their craft in New Orleans "were drawn to Chicago, New York, Los Angeles, and other cities by the chance to make a career and . . . a living."[2]

Among these émigrés was Louis Armstrong, a gifted musician who developed into "perhaps the best [jazz musician] that has ever been."[3] Armstrong played the trumpet and sang with unusual improvisational ability as well as technical mastery. As biographer Laurence Bergreen points out, Armstrong easily reached difficult high notes, the F's and G's that stymied other trumpeters.[4] His innovative singing style featured "scat," a technique that "place[s] emphasis on the human voice as an additionally important component in jazz music."[5] Eventually, Armstrong's innovations became the standard, as more and more jazz musicians took their cue from his style.

3

Armstrong's beginnings give no hint of the greatness that he would achieve. In New Orleans, he was born into poverty and received little formal education. As a youngster, Armstrong had to take odd jobs like delivering coal and selling newspapers so that he could earn money to help his family. At the age of twelve, Armstrong was placed in the Colored Waifs' Home to serve an eighteen-month sentence for firing a gun in a public place. There "Captain" Peter Davis gave him "basic musical training on the cornet."[6] Older, more established musicians soon noticed Armstrong's talent and offered him opportunities to play with them. In 1922, Joe Oliver invited Armstrong to join his band in Chicago, and the twenty-one-year-old trumpeter headed north.

It was in Chicago that Armstrong met Joe Glaser. According to Bergreen, Glaser had a reputation for being a tough but trustworthy guy who could handle any situation. He was raised in a middle-class home by parents who were Jewish immigrants from Russia. As a young man, Glaser got caught up in the Chicago underworld and soon had a rap sheet that included indictments for running a brothel as well as for statutory rape.[7] Glaser's mob connections also led to his involvement in Chicago's club scene, a business almost completely controlled by gangsters like Al Capone. During the era of Prohibition, Glaser managed the Sunset Café, a club where Armstrong often performed:

> There was a pronounced gangster element at the Sunset, but Louis, accustomed to being employed and protected by mobsters, didn't think twice about that. Mr. Capone's men ensured the flow of alcohol, and their presence reassured many whites.[8]

Notes

1. Max Jones and John Chilton, *Louis: The Louis Armstrong Story, 1900–1971* (Boston: Little, Brown, 1971), 175.

2. James N. Gregory, *The Southern Diaspora: How the Great Migrations of Black and White Southerners Transformed America* (Chapel Hill: University of North Carolina Press, 2007), 139.

3. New Orleans Tourism Marketing Corporation, "Louis Armstrong," *New Orleans Online,* http://www.neworleansonline. com/neworleans/music/musichistory/musicgreats/satchmo.html.

4. Laurence Bergreen, *Louis Armstrong: An Extravagant Life* (New York: Broadway Books, 1997), 248.

5. T. J. Anderson, "Body and Soul: Bob Kaufman's *Golden Sardine,"African American Review* 34, no. 2 (2000): 329–46, http://www.ebsco.com (accessed April 11, 2008).

6. New Orleans Tourism Marketing Corporation, "Louis Armstrong."

7. Bergreen, 372–76.

8. Ibid., 279.

Bibliography

Anderson, T. J. "Body and Soul: Bob Kaufman's *Golden Sardine.*" *African American Review* 34, no. 2 (2000): 329–46. http://www.ebsco.com (accessed April 11, 2008).

Armstrong, Louis. "Authentic American Genius." Interview by Richard Meryman. *Life,* April 15, 1966, 92–102.

———. Louis Armstrong Archives. Rosenthal Library, Queens College CUNY, Flushing, NY.

———. *Town Hall Concert Plus.* RCA INTS 5070.

Bergreen, Laurence. *Louis Armstrong: An Extravagant Life.* New York: Broadway Books, 1997.

Bogle, Donald. "Louis Armstrong: The Films." In *Louis Armstrong: A Cultural Legacy,* edited by Marc H. Miller, 147–79. Seattle: University of Washington Press and Queens Museum of Art, 1994.

Collier, James Lincoln. *Jazz: The American Theme Song.* New York: Oxford University Press, 1993.

———. *Louis Armstrong: An American Genius.* New York: Oxford University Press, 1983.

Crawford, Richard. Foreword to *The Jazz Tradition,* by Martin Williams. New York: Oxford University Press, 1993.

Davis, Miles, and Quincy Troupe. *Miles: The Autobiography.* New York: Simon & Schuster, 1989.

Gregory, James, N. *The Southern Diaspora: How the Great Migrations of Black and White Southerners Transformed America.* Chapel Hill: University of North Carolina Press, 2007.

Jones, Max, and John Chilton. *Louis: The Louis Armstrong Story, 1900–1971.* Boston: Little, Brown, 1971.

Morgenstern, Dan. "Louis Armstrong and the Development and Diffusion of Jazz." In *Louis Armstrong: A Cultural Legacy,* edited by Marc H. Miller, 95–145. Seattle: University of Washington Press and Queens Museum of Art, 1994.

Writer includes *all* sources she consulted, not just those she cited in the body of her paper.

12

26 CSE Documentation Style

The Council of Science Editors (CSE) endorses three documentation styles in the seventh edition of *Scientific Style and Format: The CSE Manual for Authors, Editors, and Publishers* (Reston, VA: CSE, 2006):

- The **name-year style** includes the last name of the author and year of publication in the text. In the list of references, sources are in alphabetical order and unnumbered.

- The **citation-sequence style** includes a superscript number or a number in parentheses in the text. In the list of references, sources are numbered and appear in order of citation.

- The **citation-name style** also uses a superscript number or a number in parentheses in the text. In the list of references, however, sources are numbered and arranged in alphabetical order.

Learn your instructor's preferred style and use it consistently within a paper. Also ask your instructor about line spacing, headings, and other design elements, which the CSE manual does not specify.

www.mhhe.com/ mhhb2

For links to Web sites for documentation styles used in various disciplines, go to

Research > Links to Documentation Sites

26a CSE style: In-text citations

Name-year style   Include the author's last name and the year of publication.

> According to Gleeson (1993), a woman loses 35% of cortical bone and 50% of trabecular bone during her lifetime.

> In epidemiologic studies, small increases in BMD and decreases in fracture risk have been reported in individuals using NSAIDS (Raisz 2001; Carbone et al. 2003).

Citation-sequence or citation-name style   Insert a superscript number immediately after the relevant name, word, or phrase, and before any punctuation. Put a space before and after the superscript unless a punctuation mark follows.

> As a group, American women over 45 years of age sustain approximately 1 million fractures each year, 70% of which are due to osteoporosis [1].

That number now belongs to that source, and you should use it if you refer to that source again in your paper.

According to Gleeson [6], a woman loses 35% of cortical bone and 50% of trabecular bone over her lifetime.

Credit more than one source at a time by referring to each source's number. Separate the numbers with a comma.

According to studies by Yomo [2], Paleg [3], and others [1,4], barley seed embryos produce a substance that stimulates the release of hydrolytic enzymes.

If more than two numbers are in sequence, however, separate them with a hyphen.

As several others [1-4] have documented, GA has an RNA-enhancing effect.

26b CSE style: List of references

Every source cited in your paper must correspond to an entry in your list of references, which should be prepared according to the guidelines in the box on page 444.

CSE STYLE: DIRECTORY to SAMPLE TYPES

Books, Reports, and Papers

1. Book with one author *444*
2. Book with two or more authors *445*
3. Book with organization as author *445*
4. Chapter in a book *445*
5. Book with editor(s) *445*
6. Selection in an edited book *446*
7. Technical report or government document *446*
8. Paper in conference proceedings *446*
9. Dissertation *447*

Periodicals

10. Article in a journal that uses only volume numbers *447*
11. Article in a journal that uses volume and issue numbers *447*
12. Article in a magazine *448*

Online Sources

13. Article in an online journal *448*
14. Online book (monograph) *448*
15. Material from a Web site *449*
16. Material from a library subscription database *449*

- Begin on a new page after your text but before any appendices, tables, and figures.
- Use the centered title "References."
- Include only references that are cited in your paper.
- Start each entry with the author's last name, followed by initials for first and middle names. Add no spaces or periods between initials.
- Abbreviate periodical titles as shown in the CSE manual, and capitalize major words.
- Use complete book and article titles; capitalize the first word and any proper nouns or proper adjectives.
- Do not use italics, underlining, or quotation marks to set off any kind of title.
- List the extent of a source (number of pages or screens) at the end of the entry if your instructor requires it.

Name-Year Style

- Always put the date after the author's name.
- List the references in alphabetical order, but do not number them.

Citation-Sequence Style

- Put the date after the name of the book publisher or periodical.
- List and number the references in the order they first appear in the text.

Citation-Name Style

- Put the date after the name of the book publisher or periodical.
- List and number the references in alphabetical order. Make the numbering of your in-text citations match.

Books, Reports, and Papers

In *name-year style*, include the author(s), last name first; publication year; title; place; and publisher. In *citation-sequence* or *citation-name style*, include the same information, but put the year after the publisher.

1. Book with one author

NAME-YEAR

Bailey C. 1991. The new fit or fat. Boston (MA): Houghton Mifflin.

CITATION-SEQUENCE OR CITATION-NAME

1. Bailey C. The new fit or fat. Boston (MA): Houghton Mifflin; 1991.

2. Book with two or more authors
List up to ten authors; if there are more than ten, use the first ten names with the phrase *and others* or *et al.* (not italicized).

NAME-YEAR

Begon M, Harper JL, Townsend CR. 1990. Ecology: individuals, populations, and communities. 2nd ed. Boston (MA): Blackwell.

CITATION-SEQUENCE OR CITATION-NAME

2. Begon M, Harper JL, Townsend CR. Ecology: individuals, populations, and communities. 2nd ed. Boston (MA): Blackwell; 1990.

3. Book with organization as author
In *name-year style*, start the entry with the organization's abbreviation, but alphabetize by the full name.

NAME-YEAR

[NIH] National Institutes of Health (US). 1993. Clinical trials supported by the National Eye Institute (US): celebrating vision research. Bethesda (MD): US Dept. of Health and Human Services.

CITATION-SEQUENCE OR CITATION-NAME

3. National Institutes of Health (US). Clinical trials supported by the National Eye Institute (US): celebrating vision research. Bethesda (MD): US Dept. of Health and Human Services; 1993.

4. Chapter in a book

NAME-YEAR

O'Connell C. 2007. The elephant's secret sense: the hidden life of the wild herds of Africa. New York: Free Press. Chapter 9, Cracking elephant Morse code; p. 119-126.

CITATION-SEQUENCE OR CITATION-NAME

4. O'Connell C. The elephant's secret sense: the hidden life of the wild herds of Africa. New York: Free Press; 2007. Chapter 9, Cracking elephant Morse code; p. 119-126.

5. Book with editor(s)

NAME-YEAR

Wilder E, editor. 1988. Obstetric and gynecologic physical therapy. New York: Churchill Livingstone.

CITATION-SEQUENCE OR CITATION-NAME

5. Wilder E, editor. Obstetric and gynecologic physical therapy. New York: Churchill Livingstone; 1988.

6. Selection in an edited book

NAME-YEAR

Bohus B, Koolhaas JM. 1993. Psychoimmunology of social factors in rodents and other subprimate vertebrates. In: Ader R, Felten DL, Cohen N, editors. Psychoneuroimmunology. San Diego (CA): Academic Press. p. 807-830.

CITATION-SEQUENCE OR CITATION-NAME

6. Bohus B, Koolhaas JM. Psychoimmunology of social factors in rodents and other subprimate vertebrates. In: Ader R, Felten DL, Cohen N, editors. Psychoneuroimmunology. San Diego (CA): Academic Press; 1993. p. 807-830.

7. Technical report or government document Include the name of the sponsoring organization or agency as well as any report or contract number.

NAME-YEAR

Bolen S, Wilson L, Vassy J, Feldman L, Yeh J, Marinopoulos S, Wilson R, Cheng D, Wiley C, Selvin E, et al. (Johns Hopkins University Evidence-based Practice Center, Baltimore, MD). 2007. Comparative effectiveness and safety of oral diabetes medications for adults with type 2 diabetes. Comparative effectiveness review No. 8. Rockville (MD): Agency for Healthcare Research and Quality (US). Contract No.: 290-02-0018. Available from: AHRQ, Rockville, MD; AHRQ Pub. No. 07-EHC010-1.

CITATION-SEQUENCE OR CITATION-NAME

7. Bolen S, Wilson L, Vassy J, Feldman L, Yeh J, Marinopoulos S, Wilson R, Cheng D, Wiley C, Selvin E, et al. (Johns Hopkins University Evidence-based Practice Center, Baltimore, MD). Comparative effectiveness and safety of oral diabetes medications for adults with type 2 diabetes. Comparative effectiveness review No. 8. Rockville (MD): Agency for Healthcare Research and Quality (US); 2007. Contract No.: 290-02-0018. Available from: AHRQ, Rockville, MD; AHRQ Pub. No. 07-EHC010-1.

8. Paper in conference proceedings

NAME-YEAR

De Jong E, Franke L, Siebes A. c2007. On the measurement of genetic interactions. In: Berthold MR, Glen RC, Feelders AJ, editors. Proceedings of the AIP 940. 3rd International Symposium on Computational Life Science; 2007 Oct 4-5; Utrecht (Netherlands). Melville (NY): American Institute of Physics. p. 16-25.

8. De Jong E, Franke L, Siebes A. On the measurement of genetic interactions. In: Berthold MR, Glen RC, Feelders AJ, editors. Proceedings of the AIP 940. 3rd International Symposium on Computational Life Science; 2007 Oct 4-5; Utrecht (Netherlands). Melville (NY): American Institute of Physics; c2007. p. 16-25.

9. Dissertation

NAME-YEAR

Bertrand KN. 2007. Fishes and floods: stream ecosystem drivers in the Great Plains [dissertation]. [Manhattan (KS)]: Kansas State University.

CITATION-SEQUENCE OR CITATION-NAME

9. Bertrand KN. Fishes and floods: stream ecosystem drivers in the Great Plains [dissertation]. [Manhattan (KS)]: Kansas State University; 2007.

Periodicals

When listing most periodical articles, include the author(s); year; title of article; title of journal (abbreviated); number of the volume; number of the issue, if available (in parentheses); and page numbers. In *name-year style*, put the year after the author(s). In *citation-sequence* or *citation-name style*, put the year after the journal title.

Up to ten authors can be listed by name. If you cannot determine the article's author, begin with the title.

10. Article in a journal that uses only volume numbers

NAME-YEAR

Devine A, Prince RL, Bell R. 1996. Nutritional effect of calcium supplementation by skim milk powder or calcium tablets on total nutrient intake in postmenopausal women. Am J Clin Nutr. 64:731-737.

CITATION-SEQUENCE OR CITATION-NAME

10. Devine A, Prince RL, Bell R. Nutritional effect of calcium supplementation by skim milk powder or calcium tablets on total nutrient intake in postmenopausal women. Am J Clin Nutr. 1996;64:731-737.

11. Article in a journal that uses volume and issue numbers

NAME-YEAR

Hummel-Berry K. 1990. Obstetric low back pain, a comprehensive review, part 2: evaluation and treatment. J Ob Gyn PT. 14(2):9-11.

CITATION-SEQUENCE OR CITATION-NAME

> 11. Hummel-Berry K. Obstetric low back pain, a comprehensive review, part 2: evaluation and treatment. J Ob Gyn PT. 1990;14(2):9-11.

12. Article in a magazine   Indicate the year, month, and day (if available) of publication.

NAME-YEAR

> Sternfeld B. 1997 Jan 1. Physical activity and pregnancy outcome. Review and recommendations. Sports Med. 33-47.

CITATION-SEQUENCE OR CITATION-NAME

> 12. Sternfeld B. Physical activity and pregnancy outcome. Review and recommendations. Sports Med. 1997 Jan 1:33-47.

Online Sources

Include information on author, title, and so forth, as with print works. Follow these special guidelines:

- Indicate the medium in brackets: [*Internet*] (not italicized).
- Include in brackets the date of the most recent update (if any) and the date you viewed the source.
- List the publisher or the sponsor, or use the bracketed phrase [*publisher unknown*] (not italicized).
- To include length of a document without page numbers, use designations such as [*16 paragraphs*] or [*4 screens*] (neither italicized).
- List the URL at the end of the reference, preceded by the phrase *Available from* (not italicized). Do not put a period after a URL unless it ends with a slash.

The following examples are in the citation-sequence or citation-name style. For name-year style, list the publication date after the author's name and do not number your references.

13. Article in an online journal

> 13. Krieger D, Onodipe S, Charles PJ, Sclabassi RJ. Real time signal processing in the clinical setting. Ann Biomed Engn [Internet]. 1998 [cited 2007 Oct 19]; 26(3): 462-472. Available from: http://www.springerlink.com/content/n31828q461h54282

14. Online book (monograph)

> 14. Kohn LT, Corrigan JM, Donaldson MS, editors. To err is human: building a safer health system [Internet]. Washington (DC): National Academy Press; c2000 [cited 2007 Oct 19]. Available from: http://www.nap.edu/books/0309068371/html

15. Material from a Web site

15. Hutchinson JR. Vertebrate flight [Internet]. Berkeley (CA): University of California; c1994-2008 [modified 2005 Sep 29; cited 2008 Jan 15]. Available from: http://www.ucmp.berkeley.edu/vertebrates/flight/flightintro.html

16. Material from a library subscription database   CSE does not specify a format. Give the information for a print article with database title and publication information.

16. Baccarelli A, Zanobetti A, Martinelli I, Grillo P, Lifang H, Lanzani G, Mannucci PM, Bertazzi PA, Schwartz, J. Air pollution, smoking, and plasma homocysteine. Environ Health Perspect [Internet]. 2007 Feb [cited 2007 Oct 23];115(2):176-181. Health Source: Nursing/Academic Edition. Birmingham (AL): EBSCO. Available from: http://www.ebsco.com

26c   Sample references list: CSE name-year style

www.mhhe.com/mhhb2
For the complete sample paper that includes these, go to
Research > Sample Research Papers > CSE Style

References

Anderson A. 1991. Early bird threatens archaeopteryx's perch. Science. 253(5015):35.

Geist N, Feduccia A. 2000. Gravity-defying behaviors: identifying models for protoaves. Am Zoologist. 40(4):664-675.

Goslow GE, Dial KP, Jenkins FA. 1990. Bird flight: insights and complications. Bioscience. 40(2):108-116.

Hinchliffe R. 1997. Evolution: the forward march of the bird-dinosaurs halted? Science. 278(5338):597-599.

Hutchinson JR. Vertebrate flight [Internet]. c1994-2008. Berkeley (CA): University of California; [modified 2005 Sep 29; cited 2008 Jan 15]. Available from: http://www.ucmp.berkeley.edu/vertebrates/flight/flightintro.html

Liem K, Bernis W, Walker W, Grande L. 2001. Functional anatomy of the vertebrates: an evolutionary perspective. New York: Harcourt College Publishers.

Padian K. 2001. Cross testing adaptive hypothesis: phylogenetic analysis and the origin of bird flight. Am Zoologist. 41(30):598-607.

(Read the complete student paper on *www.mhhe.com/mhhb2.*)

www.mhhe.com/
mhhb2
For the complete
sample paper that
include these, go to
Research > Sample
Research Papers >
CSE Style

26d Sample references list: CSE citation-name style

Here are the same references as in 26c but in citation-name style, listed and numbered in alphabetical order. Citation-sequence style would look the same, but entries would be in the order in which they were cited in the paper.

References

1. Anderson A. Early bird threatens archaeopteryx's perch. Science. 1991;253(5015):35.

2. Geist N, Feduccia A. Gravity-defying behaviors: identifying models for protoaves. Am Zoologist. 2000;40(4):664-675.

3. Goslow GE, Dial KP, Jenkins FA. Bird flight: insights and complications. Bioscience. 1990;40(2):108-116.

4. Hinchliffe R. Evolution: the forward march of the bird-dinosaurs halted? Science. 1997;278(5338):597-599.

5. Hutchinson JR. Vertebrate flight [Internet]. Berkeley (CA): University of California; c1994-2008 [modified 2005 Sep 29; cited 2008 Jan 15]. Available from: http://www.ucmp.berkeley .edu/vertebrates/flight/flightintro.html

6. Liem K, Bernis W, Walker W, Grande L. Functional anatomy of the vertebrates: an evolutionary perspective. New York: Harcourt College Publishers; 2001.

7. Padian K. Cross testing adaptive hypothesis: phylogenetic analysis and the origin of bird flight. Am Zoologist. 2001; 41(30):598-607.

The content and design of this page from one of the National Audubon Society's annual reports shows donors how their money helps this environmental organization— and why its cause matters.

The aim of education must be the training of independently acting and thinking individuals, who, however, see in the service of the community their highest life problem.
—ALBERT EINSTEIN

Writing
beyond College

27 Service Learning and Community-Service Writing

s road, writing is a way of connecting classroom, work-
nmunity.

27a Address the community on behalf of your organization.

Your ability to research and write can be of great value to organizations that serve the community. Courses at every level of the university, as well as extracurricular activities, offer opportunities to work
with organizations such as homeless shelters, tutoring centers, and
environmental groups. If you are writing a newsletter, press release, or
funding proposal for a community group, ask yourself these questions:

- What do community members talk about?
- How do they talk about these issues, and why?
- Who is an outsider (member of the community), and who is
  an insider (member of the organization)?
- How can I best write from the inside to the outside?

Your answers will help you shape your writing so that it reaches its
intended audience and moves the members of that audience to action.

WRITING OUTCOMES

Part 5: Writing beyond College
This section will help you answer questions such as:

Rhetorical Knowledge
- What is community-service writing? **(27a)**
- What should I consider when writing professional e-mail? **(29e)**

Critical Thinking, Reading, and Writing
- What kind of writing can help me address an issue in my
  community? **(28a)**
- How can I write an effective letter of complaint? **(28b)**

Processes
- How do I apply for a job? **(29b, c, d)**
- What are some online resources for job-hunting? **(29e)**

Knowledge of Conventions
- What should go on my résumé? **(29b)**
- How should I format my résumé and cover letter? **(29b, c)**

WRITING beyond COLLEGE

A Writer at Work

When Laura Amabisca entered Glendale Community College, she volunteered to be a tutor in the writing center. Upon transferring to Arizona State University West, she joined the Writing Tutors' Club. She also became a mentor for other Glendale Community College students who were trying to build the confidence to transfer to the university.

In a course in advanced expository writing, she drew on these experiences for an essay on the special needs of community-college transfer students. She also wrote a letter on the same theme to the student newspaper.

The sense of involvement Amabisca felt about her on-campus service motivated her to visit the ASU West Volunteer Office. She then became a volunteer for America Reads, a national literacy project. The Phoenix office of America Reads asked Amabisca to help design a public relations campaign. Amabisca volunteered to draft a brochure to convince other college students to join the project. In this way, she moved from involvement on her own campus to service in the wider community.

Writing on behalf of a community organization almost always involves negotiation and collaboration. A community organization may revise your draft to fit its needs. In these situations, having a cooperative attitude is as important as having strong writing skills.

Even if you are not writing on behalf of a group, you can still do community-service writing. You can write in your own name to raise an issue of concern to the community in a public forum; for example, you might write a newspaper editorial or a letter to a public official (*see Chapter 28: Letters to Raise Awareness and Share Concern*).

 27b Design brochures, newsletters, and posters with an eye to purpose and audience.

www.mhhe.com/
mhhb2

For interactive help
with document
design, go to

Writing >
Visual Rhetoric >
Document Design

If you are participating in a service learning program or an internship, you may have opportunities to design brochures and newsletters for wide distribution and posters to create awareness and promote events. To create an effective brochure, newsletter, or poster, you will need to integrate your skills in document design with what you have learned about purpose and audience.

Here are a few tips:

1. Consider how your reader will access the pages of the brochure or newsletter. Will it be distributed by mail? By hand? Electronically? What are the implications for the overall design?

2. It may be a good idea to sketch the design in pencil so that you have a plan before you start using the high-tech capabilities of the computer.

3. In making decisions about photographs, illustrations, type faces, and the design in general, think about the overall image you want to convey about the sponsoring organization.

4. If the organization has a logo, include it; if not, suggest designing one. A logo is a small visual symbol, like the Nike "swoosh" or the distinctive font used for Coca-Cola.

5. Set up a template for a brochure or newsletter so that you can create future editions easily. In word-processing and document-design programs, a template is a blank document that includes all of the formatting and codes a specific document requires. When you use a template, you just "plug in" new content and visuals—the format and design are already done.

For example, notice how the brochure for the PSFS Building in Philadelphia, Pennsylvania, shown in Figure 27.1, purposefully connects the history and importance of an architectural landmark with the prestige of Loews Hotel, into which "the world's first Modernist skyscraper" has been renovated. The brochure has an informative and also a subtly persuasive purpose. Its intent is to make readers feel that by staying at the Loews Philadelphia Hotel, they will be participating in a great tradition. The front cover is divided in half, with a striking photo of the building on the left side and an account of its history on the right. The name of the hotel appears in white letters near the bottom of the page. The interior page places a vintage photo of the revered banking establishment next to an image of hotel comfort. On both pages, quotations running vertically beside the photographs reinforce the building's architectural significance.

The Harvard Medical School newsletter entitled "Women's Health Watch," shown in Figure 27.2 on page 456, has a simple, clear design. The designer keeps in mind the newsletter's purpose and audience, which are explicitly stated in the title and the headline below it. The shaded area on the right lists the topics that are covered on the interior pages so that readers can get to the information they need quickly and easily. The Web address is prominently displayed in blue so that readers can find more information. The lead article, "Does Excess Vitamin A Cause Hip Fracture?" is designed simply in two columns, with the headline in bold type, subheadings in blue, a readable typeface, and a graphic strategically placed to break up the text and add visual interest. In all these ways, the design supports the Harvard Medical School's purpose of informing the general public about advances in medical research. (*For more information on document design, see Chapter 6, Designing Academic Papers and Preparing Portfolios, pp. 104–17.*)

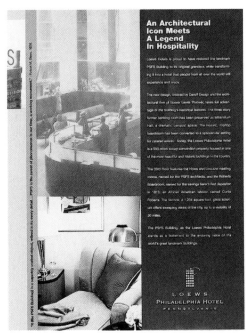

FIGURE 27.1 Example of a brochure.

HARVARD
Women's Health Watch

INFORMATION FOR ENLIGHTENED CHOICES FROM HARVARD MEDICAL SCHOOL

Does Excess Vitamin A Cause Hip Fracture?

Hip fracture is one of the most dreaded risks of aging. More than 350,000 hip fractures occur annually in the United States, mostly in women over 65. Half of these women never regain the ability to live independently. About 20% die within a year. Many others suffer chronic pain, anxiety, and depression. The consequences are so grim that many older women contacted in surveys on this subject say they'd rather die than suffer a hip fracture that would send them to a nursing home.

Current recommendations on reducing fracture risk advise women to exercise, make sure they get enough calcium and vitamin D, and, if necessary, take medications that help preserve bone strength. Some women also learn strategies for preventing falls or take classes such as tai chi to improve their balance. Now, a new study suggests that we should also pay attention to vitamin A. At high levels, this essential nutrient may actually increase our risk for hip fracture.

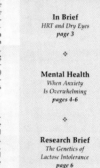

15% of women age 50 will suffer a hip fracture before age 80.

NEW STUDY FINDS LINK

Researchers at Harvard Medical School reported in the Jan. 2, 2002, *Journal of the American Medical Association* on the relationship between postmenopausal hip fracture and vitamin A intake. The data came from 72,337 women enrolled in the Nurses' Health Study. The women were divided into five groups according to their average daily consumption, over an 18-year period, of vitamin A from food and supplements.

Researchers then correlated vitamin A intake with hip fracture incidence. They found that women with the highest intake—3,000 micrograms (mcg) or more per day—had a 48% greater risk for hip fractures, compared to women with the lowest intake (1,250 mcg or less per day).

The increased risk was mainly due to *retinol*, a particular form of vitamin A. In fact, women consuming 2,000 mcg of retinol or more daily had a hip fracture risk almost *double* that of women whose daily intake was under 500 mcg. In contrast, consuming high levels of *beta-carotene*, also a source of vitamin A, had a negligible impact on hip fracture risk. Participants taking hormone replacement therapy (HRT) were somewhat protected from the effects of too much retinol.

ABOUT VITAMIN A

Vitamin A is important for vision, the immune system, and the growth of bone, hair, and skin cells. Retinol, also called "preformed vitamin A," is the active form of the vitamin. It occurs naturally in animal products such as eggs, whole milk, cheese, and liver. Other food sources of vitamin A are *carotenoids*, which are found in green leafy vegetables and in dark yellow or orange fruits and vegetables. The body can convert these plant compounds to retinol. Beta-carotene is the most plentiful carotenoid and it converts most efficiently. Even so, you need about 12 times as much beta-carotene as retinol to get the same amount of vitamin A.

Because vitamin A is lost in the process of removing fat, many fat-free dairy products are fortified with retinol. So are some margarines and ready-to-eat cereals. The vitamin A in supplements and multivitamins may come from retinol, beta-carotene, or both. Beta-carotene is preferable because it's also an antioxidant.

Although vitamin A deficiency is a leading cause of blindness in developing countries, it's not a major problem in the United States. The main concern here is excess vitamin A, which can produce birth defects, liver damage, and reduced bone mineral density (BMD). ▭

**Volume IX Number 7
March 2002**

In Brief
HRT and Dry Eyes
page 3

❖

Mental Health
*When Anxiety
Is Overwhelming*
pages 4–6

❖

Research Brief
*The Genetics of
Lactose Intolerance*
page 6

❖

Massage
*Massage Is More Than
an Indulgence*
page 7

❖

By the Way, Doctor
*Should I Still Get
Mammograms?*
page 8

www.health.harvard.edu

FIGURE 27.2 Example of a well-designed newsletter.

28 Letters to Raise Awareness and Share Concern

Your ability to write and your willingness to share your opinions and insight can influence community events and affect the way businesses treat you. A letter to a local politician regarding a current issue or to a corporation regarding customer service can accomplish much if clearly argued, concisely phrased, and appropriately directed.

28a Write about a public issue.

Your task in writing to a newspaper, community organization, or public figure is to present yourself as a polite, engaged, and reasonable person who is invested in a particular issue and who can offer a compelling case for a particular course of action.

Most publications, corporations, and nonprofit organizations include forms, links, or e-mail addresses on their Web sites for submitting letters or comments. Whenever possible, use online options instead of writing a print letter. Here are some guidelines:

- Address the appropriate person or department by name. Consult the organization's Web site for this information.

- Concisely state your area of concern in the subject line.

- Include your message in the body of your e-mail, not as an attachment: an organization's server may screen out your message as spam.

- Keep it brief. Many organizations and corporations receive millions of e-mails each week. Most publications post specific word-count limits for letters to the editor or comments.

- Follow the conventions of professional e-mail (*see pp. 471–73*). Use standard capitalization and punctuation.

- Keep your tone polite and professional (neither combative nor overly chatty).

If you send a print letter, use the following guidelines:

- Address the appropriate person(s). If you are writing to a newspaper or magazine's editorial pages, see how published letters are addressed ("To the editors," for example), and whether guidelines are available. If you are writing to an organization, consult its Web site or call the main number to find out the preferred means of address and submission. It is always best to address your letter to a specific person or department.

- Use the format for a business letter. (*See the business letter in block format on pp. 459–60.*)

457

- Write no more than three or four paragraphs. (E-mails should be shorter.)

Regardless of medium, follow this format:

- In the first paragraph, clearly and briefly state the matter you wish to address and why it is important to you. For example, if you are writing to your local school board, you should state that you are the parent of a child at the local school.

- In the second paragraph, provide clear and compelling evidence for your concern. If relevant, propose a solution.

- In your conclusion, thank the reader for considering your thoughts. Repeat any request for specific action, such as having an item added to the agenda of the next school board meeting. If you want a specific response, politely request an e-mail or telephone call. If you intend to follow up on your letter, note that you will be calling or writing again within a week (or however long is appropriate).

Below and on pages 459–60 are letters by two different writers addressing the same community issue. One e-mailed his local newspaper; the other wrote to the principal of her local school. Note how they tailor their letters for their specific audiences, purposes, and mediums.

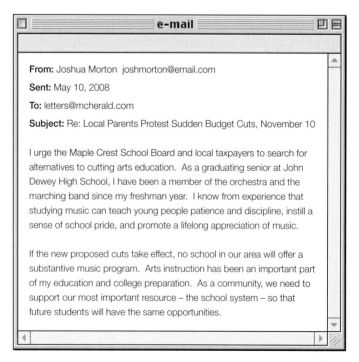

e-mail

From: Joshua Morton joshmorton@email.com

Sent: May 10, 2008

To: letters@mcherald.com

Subject: Re: Local Parents Protest Sudden Budget Cuts, November 10

I urge the Maple Crest School Board and local taxpayers to search for alternatives to cutting arts education. As a graduating senior at John Dewey High School, I have been a member of the orchestra and the marching band since my freshman year. I know from experience that studying music can teach young people patience and discipline, instill a sense of school pride, and promote a lifelong appreciation of music.

If the new proposed cuts take effect, no school in our area will offer a substantive music program. Arts instruction has been an important part of my education and college preparation. As a community, we need to support our most important resource – the school system – so that future students will have the same opportunities.

1324 Owen Drive
Maple Crest, NJ 07405
May 3, 2008

Dr. Joann Malvern
Principal
Middle Park Elementary School
47 Valley Street
Maple Crest, NJ 07405

Dear Dr. Malvern:

I am a parent of two children who attend Middle Park Elementary
School. My son is in the third grade, and my daughter is in the sixth
grade. We have lived in Maple Crest for ten years, and my children
have always attended local schools. We have been delighted with
the attention and opportunities that both children have received
in their classrooms. However, the School Board's proposed
new budget cuts would, I believe, significantly reduce both that
attention and the opportunities all children currently enjoy.

In a letter to all Middle Park parents that was sent home with
children during the last week of April, you outlined changes for
the upcoming school year. The area of greatest concern to me is
the termination of three classroom assistant positions and the
reduction of the music teacher's position from full- to part-time.
You stated that the reason for these reductions was a call from the
Board of Education to cut operating costs for the next school year.

The presence of classroom assistants has helped teachers to maintain
discipline in the classroom as well as offer additional attention
to every child in the classroom. The school's music teacher, Mr.
Jack Delvarez, has inspired both of my children to take up musical
instruments, and all parents look forward to the Fall and Spring
concerts.

I know from my conversations with other Middle Park parents
that we would appreciate the opportunity to suggest alternative
ways to save money and preserve the high quality of education
that Middle Park currently offers. I would like to request that a
special Parent-Teacher Association meeting be held within the next
two weeks in order to discuss the sudden nature of these staffing
changes as well as other options.

1"

Return address and date.

Double space.

Inside address.

Double space.

Salutation.

Double space.

Body—
paragraphs
single-
spaced,
double space
between
paragraphs.

459

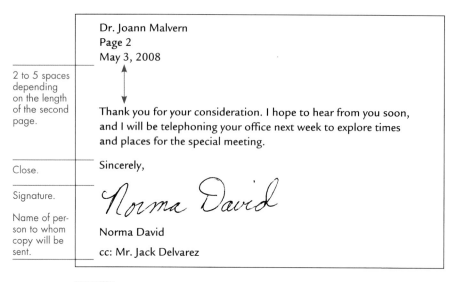

2 to 5 spaces
depending
on the length
of the second
page.

Close.

Signature.

Name of per-
son to whom
copy will be
sent.

Dr. Joann Malvern
Page 2
May 3, 2008

Thank you for your consideration. I hope to hear from you soon, and I will be telephoning your office next week to explore times and places for the special meeting.

Sincerely,

Norma David

Norma David

cc: Mr. Jack Delvarez

28b Write as a consumer.

Your ability to write can influence how you are treated as a client or a customer by large and seemingly faceless organizations. A carefully constructed message can convey a legitimate grievance or express pleasure.

1. Writing a letter of complaint

Suppose you had ordered a product from an online store as a gift, only to find your purchase delayed in transit so that it arrived too late. Following the Customer Service link on the Web site, you compose an e-mail letter of complaint like the one on page 461. In writing such a letter, present yourself as a reasonable person who has experienced unfair treatment. (If you are writing on behalf of your company or as a representative of your company, your letter should state the complaint calmly and propose a resolution.)

Here are some guidelines for writing a letter of complaint.

- If possible, send the complaint via e-mail unless you must submit supporting documentation (such as receipts).
- If you are sending a print letter, use the business format on pp. 459–60.
- Follow any procedures for submitting a complaint specified on the company's Web site.
- Address the letter to the person in charge by name. (If you do not know the correct name and title to use, consult the corporate Web site or call the company.)
- Propose reasonable recompense and enclose receipts, if appropriate. Keep the original receipts and documents,

enclosing photocopies with your letter. Do *not* send scans of receipts as e-mail attachments.

- In the first paragraph, concisely state the problem and the action you request.

- In the following paragraphs, narrate clearly and objectively what happened. Refer to details such as the date and time of the incident so that the person you are writing to can follow up.

- Recognize those who tried to help you as well as those who did not.

- Mention previous positive experiences with the organization, if you can. Your protest will have more credibility if you come across as a person who does not usually complain.

- Conclude by thanking the person you are writing to for his or her time and expressing the hope that you will be able to continue as a customer.

- Send copies to the people whom you mention.

- Keep copies of all correspondence for your records.

Consider, for example, the e-mail below written by Edward Kim.

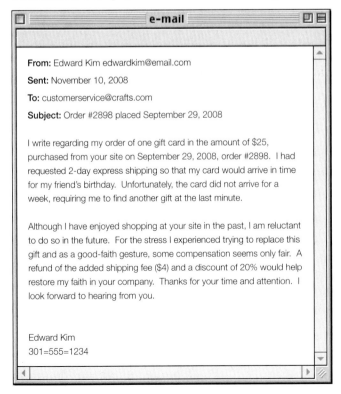

e-mail

From: Edward Kim edwardkim@email.com

Sent: November 10, 2008

To: customerservice@crafts.com

Subject: Order #2898 placed September 29, 2008

I write regarding my order of one gift card in the amount of $25, purchased from your site on September 29, 2008, order #2898. I had requested 2-day express shipping so that my card would arrive in time for my friend's birthday. Unfortunately, the card did not arrive for a week, requiring me to find another gift at the last minute.

Although I have enjoyed shopping at your site in the past, I am reluctant to do so in the future. For the stress I experienced trying to replace this gift and as a good-faith gesture, some compensation seems only fair. A refund of the added shipping fee ($4) and a discount of 20% would help restore my faith in your company. Thanks for your time and attention. I look forward to hearing from you.

Edward Kim
301=555=1234

2. Writing a letter of praise

On the other hand, suppose that you wish to thank an airline employee who has been exceptionally helpful. In the workplace, you might write a letter of praise to a colleague who worked long hours to complete a project, or to congratulate a team for bringing in new clients. The writing techniques are similar for both praise and protest letters.

- Address the letter to the person in charge by name. (If you do not know the correct name and title to use, call the corporate headquarters.)

- If you are sending a print letter, use the format for a business letter.

- In the first paragraph, concisely state the situation and the help that was provided.

- In the following paragraphs, narrate what happened, referring to details such as the date and time of the incident so that the person you are writing to can follow up with the person who helped you.

- Conclude by thanking the person you are writing to for his or her time and expressing your intention to continue doing business with the company.

- Send copies to the people whom you mention (and to the supervisor or human resources department if you are writing to a coworker).

29 Writing to Get and Keep a Job

Like many students, you may already have a job on or off campus, or you may be doing an internship or volunteering for a community-based organization. Strong writing skills will also help you find a good job once you leave college and advance in your chosen career.

29a Explore internship possibilities, and keep a portfolio of career-related writing.

www.mhhe.com/
mhhb2

For more information
on professional
writing, go to

College to Career

An internship, in which you do actual work in your chosen field, is a vital connection between the classroom and the workplace. You gain academic credit for what you learn from the job. Writing and learning go together. During your internship, keep a journal to record and analyze your experiences, as well as a file of any writing you do on the job. Your final project for the internship credit may require you to analyze the file of writing that you have produced.

Files of writing from internships, clippings of articles and editorials you have written for the student newspaper, writing you have done for a community organization—these and other documents demonstrate your ability to apply intellectual concepts to real-world demands. Organized into a portfolio, this material displays your marketable skills. Your campus career resource center may offer assistance in compiling a portfolio. The center may also keep your portfolio on file for you and send it to future employers or graduate schools.

To begin your search for a suitable internship, visit your campus career counseling center. Many local nonprofit organizations, television and radio stations, newspapers, and both small and large companies offer internship opportunities through campus career centers.

Although your internship might pay only a modest amount (or nothing at all), your employer will nonetheless have high expectations of you. If this is your first time working in an office or a professional environment, be sure that you understand not only what is expected of you in terms of work, but also how to fit in with the workplace culture.

- **Always be on time.** Your employer is making an investment in you. Even if you are not being paid, you are learning about a possible career field and picking up invaluable business skills.
- **Dress appropriately.** If, as is likely, you meet with a representative of your employer's human resources

division when you begin work, ask about any dress codes. Even if you are interning in an organization that permits informal or creative attire, it is probably best to dress conservatively.

■ **Understand what is expected.** The first few weeks of an internship might involve nothing more than filing and word processing. Once you have demonstrated your responsibility and efficiency, you might be assigned to work on more complex and interesting projects. Remember, at the end of your internship you want to have a strong reference for future positions.

■ **Ask questions.** If you want to pursue a career in the field in which you are interning, be sure to ask lots of questions of your coworkers. Find out, for example, what additional coursework you should take to prepare. What is an entry-level position like in this field? How do people rise to greater levels of responsibility? What are the field's key issues and challenges?

■ **Request a recommendation.** Ask—politely, and with plenty of advance notice—if your employer would provide you with a letter of recommendation to show potential employers in the future. (Your campus career center will probably keep such letters on file for you and will assist you with your job search after graduation.) Also ask if you may list your supervisor as a reference for future job applications.

29b Keep your résumé up-to-date and available on a computer disk.

A **résumé** is a brief summary of your education and work experience that you send to prospective employers. It is never finished. As you continue to learn, work, and write, you should be rethinking and reorganizing your résumé. You will want to emphasize different accomplishments and talents for different employers. Saving your résumé as a computer file allows you to tailor it to the needs and requirements of its readers.

Your résumé should be designed for quick reading. Expect the person reviewing it to give it no more than sixty seconds at first glance. Make that first impression count. Design a document that is easy to read, attractively formatted, and flawlessly edited.

Guidelines for writing a résumé

Always include the following *necessary* categories in a résumé:

- Heading (name, address, telephone number, e-mail address)
- Education (in reverse chronological order; do not include high school)
- Work experience (in reverse chronological order)
- References (often placed on a separate sheet; for many situations, you can add the line "References available on request" instead)

Include the following *optional* categories as appropriate:

- Objective
- Honors and awards
- Internships
- Activities and service
- Special skills

Sometimes career counselors recommend that you list a career objective right under the heading of your résumé. If you do so, be sure you know what the prospective employer is looking for and tailor your résumé accordingly.

Laura Amabisca has organized the information in her résumé (*p. 466*) by time and by categories. Within each category, she has listed items from the most to least recent. This reverse chronological order gives appropriate emphasis to what she is doing now and has just done. Because she is applying for jobs in public relations, she has highlighted her internship in that field by placing it at the top of her experience section.

The résumé on page 466 reflects appropriate formatting for print. Note the use of a line rule, alignment of text, bullet points, and bold and italic type. These elements organize the information visually, directing the reader's eye appropriately.

Amabisca's scannable résumé (*p. 467*) contains no italics, bold, or other formatting so it may be submitted electronically or entered into an employer's database (*see the box on p. 468*).

Amabisca's entire résumé is just one page. A brief, well-organized résumé is more attractive to potential employers than a rambling, multipage one.

The résumé features active verbs such as *supervised.*

LAURA AMABISCA
20650 North 58th Avenue, Apt. 15A
Glendale, AZ 85308
623-555-7310
lamabisca@peoplelink.com

Objective
To obtain a position as public relations assistant at a not-for-profit organization

Education
Arizona State University West, Phoenix
- Bachelor of Arts, History, Minor in Global Management (May 2008)
- Senior Thesis: Picturing the Hopi, 1920–1940: A Historical Analysis

Glendale Community College, Glendale, AZ (2004–2006)

Experience
Public Relations Office, Arizona State University West
Intern (Summer 2007)
- Researched and reported on university external publications.
- Created original content for print and Web.
- Assisted in planning fundraising campaign and events.

Sears, Bell Road, Phoenix, AZ
Assistant Manager, Sporting Goods Department (2006–present)
- Assist sales manager in day-to-day operations.
- Supervise team of sales associates.
- Ensure quality customer service.

Sales Associate, Sporting Goods Department (2003–2006)
- Recommended products to meet customer needs.
- Processed sales and returns.

Stock Clerk, Sporting Goods Department (2000–2003)
- Received, sorted, and tracked incoming merchandise.
- Stocked shelves to ensure appropriate supply on sales floor.

Special Skills
Language: Bilingual: Spanish/English
Computer: Windows, Mac OS, MS Office, HTML

Activities
America Reads
Tutor, Public Relations Consultant (2007)
- Taught reading to first-grade students.
- Created brochure to recruit tutors.

Multicultural Festival, Arizona State University West
Student Coordinator (2007)
Organized festival of international performances, crafts, and community organizations.

Writing Center, Glendale Community College
Tutor (2004–2006)
Met with peers to help them with writing assignments.

References
Available upon request to Career Services, Arizona State University West

LAURA AMABISCA
20650 North 58th Avenue, Apt. 15A
Glendale, AZ 85308
623-555-7310
lamabisca@peoplelink.com

OBJECTIVE
To obtain a position as public relations assistant at a not-for-profit organization

EDUCATION
Arizona State University West, Phoenix
* Bachelor of Arts, History, Minor in Global Management (May 2008)
* Senior Thesis: Picturing the Hopi, 1920-1940: A Historical Analysis

Glendale Community College, Glendale, AZ (2004–2006)

EXPERIENCE
Public Relations Office, Arizona State University West (Summer 2007)
Intern
* Researched and reported on university external publications.
* Created original content for print and Web.
* Assisted in planning fundraising campaign and events.

Sears, Bell Road, Phoenix, AZ
Assistant Manager, Sporting Goods Department (2006–present)
* Supervise team of sales associates.
* Ensure quality customer service.

Sales Associate, Sporting Goods Department (2003–2006)
* Recommended products to meet customer needs.
* Processed sales and returns.

Stock Clerk, Sporting Goods Department (2000–2003)
* Received, sorted, and tracked incoming merchandise.
* Stocked shelves to ensure appropriate supply on sales floor.

SPECIAL SKILLS
Language: Bilingual: Spanish/English
Computer: Windows, Mac OS, MS Office, HTML

ACTIVITIES
America Reads (2007)
Tutor, Public Relations Consultant
* Taught reading to first-grade students.
* Created brochure to recruit tutors.

Multicultural Festival, Arizona State University West (2007)
Student Coordinator
Organized festival of international performances, crafts, and community
organizations.

Writing Center, Glendale Community College (2004–2006)
Tutor
Met with peers to help them with writing assignments.

REFERENCES
Available upon request to Career Services, Arizona State University West

Amabisca
uses a simple
font and
no bold or
italic type,
ensuring that
the résumé
will be
scannable.

Amabisca
includes
keywords
(highlighted)
to catch
the eye of
a potential
employer or
match desired
positions in
a database.
Amabisca
knows that
a position in
public rela-
tions requires
computer
skills, com-
munication
skills, and
experience
working
with diverse
groups of
people.
Keywords
such as *sales*,
bilingual,
HTML, and
*public rela-
tions* are
critical to her
résumé.

467

29c   Write a tailored application letter.

A clear and concise **application letter** should always accompany a résumé. Before drafting your letter, do some research about the organization you are writing to. For example, even though Laura Amabisca was already familiar with the Heard Museum, she found out the name of the director of public relations. (*Amabisca's application letter appears on p. 470.*) Call the organization, or look on its Web site, and find out the name of the person responsible for your area of interest. If you are unable to identify an appropriate name, it is better to direct the letter to "Dear Director of Public Relations" than to "Dear Sir or Madam."

Here are additional guidelines for composing a letter of application:

- **Tailor your letter.** A form letter accompanied by a generic résumé is not an effective way of getting a job interview. Before writing an application letter or preparing a résumé, you should try to find out exactly what the employer is looking for. You can then tailor your documents to those precise requirements.

- **Use business style.** Use the block form shown on pages 459–60. Type your address flush at the top of the page, starting each line at the left margin. Place the date at the

TEXTCONNEX

Electronic and Scannable Résumés

Many employers now request résumés by e-mail and electronically scan print résumés. Others ask you to type your résumé into a form on the company's Web site. Here are some tips for using electronic technology to submit your résumé.

- Contact the human resources department of a potential employer and ask whether your résumé should be scannable.

- Do not include any unusual symbols or characters. Use minimal formatting and no colors, unusual fonts, or decorative flourishes.

- Include specific keywords that allow employers to locate your electronic résumé in a database. See the résumé section of *Monster.com* at http://resume.monster.com for industry-specific advice on appropriate keywords and other step-by-step advice.

- If the employer expects the résumé as an e-mail attachment, save it in a widely readable form such as rich text format (RTF) or PDF. Use a clear, common typeface in an easy-to-read size.

- Configure your e-mail program to send you an automated reply when your résumé has been successfully received.

left margin two lines above the recipient's name and address. Use a colon (:) after the greeting. Double-space between single-spaced paragraphs. Use a traditional closing (*Sincerely, Sincerely yours, Yours truly*). Make sure that the inside address and the address on the envelope match exactly.

- **Be professional.** Your letter should be crisp and to the point. Avoid personal details. Be direct and objective in presenting your educational background (starting with college, not high school) and work-related experience. Maintain a courteous and dignified tone toward the prospective employer.

- **Limit your letter to three or four paragraphs.** Focus clearly and concisely on what the employer needs to know. In the first paragraph, identify the position you are applying for, mention how you heard about it, and briefly state that you are qualified. In the following one or two paragraphs, explain your qualifications, elaborating on the most pertinent items in your résumé. Because Amabisca was applying for a public relations job at a museum of Native American culture, she chose to highlight her internship and her thesis. In an application letter for a management position at American Express, she emphasized her work experience at Sears, including the fact that she had moved up in the organization through positions of increasing responsibility.

- **State your expectation for future contact.** Conclude with a one- or two-sentence paragraph informing the reader that you are anticipating a follow-up to your letter.

- **Use *Enc.* if you are enclosing additional materials.** Decide whether it is appropriate to enclose supporting materials other than your résumé, such as samples of your writing. Amabisca decided to do so because she was applying for her ideal job and had highly relevant materials to send. If you have been instructed to send a cover letter and résumé by e-mail as attachments, include the word *Attachments* after your e-mail "signature."

For MULTILINGUAL STUDENTS

Applying for a Job

Before applying for an internship or a job in the United States, be sure that you have the appropriate visa or work permit. American employers are required by law to confirm such documentation before they hire anyone. (American citizens must prove their citizenship as well.) For more information, visit your campus international student center as well as the campus career resource center.

20650 North 58th Avenue, Apt. 15A
Glendale, AZ 85308
August 17, 2008

Amabisca writes to a specific person and uses the correct salutation (Mr., Ms., Dr., etc.). Never use someone's first name in an application letter, even if you are already acquainted.

Ms. Jaclyn Abel
Director of Public Relations
Heard Museum
2301 North Central Avenue
Phoenix, AZ 85004

Dear Ms. Abel:

I am writing to apply for the position of Public Relations Assistant that you recently advertised in the *Arizona Republic*. I believe that my experience and qualifications fit well with your needs at the Heard, a museum that I have visited and loved all my life.

Amabisca briefly sums up her work experience. This information is also available on her résumé, but she makes evident in her cover letter why she is applying for the job. Without this explanation, a potential employer might not even look at her résumé.

As the enclosed résumé indicates, I have experience in the public relations field. While at Arizona State University West, I worked as an intern in the Public Relations Office, where I was responsible for analyzing and reporting on the image projected by the university's external publications. I also had a hand in creating the brochure for the University-College Center and participated in planning ASU West's "Dream Big" campaign. In addition I assisted in organizing an opening convocation attended by 800 people. This work in the not-for-profit sector has prepared me well for employment at the Heard.

Additionally, my undergraduate major in U.S. history has helped me understand the rich heritage of Native Americans. In my senior thesis, which received the Westmarc Writing Award, I studied the history of the relationship between the Hopis and the Anglo population as reflected in photographs taken from 1920 to 1940. Although my thesis focuses on a specific tribe, I have been interested for many years in Native-American culture and have often made use of resources in the Heard. I think that I would do a superior job of presenting the Heard as the premier museum of Native American culture.

Amabisca demonstrates her familiarity with the museum to which she is applying. This shows her genuine interest in joining the organization.

Confidential reference letters are available from ASU West Career Services. I sincerely hope that we will have an opportunity to talk further about the Heard Museum and its outstanding cultural contributions to the Phoenix metropolitan area. Please contact me at 623-555-7310.

Sincerely,

Laura Amabisca

Enc.

29d Prepare in advance for the job interview.

An interview with a potential employer is like an oral presentation. You should prepare in advance, rehearse before an audience, and be prepared to answer unexpected questions. Many campus career resource centers offer free seminars on interviewing skills and can also arrange for you to role-play an interview with a career guidance counselor.

- Call to confirm your interview the day before it is scheduled. Determine how much time you will need to get there. A late appearance at an interview can count heavily against you.
- Dress modestly and professionally.
- Bring an extra copy of your résumé and cover letter.
- Expect to speak with several people—perhaps someone from human resources as well as the person for whom you would work and other people in his or her department.
- *Always* send a personalized thank-you note or e-mail to everyone who took the time to meet you. In each, mention an interesting point from the interview conversation and reiterate your enthusiasm for the job. Send these notes within twenty-four hours of your interview.

29e Apply what you learn in college to your on-the-job writing.

Once you get a job, writing is a way to establish and maintain lines of communication with your colleagues and other contacts. When you write in the workplace, you should imagine a reader who is pressed for time and wants you to get to the point immediately.

1. Writing e-mail and memos in the workplace
In the workplace, you will do much of your writing online, in the form of e-mail. *(For more on e-mail, see Chapter 1, Learning across the curriculum, pp. 11–12.)* Most e-mail programs set up messages in memo format, with "To," "From," "Date," and "Subject" lines, as in Figure 29.1 on page 472.

E-mail in the workplace requires a more formal style than the e-mail you send to family and friends. In an e-mail for a business occasion—communication with colleagues, a request for information, or a thank-you note after an interview—you should observe the same care with organization, spelling, and tone that you would in a business letter. More specifically:

- Use a concise subject line to cue the reader as to the intent of the e-mail. When replying to messages, replace subject lines that do not clearly reflect the topic.

471

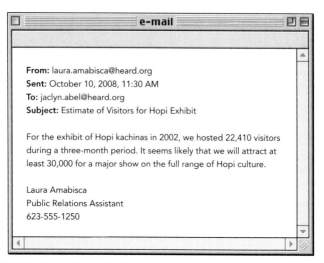

e-mail

From: laura.amabisca@heard.org
Sent: October 10, 2008, 11:30 AM
To: jaclyn.abel@heard.org
Subject: Estimate of Visitors for Hopi Exhibit

For the exhibit of Hopi kachinas in 2002, we hosted 22,410 visitors during a three-month period. It seems likely that we will attract at least 30,000 for a major show on the full range of Hopi culture.

Laura Amabisca
Public Relations Assistant
623-555-1250

FIGURE 29.1 **Sample workplace e-mail.**

▪ Maintain a courteous tone. Use joking, informality, and sarcasm cautiously, as they can cause the recipient to misunderstand your intent.

▪ Make sentences short and to the point. Use short paragraphs.

▪ Use special formatting such as italics sparingly, as not all readers will be able to view it.

▪ Use standard punctuation and capitalization.

▪ Close with your name and contact information. (*See the example above.*)

▪ Particularly when you do not know the recipient, use the conventions of letter-writing such as opening with "Dear" and ending with "Sincerely."

Business memos are used for communication with others within an organization. Like business e-mails, they are concise and formal. Memos may establish meetings, summarize information, or make announcements. (*See the example on p. 474.*) They generally contain the following elements and characteristics:

▪ A header at the top that identifies author, recipient, date, and subject

▪ Block paragraphs that are single-spaced within the paragraph and double-spaced between paragraphs

▪ Bulleted lists and other design elements (such as headers) to set off sections of longer memos

TEXTCONNEX

E-mail in the Workplace

Anything you write using a company's or an organization's computers is considered company property. If you want to gossip with a coworker, do so over lunch. If you want to e-mail your best friend about your personal life, do so from your home computer. The following guidelines will help you use e-mail wisely:

- When you are replying to an e-mail that has been sent to several people (the term *cc* means "carbon copy") determine whether your response should go to all of the original recipients or just to the original sender. Avoid cluttering other people's in-boxes.
- Open attachments from known senders only.
- File your e-mail as carefully as you would paper documents. Create separate folders in your e-mail program for each client, project, or coworker. Save any particularly important e-mails as separate files.
- Although it may be acceptable for you to browse news and shopping sites during your breaks and lunchtime, do not visit any sites while in the workplace that would embarrass you if a colleague or your supervisor suddenly looked over your shoulder.

- A section at the bottom that indicates other members of the organization who have received copies of the memo
- A professional tone

Whether you are writing an e-mail message or a conventional memo, consider both the content and the appearance of the document. For example, presenting your information as a numbered or bulleted list surrounded by white space aids readability and allows you to highlight important points and to emphasize crucial ideas. (*For more help with document design, see Chapter 6, pp. 104–17.*)

2. Writing other business genres

Readers have built-in expectations for conventional forms of business communication and know what to look for when they read them. Besides the memo, there are a number of common business genres:

- **Business letters:** Use business letters to communicate formally with people outside an organization. Typically, letters in business format have single-spaced block paragraphs with double spacing between the paragraphs. (*See the example on pp. 459–60 in Chapter 28.*)

▪ **Business reports and proposals:** Like college research papers, business reports and proposals can be used to

Heading:
Addressees'
names,
sender's
name and
initials, date,
and subject

To: Sonia Gonzalez, Grace Kim, Jonathan Jones
From: Jennifer Richer, Design Team Manager *JR*
Date: March 3, 2008
Re: Meeting on Monday

Please plan to attend a meeting on Monday at 9:00 a.m. in Room 401. At that time, we'll review our progress on the library project as well as outline future activities to ensure the following:

▪ Client satisfaction
▪ Maintenance of the current schedule
▪ Operation within budget constraints

In addition, we will discuss assignments related to other upcoming projects, such as the renovation of the gymnasium and science lab.

Person
receiving copy

Please bring design ideas and be prepared to brainstorm. Thanks.

Copy: Michael Garcia, Director, Worldwide Design

inform, analyze, and interpret. An abstract, sometimes called an *executive summary,* is almost always required, as are tables and graphs. (*For more on these visual elements, see Chapter 3: Planning and Shaping the Whole Essay, pp. 51–54.*)

▪ **Evaluations and recommendations:** You might need to evaluate a person, or you might be called on to evaluate a product or a procedure and recommend whether the company should buy or use it. Like the reviews and critiques that col-

TEXTCONNEX

Writing Connections

Monster Career Advice <http://career-advice.monster.com/resume-tips/home.aspx>: This site provides sample résumés and cover letters in addition to career advice.
Job Central <http://jobstar.org/tools/resume/samples.cfm>: This site provides samples of résumés for many different situations, as well as sample cover letters.

lege writers compose, workplace evaluations are supposed to be reasonable as well as convincing. It is important to be fair, so you should always support your account of both strengths and weaknesses with specific illustrations or examples.

■ **Presentations**: In many professions, information is presented in ways both formal and informal to groups of people. You might suddenly be asked to offer an opinion in a group meeting; or you might be given a week to prepare a formal presentation, with visuals, on an ongoing project. (*For more information on oral presentations, see Chapter 13, pp. 221–26. To learn more about PowerPoint and other presentation tools, see Chapter 14, pp. 232–37.*)

www.mhhe.com/
mhhb2

For more information
on PowerPoint, go to

Writing >
PowerPoint
Tutorial

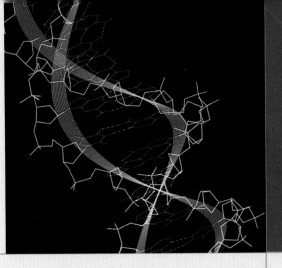

Like DNA, which provides a chemical blueprint for the construction of living organisms, grammar and syntax provide a blueprint for transforming words into intelligible sentences.

PART
6

Grammar and rhetoric are complementary. . . . Grammar maps out the possible; rhetoric narrows the possible down to the desirable or effective.

—FRANCIS CHRISTENSEN

Grammar
Basics

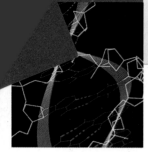

30 Parts of Speech

Written language, although based on the grammar of spoken language, has a logic and rules of its own. This chapter and the next (*Chapter 31: Sentence Basics*) explain the basic rules of standard written English.

Grammar gives us a way of talking about how sentences are put together to make sense. Take, for example, this group of words, adapted from Lewis Carroll's poem "Jabberwocky":

> The toves gimbled in the wabe.

Most of these are nonsense words: Carroll made them up. What makes a sentence meaningful, however, is not just its individual words. Because of the form of the words in this sentence and the way they relate to each other, we can answer questions about them:

www.mhhe.com/
mhhb2

For information and
exercises on parts of
speech, go to

Editing >
Parts of Speech

> What gimbled in the wabe? *The toves did.*
> What did the toves do in the wabe? *They gimbled.*
> Where did the toves gimble? *They gimbled in the wabe.*

We can answer these questions because we can tell from the form and relationship of the words what grammatical role each one plays in the sentence.

WRITING OUTCOMES

Part 6: Grammar Basics
This section will help you answer questions such as:

Rhetorical Knowledge
- When are interjections used in academic writing? (**30h**)
- How does English word order differ from that of other languages? (**31c**)

Critical Thinking, Reading, and Writing
- How do I find the subject and predicate of a sentence? (**31b, c**)
- How can I find out whether a verb is transitive or intransitive? (**31c**)

Processes
- During editing, should I add a comma after an *–ing* verb phrase that begins a sentence? (**31f**)

Knowledge of Conventions
- What are the parts of speech? (**30**)
- What are the five common sentence patterns in English? (**31c**)

Self-Assessment: *Take an online quiz at www.mhhe.com/mhhb2 to test your familiarity with the topics covered in Chapters 30–31. Pay special attention to the sections in these chapters that correspond to any questions you answer incorrectly.*